Data Science

3rd Edition

by Lillian Pierson

for
dummies®
A Wiley Brand

Data Science For Dummies®, 3rd Edition

Published by: **John Wiley & Sons, Inc.,** 111 River Street, Hoboken, NJ 07030-5774, www.wiley.com

Copyright © 2021 by John Wiley & Sons, Inc., Hoboken, New Jersey

Published simultaneously in Canada

For general information on our other products and services, please contact our Customer Care Department within the U.S. at 877-762-2974, outside the U.S. at 317-572-3993, or fax 317-572-4002. For technical support, please visit https://hub.wiley.com/community/support/dummies.

Wiley publishes in a variety of print and electronic formats and by print-on-demand. Some material included with standard print versions of this book may not be included in e-books or in print-on-demand. If this book refers to media such as a CD or DVD that is not included in the version you purchased, you may download this material at http://booksupport.wiley.com. For more information about Wiley products, visit www.wiley.com.

Library of Congress Control Number: 2021944259

ISBN 978-1-119-81155-8 (pbk); ISBN 978-1-119-81166-4 (ebk); ISBN 978-1-119-81161-9 (ebk)

SKY10029092_081321

Contents at a Glance

Table of Contents

Introduction

This book was written as much for expert data scientists as it was for aspiring ones. Its content represents a new approach to doing data science — one that puts business vision and profitably at the heart of our work as data scientists.

Data science and artificial intelligence (AI, for short) have disrupted the business world so radically that it's nearly unrecognizable compared to what things were like just 10 or 15 years ago. The good news is that most of these changes have made everyone's lives and businesses more efficient, more fun, and dramatically more interesting. The bad news is that if you don't yet have at least a modicum of data science competence, your business and employment prospects are growing dimmer by the moment.

Since 2014, when this book was first written (throughout the first two editions), I have harped on this same point. Lots of people listened! So much has changed about data science over the years, however, that this book has needed two full rewrites since it was originally published. What changed? Well, to be honest, the math and scientific approach that underlie data science haven't changed one bit. But over the years, with all the expansion of AI adoption across business and with the remarkable increase in the supply of data science workers, the data science landscape has seen a hundredfold increase in diversity with respect to what people and businesses are using data science to achieve.

The original idea behind this book when it was first published was to provide "a reference manual to guide you through the vast and expansive areas encompassed by data science." At the time, not too much information out there covered the breadth of data science in one resource. That has changed!

Data scientist as a title only really began to emerge in 2012. Most of us practitioners in the field back then were all new and still finding our way. In 2014, I didn't have the perspective or confidence I needed to write a book like the one you're holding. Thank you so much to all the readers who have read this book previously, shared positive feedback, and applied what they learned to create better lives for themselves and better outcomes for their companies. The positive transformation of my readers is a big part of what keeps me digging deep to produce the very best version of this book that I possibly can.

The Internet is full of *information for the sake of information* — information that lacks the depth, context, and relevance that's needed to transform that information to true meaning in the lives of its consumers. Publishing more of this type of content doesn't help people — it confuses them, overwhelms them, and wastes their precious time! When writing this book for a third time, I took a radical stance against "information for the sake of information."

I also want to make three further promises about the content in this book: It is meaningful, it is actionable, and it is relevant. If it isn't one of these three adjectives, I've made sure it hasn't made its way into this book.

Because this book is about data science, I spend the entirety of Parts 1 and 2 detailing what data science actually is and what its theoretical underpinnings are. Part 3 demonstrates the ways you can apply data science to support vital business functions, from finance to marketing, from decision support to operations. I've even written a chapter on how to use data science to create what may be a whole new function within your company: data monetization. (To ensure that the book's content is relevant to readers from all business functions and industries, I've included use cases and case studies from businesses a wide variety of industries and sectors.)

To enhance the relevance of this book's content, at the beginning of the book I guide readers in a self-assessment designed to help them identify which type of data science work is most appropriate for their personality — whether it's implementing data science, working in a management and leadership capacity, or even starting your own data science business.

Part 4 is the actionable part of this book — the part that shows you how to take what you've learned about data science and apply it to start getting results right away. The action you learn to take in this book involves using what you learn about data science in Parts 1 through 3 to build an implementation plan for a profit-forming data science project.

Throughout this book, you'll find references to ancillary materials that directly support what you're learning within these pages. All of these support materials are hosted on the website that companions this book, `http://businessgrowth.ai/`. I highly recommend you take advantage of those assets, as I have donated many of them from an archived, limited-edition, paid product that was only available in 2020.

Note: I have removed all coding examples from this book because I don't have adequate space here to do anything meaningful with coding demos. If you want me to show you how to implement the data science that's discussed in Part 2, I have two Python for Data Science Essential Training courses on LinkedIn Learning. You're most welcome to follow up by taking those courses. You access them both directly through my course author page on LinkedIn Learning here: `www.linkedin.com/learning/instructors/lillian-pierson-p-e`

This book is unlike any other data science book or course on the market. How do I know? Because I created it from scratch based on my own unique experience and perspective. That perspective is based on almost 15 years of technical consulting experience, almost 10 of which have been spent working as a consultant, entrepreneur, and mentor in the data science space. This book is not a remake of what some other expert wrote in *their* book — it's an original work of art and a labor of love for me. If you enjoy the contents of this book, please reach out to me at `lillian@data-mania.com` and let me know. Also, for free weekly video training on data science, data leadership, and data business-building, be sure to visit and subscribe to my YouTube channel: `https://www.youtube.com/c/Lillian Pierson_Data_Business`

Helping readers like you is my mission in life!

About This Book

In keeping with the *For Dummies* brand, this book is organized in a modular, easy-to-access format that allows you to use the book as an owner's manual. The book's chapters are structured to walk you through a clear process, so it's best to read them in order. You don't absolutely have to read the book through, from cover to cover, however. You can glean a great deal from jumping around, although now and then you might miss some important context by doing so. If you're already working in the data science space, you can skip the basic-level details about what data science is within Part 2 — but do read the rest of the book, because it's designed to present new and immensely valuable knowledge for data science practitioners of all skill levels (including experts).

Web addresses appear in monofont. If you're reading a digital version of this book on a device connected to the Internet, you can click a web address to visit that website, like this: `www.dummies.com`.

Foolish Assumptions

In writing this book, I've assumed that readers are comfortable with advanced tasks in Microsoft Excel — pivot tables, grouping, sorting, plotting, and the like. Having strong skills in algebra, basic statistics, or even business calculus helps as well. Foolish or not, it's my high hope that all readers have subject matter expertise to which they can apply the skills presented in this book. Because data scientists need to know the implications and applications of the data insights they derive, subject matter expertise is a major requirement for data science.

Icons Used in This Book

As you make your way through this book, you see the following icons in the margins:

The Tip icon marks tips (duh!) and shortcuts you can use to make subject mastery easier.

Remember icons mark information that's especially important to know. To siphon off the most important information in each chapter, just skim the material represented by these icons.

The Technical Stuff icon marks information of a highly technical nature that you can normally skip.

The Warning icon tells you to watch out! It marks important information that may save you headaches.

Beyond the Book

Data Science For Dummies, 3rd Edition, comes with a handy Cheat Sheet that lists helpful shortcuts as well as abbreviated definitions for essential processes and concepts described in the book. You can use this feature as a quick-and-easy reference when doing data science. To download the Cheat Sheet, simply go to www.dummies.com and search for *data science for dummies cheat sheet* in the Search box.

Where to Go from Here

If you're new to data science, you're best off starting from Chapter 1 and reading the book from beginning to end. If you already know the data science basics, I suggest that you read the last part of Chapter 1, skim Chapter 2, and then dig deep into all of Parts 3 and 4.

1

Getting Started with Data Science

Get introduced to the field of data science.

Delve into vital data engineering details.

Discover your inner data superhero archetype.

Chapter **1**

Wrapping Your Head Around Data Science

For over a decade now, *everyone* has been absolutely deluged by data. It's coming from every computer, every mobile device, every camera, and every imaginable sensor — and now it's even coming from watches and other wearable technologies. Data is generated in every social media interaction we humans make, every file we save, every picture we take, and every query we submit; data is even generated when we do something as simple as ask a favorite search engine for directions to the closest ice cream shop.

Although data immersion is nothing new, you may have noticed that the phenomenon is accelerating. Lakes, puddles, and rivers of data have turned to floods and veritable tsunamis of structured, semistructured, and unstructured data that's streaming from almost every activity that takes place in both the digital and physical worlds. It's just an unavoidable fact of life within the information age.

If you're anything like I was, you may have wondered, "What's the point of all this data? Why use valuable resources to generate and collect it?" Although even just two decades ago, no one was in a position to make much use of most of the data that's generated, the tides today have definitely turned. Specialists known as *data engineers* are constantly finding innovative and powerful new ways to capture, collate, and condense unimaginably massive volumes of data, and other specialists, known as *data scientists,* are leading change by deriving valuable and actionable insights from that data.

In its truest form, data science represents the optimization of processes and resources. Data science produces *data insights* — actionable, data-informed conclusions or predictions that you can use to understand and improve your business, your investments, your health, and even your lifestyle and social life. Using data science insights is like being able to see in the dark. For any goal or pursuit you can imagine, you can find data science methods to help you predict the most direct route from where you are to where you want to be — and to anticipate every pothole in the road between both places.

Seeing Who Can Make Use of Data Science

The terms *data science* and *data engineering* are often misused and confused, so let me start off by clarifying that these two fields are, in fact, separate and distinct domains of expertise. *Data science* is the computational science of extracting meaningful insights from raw data and then effectively communicating those insights to generate value. *Data engineering,* on the other hand, is an engineering domain that's dedicated to building and maintaining systems that overcome data processing bottlenecks and data handling problems for applications that consume, process, and store large volumes, varieties, and velocities of data. In both data science and data engineering, you commonly work with these three data varieties:

- » **Structured:** Data that is stored, processed, and manipulated in a traditional *relational database management system (RDBMS)* – an example of this would be a MySQL database that uses a tabular schema of rows and columns, making it easier to identify specific values within data that's stored within the database.

- » **Unstructured:** Data that is commonly generated from human activities and doesn't fit into a structured database format. Examples of unstructured data is data that comprises email documents, Word documents or audio / video files.

- » **Semistructured:** Data that doesn't fit into a structured database system but is nonetheless organizable by tags that are useful for creating a form of order and hierarchy in the data. XML and JSON files are examples of data that comes in semi-structured form.

It used to be that only large tech companies with massive funding had the skills and computing resources required to implement data science methodologies to optimize and improve their business, but that's not been the case for quite a while now. The proliferation of data has created a demand for insights, and this demand is embedded in many aspects of modern culture — from the Uber passenger who expects the driver to show up exactly at the time and location predicted by the Uber application to the online shopper who expects the Amazon platform to recommend the best product alternatives for comparing similar goods before making a purchase. Data and the need for data-informed insights are ubiquitous. Because organizations of all sizes are beginning to recognize that they're immersed in a sink-or-swim, data-driven, competitive environment, data know-how has emerged as a core and requisite function in almost every line of business.

What does this mean for the average knowledge worker? First, it means that everyday employees are increasingly expected to support a progressively advancing set of technological and data requirements. Why? Well, that's because almost all industries are reliant on data technologies and the insights they spur. Consequently, many people are in continuous need of upgrading their data skills, or else they face the real possibility of being replaced by a more data-savvy employee.

The good news is that upgrading data skills doesn't usually require people to go back to college, or — God forbid — earn a university degree in statistics, computer science, or data science. The bad news is that, even with professional training or self-teaching, it always takes extra work to stay industry-relevant and tech-savvy. In this respect, the data revolution isn't so different from any other change that has hit industry in the past. The fact is, in order to stay relevant, you need to take the time and effort to acquire the skills that keep you current. When you're learning how to do data science, you can take some courses, educate yourself using online resources, read books like this one, and attend events where you can learn what you need to know to stay on top of the game.

Who can use data science? You can. Your organization can. Your employer can. Anyone who has a bit of understanding and training can begin using data insights to improve their lives, their careers, and the well-being of their businesses. Data science represents a change in the way you approach the world. When determining outcomes, people once used to make their best guess, act on that guess, and then hope for the desired result. With data insights, however, people now have access to the predictive vision that they need to truly drive change and achieve the results they want.

Here are some examples of ways you can use data insights to make the world, and your company, a better place:

>> **Business systems:** Optimize returns on investment (those crucial ROIs) for any measurable activity.

>> **Marketing strategy development:** Use data insights and predictive analytics to identify marketing strategies that work, eliminate under-performing efforts, and test new marketing strategies.

>> **Keep communities safe:** Predictive policing applications help law enforcement personnel predict and prevent local criminal activities.

>> **Help make the world a better place for those less fortunate:** Data scientists in developing nations are using social data, mobile data, and data from websites to generate real-time analytics that improve the effectiveness of humanitarian responses to disaster, epidemics, food scarcity issues, and more.

Inspecting the Pieces of the Data Science Puzzle

To practice data science, in the true meaning of the term, you need the analytical know-how of math and statistics, the coding skills necessary to work with data, and an area of subject matter expertise. Without this expertise, you might as well call yourself a mathematician or a statistician. Similarly, a programmer without subject matter expertise and analytical know-how might better be considered a software engineer or developer, but not a data scientist.

The need for data-informed business and product strategy has been increasing exponentially for about a decade now, thus forcing all business sectors and industries to adopt a data science approach. As such, different flavors of data science have emerged. The following are just a few titles under which experts of every discipline are required to know and regularly do data science: director of data science–advertising technology, digital banking product owner, clinical biostatistician, geotechnical data scientist, data scientist–geospatial and agriculture analytics, data and tech policy analyst, global channel ops–data excellence lead, and data scientist–healthcare.

Nowadays, it's almost impossible to differentiate between a proper data scientist and a subject matter expert (SME) whose success depends heavily on their ability to use data science to generate insights. Looking at a person's job title may or may not be helpful, simply because many roles are titled data scientist when they may as well be labeled data strategist or product manager, based on the actual requirements. In addition, many knowledge workers are doing daily data science and not working under the title of data scientist. It's an overhyped, often misleading label that's not always helpful if you're trying to find out what a data scientist does by looking at online job boards. To shed some light, in the following sections I spell out the key components that are part of any data science role, regardless of whether that role is assigned the data scientist label.

Collecting, querying, and consuming data

Data engineers have the job of capturing and collating large volumes of structured, unstructured, and semi structured *big data* — an outdated term that's used to describe data that exceeds the processing capacity of conventional database systems because it's too big, it moves too fast, or it lacks the structural requirements of traditional database architectures. Again, data engineering tasks are separate from the work that's performed in data science, which focuses more on analysis, prediction, and visualization. Despite this distinction, whenever data scientists collect, query, and consume data during the analysis process, they perform work similar to that of the data engineer (the role I tell you about earlier in this chapter).

Although valuable insights can be generated from a single data source, often the combination of several relevant sources delivers the contextual information required to drive better data-informed decisions. A data scientist can work from several datasets that are stored in a single database, or even in several different data storage environments. At other times, source data is stored and processed on a cloud-based platform built by software and data engineers.

No matter how the data is combined or where it's stored, if you're a data scientist, you almost always have to *query* data — write commands to extract relevant datasets from data storage systems, in other words. Most of the time, you use Structured Query Language (SQL) to query data. (Chapter 7 is all about SQL, so if the acronym scares you, jump ahead to that chapter now.)

Whether you're using a third-party application or doing custom analyses by using a programming language such as R or Python, you can choose from a number of universally accepted file formats:

>> **Comma-separated values (CSV):** Almost every brand of desktop and web-based analysis application accepts this file type, as do commonly used scripting languages such as Python and R.

>> **Script:** Most data scientists know how to use either the Python or R programming language to analyze and visualize data. These script files end with the extension .ply or .ipynb (Python) or .r (R).

>> **Application:** Excel is useful for quick-and-easy, spot-check analyses on small- to medium-size datasets. These application files have the .xls or .xlsx extension.

>> **Web programming:** If you're building custom, web-based data visualizations, you may be working in D3.js — or data-driven documents, a JavaScript library for data visualization. When you work in D3.js, you use data to manipulate web-based documents using `.html`, `.svg`, and `.css` files.

Applying mathematical modeling to data science tasks

Data science relies heavily on a practitioner's math skills (and statistics skills, as described in the following section) precisely because these are the skills needed to understand your data and its significance. These skills are also valuable in data science because you can use them to carry out predictive forecasting, decision modeling, and hypotheses testing.

REMEMBER

Mathematics uses deterministic methods to form a *quantitative* (or *numerical*) description of the world; *statistics* is a form of science that's derived from mathematics, but it focuses on using a *stochastic* (probabilities) approach and inferential methods to form a quantitative description of the world. I tell you more about both in Chapter 4. Data scientists use mathematical methods to build decision models, generate approximations, and make predictions about the future. Chapter 4 presents many mathematical approaches that are useful when working in data science.

REMEMBER

In this book, I assume that you have a fairly solid skill set in basic math — you will benefit if you've taken college-level calculus or even linear algebra. I try hard, however, to meet readers where they are. I realize that you may be working based on a limited mathematical knowledge (advanced algebra or maybe business calculus), so I convey advanced mathematical concepts using a plain-language approach that's easy for everyone to understand.

Deriving insights from statistical methods

In data science, statistical methods are useful for better understanding your data's significance, for validating hypotheses, for simulating scenarios, and for making predictive forecasts of future events. Advanced statistical skills are somewhat rare, even among quantitative analysts, engineers, and scientists. If you want to go places in data science, though, take some time to get up to speed in a few basic statistical methods, like linear and logistic regression, naïve Bayes classification, and time series analysis. These methods are covered in Chapter 4.

Coding, coding, coding — it's just part of the game

Coding is unavoidable when you're working in data science. You need to be able to write code so that you can instruct the computer in how to manipulate, analyze, and visualize your data. Programming languages such as Python and R are important for writing scripts for data manipulation, analysis, and visualization. SQL, on the other hand, is useful for data querying. Finally, the JavaScript library D3.js is often required for making cool, custom, and interactive web-based data visualizations.

Although coding is a requirement for data science, it doesn't have to be this big, scary *thing* that people make it out to be. Your coding can be as fancy and complex as you want it to be, but you can also take a rather simple approach. Although these skills are paramount to success, you can pretty easily learn enough coding to practice high-level data science. I've dedicated Chapters 6 and 7 to helping you get to know the basics of what's involved in getting started in Python and R, and querying in SQL (respectively).

Applying data science to a subject area

Statisticians once exhibited some measure of obstinacy in accepting the significance of data science. Many statisticians have cried out, "Data science is nothing new — it's just another name for what we've been doing all along!" Although I can sympathize with their perspective, I'm forced to stand with the camp of data scientists who markedly declare that data science is separate, and definitely distinct, from the statistical approaches that comprise it.

My position on the unique nature of data science is based to some extent on the fact that data scientists often use computer languages not used in traditional statistics and take approaches derived from the field of mathematics. But the main point of distinction between statistics and data science is the need for subject matter expertise.

Because statisticians usually have only a limited amount of expertise in fields outside of statistics, they're almost always forced to consult with a SME to verify exactly what their findings mean and to determine the best direction in which to proceed. Data scientists, on the other hand, should have a strong subject matter expertise in the area in which they're working. Data scientists generate deep insights and then use their domain-specific expertise to understand exactly what those insights mean with respect to the area in which they're working.

The following list describes a few ways in which today's knowledge workers are coupling data science skills with their respective areas of expertise in order to amplify the results they generate.

>> **Clinical informatics scientists** combine their healthcare expertise with data science skills to produce personalized healthcare treatment plans. They use healthcare informatics to predict and preempt future health problems in at-risk patients.

>> **Marketing data scientists** combine data science with marketing expertise to predict and preempt customer *churn* (the loss of customers from a product or service to that of a competitor's, in other words). They also optimize marketing strategies, build recommendation engines, and fine-tune marketing mix models. I tell you more about using data science to increase marketing ROI in Chapter 11.

>> **Data journalists** *scrape* websites (extract data in bulk directly from the pages on a website, in other words) for fresh data in order to discover and report the latest breaking-news stories. (I talk more about data storytelling in Chapter 8.)

>> **Directors of data science** bolster their technical project management capabilities with an added expertise in data science. Their work includes leading data projects and working to protect the profitability of the data projects for which they're responsible. They also act to ensure transparent communication between C-suite executives, business managers, and the data personnel on their team who actually do the implementation work. (I share more details in Part 4 about leading successful data projects; check out Chapter 18 for details about data science leaders.)

>> **Data product managers** supercharge their product management capabilities with the power of data science. They use data science to generate predictive insights that better inform decision-making around product design, develop-ment, launch, and strategy. This is a classic type of data leadership role, the likes of which are covered in Chapter 18. For more on developing effective data strategy, take a gander at Chapters 15 through 17.

>> **Machine learning engineers** combine software engineering superpowers with data science skills to build predictive applications. This is a classic data implementation role, more of which is discussed in Chapter 2.

Communicating data insights

As a data scientist, you must have sharp verbal communication skills. If a data scientist can't communicate, all the knowledge and insight in the world does *nothing* for the organization. Data scientists need to be able to explain data insights in a way that staff members can understand. Not only that, data scientists need to be able to produce clear and meaningful data visualizations and written narratives. Most of the time, people need to see a concept for themselves in order to truly understand it. Data scientists must be creative and pragmatic in their means and methods of communication. (I cover the topics of data visualization and data-driven storytelling in much greater detail in Chapter 8.)

Exploring Career Alternatives That Involve Data Science

Not to cause alarm, but it's fully possible for you to develop deep and sophisticated data science skills and then come away with a gut feeling that you know you're meant to do something more.

Earlier in my data career, I was no stranger to this feeling. I'd just gone and pumped up my data science skills. It was the "sexiest" career path — according to *Harvard Business Review* in 2012 — and offered so many opportunities. The money was good and the demand was there. What's not to love about opportunities with big tech giants, start-ups, and multiple six-figure salaries, right?

But very quickly, I realized that, although I had the data skills and education I needed to land some sweet opportunities (including interview offers from Facebook!), I soon realized that coding away and working only on data implementation simply weren't what I was meant to do for the rest of my life.

Something about getting lost in the details felt disempowering to me. My personality craved more energy, more creativity — plus, I needed to see the big-picture impact that my data work was making.

In short, I hadn't yet discovered my inner data superhero. I coined this term to describe that juicy combination of a person's data skills, coupled with their personality, passions, goals, and priorities. When all these aspects are in sync, you'll find that you're absolutely on fire in your data career. These days, I'm a data entrepreneur. I get to spend my days doing work that I absolutely adore and that's truly aligned with my mission and vision for my data career and life-at-large. I want the same thing for you, dear reader.

TIP

Over on the companion site to this book (https://businessgrowth.ai/), you can find free access to a fun, 45-second quiz about data career paths. It helps you uncover your own inner data superhero type. Take the quiz to receive personalized data career recommendations that directly align with your unique combination of data skills, personality, and passions.

For now, let's take a look at the three main data superhero archetypes that I've seen evolving and developing over the past decade.

The data implementer

Some data science professionals were simply *born* to be implementers. If that's you, then your secret superpower is building data and artificial intelligence (AI) solutions. You have a meticulous attention to detail that naturally helps you in coding up innovative solutions that deliver reliable and accurate results — almost every time. When you're facing a technical challenge, you can be more than a little stubborn. You're able to accomplish the task, no matter how complex.

Without implementers, none of today's groundbreaking technologies would even exist. Their unparalleled discipline and inquisitiveness keep them in the problem-solving game all the way until project completion. They usually start off a project with a simple request and some messy data, but through sheer perseverance and brainpower, they're able to turn them into clear and accurate predictive data insights — or a data system, if they prefer to implement data engineering rather than data science tasks. If you're a data implementer, math and coding are your bread-and-butter, so to speak.

Part 2 of this book are dedicated to showing you the basics of data science and the skills you need to take on to get started in a career in data science implementation. You may also be interested in how your work in this area is applied to improve a business's profitability. You can read all about this topic in Part 3.

The data leader

Other data science professionals naturally gravitate more toward business, strategy, and product. They take their data science expertise and apply it to lead profit-forming data science projects and products. If you're a natural data leader, then you're gifted at leading teams and project stakeholders through the process of building successful data solutions. You're a meticulous planner and organizer, which empowers you to show up at the right place and the right time, and hopefully keep your team members moving forward without delay.

Data leaders love data science just as much as data implementers and data entrepreneurs — you can read about them in the later section "The data entrepreneur." The difference between most data implementers and data leaders is that leaders generally love data science for the incredible outcomes that it makes possible. They have a deep passion for using their data science expertise and leadership skills to create tangible results. Data leaders love to collaborate with smart people across the company to get the job done right. With teamwork, and some input from the data implementation team, they form brilliant plans for accomplishing any task, no matter how complex. They harness manpower, data science savvy, and serious business acumen to produce some of the most innovative technologies on the planet.

Chapters 7 through 9 and Chapters 15 through 17 in this book are dedicated to showing you the basics of the data science leadership-and-strategy skills you need in order to nail down a job as a data science leader.

That said, to lead data science projects, you should know what's involved in implementing them — you'll lead a team of data implementers, after all. See Part 2 — it covers all the basics on data science implementation. You also need to know prominent data science use cases, which you can explore over in Part 3.

The data entrepreneur

The third data superhero archetype that has evolved over the past decade is the data entrepreneur. If you're a data entrepreneur, your secret superpower is building up businesses by delivering exceptional data science services and products.

You have the same type of focus and drive as the data implementer, but you apply it toward bringing your business vision to reality. But, like the data leader, your love for data science is inspired mostly by the incredible outcomes that it makes possible. A data entrepreneur has many overlapping traits and a greater affinity for either the data implementer or the data leader, but with one important difference:

> Data entrepreneurs crave the creative freedom that comes with being a founder.

Data entrepreneurs are more risk-tolerant than their data implementer or data leader counterparts. This risk tolerance and desire for freedom allows them to do what they do — which is to create a vision for a business and then use their data science expertise to guide the business to turn that vision into reality.

For more information on how to transform data science expertise into a profitable product or business, jump over to Part 3.

Using my own data science career to illustrate what this framework looks like in action, (as mentioned earlier in this chapter) I started off as a data science implementer, and quickly turned into a data entrepreneur. Within my data business, however, my focus has been on data science training services, data strategy services, and mentoring data entrepreneurs to build world-class businesses. I've helped educate more than a million data professionals on data science and helped grow existing data science communities to more than 650,000 data professionals — and counting. Stepping back, you could say that although I call myself a data entrepreneur, the work I do has a higher degree of affinity to data leadership than data implementation.

TIP

I encourage you to go to the companion site to this book at `https://businessgrowth.ai/` and take that career path quiz I mention earlier in this section. The quiz can give you a head-start in determining where you best fit within the spectrum of data science superhero archetypes.

Chapter **2**

Tapping into Critical Aspects of Data Engineering

Though data and artificial intelligence (AI) are extremely interesting topics in the eyes of the public, most laypeople aren't aware of what data really is or how it's used to improve people's lives. This chapter tells the full story about big data, explains where big data comes from and how it's used, and then outlines the roles that machine learning engineers, data engineers, and data scientists play in the modern data ecosystem. In this chapter, I introduce the fundamental concepts related to storing and processing data for data science so that this information can serve as the basis for laying out your plans for leveraging data science to improve business performance.

Defining Big Data and the Three Vs

I am reluctant to even mention big data in this, the third, edition of *Data Science For Dummies*. Back about a decade ago, the industry hype was huge over what people called *big data* — a term that characterizes data that exceeds the processing capacity of conventional database systems because it's too big, it moves too fast, or it lacks the structural requirements of traditional database architectures.

My reluctance stems from a tragedy I watched unfold across the second decade of the 21st century. Back then, the term *big data* was so overhyped across industry that countless business leaders made misguided impulse purchases. The narrative in those days went something like this: "If you're not using big data to develop a competitive advantage for your business, the future of your company is in great peril. And, in order to use big data, you need to have big data storage and processing capabilities that are available only if you invest in a Hadoop cluster."

REMEMBER

Hadoop is a data processing platform that is designed to boil down big data into smaller datasets that are more manageable for data scientists to analyze. For reasons you're about to see, Hadoop's popularity has been in steady decline since 2015.

Despite its significant drawbacks, Hadoop is, and was, powerful at satisfying one requirement: batch-processing and storing large volumes of data. That's great if your situation requires precisely this type of capability, but the fact is that technology is never a one-size-fits-all sort of thing. If I learned anything from the years I spent building technical and strategic engineering plans for government institutions, it's this: Before investing in any sort of technology solution, you must always assess the current state of your organization, select an optimal use case, and thoroughly evaluate competing alternatives, all before even considering whether a purchase should be made. This process is so vital to the success of data science initiatives that I cover it extensively in Part 4.

Unfortunately, in almost all cases back then, business leaders bought into Hadoop before having evaluated whether it was an appropriate choice. Vendors sold Hadoop and made lots of money. Most of those projects failed. Most Hadoop vendors went out of business. Corporations got burned on investing in data projects, and the data industry got a bad rap. For any data professional who was working in the field between 2012 and 2015, the term *big data* represents a blight on the industry.

Despite the setbacks the data industry has faced due to overhype, this fact remains: If companies want to stay competitive, they must be proficient and adept at infusing data insights into their processes, products, as well as their growth and management strategies. This is especially true in light of the digital adoption explosion that occurred as a direct result of the COVID-19 pandemic. Whether your data volumes rank on the terabyte or petabyte scales, data-engineered solutions must be designed to meet requirements for the data's intended destination and use.

TECHNICAL STUFF

When you're talking about regular data, you're likely to hear the words *kilobyte* and *gigabyte* used as measurements. Kilobyte refers to 1024 bytes, or 2^{10} B.) A *byte* is an 8-bit unit of data.

Three characteristics — also called "the three Vs" — define big data: volume, velocity, and variety. Because the three Vs of big data are continually expanding, newer, more innovative data technologies must continuously be developed to manage big data problems.

REMEMBER

In a situation where you're required to adopt a big data solution to overcome a problem that's caused by your data's velocity, volume, or variety, you have moved past the realm of regular data — you have a big data problem on your hands.

Grappling with data volume

The lower limit of big data volume starts as low as 1 terabyte, and it has no upper limit. If your organization owns at least 1 terabyte of data, that data technically qualifies as big data.

WARNING

In its raw form, most big data is *low value* — in other words, the value-to-data-quantity ratio is low in raw big data. Big data is composed of huge numbers of very small transactions that come in a variety of formats. These incremental components of big data produce true value only after they're aggregated and analyzed. Roughly speaking, data engineers have the job of aggregating it, and data scientists have the job of analyzing it.

Handling data velocity

A lot of big data is created by using automated processes and instrumentation nowadays, and because data storage costs are relatively inexpensive, system velocity is, many times, the limiting factor. Keep in mind that big data is low-value. Consequently, you need systems that are able to ingest a lot of it, on short order, to generate timely and valuable insights.

In engineering terms, *data velocity* is data volume per unit time. Big data enters an average system at velocities ranging between 30 kilobytes (K) per second to as much as 30 *gigabytes* (GB) per second. Latency is a characteristic of all data systems, and it quantifies the system's delay in moving data after it has been instructed to do so. Many data-engineered systems are required to have latency less than 100 milliseconds, measured from the time the data is created to the time the system responds.

Throughput is a characteristic that describes a systems capacity for work per unit time. Throughput requirements can easily be as high as 1,000 messages per second in big data systems! High-velocity, real-time moving data presents an obstacle to timely decision-making. The capabilities of data-handling and data-processing technologies often limit data velocities.

Tools that intake data into a system — otherwise known as data ingestion tools — come in a variety of flavors. Some of the more popular ones are described in the following list:

>> **Apache Sqoop:** You can use this data transference tool to quickly transfer data back-and-forth between a relational data system and the *Hadoop distributed file system (HDFS)* — it uses clusters of commodity servers to store big data. HDFS makes big data handling and storage financially feasible by distributing storage tasks across clusters of inexpensive commodity servers.

>> **Apache Kafka:** This distributed messaging system acts as a message broker whereby messages can quickly be pushed onto, and pulled from, HDFS. You can use Kafka to consolidate and facilitate the data calls and pushes that consumers make to and from the HDFS.

>> **Apache Flume:** This distributed system primarily handles log and event data. You can use it to transfer massive quantities of unstructured data to and from the HDFS.

Dealing with data variety

Big data gets even more complicated when you add unstructured and semistructured data to structured data sources. This *high-variety* data comes from a multitude of sources. The most salient point about it is that it's composed of a combination of datasets with differing underlying structures (structured, unstructured, or semistructured). Heterogeneous, high-variety data is often composed of any combination of graph data, JSON files, XML files, social media data, structured tabular data, weblog data, and data that's generated from user clicks on a web page — otherwise known as click-streams.

Structured data can be stored, processed, and manipulated in a traditional relational database management system (RDBMS) — an example of this would be a PostgreSQL database that uses a tabular schema of rows and columns, making it easier to identify specific values within data that's stored within the database. This data, which can be generated by humans or machines, is derived from all sorts of sources — from click-streams and web-based forms to point-of-sale transactions and sensors. *Unstructured* data comes completely unstructured — it's commonly generated from human activities and doesn't fit into a structured database format. Such data can be derived from blog posts, emails, and Word documents. *Semistructured* data doesn't fit into a structured database system, but is nonetheless structured, by tags that are useful for creating a form of order and hierarchy in the data. Semistructured data is commonly found in databases and file systems. It can be stored as log files, XML files, or JSON data files.

TIP

Become familiar with the term *data lake* — this term is used by practitioners in the big data industry to refer to a nonhierarchical data storage system that's used to hold huge volumes of multistructured, raw data within a flat storage architecture — in other words, a collection of records that come in uniform format and that are not cross-referenced in any way. HDFS can be used as a data lake storage repository, but you can also use the Amazon Web Services (AWS) S3 platform — or a similar cloud storage solution — to meet the same requirements on the cloud. (The Amazon Web Services S3 platform is one of the more popular cloud architectures available for storing big data.)

WARNING

Although both data lake and data warehouse are used for storing data, the terms refer to different types of systems. Data lake was defined above and a data warehouse is a centralized data repository that you can use to store and access only structured data. A more traditional data warehouse system commonly employed in business intelligence solutions is a *data mart* — a storage system (for structured data) that you can use to store one particular focus area of data, belonging to only one line of business in the company.

Identifying Important Data Sources

Vast volumes of data are continually generated by humans, machines, and sensors everywhere. Typical sources include data from social media, financial transactions, health records, click-streams, log files, and the *Internet of things* — a web of digital connections that joins together the ever-expanding array of electronic devices that consumers use in their everyday lives. Figure 2-1 shows a variety of popular big data sources.

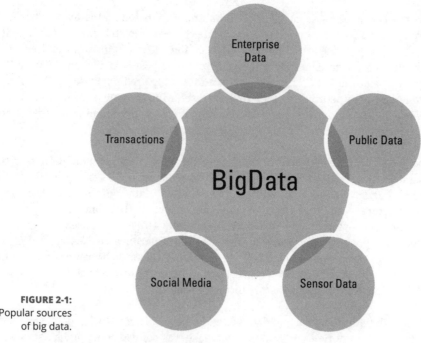

FIGURE 2-1:
Popular sources of big data.

Grasping the Differences among Data Approaches

Data science, machine learning engineering, and data engineering cover different functions within the *big data paradigm* — an approach wherein huge velocities, varieties, and volumes of structured, unstructured, and semistructured data are being captured, processed, stored, and analyzed using a set of techniques and technologies that are completely novel compared to those that were used in decades past.

All these functions are useful for deriving knowledge and actionable insights from raw data. All are essential elements for any comprehensive decision-support system, and all are extremely helpful when formulating robust strategies for future business growth. Although the terms *data science* and *data engineering* are often used interchangeably, they're distinct domains of expertise. Over the past five years, the role of machine learning engineer has risen up to bridge a gap that exists between data science and data engineering. In the following sections, I introduce concepts that are fundamental to data science and data engineering, as well as the hybrid machine learning engineering role, and then I show you the differences in how these roles function in an organization's data team.

Defining data science

If *science* is a systematic method by which people study and explain domain-specific phenomena that occur in the natural world, you can think of *data science* as the scientific domain that's dedicated to knowledge discovery via data analysis.

TECHNICAL STUFF

With respect to data science, the term *domain-specific* refers to the industry sector or subject matter domain that data science methods are being used to explore.

Data scientists use mathematical techniques and algorithmic approaches to derive solutions to complex business and scientific problems. Data science practitioners use its predictive methods to derive insights that are otherwise unattainable. In business and in science, data science methods can provide more robust decision-making capabilities:

>> **In business,** the purpose of data science is to empower businesses and organizations with the data insights they need in order to optimize organizational processes for maximum efficiency and revenue generation.

>> **In science,** data science methods are used to derive results and develop protocols for achieving the specific scientific goal at hand.

Data science is a vast and multidisciplinary field. To call yourself a true data scientist, you need to have expertise in math and statistics, computer programming, and your own domain-specific subject matter.

Using data science skills, you can do cool things like the following:

>> Use machine learning to optimize energy usage and lower corporate carbon footprints.

>> Optimize tactical strategies to achieve goals in business and science.

>> Predict for unknown contaminant levels from sparse environmental datasets.

>> Design automated theft- and fraud-prevention systems to detect anomalies and trigger alarms based on algorithmic results.

>> Craft site-recommendation engines for use in land acquisitions and real estate development.

>> Implement and interpret predictive analytics and forecasting techniques for net increases in business value.

Data scientists must have extensive and diverse quantitative expertise to be able to solve these types of problems.

Machine learning is the practice of applying algorithms to learn from — and make automated predictions from — data.

Defining machine learning engineering

A *machine learning engineer* is essentially a software engineer who is skilled enough in data science to deploy advanced data science models within the applications they build, thus bringing machine learning models into production in a live environment like a Software as a Service (SaaS) product or even just a web page. Contrary to what you may have guessed, the role of machine learning engineer is a hybrid between a data scientist and a software engineer, *not* a data engineer. A machine learning engineer is, at their core, a well-rounded software engineer who also has a solid foundation in machine learning and artificial intelligence. This person doesn't need to know as much data science as a data scientist but should know much more about computer science and software development than a typical data scientist.

Software as a Service (SaaS) is a term that describes cloud-hosted software services that are made available to users via the Internet. Examples of popular SaaS companies include Salesforce, Slack, HubSpot, and so many more.

Defining data engineering

If *engineering* is the practice of using science and technology to design and build systems that solve problems, you can think of *data engineering* as the engineering domain that's dedicated to building and maintaining data systems for overcoming data processing bottlenecks and data handling problems that arise from handling the high volume, velocity, and variety of big data.

Data engineers use skills in computer science and software engineering to design systems for, and solve problems with, handling and manipulating big datasets. Data engineers often have experience working with (and designing) real-time processing frameworks and massively parallel processing (MPP) platforms (discussed later in this chapter), as well as with RDBMSs. They generally code in Java, C++, Scala, or Python. They know how to deploy Hadoop MapReduce or Spark to handle, process, and refine big data into datasets with more manageable sizes. Simply put, with respect to data science, the purpose of data engineering is to engineer large-scale data solutions by building coherent, modular, and scalable data processing platforms from which data scientists can subsequently derive insights.

REMEMBER

Most engineered systems are *built* systems — they are constructed or manufactured in the physical world. Data engineering is different, though. It involves designing, building, and implementing software solutions to problems in the data world — a world that can seem abstract when compared to the physical reality of the Golden Gate Bridge or the Aswan Dam.

Using data engineering skills, you can, for example:

>> Integrate data pipelines with the natural language processing (NLP) services that were built by data scientists at your company.

>> Build mission-critical data platforms capable of processing more than 10 billion transactions per day.

>> Tear down data silos by finally migrating your company's data from a more traditional on-premise data storage environment to a cutting-edge cloud warehouse.

>> Enhance and maintain existing data infrastructure and data pipelines.

Data engineers need solid skills in computer science, database design, and software engineering to be able to perform this type of work.

Comparing machine learning engineers, data scientists, and data engineers

The roles of data scientist, machine learning engineer, and data engineer are frequently conflated by hiring managers. If you look around at most position descriptions for companies that are hiring, they often mismatch the titles and roles or simply expect applicants to be the Swiss army knife of data skills and be able to do them all.

TIP

If you're hiring someone to help make sense of your data, be sure to define the requirements clearly before writing the position description. Because data scientists must also have subject matter expertise in the particular areas in which they work, this requirement generally precludes data scientists from also having much expertise in data engineering. And, if you hire a data engineer who has data science skills, that person generally won't have much subject matter expertise outside of the data domain. Be prepared to call in a subject matter expert (SME) to help out.

Because many organizations combine and confuse roles in their data projects, data scientists are sometimes stuck having to learn to do the job of a data engineer — and vice versa. To come up with the highest-quality work product in the least amount of time, hire a data engineer to store, migrate, and process your data; a data scientist to make sense of it for you; and a machine learning engineer to bring your machine learning models into production.

Lastly, keep in mind that data engineer, machine learning engineer, and data scientist are just three small roles within a larger organizational structure. Managers, middle-level employees, and business leaders also play a huge part in the success of any data-driven initiative.

Storing and Processing Data for Data Science

A lot has changed in the world of big data storage options since the Hadoop debacle I mention earlier in this chapter. Back then, almost all business leaders clamored for on-premise data storage. Delayed by years due to the admonitions of traditional IT leaders, corporate management is finally beginning to embrace the notion that storing and processing big data with a reputable cloud service provider is the most cost-effective and secure way to generate value from enterprise data. In the following sections, you see the basics of what's involved in both cloud and on-premise big data storage and processing.

Storing data and doing data science directly in the cloud

After you have realized the upside potential of storing data in the cloud, it's hard to look back. Storing data in a cloud environment offers serious business advantages, such as these:

>> **Faster time-to-market:** Many big data cloud service providers take care of the bulk of the work that's required to configure, maintain, and provision the computing resources that are required to run jobs within a defined system – also known as a compute environment. This dramatically increases ease of use, and ultimately allows for faster time-to-market for data products.

>> **Enhanced flexibility:** Cloud services are extremely flexible with respect to usage requirements. If you set up in a cloud environment and then your project plan changes, you can simply turn off the cloud service with no further charges incurred. This isn't the case with on-premise storage, because once you purchase the server, you own it. Your only option from then on is to extract the best possible value from a noncancelable resource.

>> **Security:** If you go with reputable cloud service providers — like Amazon Web Services, Google Cloud, or Microsoft Azure — your data is likely to be a whole lot more secure in the cloud than it would be on-premise. That's because of the sheer number of resources that these megalith players dedicate to protecting and preserving the security of the data they store. I can't think of a multinational company that would have more invested in the security of its data infrastructure than Google, Amazon, or Microsoft.

A lot of different technologies have emerged in the wake of the cloud computing revolution, many of which are of interest to those trying to leverage big data. The next sections examine a few of these new technologies.

Using serverless computing to execute data science

When we talk about serverless computing, the term *serverless* is quite misleading because the computing indeed takes place on a server. Serverless computing really refers to computing that's executed in a cloud environment rather than on your desktop or on-premise at your company. The physical host server exists, but it's 100 percent supported by the cloud computing provider retained by you or your company.

One great tragedy of modern-day data science is the amount of time data scientists spend on non-mission-critical tasks like data collection, data cleaning and reformatting, data operations, and data integration. By most estimates, only 10 percent of a data scientist's time is spent on predictive model building — the rest of it is spent trying to prepare the data and the data infrastructure for that mission-critical task they've been retained to complete. Serverless computing has been a game-changer for the data science industry because it decreases the downtime that data scientists spend in preparing data and infrastructure for their predictive models.

Earlier in this chapter, I talk a bit about SaaS. Serverless computing offers something similar, but this is Function as a Service (FaaS) — a containerized cloud computing service that makes it much faster and simpler to execute code and predictive functions directly in a cloud environment, without the need to set up complicated infrastructure around that code. With serverless computing, your data science model runs directly within its container, as a sort of stand-alone function. Your cloud service provider handles all the provisioning and adjustments that need to be made to the infrastructure to support your functions.

Examples of popular serverless computing solutions are AWS Lambda, Google Cloud Functions, and Azure Functions.

Containerizing predictive applications within Kubernetes

Kubernetes is an open-source software suite that manages, orchestrates, and coordinates the deployment, scaling, and management of containerized applications across clusters of worker nodes. One particularly attractive feature about Kubernetes is that you can run it on data that sits in on-premise clusters, in the cloud, or in a hybrid cloud environment.

Kubernetes' chief focus is helping software developers build and scale apps quickly. Though it does provide a fault-tolerant, extensible environment for deploying and scaling predictive applications in the cloud, it also requires quite a bit of data engineering expertise to set them up correctly.

REMEMBER

A system is fault tolerant if it is built to continue successful operations despite the failure of one or more of its subcomponents. This requires redundancy in computing nodes. A system is described as extensible if it is flexible enough to be extended or shrunk in size without disrupting its operations.

To overcome this obstacle, Kubernetes released its KubeFlow product, a machine learning toolkit that makes it simple for data scientists to directly deploy predictive models within Kubernetes containers, without the need for outside data engineering support.

Sizing up popular cloud-warehouse solutions

You have a number of products to choose from when it comes to cloud-warehouse solutions. The following list looks at the most popular options:

>> **Amazon Redshift:** A popular big data warehousing service that runs atop data sitting within the Amazon Cloud, it is most notable for the incredible speed at which it can handle data analytics and business intelligence workloads. Because it runs on the AWS platform, Redshift's fully managed data warehousing service has the incredible capacity to support petabyte-scale cloud storage requirements. If your company is already using other AWS services — like Amazon EMR, Amazon Athena, or Amazon Kinesis — Redshift is the natural choice to integrate nicely with your existing technology. Redshift offers both pay-as-you-go as well as on-demand pricing structures that you'll want to explore further on its website: https://aws.amazon.com/redshift

TECHNICAL STUFF

Parallel processing refers to a powerful framework where data is processed very quickly because the work required to process the data is distributed across multiple nodes in a system. This configuration allows for the simultaneous processing of multiple tasks across different nodes in the system.

>> **Snowflake**: This SaaS solution provides powerful, parallel-processing analytics capabilities for both structured and semistructured data stored in the cloud on Snowflake's servers. Snowflake provides the ultimate 3-in-1 with its cost-effective big data storage, analytical processing capabilities, and all the built-in cloud services you might need. Snowflake integrates well with analytics tools like Tableau and Qlik, as well as with traditional big data technologies like Apache Spark, Pentaho, and Apache Kafka, but it wouldn't make sense if you're already relying mostly on Amazon services. Pricing for the Snowflake service is based on the amount of data you store as well as on the execution time for compute resources you consume on the platform.

>> **Google BigQuery:** Touted as a serverless data warehouse solution, BigQuery is a relatively cost-effective solution for generating analytics from big data sources stored in the Google Cloud. Similar to Snowflake and Redshift, BigQuery provides fully managed cloud services that make it fast and simple for data scientists and analytics professionals to use the tool without the need for assistance from in-house data engineers. Analytics can be generated on petabyte-scale data. BigQuery integrates with Google Data Studio, Power BI, Looker, and Tableau for ease of use when it comes to post-analysis data storytelling. Pricing for Google BigQuery is based on the amount of data you store as well as on the compute resources you consume on the platform, as represented by the amount of data your queries return from the platform.

Introducing NoSQL databases

A traditional RDBMS isn't equipped to handle big data demands. That's because it's designed to handle only relational datasets constructed of data that's stored in clean rows and columns and thus is capable of being queried via SQL. RDBMSs are incapable of handling unstructured and semistructured data. Moreover, RDBMSs simply lack the processing and handling capabilities that are needed for meeting big data volume-and-velocity requirements.

This is where *NoSQL* comes in — its databases are nonrelational, distributed database systems that were designed to rise to the challenges involved in storing and processing big data. They can be run on-premise or in a cloud environment. NoSQL databases step out past the traditional relational database architecture and offer a much more scalable, efficient solution. NoSQL systems facilitate non-SQL data querying of nonrelational or schema-free, semistructured and unstructured data. In this way, NoSQL databases are able to handle the structured, semistructured, and unstructured data sources that are common in big data systems.

TECHNICAL STUFF

A key-value pair is a pair of data items, represented by a key and a value. The key is a data item that acts as the record identifier and the *value* is the data that's identified (and retrieved) by its respective key.

NoSQL offers four categories of nonrelational databases: graph databases, document databases, key-values stores, and column family stores. Because NoSQL offers native functionality for each of these separate types of data structures, it offers efficient storage and retrieval functionality for most types of nonrelational data. This adaptability and efficiency make NoSQL an increasingly popular choice for handling big data and for overcoming processing challenges that come along with it.

NoSQL applications like Apache Cassandra and MongoDB are used for data storage and real-time processing. Apache Cassandra is a popular type of key-value store NoSQL database, and MongoDB is the most-popular document-oriented type of NoSQL database. It uses dynamic schemas and stores JSON-esque documents.

TECHNICAL STUFF

A document-oriented database is a NoSQL database that houses, retrieves, and manages the JSON files and XML files that you heard about back in Chapter 1, in the definition of semistructured data. A document-oriented database is otherwise known as a document store.

TECHNICAL STUFF

Some people argue that the term *NoSQL* stands for Not Only SQL, and others argue that it represents non-SQL databases. The argument is rather complex and has no cut-and-dried answer. To keep things simple, just think of NoSQL as a class of nonrelational systems that don't fall within the spectrum of RDBMSs that are queried using SQL.

Storing big data on-premise

Although cloud storage and cloud processing of big data is widely accepted as safe, reliable, and cost-effective, companies have a multitude of reasons for using on-premise solutions instead. In many instances of the training and consulting work I've done for foreign governments and multinational corporations, cloud data storage was the ultimate "no-fly zone" that should never be breached. This is particularly true of businesses I've worked with in the Middle East, where local security concerns were voiced as a main deterrent for moving corporate or government data to the cloud.

Though the popularity of storing big data on-premise has waned in recent years, many companies have their reasons for not wanting to move to a cloud environment. If you find yourself in circumstances where cloud services aren't an option, you'll probably appreciate the following discussion about on-premise alternatives.

REMEMBER

The Kubernetes and NoSQL databases described earlier in this chapter can be deployed on-premise as well as in a cloud environment.

Reminiscing about Hadoop

Because big data's three Vs (volume, velocity, and variety) don't allow for the handling of big data using traditional RDMSs, data engineers had to become innovative. To work around the limitations of relational systems, data engineers originally turned to the Hadoop data processing platform to boil down big data into smaller datasets that are more manageable for data scientists to analyze. This was all the rage until about 2015, when market demands had changed to the point that the platform was no longer able to meet them.

REMEMBER

When people refer to *Hadoop*, they're generally referring to an on-premise Hadoop storage environment that includes the HDFS (for data storage), MapReduce (for bulk data processing), Spark (for real-time data processing), and YARN (for resource management).

Incorporating MapReduce, the HDFS, and YARN

MapReduce is a parallel distributed processing framework that can process tremendous volumes of data *in-batch* — where data is collected and then processed as one unit with processing completion times on the order of hours or days. MapReduce works by converting raw data down to sets of tuples and then combining and reducing those tuples into smaller sets of tuples. (With respect to MapReduce, *tuples* refers to key-value pairs by which data is grouped, sorted, and processed.) In layperson terms, MapReduce uses parallel distributed computing to transform big data into data of a manageable size.

TECHNICAL STUFF

In Hadoop, *parallel distributed processing* refers to a powerful framework in which data is processed quickly via the distribution and parallel processing of tasks across clusters of commodity servers.

Storing data on the Hadoop distributed file system (HDFS)

The HDFS uses clusters of commodity hardware for storing data. Hardware in each cluster is connected, and this hardware is composed of *commodity servers* — low-cost, low-performing generic servers that offer powerful computing capabilities when run in parallel across a shared cluster. These commodity servers are also called *nodes*. Commoditized computing dramatically decreases the costs involved in storing big data.

The HDFS is characterized by these three key features:

>> **HDFS blocks:** In data storage, a block is a storage unit that contains some maximum number of records. HDFS blocks can store 64 megabytes of data, by default.

>> **Redundancy:** Datasets that are stored in HDFS are broken up and stored on blocks. These blocks are then replicated (three times, by default) and stored on several different servers in the cluster, as backup, or as redundancy.

>> **Fault-tolerance:** As mentioned earlier, a system is described as fault-tolerant if it's built to continue successful operations despite the failure of one or more of its subcomponents. Because the HDFS has built-in redundancy across multiple servers in a cluster, if one server fails, the system simply retrieves the data from another server.

Putting it all together on the Hadoop platform

The Hadoop platform was designed for large-scale data processing, storage, and management. This open-source platform is generally composed of the HDFS, MapReduce, Spark, and YARN (a resource manager) all working together.

Within a Hadoop platform, the workloads of applications that run on the HDFS (like MapReduce and Spark) are divided among the nodes of the cluster, and the output is stored on the HDFS. A Hadoop cluster can be composed of thousands of nodes. To keep the costs of input/output (I/O) processes low, MapReduce jobs are performed as close as possible to the data — the task processors are positioned as closely as possible to the outgoing data that needs to be processed. This design facilitates the sharing of computational requirements in big data processing.

Introducing massively parallel processing (MPP) platforms

Massively parallel processing (MPP) platforms can be used instead of MapReduce as an alternative approach for distributed data processing. If your goal is to deploy parallel processing on a traditional on-premise data warehouse, an MPP may be the perfect solution.

To understand how MPP compares to a standard MapReduce parallel-processing framework, consider that MPP runs parallel computing tasks on costly custom hardware, whereas MapReduce runs them on inexpensive commodity servers. Consequently, MPP processing capabilities are cost restrictive. MPP is quicker and easier to use than standard MapReduce jobs. That's because MPP can be queried using Structured Query Language (SQL), but native MapReduce jobs are controlled by the more complicated Java programming language.

Processing big data in real-time

A *real-time processing framework* is — as its name implies — a framework that processes data in real-time (or near-real-time) as the data streams and flows into the system. Real-time frameworks process data in microbatches — they return results in a matter of seconds rather than the hours or days it typically takes batch processing frameworks like MapReduce. Real-time processing frameworks do one of the following:

>> **Increase the overall time efficiency of the system:** Solutions in this category include Apache Storm and Apache Spark for near-real-time stream processing.

>> **Deploy innovative querying methods to facilitate the real-time querying of big data:** Some solutions in this category are Google's Dremel, Apache Drill, Shark for Apache Hive, and Cloudera's Impala.

TECHNICAL STUFF

In-memory refers to processing data within the computer's memory, without actually reading and writing its computational results onto the disk. In-memory computing provides results a lot faster but cannot process much data per processing interval.

Apache Spark is an in-memory computing application that you can use to query, explore, analyze, and even run machine learning algorithms on incoming streaming data in near-real-time. Its power lies in its processing speed: The ability to process and make predictions from streaming big data sources in three seconds flat is no laughing matter.

TIP

Real-time, stream-processing frameworks are quite useful in a multitude of industries — from stock and financial market analyses to e-commerce optimizations and from real-time fraud detection to optimized order logistics. Regardless of the industry in which you work, if your business is impacted by real-time data streams that are generated by humans, machines, or sensors, a real-time processing framework would be helpful to you in optimizing and generating value for your organization.

2

Using Data Science to Extract Meaning from Your Data

Chapter **3**

Machine Learning Means . . . Using a Machine to Learn from Data

I f you've been watching any news for the past decade, you've no doubt heard of a concept called machine learning — often referenced when reporters are covering stories on the newest amazing invention from artificial intelligence. In this chapter, you dip your toes into the area called machine learning, and in Part 3 you see how machine learning and data science are used to increase business profits.

Defining Machine Learning and Its Processes

Machine learning is the practice of applying algorithmic models to data over and over again so that your computer discovers hidden patterns or trends that you can use to make predictions. It's also called *algorithmic learning*. Machine learning has a vast and ever-expanding assortment of use cases, including

>> Real-time Internet advertising

>> Internet marketing personalization

>> Internet search

>> Spam filtering

>> Recommendation engines

>> Natural language processing and sentiment analysis

>> Automatic facial recognition

>> Customer churn prediction

>> Credit score modeling

>> Survival analysis for mechanical equipment

Walking through the steps of the machine learning process

Three main steps are involved in machine learning: setup, learning, and application. Setup involves acquiring data, preprocessing it, selecting the most appropriate variables for the task at hand (called *feature selection*), and breaking the data into training and test datasets. You use the *training data* to train the model, and the *test data* to test the accuracy of the model's predictions. The learning step involves model experimentation, training, building, and testing. The application step involves model deployment and prediction.

REMEMBER

Here's a rule of thumb for breaking data into test-and-training sets: Apply random sampling to two-thirds of the original dataset in order to use that sample to train the model. Use the remaining one-third of the data as test data, for evaluating the model's predictions.

A random sample contains observations that all each have an equal probability of being selected from the original dataset. A simple example of a random sample is illustrated by Figure 3-1 below. You need your sample to be randomly chosen so that it represents the full data set in an unbiased way. Random sampling allows you to test and train an output model without selection bias.

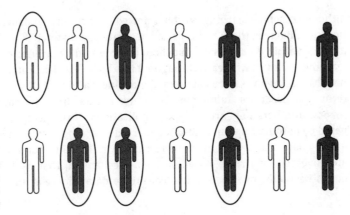

FIGURE 3-1:
A example of a simple random sample

Becoming familiar with machine learning terms

Before diving too deeply into a discussion of machine learning methods, you need to know about the (sometimes confusing) vocabulary associated with the field. Because machine learning is an offshoot of both traditional statistics and computer science, it has adopted terms from both fields and added a few of its own. Here is what you need to know:

>> **Instance:** The same as a *row* (in a data table), an *observation* (in statistics), and a *data point*. Machine learning practitioners are also known to call an instance a *case*.

>> **Feature:** The same as a *column* or *field* (in a data table) and a *variable* (in statistics). In regression methods, a feature is also called an *independent variable* (IV).

>> **Target variable:** The same as a *predictant* or *dependent* variable (DV) in statistics.

REMEMBER

In machine learning, *feature selection* is a somewhat straightforward process for selecting appropriate variables; for *feature engineering*, you need substantial domain expertise and strong data science skills to manually design input variables from the underlying dataset. You use feature engineering in cases where your model needs a better representation of the problem being solved than is available in the raw dataset.

WARNING

Although machine learning is often referred to in context of data science and artificial intelligence, these terms are all separate and distinct. Machine learning is a practice within data science, but there is more to data science than just machine learning — as you will learn throughout this book. Artificial intelligence often, but not always, involves data science and machine learning. Artificial intelligence is a term that describes autonomously acting agents. In some case AI agents are robots, in others they are software applications. If the agent's actions are triggered by outputs from an embedded machine learning model, then the AI is powered by data science and machine learning. On the other hand, if the AI's actions are governed by a rules-based decision mechanism, then you can have AI that doesn't actually involve machine learning or data science at all.

Considering Learning Styles

Machine learning can be applied in three main styles: supervised, unsupervised, and semisupervised. Supervised and unsupervised methods are behind most modern machine learning applications, and semisupervised learning is an up-and-coming star.

Learning with supervised algorithms

Supervised learning algorithms require that input data has labeled features. These algorithms learn from known features of that data to produce an output model that successfully predicts labels for new incoming, unlabeled data points. You use supervised learning when you have a labeled dataset composed of historical values that are good predictors of future events. Use cases include survival analysis and fraud detection, among others. Logistic regression is a type of supervised learning algorithm, and you can read more on that topic in the next section.

TECHNICAL STUFF

Survival analysis, also known as event history analysis in social science, is a statistical method that attempts to predict the time of a particular event — such as a mother's age at first childbirth in the case of demography, or age at first incarceration for criminologists.

Learning with unsupervised algorithms

Unsupervised learning algorithms accept unlabeled data and attempt to group observations into categories based on underlying similarities in input features, as shown in Figure 3-2. Principal component analysis, k-means clustering, and singular value decomposition are all examples of unsupervised machine learning algorithms. Popular use cases include recommendation engines, facial recognition systems, and customer segmentation.

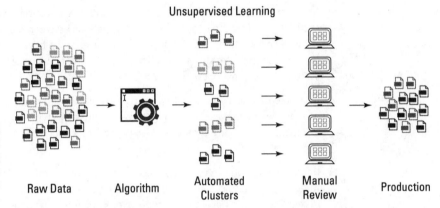

FIGURE 3-2: Unsupervised machine learning breaks down unlabeled data into subgroups.

Learning with reinforcement

Reinforcement learning is a behavior-based learning model. It's based on a mechanic similar to how humans and animals learn. The model is given "rewards" based on how it behaves, and it subsequently learns to maximize the sum of its rewards by adapting the decisions it makes to earn as many rewards as possible.

Seeing What You Can Do

Whether you're just becoming familiar with the algorithms that are involved in machine learning or you're looking to find out more about what's happening in cutting-edge machine learning advancements, this section has something for you. First, I give you an overview of machine learning algorithms, broken down by function, and then I describe more about the advanced areas of machine learning that are embodied by deep learning and Apache Spark.

Selecting algorithms based on function

When you need to choose a class of machine learning algorithms, it's helpful to consider each model class based on its functionality. For the most part, algorithmic functionality falls into the categories shown in Figure 3-3.

>> **Regression:** You can use this type to model relationships between features in a dataset. You can read more on linear and logistic regression methods and ordinary least squares in Chapter 4.

>> **Association rule learning:** This type of algorithm is a rule-based set of methods that you can use to discover associations between features in a dataset. For an in-depth training and demonstration on how to use association rules in Excel, be sure to check out the companion website to this book (https://businessgrowth.ai/).

>> **Instance-based:** If you want to use observations in your dataset to classify new observations based on similarity, you can use this type. To model with instances, you can use methods like k-nearest neighbor classification, covered in Chapter 5.

>> **Regularizing:** You can use regularization to introduce added information as a means by which to prevent model overfitting or to solve an ill-posed problem. In case the term is new to you, model overfitting is a situation in which a model is so tightly fit to its underlying dataset, as well as its noise or random error, that the model performs poorly as a predictor for new observations.

>> **Naïve Bayes:** If you want to predict the likelihood of an event's occurrence based on some evidence in your data, you can use this method, based on classification and regression. Naïve Bayes is covered in Chapter 4.

>> **Decision tree:** A tree structure is useful as a decision-support tool. You can use it to build models that predict for potential downstream implications that are associated with any given decision.

>> **Clustering:** You can use this type of unsupervised machine learning method to uncover subgroups within an unlabeled dataset. Both k-means clustering and hierarchical clustering are covered in Chapter 5.

>> **Dimension reduction:** If you're looking for a method to use as a filter to remove redundant information, unexplainable random variation, and outliers from your data, consider dimension reduction techniques such as factor analysis and principal component analysis. These topics are covered in Chapter 4.

>> **Neural network:** A neural network mimics how the brain solves problems, by using a layer of interconnected neural units as a means by which to learn — and infer rules — from observational data. It's often used in image recognition and computer vision applications.

Imagine that you're deciding whether you should go to the beach. You never go to the beach if it's raining, and you don't like going if it's colder than 75 degrees (Fahrenheit) outside. These are the two inputs for your decision. Your preference to not go to the beach when it's raining is a lot stronger than your preference to not go to the beach when it's colder than 75 degrees, so you weight these two inputs accordingly. For any given instance where you decide whether you're going to the beach, you consider these two criteria, add up the result, and then decide whether to go. If you decide to go, your decision threshold has been satisfied. If you decide not to go, your decision threshold was not satisfied. This is a simplistic analogy for how neural networks work.

Now, for a more technical definition. The simplest type of neural network is the *perceptron*. It accepts more than one input, weights them, adds them up on a processor layer, and then — based on the activation function and the threshold you set for it — outputs a result. An *activation function* is a mathematical function that transforms inputs into an output signal. The processor layer is called a *hidden layer*. A *neural network* is a layer of connected perceptrons that all work together as a unit to accept inputs and return outputs that signal whether some criteria is met. A key feature of neural nets is that they're *self-learning* — in other words, they adapt, learn, and optimize per changes in input data. Figure 3-4 is a schematic layout that depicts how a perceptron is structured.

>> **Deep learning method:** This method incorporates traditional neural networks in successive layers to offer deep-layer training for generating predictive outputs. I tell you more about this topic in the next section.

>> **Ensemble algorithm:** You can use ensemble algorithms to combine machine learning approaches to achieve results that are better than would be available from any single machine learning method on its own.

Visit the companion website to this book (`https://businessgrowth.ai/`) to get a quick-start guide to selecting the best deep learning network for your most immediate needs.

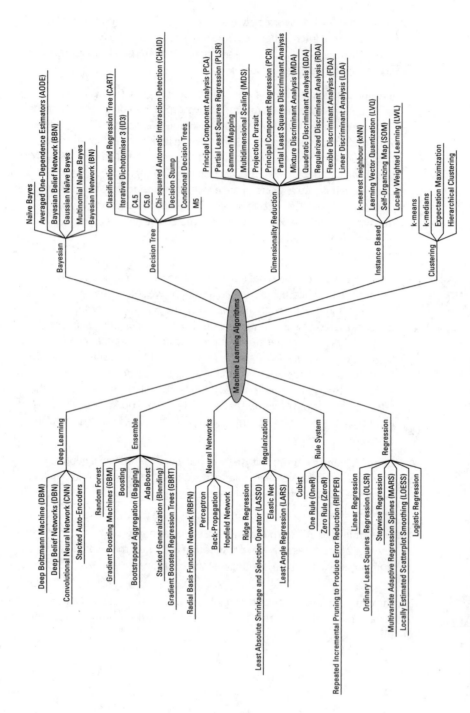

FIGURE 3-3: Machine learning algorithms can be broken down by function.

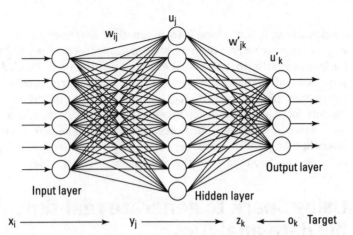

FIGURE 3-4: Neural networks are connected layers of artificial neural units.

If you use Gmail, you must be enjoying its autoreply functionality. You know — the three 1-line messages from which you can choose an autoreply to a message someone sent you? Well, this autoreply functionality within Gmail is called Smart-Reply, and it is built on deep learning algorithms. Another innovation built on deep learning is Facebook DeepFace, the Facebook feature that automatically recognizes and suggests tags for the people who appear in your Facebook photos. Figure 3-5 is a schematic layout that depicts how a deep learning network is structured.

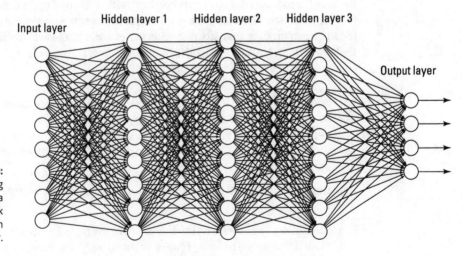

FIGURE 3-5: A deep learning network is a neural network with more than one hidden layer.

Deep learning is a machine learning method that uses hierarchical neural networks to learn from data in an iterative and adaptive manner. It's an ideal approach for learning patterns from unlabeled and unstructured data. It's essentially the same concept as the neural network, except that deep learning algorithms have two or more hidden layers. In fact, computer vision applications — like those that support facial recognition for images uploaded to Facebook, or the self-driving cars produced by Tesla — have been known to implement more than 150 hidden layers in a single deep neural network. The more hidden layers there are, the more complex a decision the algorithm can make.

Using Spark to generate real-time big data analytics

Apache Spark is an in-memory distributed computing application that you can use to deploy machine learning algorithms on big data sources in near-real-time to generate analytics from streaming big data sources. Whew!

TECHNICAL STUFF

In-memory refers to processing data within the computer's memory, without actually reading and writing its computational results onto the disk. In-memory computing provides its results a lot faster but cannot process much data per processing interval.

Because it processes data in microbatches, with 3-second cycle times, you can use it to significantly decrease time-to-insight in cases where time is of the essence. It can be run on data that sits in a wide variety of storage architectures, including Hadoop HDFS, Amazon Redshift, MongoDB, Cassandra, Solr and AWS. Spark is composed of the following submodules:

» **Spark SQL:** You use this module to work with and query structured data using Spark. Within Spark, you can query data using Spark's built-in SQL package: SparkSQL. You can also query structured data using Hive, but then you'd use the HiveQL language and run the queries using the Spark processing engine.

» **GraphX:** The GraphX library is how you store and process network data from within Spark.

» **Streaming:** The Streaming module is where the big data processing takes place. This module basically breaks a continuously streaming data source into much smaller data streams, called *Dstreams* — discreet data streams, in other words. Because the Dstreams are small, these batch cycles can be completed within three seconds, which is why it's called microbatch processing.

» **MLib:** The MLib submodule is where you analyze data, generate statistics, and deploy machine learning algorithms from within the Spark environment. MLib has APIs for Java, Scala, Python, and R. The MLib module allows data professionals to work within Spark to build machine learning models in Python or R, and those models will then pull data directly from the requisite data storage repository, whether that be on-premise, in a cloud, or even a multicloud environment. This helps reduce the reliance that data scientists sometimes have on data engineers. Furthermore, computations are known to be 100 times faster when processed in-memory using Spark as opposed to the traditional MapReduce framework.

You can deploy Spark on-premise by downloading the open-source framework from the Apache Spark website, at http://spark.apache.org/downloads.html. Another option is to run Spark on the cloud via the Apache Databricks service, at https://databricks.com.

Chapter **4**

Math, Probability, and Statistical Modeling

Math and statistics are not the scary monsters that many people make them out to be. In data science, the need for these quantitative methods is simply a fact of life — and nothing to get alarmed over. Although you must have a handle on the math and statistics that are necessary to solve a problem, you don't need to go study for degrees in those fields.

Contrary to what many pure statisticians would have you believe, the data science field isn't the same as the statistics field. Data scientists have substantive knowledge in one field or several fields, and they use statistics, math, coding, and strong communication skills to help them discover, understand, and communicate data insights that lie within raw datasets related to their field of expertise. Statistics is a vital component of this formula, but not more vital than the others. In this chapter, I introduce you to the basic ideas behind probability, correlation analysis, dimensionality reduction, decision modeling, regression analysis, outlier detection, and time series analysis.

Exploring Probability and Inferential Statistics

Probability is one of the most fundamental concepts in statistics. To even get started making sense of your data by using statistics, you need to be able to identify something as basic as whether you're looking at *descriptive* or *inferential* statistics. You also need a firm grasp of the basics of probability distribution. The following sections cover these concepts and more.

A *statistic* is a result that's derived from performing a mathematical operation on numerical data. In general, you use statistics in decision-making. Statistics come in two flavors:

>> **Descriptive:** Descriptive statistics provide a description that illuminates some characteristic of a numerical dataset, including dataset distribution, central tendency (such as mean, min, or max), and dispersion (as in standard deviation and variance). For clarification, the mean of a data set is the average value of its data points, its min is the minimum value of its data points and the max is the maximum value. Descriptive statistics are not meant to illustrate any causal claims.

REMEMBER

Descriptive statistics can highlight relationships between X and Y, but they do not posit that X causes Y.

>> **Inferential:** Rather than focus on pertinent descriptions of a dataset, inferential statistics carve out a smaller section of the dataset and attempt to deduce significant information about the larger dataset. Unlike descriptive statistics, inferential methods, such as regression analysis, DO try to predict by studying causation. Use this type of statistics to derive information about a real-world measure in which you're interested.

It's true that descriptive statistics describe the characteristics of a numerical dataset, but that doesn't tell you why you should care. In fact, most data scientists are interested in descriptive statistics only because of what they reveal about the real-world measures they describe. For example, a descriptive statistic is often associated with a *degree of accuracy*, indicating the statistic's value as an estimate of the real-world measure.

To better understand this concept, imagine that a business owner wants to estimate the upcoming quarter's profits. The owner might take an average of the past few quarters' profits to use as an estimate of how much profit they'll make during the next quarter. But if the previous quarters' profits varied widely, a descriptive statistic that estimated the *variation* of this predicted profit value (the amount by which this dollar estimate could differ from the actual profits earned) would indicate just how far the predicted value could be from the actual one. (Not bad information to have, right?)

TIP

You can use descriptive statistics in many ways — to detect outliers, for example, or to plan for feature preprocessing requirements or to quickly identify which features you may want — or not want — to use in an analysis.

Like descriptive statistics, *inferential statistics* are used to reveal something about a real-world measure. Inferential statistics do this by providing information about a small data selection, so you can use this information to infer something about the larger dataset from which it was taken. In statistics, this smaller data selection is known as a *sample,* and the larger, complete dataset from which the sample is taken is called the *population.*

If your dataset is too big to analyze in its entirety, pull a smaller sample of this dataset, analyze it, and then make inferences about the entire dataset based on what you learn from analyzing the sample. You can also use inferential statistics in situations where you simply can't afford to collect data for the entire population. In this case, you'd use the data you do have to make inferences about the population at large. At other times, you may find yourself in situations where complete information for the population isn't available. In these cases, you can use inferential statistics to estimate values for the missing data based on what you learn from analyzing the data that's available.

WARNING

For an inference to be valid, you must select your sample carefully so that you form a true representation of the population. Even if your sample is representative, the numbers in the sample dataset will always exhibit some *noise* — random variation, in other words — indicating that the sample statistic isn't exactly identical to its corresponding population statistic. For example, if you're constructing a sample of data based on the demographic makeup of Chicago's population, you would want to ensure that proportions of racial/ethnic groups in your sample match up to proportions in the population overall.

Probability distributions

Imagine that you've just rolled into Las Vegas and settled into your favorite roulette table over at the Bellagio. When the roulette wheel spins off, you intuitively understand that there is an equal chance that the ball will fall into any of the slots of the cylinder on the wheel. The slot where the ball lands is totally random, and the *probability,* or likelihood, of the ball landing in any one slot over another is the same. Because the ball can land in any slot, with equal probability, there is an equal probability distribution, or a *uniform probability distribution* — the ball has an equal probability of landing in any of the slots in the wheel.

But the slots of the roulette wheel aren't all the same — the wheel has 18 black slots and 20 slots that are either red or green.

Probability $(\text{black}) = {}^{18}\!/_{38} = .4736$

Because of this arrangement, the probability that your ball will land on a black slot is 47.4%.

Your net winnings here can be considered a *random variable*, which is a measure of a trait or value associated with an object, a person, or a place (something in the real world) that is unpredictable. Because this trait or value is unpredictable, however, doesn't mean that you know nothing about it. What's more, you can use what you do know about this thing to help you in your decision-making. Keep reading to find out how.

A *weighted average* is an average value of a measure over a very large number of data points. If you take a weighted average of your winnings (your random variable) across the probability distribution, this would yield an *expectation value* — an expected value for your net winnings over a successive number of bets. (An expectation can also be thought of as the best guess, if you had to guess.) To describe it more formally, an *expectation* is a weighted average of some measure associated with a random variable. If your goal is to model an unpredictable variable so that you can make data-informed decisions based on what you know about its probability in a population, you can use random variables and probability distributions to do this.

REMEMBER

When considering the probability of an event, you must know what other events are possible. Always define the set of events as *mutually exclusive* — only one can occur at a time. (Think of the six possible results of rolling a die.) Probability has these two important characteristics:

>> The probability of any single event never goes below 0.0 or exceeds 1.0.

>> The probability of all events always sums to exactly 1.0.

Probability distribution is classified per these two types:

>> **Discrete:** A random variable where values can be counted by groupings

>> **Continuous:** A random variable that assigns probabilities to a range of value

REMEMBER

To understand discrete and continuous distribution, think of two variables from a dataset describing cars. A "color" variable would have a discrete distribution because cars have only a limited range of colors (black, red, or blue, for example). The observations would be countable per the color grouping. A variable describing cars' miles per gallon, or mpg, would have a continuous distribution because each car could have its own, separate value for miles per gallon (mpg) that it gets on average.

» **Normal distributions (numeric continuous):** Represented graphically by a symmetric bell-shaped curve, these distributions model phenomena that tend toward some most-likely observation (at the top of the bell in the bell curve); observations at the two extremes are less likely.

» **Binomial distributions (numeric discrete):** These distributions model the number of successes that can occur in a certain number of attempts when only two outcomes are possible (the old heads-or-tails coin flip scenario, for example). Binary variables — variables that assume only one of two values — have a binomial distribution.

» **Categorical distributions (non-numeric):** These represent either non-numeric categorical variables or *ordinal variables* (an ordered categorical variable, for example the level of service offered by most airlines is ordinal because they offer first class, business class, and economy class seats).

Conditional probability with Naïve Bayes

You can use the Naïve Bayes machine learning method, which was borrowed straight from the statistics field, to predict the likelihood that an event will occur, given evidence defined in your data features — something called *conditional probability*. Naïve Bayes, which is based on classification and regression, is especially useful if you need to classify text data.

To better illustrate this concept, consider the Spambase dataset that's available from University of California, Irvine's machine learning repository (https://archive.ics.uci.edu/ml/datasets/Spambase). That dataset contains 4,601 records of emails and, in its last field, designates whether each email is spam. From this dataset, you can identify common characteristics between spam emails. After you've defined common features that indicate spam email, you can build a Naïve Bayes classifier that reliably predicts whether an incoming email is spam, based on the empirical evidence supported in its content. In other words, the model predicts whether an email is spam — the *event* — based on features gathered from its content — the *evidence*.

TECHNICAL
STUFF

When it comes to experimentation, multinomial and binomial distributions behave similarly, except those multinomial distributions can produce two or more outcomes, and binomial distributions can only produce two outcomes.

Naïve Bayes comes in these three popular flavors:

>> **MultinomialNB:** Use this version if your variables (categorical or continuous) describe discrete frequency counts, like word counts. This version of Naïve Bayes assumes a multinomial distribution, as is often the case with text data. It does not accept negative values.

>> **BernoulliNB:** If your features are binary, you can use multinomial Bernoulli Naïve Bayes to make predictions. This version works for classifying text data but isn't generally known to perform as well as MultinomialNB. If you want to use BernoulliNB to make predictions from continuous variables, that will work, but you first need to subdivide the variables into discrete interval groupings (also known as *binning*).

>> **GaussianNB:** Use this version if all predictive features are normally distributed. It's not a good option for classifying text data, but it can be a good choice if your data contains both positive and negative values (and if your features have a normal distribution, of course).

WARNING

Before building a Bayes classifier naïvely, consider that the model holds an *a priori* assumption — meaning that its predictions are based on an assumption that past conditions still hold true. Predicting future values from historical ones generates incorrect results when present circumstances change.

Quantifying Correlation

Many statistical and machine learning methods assume that your features are independent. To test whether they're independent, though, you need to evaluate their *correlation* — the extent to which variables demonstrate interdependency. In this section, you get a brief introduction to Pearson correlation and Spearman's rank correlation.

TIP

Correlation is quantified per the value of a variable called r, which ranges between −1 and 1. The closer the r-value is to 1 or −1, the more correlation there is between two variables. If two variables have an r-value that's close to 0, it could indicate that they're independent variables.

Calculating correlation with Pearson's r

If you want to uncover dependent relationships between continuous variables in a dataset, you'd use statistics to estimate their correlation. The simplest form of correlation analysis is the *Pearson correlation*, which assumes that

>> Your data is normally distributed.

>> You have continuous, numeric variables.

>> Your variables are linearly related. You can identify a linear relationship by plotting the data points on a chart and looking to see if there is a clear increasing or decreasing trend within the values of the data points, such that a straight line can be drawn to summarize that trend. See Figure 4-1 for an illustration of what a linear relationship looks like.

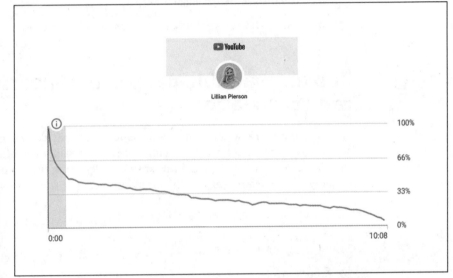

FIGURE 4-1:
An example
of a linear
relationship
between months
and YouTube
subscribers.

WARNING

Because the Pearson correlation has so many conditions, use it *only* to determine whether a relationship between two variables exists, but not to rule out possible relationships. If you were to get an r-value that is close to 0, it indicates that there is no linear relationship between the variables but that a nonlinear relationship between them still could exist.

To use the Pearson's r to test for linear correlation between two variables, you'd simply plug your data into the following formula and calculate the result.

$$r = \frac{\sum(x-\bar{x})(y-\bar{y})}{\sqrt{\sum(x-\bar{x})^2 \sum(y-\bar{y})^2}}$$

>> $\bar{x}$ = mean of x variable

>> $\bar{y}$ = mean of y variable

>> r = Pearson r coefficient of correlation

Once you get a value for your Pearson r, you'd interpret it value according to the following standards:

>> **if r close to +1:** Strong positive correlation between variables

>> **if r = 0:** Variables are not linearly correlated

>> **if r close to -1:** Strong negative correlation between variables

Ranking variable-pairs using Spearman's rank correlation

The Spearman's rank correlation is a popular test for determining correlation between ordinal variables. By applying Spearman's rank correlation, you're converting numeric variable–pairs into ranks by calculating the strength of the relationship between variables and then ranking them per their correlation.

The Spearman's rank correlation assumes that

>> Your variables are ordinal.

>> Your variables are related nonlinearly. You can identify nonlinearity between variables by looking at a graph. If the graph between two variables produces a curve (for example, like the one shown in Figure 4-2) then the variables have a nonlinear relationship. This curvature occurs because, with variables related in a non-linear manner, a change in the value of x does not necessarily correspond to the same change in dataset's y-value.

>> Your data is nonnormally distributed.

To use Spearman Rank to test for correlation between ordinal variables, you'd simply plug the values for your variables into the following formula and calculate the result.

$$\rho = 1 - \frac{6\sum d^2}{n\left(n^2 - 1\right)}$$

>> ρ = Spearman's rank correlation coefficient

>> *d* = difference between the two ranks of each data point

>> *n* = total number of data points in the data set

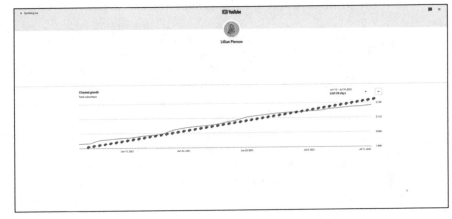

FIGURE 4-2:
An example of a non-linear relationship between watch time and % viewership.

Reducing Data Dimensionality with Linear Algebra

Any intermediate-level data scientist should have a good understanding of linear algebra and how to do math using matrices. Array and matrix objects are the primary data structure in analytical computing. You need them in order to perform mathematical and statistical operations on large and *multidimensional* datasets — datasets with many different features to be tracked simultaneously. In this section, you see exactly what is involved in using linear algebra and machine learning methods to reduce a dataset's dimensionality — in other words, to reduce a dataset's feature count, without losing the important information the dataset contains, by compressing its features' information into synthetic variables that you can subsequently utilize to make predictions or as input into another machine learning model.

Decomposing data to reduce dimensionality

Okay, what can you do with all this theory? Well, for starters, using a linear algebra method called *singular value decomposition (SVD)*, you can reduce the dimensionality of your dataset — reduce the number of features that you track when carrying out an analysis, in other words. Dimension reduction algorithms are ideal options if you need to compress your dataset while also removing redundant information and noise. In data science, SVD is applied to analyze principal components from with large, noisy, sparse data sets — an approach machine learning folks call *Principal Component Analysis (PCA)*. Since the linear algebra involved in PCA is rooted in SVD, let's look at how SVD works.

TECHNICAL STUFF

The difference between SVD and PCA is just this: PCA assumes that you are working with a square (1x1) input matrix. If your input matrix is not square, then use SVD instead, because SVD does not make this assumption. PCA is covered in greater detail later in this chapter.

The SVD linear algebra method decomposes the data matrix into the three resultant matrices shown in Figure 4-4. The product of these matrices, when multiplied together, gives you back your original matrix. SVD is handy when you want to compress or clean your dataset. Using SVD enables you to uncover *latent variables* — inferred variables hidden within your dataset that affect how that dataset behaves. Two main ways to use the SVD algorithm include

>> **Compressing sparse matrices:** If you have a clean yet sparse dataset then, you don't want to remove any of the information that the dataset holds, but you do need to compress that information down into a manageable number of variables, so that you can use them to make predictions. A handy thing about SVD is that it allows you to set the number of variables, or components, it creates from your original dataset. And if you don't remove any of those components, then you will reduce the size of your dataset without losing any of its important information. This process is illustrated in Figure 4-3.

>> **Cleaning and compressing dirty data:** In other cases, you can use SVD to do an algorithmic cleanse of a dirty, noisy dataset. In this case you'd apply SVD to uncover your components, and then decide which of them to keep by looking at their variance. The industry standard is that explained variance of the components you keep should add up to at least 75 percent or more. This ensures that at least 75 percent of the dataset's original information has been retained within the components you've kept. This process is illustrated in Figure 4-4.

WARNING

If the sum of the explained variance — or *cumulative variance explained (CVE)* — for the components you keep is less than 95 percent, do not use the components as derived features further downstream in other machine learning models. In this case, the information lost within these derived features will cause the machine learning model to generate inaccurate, unreliable predictions. These derived components are, however, useful as a source for descriptive statistics or for building more general *descriptive analytics* — in other words, analytics that describe what happened in the past, and answer questions like "what happened" "when" "how many", and "where."

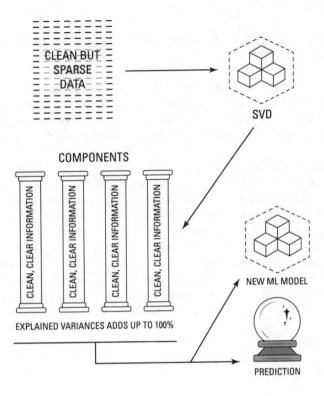

FIGURE 4-3: Applying SVD to compress a sparse, clean dataset.

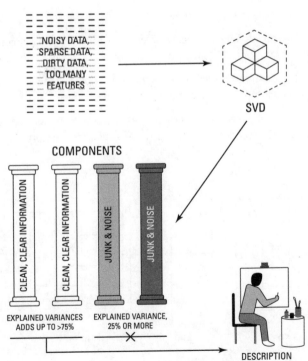

FIGURE 4-4: Applying SVD to clean and compress a sparse, dirty dataset.

REMEMBER

The lower the CVE, the more you should take your model's results with a grain of salt.

WARNING

If you remove some components, then when you go to reconstruct your matrix, you'll probably notice that the resulting matrix isn't an exact match to your original dataset. Worry not! That is the data that remains after much of the information redundancy and noise was filtered out by SVD and removed by you.

Getting a little nitty-gritty about SVD, let's look at the formula for SVD, but keep in mind — this is linear algebra not regular algebra, so we are looking at matrix math not regular math. To take it from the beginning, you need to understand the concept of eigenvector. To do that, think of a matrix called A. Now consider a non-zero vector called x and that $Ax = \lambda x$ for a scalar λ. In this scenario, scalar λ is what's called an *eigenvalue* of matrix A. It's permitted to take on a value of 0. Furthermore, x is the eigenvector that corresponds to λ, and again, it's not permitted to be a zero value. λ is simply the scale factor of the eigenvector. SVD decomposes the matrix down into three resultant matrices shown in Figure 4-5. The product of these matrices, when multiplied together, gives you back your original matrix.

Take a closer look at Figure 4-5:

$$A = u * S * v$$

>> **A:** This is the matrix that holds all your original data.

>> **u:** This is a left-singular vector (an eigenvector) of A, and it holds all the important, nonredundant information about your data's observations.

>> **v:** This is a right-singular eigenvector of A. It holds all the important, nonredundant information about columns in your dataset's features.

>> **S:** This is the square root of the eigenvalue of A. It contains all the information about the procedures performed during the compression.

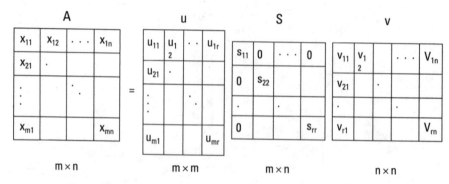

FIGURE 4-5: You can use SVD to decompose data down to u, S, and V matrices.

Reducing dimensionality with factor analysis

Factor analysis is along the same lines as SVD in that it's a method you can use for filtering out redundant information and noise from your data. An offspring of the psychometrics field, this method was developed to help you derive a root cause in cases where a shared root cause results in *shared variance* — when a variable's variance correlates with the variance of other variables in the dataset.

TECHNICAL STUFF

A variable's variability measures how much variance it has around its mean. The greater a variable's variance, the more information that variable contains.

When you find shared variance in your dataset, that means information redundancy is at play. You can use factor analysis or principal component analysis to clear your data of this information redundancy. You see more on principal component analysis in the following section, but for now, focus on factor analysis and the fact that you can use it to compress your dataset's information into a reduced set of meaningful, non-information-redundant *latent variables* — meaningful inferred variables that underlie a dataset but are not directly observable.

Factor analysis makes the following assumptions:

>> Your features are *metric* — numeric variables on which meaningful calculations can be made.

>> Your features should be continuous or *ordinal* (if you're not sure what ordinal is, refer back to the first class, business class, and economy class analogy in the probability distributions section of this chapter).

>> You have more than 100 observations in your dataset and at least 5 observations per feature.

>> Your sample is homogenous.

>> There is r > 0.3 correlation between the features in your dataset.

In factor analysis, you do a regression — a topic covered later in this chapter — on features to uncover underlying latent variables, or *factors*. You can then use those factors as variables in future analyses, to represent the original dataset from which they're derived. At its core, factor analysis is the process of fitting a model to prepare a dataset for analysis by reducing its dimensionality and information redundancy.

Decreasing dimensionality and removing outliers with PCA

Principal component analysis (PCA) is another dimensionality reduction technique that's closely related to SVD: This unsupervised statistical method finds relationships between features in your dataset and then transforms and reduces them to a set of non–information–redundant *principal components* — uncorrelated features that embody and explain the information that's contained within the dataset (that is, its variance). These components act as a synthetic, refined representation of the dataset, with the information redundancy, noise, and outliers stripped out. You can then use those reduced components as input for your machine learning algorithms to make predictions based on a compressed representation of your data. (For more on outliers, see the "Detecting Outliers" section, later in this chapter.)

The PCA model makes these two assumptions:

>> *Multivariate normality* (MVN) — or a set of real-valued, correlated, random variables that are each clustered around a mean — is desirable, but not required.

>> Variables in the dataset should be continuous.

Although PCA is like factor analysis, they have two major differences: One difference is that PCA does not regress to find some underlying cause of shared variance, but instead decomposes a dataset to succinctly represent its most important information in a reduced number of features. The other key difference is that, with PCA, the first time you run the model, you don't specify the number of components to be discovered in the dataset. You let the initial model results tell you how many components to keep, and then you rerun the analysis to extract those features.

REMEMBER

Similar to the CVE discussion in the SVD part of this chapter, the amount of variance you retain depends on how you're applying PCA, as well as the data you're inputting into the model. Breaking it down based on how you're applying PCA, the following rules of thumb become relevant:

>> **Used for descriptive analytics**: If PCA is being used for descriptive purposes only (for example, when working to build a descriptive avatar of your company's ideal customer) the CVE can be lower than 95 percent. In this case you can get away with a CVE as low as 75-80 percent.

>> **Used for diagnostic, predictive or prescriptive analytics**: If principal components are meant for downstream models that generate diagnostic, predictive or prescriptive analytics, then CVE should be 95 percent or higher.

Just realize that the lower the CVE, the less reliable your model results will be downstream. Each percentage of CVE that's lost represents a small amount of information from your original dataset that won't be captured by the principal components.

TIP

When using PCA for outlier detection, simply plot the principal components on an x-y scatter plot and visually inspect for areas that might have outliers. Those data points correspond to potential outliers that are worth investigating.

Modeling Decisions with Multiple Criteria Decision-Making

Life is complicated. We're often forced to make decisions where several different criteria come into play, and it often seems unclear which criterion should have priority. Mathematicians, being mathematicians, have come up with quantitative approaches that you can use for decision support whenever you have several criteria or alternatives on which to base your decision. You see those approaches in Chapter 3, where I talk about neural networks and deep learning — another method that fulfills this same decision-support purpose is *multiple criteria decision-making* (or *MCDM*, for short).

Turning to traditional MCDM

You can use MCDM methods in anything from stock portfolio management to fashion-trend evaluation, from disease outbreak control to land development decision-making. Anywhere you have two or more criteria on which you need to base your decision, you can use MCDM methods to help you evaluate alternatives.

To use multiple criteria decision-making, the following two assumptions must be satisfied:

>> **Multiple criteria evaluation:** You must have more than one criterion to optimize.

>> **Zero-sum system:** Optimizing with respect to one criterion must come at the sacrifice of at least one other criterion. This means that there must be trade-offs between criteria — to gain with respect to one means losing with respect to at least one other.

Another important thing to note about MCDM is that it's characterized by binary membership. In mathematics, a *set* is a group of numbers that share a similar characteristic. In traditional set theory, membership is *binary* — in other words, an individual is either a member of a set or it's not. If the individual is a member, it's represented by the number 1, representing a "yes." If it is not a member, it's represented by the number 0, for "no."

The best way to gain a solid grasp on MCDM is to see how it's used to solve a real-world problem. MCDM is commonly used in investment portfolio theory. Pricing of individual financial instruments typically reflects the level of risk you incur, but an entire portfolio can be a mixture of virtually riskless investments (US government bonds, for example) and minimum-, moderate-, and high-risk investments. Your level of risk aversion dictates the general character of your investment portfolio. Highly risk-averse investors seek safer and less lucrative investments, and less risk-averse investors choose riskier, more lucrative investments. In the process of evaluating the risk of a potential investment, you'd likely consider the following criteria:

>> **Earnings growth potential:** Using a binary variable to score the earnings growth potential, then you could say that an investment that falls under a specific earnings growth potential threshold gets scored as 0 (as in "no — the potential is not enough"); anything higher than that threshold gets a 1 (for "yes — the potential is adequate").

>> **Earnings quality rating:** Using a binary variable to score earnings quality ratings, then you could say that an investment falling within a particular ratings class for earnings quality gets scored as 1 (for "yes — the rating is adequate"); otherwise, it gets scored as a 0 (as in "no — it's earning quality rating is not good enough").

For you non-Wall Street types out there, *earnings quality* refers to various measures used to determine how kosher a company's reported earnings are; such measures attempt to answer the question, "Do these reported figures pass the smell test?"

>> **Dividend performance:** Using a binary variable to score dividend performance, then you could say that when an investment fails to reach a set dividend performance threshold, it gets a 0 (as in "no — it's dividend performance is not good enough"); if it reaches or surpasses that threshold, it gets a 1 (for "yes — the performance is adequate").

Imagine that you're evaluating 20 different potential investments. In this evaluation, you'd score each criterion for each of the investments. To eliminate poor investment choices, simply sum the criteria scores for each of the alternatives and then dismiss any investments that don't earn a total score of 3 — leaving you with the investments that fall within a certain threshold of earning growth potential, that have good earnings quality, and whose dividends perform at a level that's acceptable to you.

TIP

For some hands-on practice doing multiple criteria decision-making, go to the companion website to this book (www.businessgrowth.ai) and check out the MCDM practice problem I've left for you there.

Focusing on fuzzy MCDM

If you prefer to evaluate suitability within a range, rather than use binary membership terms of 0 or 1, you can use *fuzzy multiple criteria decision-making (FMCDM)* to do that. With FMCDM you can evaluate all the same types of problems as you would with MCDM. The term *fuzzy* refers to the fact that the criteria being used to evaluate alternatives offer a range of acceptability — instead of the binary, crisp set criteria associated with traditional MCDM. Evaluations based on fuzzy criteria lead to a range of potential outcomes, each with its own level of suitability as a solution.

TIP

One important feature of FMCDM: You're likely to have a list of several fuzzy criteria, but these criteria might not all hold the same importance in your evaluation. To correct for this, simply assign weights to criteria to quantify their relative importance.

Introducing Regression Methods

Machine learning algorithms of the regression variety were adopted from the statistics field in order to provide data scientists with a set of methods for describing and quantifying the relationships between variables in a dataset. Use regression techniques if you want to determine the strength of correlation between variables in your data. As for using regression to predict future values from historical values, feel free to do it, but be careful: Regression methods assume a cause-and-effect relationship between variables, but present circumstances are always subject to flux. Predicting future values from historical ones will generate incorrect results when present circumstances change. In this section, I tell you all about linear regression, logistic regression, and the ordinary least squares method.

Linear regression

Linear regression is a machine learning method you can use to describe and quantify the relationship between your target variable, y — the *predictant*, in statistics lingo — and the dataset features you've chosen to use as predictor variables (commonly designated as *dataset X* in machine learning). When you use just one variable as your predictor, linear regression is as simple as the middle school algebra formula y=mx+b. A classic example of linear regression is its usage in predicting home prices, as shown in Figure 4-6. You can also use linear regression to quantify correlations between several variables in a dataset — called *multiple linear regression*. Before getting too excited about using linear regression, though, make sure you've considered its limitations:

>> Linear regression works with only numerical variables, not categorical ones.

>> If your dataset has missing values, it will cause problems. Be sure to address your missing values before attempting to build a linear regression model.

>> If your data has outliers present, your model will produce inaccurate results. Check for outliers before proceeding.

>> The linear regression model assumes that a linear relationship exists between dataset features and the target variable.

>> The linear regression model assumes that all features are independent of each other.

>> Prediction errors, or *residuals,* should be normally distributed.

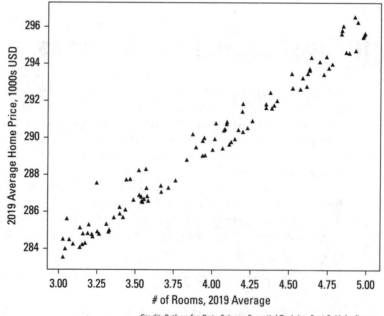

FIGURE 4-6:
Linear regression used to predict home prices based on the number of rooms in a house.

Credit: *Python for Data Science Essential Training Part 2, LinkedIn.com*

REMEMBER

Don't forget dataset size! A good rule of thumb is that you should have at least 20 observations per predictive feature if you expect to generate reliable results using linear regression.

Logistic regression

Logistic regression is a machine learning method you can use to estimate values for a categorical target variable based on your selected features. Your target variable should be numeric and should contain values that describe the target's class — or category. One cool aspect of logistic regression is that, in addition to predicting the class of observations in your target variable, it indicates the probability for each of its estimates. Though logistic regression is like linear regression, its requirements are simpler, in that:

>> There doesn't need to be a linear relationship between the features and target variable.

>> Residuals don't have to be normally distributed.

>> Predictive features aren't required to have a normal distribution.

When deciding whether logistic regression is a good choice for you, consider the following limitations:

REMEMBER

>> Missing values should be treated or removed.

>> Your target variable must be binary or ordinal.

Binary classification assigns a 1 for "yes" and a 0 for "no."

>> Predictive features should be independent of each other.

Logistic regression requires a greater number of observations than linear regression to produce a reliable result. The rule of thumb is that you should have at least 50 observations per predictive feature if you expect to generate reliable results.

TIP

Predicting survivors on the Titanic is the classic practice problem for newcomers to learn logistic regression. You can practice it and see lots of examples of this problem worked out over on Kaggle. (www.kaggle.com/c/titanic).

Ordinary least squares (OLS) regression methods

Ordinary least squares (OLS) is a statistical method that fits a linear regression line to a dataset. With OLS, you do this by squaring the vertical distance values that describe the distances between the data points and the best-fit line, adding up those squared distances, and then adjusting the placement of the best-fit line so that the summed squared distance value is minimized. Use OLS if you want to construct a function that's a close approximation to your data.

REMEMBER

As always, don't expect the actual value to be identical to the value predicted by the regression. Values predicted by the regression are simply estimates that are most similar to the actual values in the model.

OLS is particularly useful for fitting a regression line to models containing more than one independent variable. In this way, you can use OLS to estimate the target from dataset features.

WARNING

When using OLS regression methods to fit a regression line that has more than one independent variable, two or more of the variables may be interrelated. When two or more independent variables are strongly correlated with each other, this is called *multicollinearity*. Multicollinearity tends to adversely affect the reliability of the variables as predictors when they're examined apart from one another. Luckily, however, multicollinearity doesn't decrease the overall predictive reliability of the model when it's considered collectively.

Detecting Outliers

Many statistical and machine learning approaches assume that your data has no outliers. Outlier removal is an important part of preparing your data for analysis. In this section, you see a variety of methods you can use to discover outliers in your data.

Analyzing extreme values

Outliers are data points with values that are significantly different from the majority of data points comprising a variable. It's important to find and remove outliers because, left untreated, they skew variable distribution, make variance appear falsely high, and cause a misrepresentation of intervariable correlations.

You can use outlier detection to spot anomalies that represent fraud, equipment failure, or cybersecurity attacks. In other words, outlier detection is a data preparation method and an analytical method in its own right.

Outliers fall into the following three categories:

» **Point:** Point outliers are data points with anomalous values compared to the normal range of values in a feature.

» **Contextual:** Contextual outliers are data points that are anomalous only within a specific context. To illustrate, if you're inspecting weather station data from January in Orlando, Florida, and you see a temperature reading of 23 degrees F, this would be quite anomalous because the average temperature there is 70 degrees F in January. But consider if you were looking at data from January at a weather station in Anchorage, Alaska — a temperature reading of 23 degrees F in this context isn't anomalous at all.

» **Collective:** These outliers appear nearby one another, all having similar values that are anomalous to the majority of values in the feature.

You can detect outliers using either a univariate or multivariate approach, as spelled out in the next two sections.

Detecting outliers with univariate analysis

Univariate outlier detection is where you look at features in your dataset and inspect them individually for anomalous values. You can choose from two simple methods for doing this:

» Tukey outlier labeling

» Tukey boxplotting

Tukey boxplotting is an exploratory data analysis technique that's useful for visualizing the distribution of data within a numeric variable by visualizing that distribution with quartiles. As you might guess, the Tukey boxplot was named after its inventor, John Tukey, an American mathematician who did most of his work back in the 1960s and 70s. Tukey outlier labeling refers to labeling data points (that lie beyond the minimum and maximum extremes of a box plot) as outliers.

It is cumbersome to use the Tukey method to manually calculate, identify, and label outliers, but if you want to do it, the trick is to look at how far the minimum and maximum values are from the 25 and 75 percentiles. The distance between the *1st quartile* (at 25 percent) and the *3rd quartile* (at 75 percent) is called the *inter-quartile range (IQR)*, and it describes the data's spread. When you look at a variable, consider its spread, its Q1 / Q3 values, and its minimum and maximum values to decide whether the variable is suspect for outliers.

TIP

Here's a good rule of thumb:

a = Q1 – 1.5*IQR

and

b = Q3 + 1.5*IQR.

If your minimum value is less than a, or your maximum value is greater than b, the variable probably has outliers.

On the other hand, it is quite easy to generate a Tukey boxplot and spot outliers using Python or R. Each boxplot has whiskers that are set at 1.5*IQR. Any values that lie beyond these whiskers are outliers. Figure 4-7 shows outliers as they appear within a Tukey boxplot that was generated in Python.

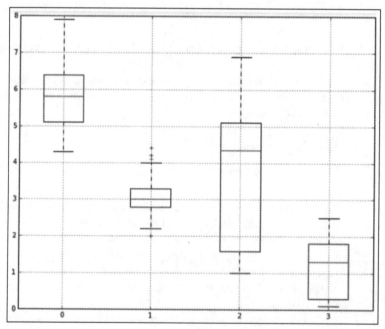

FIGURE 4-7: Spotting outliers with a Tukey boxplot.

Credit: Python for Data Science Essential Training Part 1, LinkedIn.com

Detecting outliers with multivariate analysis

Sometimes outliers show up only within combinations of data points from disparate variables. These outliers wreak havoc on machine learning algorithms, so it's important to detect and remove them. You can use multivariate analysis of outliers to do this. A multivariate approach to outlier detection involves considering two or more variables at a time and inspecting them together for outliers. You can use one of several methods, including:

» A scatter-plot matrix

» Boxplotting

» Density-based spatial clustering of applications with noise (DBScan) — as discussed in Chapter 5

» Principal component analysis (PCA, as shown in Figure 4-8)

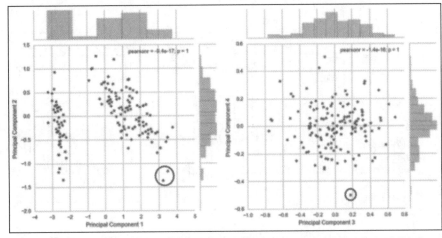

FIGURE 4-8:
Using PCA to spot outliers.

Credit: Python for Data Science Essential Training Part 2, LinkedIn.com

Introducing Time Series Analysis

A *time series* is just a collection of data on attribute values over time. Time series analysis is performed to predict future instances of the measure based on the past observational data. To forecast or predict future values from data in your dataset, use time series techniques.

Identifying patterns in time series

Time series exhibit specific patterns. Take a look at Figure 4-9 to gain a better understanding of what these patterns are all about. *Constant* time series remain at roughly the same level over time but are subject to some random error. In contrast, *trended* series show a stable linear movement up or down. Whether constant or trended, time series may also sometimes exhibit *seasonality* — predictable, cyclical fluctuations that reoccur seasonally throughout a year. As an example of seasonal time series, consider how many businesses show increased sales during the holiday season.

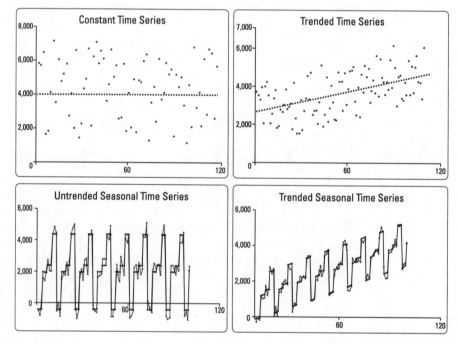

FIGURE 4-9: A comparison of patterns exhibited by time series.

If you're including seasonality in your model, incorporate it in the quarterly, monthly, or even biannual period — wherever it's appropriate. Time series may show *nonstationary processes* — unpredictable cyclical behavior that isn't related to seasonality and that results from economic or industry-wide conditions instead.

Because they're not predictable, nonstationary processes can't be forecasted. You must transform nonstationary data to stationary data before moving forward with an evaluation.

Take a look at the solid lines shown earlier, in Figure 4-9. These represent the mathematical models used to forecast points in the time series. The mathematical models shown represent good, precise forecasts because they're a close fit to the actual data. The actual data contains some random error, thus making it impossible to forecast perfectly.

TIP

For help getting started with time series within the context of the R programming language, be sure to visit the companion website to this book (`http://businessgrowth.ai/`), where you'll find a free training and coding demonstration of time series data visualization in R.

Modeling univariate time series data

Similar to how multivariate analysis is the analysis of relationships between multiple variables, *univariate analysis* is the quantitative analysis of only one variable at a time. When you model univariate time series, you're modeling time series changes that represent changes in a single variable over time.

Autoregressive moving average (ARMA) is a class of forecasting methods that you can use to predict future values from current and historical data. As its name implies, the family of ARMA models combines *autoregression* techniques (analyses that assume that previous observations are good predictors of future values and perform an autoregression analysis to forecast for those future values) and *moving average* techniques — models that measure the level of the constant time series and then update the forecast model if any changes are detected. If you're looking for a simple model or a model that will work for only a small dataset, the ARMA model isn't a good fit for your needs. An alternative in this case might be to just stick with simple linear regression. In Figure 4-10, you can see that the model forecast data and the actual data are a close fit.

REMEMBER

To use the ARMA model for reliable results, you need to have at least 50 observations.

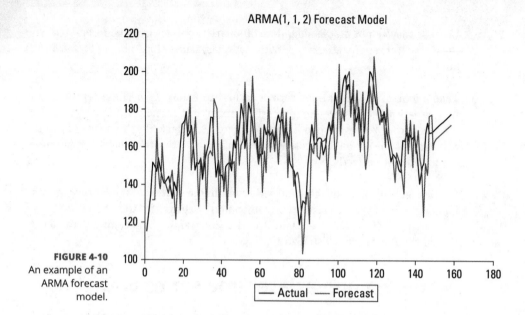

FIGURE 4-10
An example of an
ARMA forecast
model.

Chapter **5**

Grouping Your Way into Accurate Predictions

When it comes to making predictions from data, grouping techniques can be a simple and powerful way to generate valuable insights quickly. Although grouping methods tend to be relatively simple, you can choose from quite a few approaches. In this chapter, I introduce you to classification, and clustering algorithms, as well as decision trees and random forests.

Data scientists use *clustering* to help them divide their unlabeled data into subsets. If they're starting with labeled data, they can use *classification methods* to build predictive models that they can then use to forecast the classification of future observations. Classification is a form of *supervised machine learning* — the classification algorithm essentially learns from your labeled data.

Though the basics behind clustering and classification seem relatively easy to understand at first, things get tricky fast when you get into using some of the more advanced algorithms. I start you out with the simplest approach — clustering — and then lightly touch on decision trees and random forests before I help you, lastly, tackle instance-based learning classification algorithms.

Starting with Clustering Basics

To grasp advanced methods for use in clustering your data, first take a few moments to grasp the basics that underlie all forms of clustering. Clustering is a form of *machine learning* — the machine in this case is your computer, and *learning* refers to an algorithm that's repeated over and over until a certain set of predetermined conditions is met. Learning algorithms are generally run until the point that the final analysis results won't change, no matter how many additional times the algorithm is passed over the data.

Clustering is one of the two main types of machine learning: unsupervised machine learning. In *unsupervised* machine learning, the data in the dataset is unlabeled. Because the data is unlabeled, the algorithms must use inferential methods to discover patterns, relationships, and correlations within the raw dataset. To put clustering through its paces, I want to use a readily available sample dataset from the World Bank's open datasets on country income and education. This data shows the percentage of income earned by the bottom 10 percent of the population in each country and the percentage of children who complete primary school in each country.

TECHNICAL STUFF

For this chapter's discussion, I'm isolating the median reported statistic from the years 2000 to 2003. (Some countries report on these statistics only every few years, and during 2000 to 2003, this data was fully reported by 81 of 227 countries.)

WARNING

In datasets about the percentage of children who complete primary school, some are reported at more than 100 percent. That's because some countries count this statistic at different ages, but the data was *normalized* so that the percentage distribution is proportionally scaled across the range of countries represented in the dataset. In other words, although the total scale exceeds 100 percent, the values have been normalized so that they're proportional to one another and you're getting an apples-to-apples comparison. Thus, the fact that some countries report completion rates greater than 100 percent has no adverse effect on the analysis you make in this chapter.

Getting to know clustering algorithms

You use clustering algorithms to subdivide unlabeled datasets into clusters of observations that are most similar for a predefined feature. If you have a dataset that describes multiple features about a set of observations and you want to group your observations by their feature similarities, use clustering algorithms.

TIP

Over on the companion website to this book (`http://www.businessgrowth.ai/`), you'll find a free training-and-coding demonstration of how to use clustering in Python for a popular use case — customer profiling and segmentation.

You can choose from various clustering methods, depending on how you want your dataset to be divided. The two main types of clustering algorithms are

>> **Partitional:** Algorithms that create only a single set of clusters

>> **Hierarchical:** Algorithms that create separate sets of nested clusters, each in its own hierarchical level

You can read about both approaches later in this chapter, but for now, start by looking at Figure 5-1, a simple scatterplot of the Country Income and Education datasets.

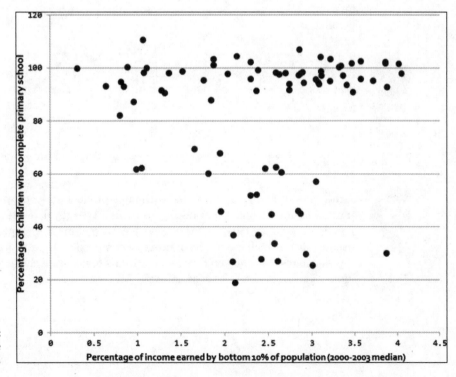

FIGURE 5-1:
A simple
scatterplot.

In unsupervised clustering, you start with this data and then proceed to divide it into subsets. These subsets, called *clusters*, are composed of observations that are most similar to one another. In Figure 5-1, it appears that the scatterplot has at least two clusters, and probably three — one at the bottom with low income and education, and then the high-education countries look like they might be split between low and high incomes.

Figure 5-2 shows the result of *eyeballing*, or making a visual estimate of, clusters in this dataset.

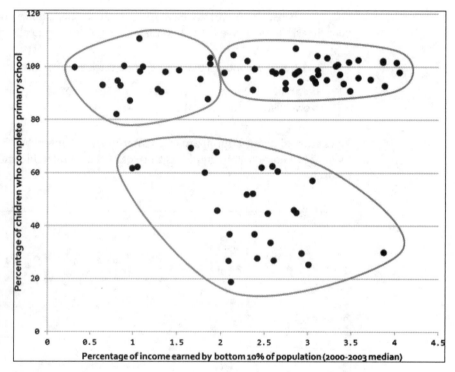

FIGURE 5-2:
A simple
scatterplot,
showing
eyeballed
estimations of
clustering.

TIP

Although you can generate visual estimates of clusters, you can achieve much more accurate results when dealing with much larger datasets by using algorithms to generate clusters for you. Visual estimation is a rough method that's useful only on smaller datasets of minimal complexity. Algorithms produce exact, repeatable results, and you can use algorithms to generate clusters from multiple dimensions of data within your dataset.

Clustering algorithms are appropriate in situations where the following characteristics are true:

>> You know and understand the dataset you're analyzing.

>> Before running the clustering algorithm, you don't have an exact idea of the nature of the subsets (clusters). Often, you don't even know how many subsets are in the dataset before you run the algorithm.

>> The subsets (clusters) are determined by only the single dataset you're analyzing.

>> Your goal is to determine a model that describes the subsets in a single dataset and only this dataset.

TIP

If you add more data to your dataset after you've already built the model, be sure to rebuild the model from scratch to produce more complete and accurate model results.

Examining clustering similarity metrics

Clustering is based on calculating the similarity or difference between two observations. If your dataset is *numeric* — composed of only numerical features — and can be portrayed on an *n*-dimensional plot, you can use various geometric metrics to scale your multidimensional data.

REMEMBER

An *n-dimensional plot* is a multidimensional scatterplot that you can use to plot *n* number of dimensions of data.

Some popular geometric metrics, used for calculating distances between observations include:

>> **Euclidean:** A measure of the distance between points plotted on a Euclidean plane.

>> **Manhattan:** A measure of the distance between points where distance is calculated as the sum of the absolute value of the differences between two points' Cartesian coordinates.

>> **Minkowski distance:** A generalization of the Euclidean and Manhattan distance metrics. Quite often, these metrics can be used interchangeably.

>> **Cosine similarity:** The cosine metric measures the similarity of two data points based on their orientation, as determined by calculating the cosine of the angle between them.

Lastly, for nonnumeric data, you can use metrics like the *Jaccard distance metric,* an index that compares the number of features that two observations have in common. For example, to illustrate a Jaccard distance, look at these two text strings:

```
Saint Louis de Ha-ha, Quebec
St-Louis de Ha!Ha!, QC
```

What features do these text strings have in common? And what features are different between them? The Jaccard metric generates a numerical index value that quantifies the similarity between text strings.

Identifying Clusters in Your Data

You can use many different algorithms for clustering, but the speed and robustness of the k-means algorithm make it a popular choice among experienced data scientists. As alternatives, kernel density estimation methods, hierarchical algorithms, and neighborhood algorithms are also available to help you identify clusters in your dataset.

Clustering with the k-means algorithm

The *k-means* clustering algorithm is a simple, fast, unsupervised learning algorithm that you can use to predict groupings within a dataset. For getting started with k-means clustering, you first need to be familiar with the concept of centroid. A *centroid* is the most representative point within any given cluster group. With k-means, you define the number of centroids the model should find as it generates its prediction. The *number of centroids* is represented by k, and the clusters are formed by calculating the nearest mean values to those centroids, measured by the Euclidean distance between observations.

WARNING

Because the features of a dataset are usually on different scales, the difference of scales can distort the results of this distance calculation. To avoid this problem, scale your variables before using k-means to predict data groupings.

The quality of the clusters is heavily dependent on the correctness of the k value you specify. If your data is 2- or 3-dimensional, a plausible range of k values may be visually determinable. In the eyeballed approximation of clustering from the World Bank Income and Education data scatterplot (refer to Figure 5-2), a visual estimation of the k value would equate to three clusters, or $k = 3$.

REMEMBER

When defining the k value, it may be possible to choose the number of centroids by looking at a scatterplot (if your dataset is 2- or 3-dimensional) or by looking for obvious, significant groupings within your dataset's variables. You can pick the number of centroids based on the number of groupings that you know exist in the dataset or by the number of groupings that you want to exist in the dataset. Whatever the case, use your subjective knowledge about the dataset when choosing the number of clusters to be modeled.

If your dataset has more than three dimensions, however, you can use computational methods to generate a good value for k. One such method is the *silhouette coefficient* — a method that calculates the average distance of each point from all other points in a cluster and then compares that value with the average distance to every point in every other cluster. Luckily, because the k-means algorithm is efficient, it doesn't require much computer processing power and you can easily calculate this coefficient for a wide range of k values.

The k-means algorithm works by placing sample cluster centers on an n-dimensional plot and then evaluating whether moving them in any single direction would result in a new center with higher *density* — with more observations closer to it, in other words. The centers are moved from regions of lower density to regions of higher density until all centers are within a region of *local maximum density* — a true center of the cluster, where each cluster has a maximum number of data points closest to its cluster center. Whenever possible, try to place the centers yourself, manually. If that's impossible, simply place the centers randomly and run the algorithm several times to see how often you end up with the same clusters.

One weakness of the k-means algorithm is that it may produce incorrect results by placing cluster centers in areas of *local minimum density*. This happens when centers get lost in *low-density regions* (in other words, regions of the plot that have relatively few points plotted in them) and the algorithm-driven *directional movement* (the movement that's meant to increase point density) starts to bounce and oscillate between faraway clusters. In these cases, the center gets caught in a low-density space that's located between two high-point density zones. This results in erroneous clusters based around centers that converge in areas of low, local minimum density. Ironically, this happens most often when the underlying data is very well-clustered, with tight, dense regions that are separated by wide, sparse areas.

TIP

Get hands-on experience with the free k-means clustering coding demo that's hosted on the companion website for this book (http://www.businessgrowth.ai/).

TIP

To try things out for yourself, start clustering your data with the k-means methods by using either R's `cluster` package or Python's Scikit-learn library. For more on R's cluster package, check out `http://cran.r-project.org/web/packages/cluster/cluster.pdf`; for more on Scikit-learn, check out `http://scikit-learn.org`.

Estimating clusters with kernel density estimation (KDE)

If the k-means algorithm doesn't appeal to you, one alternative way to identify clusters in your data is to use a density smoothing function instead. *Kernel density estimation* (KDE) is that smoothing method; it works by placing a *kernel* — a weighting function that is useful for quantifying density — on each data point in the dataset and then summing the kernels to generate a kernel density estimate for the overall region. Areas of greater point density will sum out with greater kernel density, and areas of lower point density will sum out with less kernel density.

Because kernel smoothing methods don't rely on cluster center placement and clustering techniques to estimate clusters, they don't exhibit a risk of generating erroneous clusters by placing centers in areas of local minimum density. Where k-means algorithms generate hard-lined definitions between points in different clusters, KDE generates a plot of gradual density change between observations. For this reason, it's a helpful aid when eyeballing clusters. Figure 5-3 shows what the World Bank Income and Education scatterplot looks like after KDE has been applied.

In Figure 5-3, you can see that the white spaces between clusters have been reduced. When you look at the figure, it's fairly obvious that you can see at least three clusters, and possibly more, if you want to allow for small clusters.

Clustering with hierarchical algorithms

A hierarchical clustering algorithm is yet another alternative to k-means clustering. In comparison to k-means clustering, the hierarchical clustering algorithm is a slower, clunkier unsupervised clustering algorithm. It predicts groupings within a dataset by calculating the distance and generating a link between each singular observation and its nearest neighbor. It then uses those distances to predict subgroups within a dataset. If you're carrying out a statistical study or analyzing biological or environmental data, hierarchical clustering might be your ideal machine learning solution.

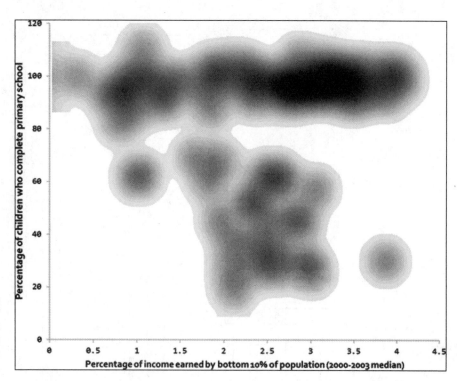

FIGURE 5-3:
KDE smoothing of the World Bank's Income and Education data scatterplot.

To visually inspect the results of your hierarchical clustering, generate a *dendrogram* — a visualization tool that depicts the similarities and branching between groups in a data cluster. You can use several different algorithms to build a dendrogram, and the algorithm you choose dictates where and how branching occurs within the clusters. Additionally, dendrograms can be built either *bottom-up* (by assembling pairs of points and then aggregating them into larger and larger groups) or *top-down* (by starting with the full dataset and splitting it into smaller and smaller groups). Looking at the dendrogram results makes it easier to decide the appropriate number of clusters for your dataset. In the dendrogram example shown in Figure 5-4, the underlying dataset appears to have either three or four clusters.

In hierarchical clustering, the distance between observations is measured in three different ways: Euclidean, Manhattan, or Cosine. Additionally, linkage is formed by three different methods: Ward, Complete, and Average. When deciding what distance and linkage parameters to use, trial-and-error is an easy approach. Just try each combination and then compare all your model results. Go with the model that produces the most accurate prediction.

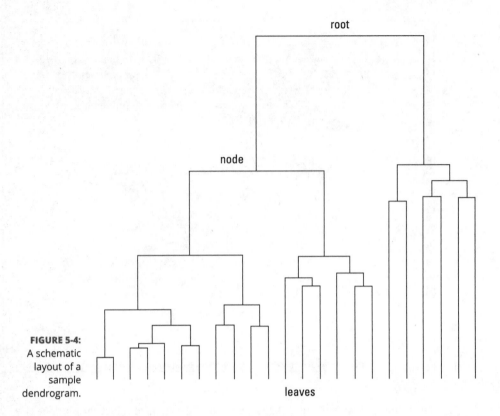

FIGURE 5-4:
A schematic layout of a sample dendrogram.

Hierarchical clustering algorithms require more computing resources than k-means algorithms because, with each iteration of hierarchical clustering, many observations must be compared to many other observations. The benefit, however, is that hierarchical clustering algorithms are not subject to errors caused by center convergence at areas of local minimum density (as exhibited with the k-means clustering algorithms).

WARNING

If you're working with a large dataset, watch out! Hierarchical clustering will probably be *way* too slow.

TIP

If you want to get started working with hierarchical clustering algorithms, check out R's `hclust` package or (again) Python's `Scikit-learn` library. (If you're curious about `hclust`, check out this page:

```
https://stat.ethz.ch/R-manual/R-patched/library/stats/html/hclust.html
```

Neither k-means nor hierarchical clustering algorithms perform well when clusters are *nonglobular* — a configuration where some points in a cluster are closer to points in a different cluster than they are to points in the center of their own cluster. If your dataset shows nonglobular clustering, you can use neighborhood clustering algorithms, like DBScan, to determine whether each point is closer to its neighbors in the same cluster or closer to its neighboring observations in other clusters. (Figure 5-5, in the following section, shows an example of using the DBScan neighborhood clustering algorithm to detect outliers in the classical practice dataset called "Iris," and the next section covers neighborhood clustering in greater detail.)

Dabbling in the DBScan neighborhood

Density-based spatial clustering of applications with noise (DBScan) is an unsupervised learning method that works by clustering *core samples* (dense areas of a dataset) while simultaneously demarking *noncore samples* (portions of the dataset that are comparatively sparse). It's a neighborhood clustering algorithm that's ideal for examining two or more variables together to identify outliers. It's particularly useful for identifying *collective* outliers — outliers that appear nearby to one another, all having similar values that are anomalous to most values in the variable. (Figure 5-5 shows DBScan at work.)

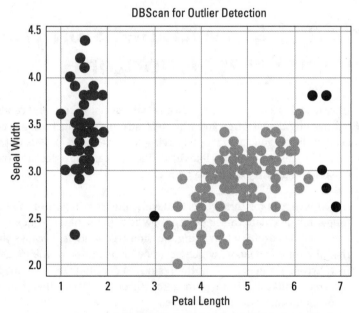

Credit: Python for Data Science Essential Training Part 2, LinkedIn.com

FIGURE 5-5:
Using DBScan to detect outliers (in black) within the Iris dataset.

REMEMBER

With DBScan, you take an iterative, trial-and-error approach to find the ideal number of outliers for inspection. When experimenting with the DBScan model, outliers should comprise 5 percent or less of the dataset's observations. You must adjust the model parameters until you've isolated this small select group of observations.

Neighborhood clustering algorithms are generally effective, but they are subject to the following two weaknesses:

>> **Neighborhood clustering can be computationally expensive.** With every iteration of this method, every data point might have to be compared to every other data point in the dataset.

>> **With neighborhood clustering, you might have to provide the model with empirical parameter values for expected cluster size and cluster density.** If you guess either of these parameters incorrectly, the algorithm misidentifies clusters, and you must start the whole long process over again to fix the problem. If you choose to use the DBScan method, you're required to specify these parameters. (As an alternative, you could try the average nearest neighbor and k-nearest neighbor algorithms, which are discussed later in this chapter.)

TIP

To avoid making poor guesses for the cluster size and cluster density parameters, you can first use a quick k-means algorithm to determine plausible values.

Categorizing Data with Decision Tree and Random Forest Algorithms

In cases where clustering algorithms fail, decision tree and random forest algorithms might just offer you a perfect alternative machine learning solution. At certain times, you can get stuck trying to cluster and classify data from a nonnumerical dataset. It's times like these that you can use a decision tree model to help cluster and classify your data correctly.

A *decision tree* algorithm works by developing a set of yes-or-no rules that you can follow for new data to see exactly how it will be characterized by the model. But you must be careful when using decision tree models, because they run the high risk of *error propagation*, which occurs whenever one of the model rules is incorrect. Errors are generated in the results of decisions that are made based on that incorrect rule, and then propagated through every other subsequent decision made along that branch of the tree.

To illustrate this type of algorithm, consider a dataset that's often used in machine learning demonstrations — the list of passenger names from the *Titanic*. Using a simple decision tree model, you can predict that if a passenger were female or were a male child with a large family, that person probably survived the catastrophe. Figure 5-6 illustrates this determination.

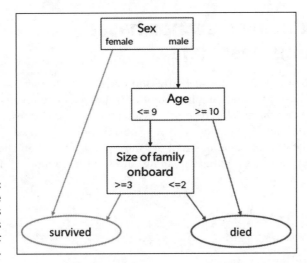

FIGURE 5-6:
A decision tree model predicts survival rates from the *Titanic* catastrophe.

Lastly, random forest algorithms are a slower but more powerful alternative. Rather than build a tree from the data, the algorithm creates random trees and then determines which one best classifies the testing data. This method eliminates the risk of error propagation that is inherent in decision tree models.

Drawing a Line between Clustering and Classification

The purpose of both clustering and classification algorithms is to make sense of, and extract value from, large sets of structured and unstructured data. If you're working with huge volumes of unstructured data, it only makes sense to try to partition the data into some sort of logical groupings before attempting to analyze it. Both clustering and classification methods allow you to take a sweeping glance of your data all at once and then form some logical structures based on what you find there, before digging deeper into the nuts-and-bolts analysis.

Though your plain-vanilla clustering algorithm — like the k-means method discussed earlier in this chapter — can help you predict subgroups from within *unlabeled datasets*, there's way more to life than plain vanilla. I think it's about time to take things one step further, by exploring how we can make predictions by grouping *labeled data* instead. Enter instance-based learning classifiers!

Introducing instance-based learning classifiers

Instance-based learning classifiers are supervised, *lazy learners* — they have no training phase, and they simply memorize training data to predict classifications for new data points. This type of classifier looks at instances — observations within a dataset — and, for each new observation, the classifier searches the training data for observations that are most similar and then classifies the new observation based on its similarity to instances in the training set. Instance-based classifiers include

>> k-nearest neighbor (kNN)

>> Self-organizing maps

>> Locally weighted learning

If you're unsure about your dataset's distribution, instance-based classifiers might be a good option, but first make sure that you know their limitations. These classifiers aren't well-suited for

>> Noisy data (data with unexplainable random variation)

>> Datasets with unimportant or irrelevant features

>> Datasets with missing values

To simplify this introduction as much as possible, I stick to explaining the k-nearest neighbor classification algorithm (known affectionately as kNN). The concepts involved in kNN are a bit tricky, though, so first I introduce you to the simpler average nearest neighbor methods before going into the kNN approach.

Getting to know classification algorithms

You might have heard of classification and thought that it's the same concept as clustering. Many people do, but this isn't the case. In *classification*, your data is *labeled*, so before you analyze it, you already know the number of classes into which it should be grouped. You also already know which class you want assigned to each data point. In contrast, with *clustering* methods, your data is *unlabeled*, so you have no predefined concept of how many clusters are appropriate. You must rely on the clustering algorithms to sort and cluster the data in the most appropriate way.

With classification algorithms, you use what you know about an existing labeled dataset to generate a predictive model for classifying future observations. If your goal is to use your dataset and its known subsets to build a model for predicting the categorization of future observations, you'll want to use classification algorithms. When implementing supervised classification, you already know your dataset's *labels* — the criteria you use to subset observations into *classes*. Classification helps you see how well your data fits into the dataset's predefined classes so that you can then build a predictive model for classifying future observations.

Figure 5-7 illustrates how it looks to classify the World Bank's Income and Education datasets geographically according to continent.

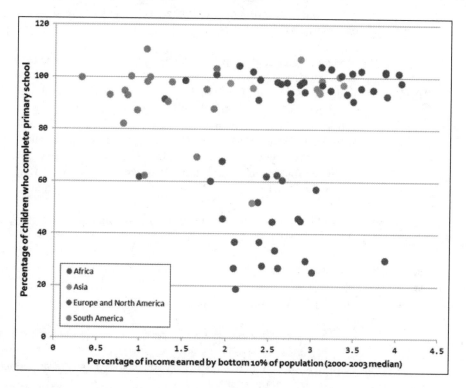

FIGURE 5-7:
Using the
Continent feature
to classify World
Bank data.

In Figure 5-7, you can see that, in some cases, the subsets you might identify with a clustering technique do correspond to the Continent category, but in other cases, they don't. For example, look at the lone Asian country in the middle of the African observations. That's Bhutan. You could use the data in this dataset to build a model that would predict a Continent class for incoming observations, but if you introduced a data point for a new country that showed statistics similar to those of Bhutan, the new country could be categorized as being part of either the Asian continent or the African continent, depending on how you define your model.

Now imagine a situation in which the original data doesn't include Bhutan and you use the model to predict Bhutan's continent as a new data point. In this scenario, the model would incorrectly predict that Bhutan is part of the African continent. This is an example of *model overfitting* — a situation in which a model is so tightly fit to its underlying dataset, as well as its noise or random error, that the model performs poorly as a predictor for new observations.

To avoid overfitting your models, divide the data into a training set and a test set. A typical ratio is to assign 70 percent (or more) of the data to the training set and the remaining 30 percent to the test set. Build your model with the training set, and then use the test set to evaluate the model by pretending that the test set observations are unknown. You can evaluate the accuracy of your model by comparing the classes assigned to the test set observations to the true classes of these observations.

Model overgeneralization can also be a problem. *Overgeneralization* is the opposite of overfitting: If you don't train a machine learning model enough, it will be underfit. As a result, it will make inaccurate, overly general predictions. Naturally it follows that, overly general models end up assigning every class a low degree of confidence. To illustrate model overgeneralization, consider again the World Bank Income and Education datasets. If the model used the presence of Bhutan to cast doubt on every new data point in its nearby vicinity, you end up with a wishy-washy model that treats all nearby points as African, but with a low probability. This model would be a poor predictive performer.

I can illustrate a good metaphor for overfitting and overgeneralization by using this well-known maxim:

If it walks like a duck and talks like a duck, then it's a duck.

Overfitting would turn the maxim into this statement:

It's a duck if, and only if, it walks and quacks exactly in the ways that I have personally observed a duck to walk and quack. Since I've never observed the way an Australian spotted duck walks and quacks, an Australian spotted duck must not really be a duck at all.

In contrast, overgeneralization would say:

If it moves around on two legs and emits any high-pitched, nasal sound, it's a duck. Therefore, Fran Fine, who was Fran Drescher's character in the 1990s American sitcom *The Nanny,* must be a duck.

REMEMBER

Be aware of the constant danger of overfitting and overgeneralization. Find a happy medium between the two.

When classifying data, keep these two points in mind:

>> **Model predictions are only as good as the model's underlying data.** In the World Bank data example, it could be the case that, if other factors such as life expectancy or energy use per capita were added to the model, its predictive strength would increase.

>> **Model predictions are only as good as the categorization of the underlying dataset.** For example, what do you do with countries, like Russia, that span two continents? Do you distinguish North Africa from sub-Saharan Africa? Do you lump North America in with Europe because they tend to share similar features? Do you consider Central America to be part of North America or South America?

Making Sense of Data with Nearest Neighbor Analysis

At their core, nearest neighbor methods work by taking the value of an observation's attribute (or feature) — also called an *attribute value* — and then locating another observation whose attribute value is numerically nearest to it. Because the nearest neighbor technique is a classification method, you can use it to perform tasks as scientifically oriented as deducing the molecular structure of a vital human protein or uncovering key biological evolutionary relationships or as business-driven as designing recommendation engines for e-commerce sites or building predictive models for consumer transactions. The applications are limitless.

A good analogy for the nearest neighbor concept is illustrated in GPS technology. Imagine that you're in desperate need of a Starbucks iced latte but you have no idea where the nearest store is located. What to do? One easy solution is simply to ask your smartphone where the nearest one is located.

When you do that, the system looks for businesses named Starbucks within a reasonable proximity of your current location. After generating a results listing, the system reports back to you with the address of the Starbucks coffeehouse closest to your current location — the one that is your nearest neighbor, in other words.

As the term *nearest neighbor* implies, the primary purpose of a nearest neighbor analysis is to examine your dataset and find the observation that's quantitatively most similar to your observation. Note that similarity comparisons can be based on any quantitative attribute, whether that is distance, age, income, weight, or any other factor that can describe the observation you're investigating. The simplest comparative attribute is distance.

In my Starbucks analogy, the x, y, z coordinates of the store reported to you by your smartphone are the most similar to the x, y, z coordinates of your current location. In other words, its location is closest in actual physical distance. The quantitative *attribute* being compared is distance, your current location is the *observation,* and the reported Starbucks coffeehouse is the *most similar observation.*

REMEMBER

Modern nearest neighbor analyses are almost always performed using computational algorithms. The nearest neighbor algorithm is known as a *single-link algorithm* — an algorithm that merges clusters if the clusters share between them at least one *connective edge* (a shared boundary line, in other words). In the following sections, you can learn the basics of the average nearest neighbor algorithm and the k-nearest neighbor algorithm.

Classifying Data with Average Nearest Neighbor Algorithms

Average nearest neighbor algorithms are basic yet powerful classification algorithms. They're useful for finding and classifying observations that are most similar on average. Average nearest neighbor algorithms are used in pattern recognition, in chemical and biological structural analysis, and in spatial data modeling. They're most often used in biology, chemistry, engineering, and geosciences.

In this section, you can find out how to use average nearest neighbor algorithms to compare multiple attributes between observations and, subsequently, identify which of your observations are most similar. You can also find out how to use average nearest neighbor algorithms to identify significant patterns in the dataset.

The purpose of using an average nearest neighbor algorithm is to classify observations based on the average of the arithmetic distances between them. If your goal is to identify and group observations by average similarity, the average nearest neighbor algorithm is a useful way to do that.

With respect to nearest neighbor classifiers, a dataset is composed of observations, each of which has an x- and y-variable. An x-variable represents the input value, or *feature*, and the y-variable represents the data label, or target variable. To keep all these terms straight, consider the following example.

Suppose that your friendly neighborhood business analyst, Business Analyst Stu, is using average nearest neighbor algorithms to perform a classification analysis of datasets in his organization's database. Stu is comparing employees based on the following five features:

>> Age

>> Number of children

>> Annual income

>> Seniority

>> Eligibility to Retire

Shown below, you can see that each employee in Stu's organization is represented by a 5-dimensional *tuple* — a finite ordered list (or *sequence*).

>> **Employee Mike:** (34, 1, 120000, 9, 0)

>> **Employee Liz:** (42, 0, 90000, 5, 0)

>> **Employee Jin:** (22, 0, 60000, 2, 0)

>> **Employee Mary:** (53, 3, 180000, 30, 1)

These tuples were created from the data in the dataset that's shown in Table 5-1 below. Each tuple consists of data on the following five features: Age, Number of Children, Annual Income, and Seniority as predictive features, Business Analyst Stu calculates the average arithmetic differences between each of the employees. Figure 5-8 shows the calculated distances between each of the employees.

TABLE 5-1: **Business Analyst Stu's Employee Data**

Employee Name	Age	Number of Children	Annual Income	Seniority	Eligible to Retire
Mike	34	1	$120,000	9	0
Liz	42	0	$90,000	5	0
Jin	22	0	$60,000	2	0
Mary	53	3	$180,000	30	1

Mike	34	1	120000	9
Liz	42	0	90000	5
Distance between employees	**8**	**1**	**30000**	**4**
Mike	34	1	120000	9
Jin	22	0	60000	2
Distance between employees	**12**	**1**	**60000**	**7**
Mike	34	1	120000	9
Mary	53	3	180000	30
Distance between employees	**19**	**2**	**60000**	**21**
Liz	42	0	90000	5
Jin	22	0	60000	2
Distance between employees	**20**	**0**	**30000**	**3**
Liz	42	0	90000	5
Mary	53	3	180000	30
Distance between employees	**11**	**3**	**90000**	**25**
Jin	22	0	60000	2
Mary	53	3	180000	30
Distance between employees	**31**	**3**	**120000**	**28**

FIGURE 5-8: The distances between the employees' tuples.

After Business Analyst Stu has this arithmetic measure of distance between the employees, he finds the *average nearest neighbor* by taking an average of these separation distances. Figure 5-9 shows that average similarity.

Finding Average Similarities	
Average Distance (Mike - Liz)	
Average Distance Value - (Average of 8, 1, 30000, 4)	7503.25
Average Distance (Mike - Jin)	
Average Distance Value - (Average of 12, 1, 60000, 7)	15005
Average Distance (Mike - Mary)	
Average Distance Value - (Average of 19, 2, 60000, 21)	15010.5
Average Distance (Liz - Jin)	
Average Distance Value - (Average of 20, 0, 30000, 3)	7505.75
Average Distance (Liz - Mary)	
Average Distance Value - (Average of 11, 3, 90000, 25)	22509.75
Average Distance (Jin - Mary)	
Average Distance Value - (Average of)	30015.5

FIGURE 5-9: Finding the average similarity between employees.

Stu then groups the employees by the average separation distance between them. Because the average separation distance values between Mike, Liz, and Jin are the smallest, they're grouped into class 0. Mary's average separation distances are quite unlike the others, so she is put into her own class — Class 1.

Does this make sense? Well, you're working with a labeled dataset and you can see that the attribute Eligible to Retire assumes only one of two possible values. So, yes. If the algorithm predicts two classifications within the data, that's a reasonable prediction. Furthermore, if Stu gets new incoming data points that are unlabeled with respect to a person's eligibility to retire, he could probably use this algorithm to predict for that eligibility, based on the other four features.

Classifying with K-Nearest Neighbor Algorithms

The best way to define a k-nearest neighbor is to call it a supervised machine learning classifier that uses the observations it memorizes from within a test dataset to predict classifications for new, unlabeled observations. kNN makes its predictions based on *similarity* — the more similar the training observations are to the new, incoming observations, the more likely it is that the classifier will assign them both the same class. kNN works best if the dataset is

>> Low on noise

>> Free of outliers

>> Labeled

>> Composed only of relevant selected features

>> Composed of distinguishable groups

If you're working with a large dataset, you may want to avoid using kNN, because it will probably take way too long to make predictions from larger datasets.

WARNING

Over on the companion website to this book (`http://www.businessgrowth.ai/`), you'll find a free training-and-coding demonstration of how to build a quick-and-easy k-nearest neighbor classifier in Python.

TIP

In the larger context of machine learning, kNN (like all instance-based learning classifiers) is known as a *lazy* machine learning algorithm — in other words, it has little to no training phase. It simply memorizes training data and then uses that information as the basis on which to classify new observations. The goal of the kNN is to estimate the class of the query point *P* based on the classes of its k-nearest neighbors.

The kNN algorithm is a generalization of the nearest neighbor algorithm. Rather than consider the nearest neighbor, you consider k numbers of nearest neighbors from within a dataset that contains n number of data points — k defines how many nearest neighbors will have an influence on the classification process. In kNN, the classifier classifies the query point P per the classification labels found in a majority of k-nearest points surrounding the query point.

If you know little about the distribution of your dataset, kNN is definitely a good classification method for you to use. What's more, if you do have a solid idea about your dataset's distribution and *feature selection criteria* — the criteria you're using to identify and remove noise in the dataset — you can leverage this information to create significant enhancements in the algorithm's performance.

REMEMBER

Even though kNN is among the simplest and most easy-to-implement classification methods, it nevertheless yields competitive results when compared to some of the more sophisticated machine learning methods. Probably because of its simplicity and the competitive results it provides, the kNN algorithm has been ranked among the top ten most influential data mining algorithms by the academic research community.

Understanding how the k-nearest neighbor algorithm works

To use kNN, you simply need to pick a query point — usually called P — in the sample dataset and then compute the k-nearest neighbors to this point. The query point P is classified with a label that's the same as the label of most k-nearest points that surround it. (Figure 5-10 gives a bird's-eye view of the process.)

REMEMBER

K-nearest neighbors are quantified by either distance or similarity based on another quantitative attribute.

Consider the following example: A dataset is given by [1, 1, 4, 3, 5, 2, 6, 2, 4], and point P is equal to 5. Figure 5-10 shows how kNN would be applied to this dataset. By specifying that k is equal to 3, the figure shows that, based on distance, there are three nearest neighbors to the point 5. Those neighbors are 4, 4, and 6. So, based on the kNN algorithm, query point P will be classified as 4 because 4 is the majority number in the k number of points nearest to it. Similarly, kNN continues defining other query points using the same majority principle.

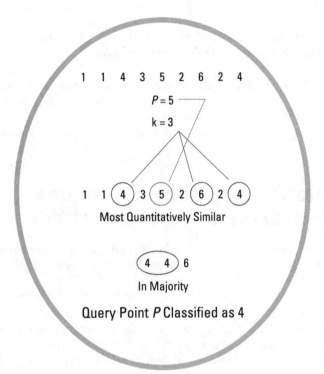

FIGURE 5-10:
How kNN works.

REMEMBER

When using kNN, it's crucial to choose a *k* value that minimizes *noise* — unexplainable random variation, in other words. At the same time, you must choose a *k* value that includes sufficient data points in the selection process. If the data points aren't uniformly distributed, it's generally harder to predetermine a good *k* value. Be careful to select an optimum *k* value for each dataset you're analyzing.

TIP

Large *k* values tend to produce less noise and more *boundary smoothing* — clearer definition and less overlap — between classes than small *k* values do.

Knowing when to use the k-nearest neighbor algorithm

kNN is particularly useful for *multi-label learning* — supervised learning where the algorithm is applied so that it automatically *learns from* (detects patterns in) multiple sets of instances. Each of these sets could potentially have several classes of their own. With multi-label learning, the algorithm learns to predict multiple class labels for each new instance it encounters.

The problem with kNN is that it takes a lot longer than other classification methods to classify a sample. Nearest neighbor classifier performance depends on calculating the distance function as well as on the value of the neighborhood parameter k. You can try to speed things up by specifying optimal values for k and n.

Exploring common applications of k-nearest neighbor algorithms

kNN is often used for Internet database management purposes. In this capacity, kNN is useful for website categorization, web page ranking, and other user dynamics across the web.

kNN classification techniques are also quite beneficial in *customer relationship management (CRM)*, a set of processes that ensure a business sustains improved relationships with its clients while simultaneously experiencing increased business revenues. Most CRMs gain tremendous benefit from using kNN to data-mine customer information to find patterns that are useful in boosting customer retention.

The method is so versatile that even if you're a small-business owner or a marketing department manager, you can easily use kNN to boost your own marketing return on investment. Simply use kNN to analyze your customer data for purchasing patterns, and then use those findings to customize marketing initiatives so that they're more exactly targeted for your customer base.

Solving Real-World Problems with Nearest Neighbor Algorithms

Nearest neighbor methods are used extensively to understand and create value from patterns in retail business data. In the following sections, I present two powerful cases where kNN and average-NN algorithms are being used to simplify management and security in daily retail operations.

Seeing k-nearest neighbor algorithms in action

Techniques associated with k-nearest neighbor algorithms are often used for theft prevention in the modern retail business. Of course, you're accustomed to seeing CCTV cameras around almost every store you visit, but most people have no idea how the data gathered from these devices is being used.

You might picture someone in the back room resolutely monitoring these cameras for suspicious activity for hours at a time, and perhaps that is how things were done in the past. But now a modern surveillance system is intelligent enough to analyze and interpret video data on its own, without the need for human assistance. The modern systems can now use k-nearest neighbor for visual pattern recognition to scan and detect hidden packages in the bottom bin of a shopping cart at checkout. If an object is detected that is an exact match with an object listed in the database, the price of the spotted product can even automatically be added to the customer's bill. Though this automated billing practice isn't used extensively now, the technology has been developed and is available for use.

Retail stores also use k-nearest neighbor to detect patterns in credit card use. Many new transaction-scrutinizing software applications use kNN algorithms to analyze register data and spot unusual patterns that indicate suspicious activity. For example, if register data indicates that a lot of customer information is being entered manually rather than by automated scanning and swiping, it can indicate that the employee who's using that register is in fact stealing a customer's personal information. Or, if register data indicates that a particular good is being returned or exchanged multiple times, it can indicate that employees are misusing the return policy or trying to make money from making fake returns.

Seeing average nearest neighbor algorithms in action

Average nearest neighbor algorithm classification and point pattern detection can be used in grocery retail to identify key patterns in customer purchasing behavior, and subsequently increase sales and customer satisfaction by anticipating customer behavior. Consider the following story:

> As with other grocery stores, buyer behavior at (the fictional) Waldorf Food Co-op tends to follow fixed patterns. Managers have even commented on the odd fact that members of a particular age group tend to visit the store during the same

particular time window, and they even tend to buy the same types of products. One day, Manager Mike became extremely proactive and decided to hire a data scientist to analyze customer data and provide exact details about some recent trends that were noticeably odd. Data Scientist Dan got in there and quickly uncovered a pattern among employed middle-aged male adults: They tended to visit the grocery store only during the weekends or at the end of the day on weekdays, and if they entered the store on a Thursday, they almost always bought beer.

Armed with these facts, Manager Mike quickly used this information to maximize beer sales on Thursday evenings by offering discounts, bundles, and specials. Not only was the store owner happy with the increased revenues, but Waldorf Food Co-op's male customers were also happy because they got more of what they wanted, when they wanted it.

Chapter **6**

Coding Up Data Insights and Decision Engines

I f you've managed to dip into any part of this book, you've surely seen how data science involves the skillful application of math, coding, and subject matter expertise in ways that allow data scientists to generate reliable and accurate predictions from data. While the last element — subject matter expertise — is unique to each practitioner, if you apply data science within a business context, then you'd want to make sure you've got a good handle on the business acumen that's discussed in Chapter 9. We discuss the math-and-statistics requirements of data science earlier, in Chapters 4 and 5. The other important data science constituent to discuss is coding — in particular, using either the R or Python programming language to build models and generate predictive insights.

In this chapter, I introduce you to the fundamental concepts of programming with Python and R (such as data types, functions, and classes). The machine learning models you build with either of these two languages can serve as the *decision engines* within AI SaaS products you build for your company. I also introduce some of the best Python libraries, and R packages for manipulating data, performing statistical computations, creating data visualizations, and completing other data science tasks.

Seeing Where Python and R Fit into Your Data Science Strategy

Would you be surprised to hear that not all data projects that are out there trying to turn a profit necessarily require data science? It may seem odd, but it's true! Think about LinkedIn for a second: Imagine how much less useful that platform would be if it didn't allow direct messaging between users. That feature directly improves the user experience, keeping users returning more often and keeping them more active on the platform for longer periods, thus increasing the overall profitability of the LinkedIn platform.

The longer users stay active on the platform and the more often they return, the more likely they are to generate revenues for the platform — by either subscribing to LinkedIn Learning or using Open to Work, a LinkedIn designation that encourages recruiters to contact them. (With Open to Work, the contacting of users is paid for by the recruiter as a form of indirect monetization of users on the platform.) The popular LinkedIn Premium feature allows users to message others directly on the platform, regardless of whether they know them. All these monetization features rely directly on LinkedIn's direct messaging product. And do you know what it's built on? It's the data engineering technology called Apache Kafka. Not advanced machine learning models, not deep learning — just traditional, tried-and-tested data engineering, which we talk about in Chapter 2.

But, for those for-profit data projects that involve data science, you'll want to make sure you have a well-formed and effective data science strategy in place, governing project implementation. A *data science strategy* is a technical plan that maps out each and every element required to lead data science projects in ways that increase the profitability of a business. Because R and Python are the lifeblood by which data science produces predictive insights designed to increase profits, you'd be hard-pressed to find a place where they don't fit within an effective data science strategy.

Using Python for Data Science

Although popular programming languages like Java and C++ are good for developing stand-alone desktop applications, Python's versatility makes it an ideal programming language for processing, analyzing, and visualizing data. For this reason, Python has earned a reputation of excellence in the data science field, where it has been widely adopted over the past decade. In fact, Python has become so popular that it's actually stolen a lot of ground from R — the other free, widely adopted programming language for data science applications. Python's status as one of the more popular programming languages out there can be linked to the fact that it's relatively easy to learn and it allows users to accomplish several tasks using just a few lines of code.

TIP

Though this book wasn't designed to teach readers either the mechanics of programming or the implementation of machine learning algorithms, I have included plenty of helpful coding demonstrations and course recommendations over on the companion website, `www.businessgrowth.ai`. If you want to learn to get started with using Python to implement data science, you may want to check it out.

You can use Python to do anything, from simple mathematical operations to data visualizations and even machine learning and predictive analytics. Here's an example of a basic math operation in Python:

```
>>> 2.5+3
5.5
```

Figure 6-1 shows an example — taken from Python's MatPlotLib library — of a more advanced output based on topographical data sets created by the National Oceanic and Atmospheric Administration (NOAA).

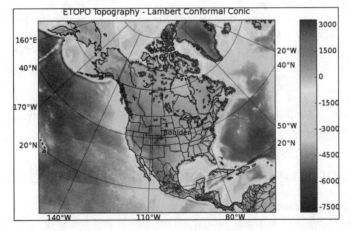

FIGURE 6-1:
Sample output from Python's MatPlotLib library.

Regardless of the task at hand, you should always study the most basic concepts of a language before attempting to delve into its more specialized libraries. So, to start you off, keep in mind that, because Python is an object-oriented programming language, everything in Python is considered an object. In Python, an *object* is anything that can be assigned to a variable or passed as an argument to a function. The following items are all considered objects in the Python programming language:

>> Numbers

>> Strings

>> Lists

>> Tuples

>> Sets

>> Dictionaries

>> Functions

>> Classes

Additionally, all these items (except for the last two in the list) function as basic data types in plain ol' Python, which is Python with no external extensions added to it. (I introduce you to the external Python libraries NumPy, SciPy, Pandas, MatPlotLib, and Scikit-learn in the later section "Checking out some useful Python libraries." When you add these libraries, additional data types become available to you.)

In Python, functions do basically the same thing as they do in plain math — they accept data inputs, process them, and output the result. Output results depend wholly on the task the function was programmed to do. Classes, on the other hand, are prototypes of objects that are designed to output additional objects.

REMEMBER

If your goal is to write fast, reusable, easy-to-modify code in Python, you must use functions and classes. Doing so helps to keep your code efficient and organized.

Sorting out the various Python data types

If you do much work with Python, you need to know how to work with different data types. The main data types in Python and the general forms they take are described in this list:

>> **Numbers:** Plain old numbers, obviously

>> **Strings:** '. . .' or ". . ."

>> **Lists:** [. . .] or [. . ., . . ., . . .]

>> **Tuples:** (. . .) or (. . ., . . ., . . .)

>> **Sets:** Rarely used

>> **Dictionaries:** {'Key': 'Value', . . .}.

Numbers and strings are the most basic data types. You can incorporate them inside other, more complicated data types. All Python data types can be assigned to variables.

REMEMBER

In Python, numbers, strings, lists, tuples, sets, and dictionaries are classified as both object types and data types.

Numbers in Python

The Numbers data type represents numeric values that you can use to handle all types of mathematical operations. Numbers come in the following types:

>> **Integer:** A whole-number format

>> **Long:** A whole-number format with an unlimited digit size

>> **Float:** A real-number format, written with a decimal point

>> **Complex:** An imaginary-number format, represented by the square root of –1

Strings in Python

Strings are the most often used data type in Python — and in every other programming language, for that matter. Simply put, a *string* consists of one or more characters written inside single or double quotes. The following code represents a string:

```
>>> variable1='This is a sample string'
>>> print(variable1)
This is a sample string
```

In this code snippet, the string is assigned to a variable and the variable subsequently acts like a storage container for the string value.

To print the characters contained inside the variable, simply use the predefined function, `print`.

TIP

Python coders often refer to lists, tuples, sets, and dictionaries as data *structures* rather than data *types*. *Data structures* are basic functional units that organize data so that it can be used efficiently by the program or application you're working with.

REMEMBER

Lists, tuples, sets, and dictionaries are data structures, but keep in mind that they're still composed of one or more basic data types (numbers and/or strings, for example).

Lists in Python

A *list* is a sequence of numbers and/or strings. To create a list, you simply enclose the elements of the list (separated by commas) within square brackets. Here's an example of a basic list:

```
>>> variable2=["ID","Name","Depth","Latitude","Longitude"]
>>> depth=[0,120,140,0,150,80,0,10]
>>> variable2[3]
'Latitude'
```

Every element of the list is automatically assigned an index number, starting from 0. You can access each element using this index, and the corresponding value of the list is returned. If you need to store and analyze long arrays of data, use lists — storing your data inside a list makes it fairly easy to extract statistical information. The following code snippet is an example of a simple computation to pull the mean value from the elements of the depth list created in the preceding code example:

```
>>> sum(depth)/len(depth)
62.5
```

In this example, the average of the list elements is computed by first summing up the elements, via the sum function, and then dividing them by the number of the elements contained in the list — a number you determine with the help of the len function, which returns the *length* (the number of elements, in other words) in a string, an array, or a list. The len function in the denominator here is what's returning the average value of items in the object. See? it's as simple as 1-2-3!

Tuples in Python

Tuples are just like lists, except that you can't modify their content after you create them. Also, to create tuples, you need to use normal brackets instead of squared ones.

REMEMBER

"Normal brackets" refers to refers to parentheses in the form of (. . .) or (. . ., . . ., . . .)

Here's an example of a tuple:

```
>>> depth=(0,120,140,0,150,80,0,10)
```

In this case, you can't modify any of the elements, as you would with a list. To ensure that your data stays in a read-only format, use tuples.

Sets in Python

A *set* is another data structure that's similar to a list. In contrast to lists, however, elements of a *set* are unordered. This disordered characteristic of a set makes it impossible to index, so it's not a commonly used data type.

Dictionaries in Python

Dictionaries are data structures that consist of pairs of keys and values. In a dictionary, every value corresponds to a certain key, and consequently, each value can be accessed using that key. The following code snippet shows a typical key/value pairing:

```
>>> variable4={"ID":1,"Name":"Valley City","Depth":0,"Latitude":49.6,
    "Longitude":-98.01}
>>> variable4["Longitude"]
-98.01
```

Putting loops to good use in Python

When working with lists in Python, you typically access a list element by using the element index number. In a similar manner, you can access other elements of the list by using their corresponding index numbers. The following code snippet illustrates this concept:

```
>>>variable2=["ID","Name","Depth","Latitude","Longitude"]
>>> print(variable2[3])
Latitude
>>> print(variable2[4])
Longitude
```

WARNING

Don't let the index numbering system confuse you. Every element of the list is automatically assigned an index number starting from 0 — *not* starting from 1. That means the fourth element in an index actually bears the index number 3.

When you're analyzing considerable amounts of data and you need to access each element of a list, this technique becomes quite inefficient. In these cases, you should use a looping technique instead.

You can use *looping* to execute the same block of code multiple times for a sequence of items. Consequently, rather than manually access all elements one by one, you simply create a loop to automatically *iterate* (or pass through in successive cycles) each element of the list.

You can use two types of loops in Python: the for loop and the while loop. The most often used looping technique is the for loop — designed especially to iterate through sequences, strings, tuples, sets, and dictionaries. The following code snippet illustrates a for loop iterating through the variable2 list created in the preceding code snippet:

```
>>> for element in variable2:print(element)
ID
Name
Depth
Latitude
Longitude
```

The other available looping technique in Python is the while loop. Use a while loop to perform actions while a given condition is true.

REMEMBER

Looping is crucial when you work with long arrays of data, such as when you're working with raster images. Looping lets you apply certain actions to all data or to apply those actions to only predefined groups of data.

Having fun with functions

Functions (and classes, which I describe in the following section) are the crucial building blocks of almost every programming language. They provide a way to build organized, reusable code. Functions are blocks of code that take an input, process it, and return an output. Function inputs can be numbers, strings, lists, objects, or other functions. Python has two types of functions: built-in and custom. *Built-in* functions are predefined inside Python. You can use them by just typing their names.

The following code snippet is an example of the built-in function print:

```
>>> print("Hello")
Hello
```

This oft-used, built-in function `print` prints a given input. The code behind `print` has already been written by the people who created Python. Now that this code stands in the background, you don't need to know how to code it yourself — you simply call the `print` function. The people who created the Python library couldn't guess every possible function to satisfy everyone's needs, but they managed to provide users with a way to create and reuse their own functions when necessary.

In the section "Sorting out the various Python data types," earlier in this chapter, the following code snippet from that section (listed again here) was used to sum up the elements in a list and calculate the average:

```
>>> depth=[0,120,140,0,150,80,0,10]
>>> sum(depth)/len(depth)
62.5
```

The preceding data represents snowfall and snow depth records from multiple point locations. As you can see, the points where snow depth measurements were collected have an average depth of 62.5 units. These are depth measurements taken at only one time, though. In other words, all the data bears the same time-stamp. When modeling data using Python, you often see scenarios in which sets of measurements were taken at different times — known as *time-series* data.

Here's an example of time-series data:

```
>>> december_depth=[0,120,140,0,150,80,0,10]
>>> january_depth=[20,180,140,0,170,170,30,30]
>>> february_depth=[0,100,100,40,100,160,40,40]
```

You could calculate December, January, and February average snow depth in the same way you averaged values in the previous list, but that would be cumbersome. This is where custom functions come in handy:

```
>>> def average(any_list):return(sum(any_list)/len(any_list))
```

This code snippet defines a function named `average`, which takes any list as input and calculates the average of its elements. The function isn't executed yet, but the code defines what the function does when it later receives some input values. In this snippet, `any_list` is just a variable that's later assigned the given value when the function is executed. To execute the function, all you need to do is pass it a value. In this case, the value is a real list with numerical elements:

```
>>> average(february_depth)
72
```

Executing a function is straightforward. You can use functions to do the same thing repeatedly, as many times as you need, for different input values. The beauty here is that, once the functions are constructed, you can reuse them without having to rewrite the calculating algorithm.

Keeping cool with classes

Classes are blocks of code that put together functions and variables to produce other objects. As such, they're slightly different from functions, which take an input and produce an output. The set of functions and classes tied together inside a class describes the blueprint of a certain object. In other words, classes spell out what has to happen in order for an object to be created. After you come up with a class, you can generate the actual object instance by calling a class instance. In Python, this is referred to as *instantiating* an object — creating an instance of that class, in other words.

REMEMBER

Functions that are created inside of a class are called *methods,* and variables within a class are called *attributes.* Methods describe the actions that generate the object, and attributes describe the actual object properties.

To better understand how to use classes for more efficient data analysis, consider the following scenario: Imagine that you have snow depth data from different locations and times and you're storing it online on an FTP server. The dataset contains different ranges of snow depth data, depending on the month of the year. Now imagine that every monthly range is stored in a different location on the FTP server.

Your task is to use Python to fetch all monthly data and then analyze the entire dataset, so you need to use different operations on the data ranges. First, you need to download the data from within Python by using an FTP handling library, such as `ftplib`. Then, to be able to analyze the data in Python, you need to store it in proper Python data types (in lists, tuples, or dictionaries, for example). After you fetch the data and store it as recognizable data types in a Python script, you can then apply more advanced operations that are available from specialized libraries such as NumPy, SciPy, Pandas, MatPlotLib, and Scikit-learn.

In this scenario, you want to create a class that creates a list containing the snow depth data for each month. Every monthly list would be an object instance generated by the class. The class itself would tie together the FTP downloading functions and the functions that store the downloaded records inside the lists. You can then instantiate the class for as many months as you need in order to carry out a thorough analysis. The code to do something like this is shown in Listing 6-1.

LISTING 6-1: **Defining a Class in Python**

```
class Download:
    def __init__(self,ftp=None,site,dir,fileList=[]):
        self.ftp =ftp
        self.site=site
        self.dir=dir
        self.fileList=fileList
        self.Login_ftp()
                self.store_in_list()
    def Login_ftp(self):
        self.ftp=ftplib.FTP(self.site)
        self.ftp.login()
    def store_in_list(self):
        fileList=[]
        self.ftp.cwd("/")
        self.ftp.cwd(self.dir)
        self.ftp.retrlines('NLST',fileList.append)
        return fileList
```

Defining a class probably looks intimidating right now, but I simply want to give you a feeling for the basic structure and point out the class methods involved.

Delving into Listing 6-1, the keyword `class` defines the class, and the keyword `def` defines the class methods. The init function is a default function that you should always define when creating classes, because you use it to declare class variables. The `Login_ftp` method is a custom function that you define to log in to the FTP server. After you log in using the `Login_ftp` method and set the required directory where the data tables are located, you then store the data in a Python list using the custom function `store_in_list`.

After you finish defining the class, you can use it to produce objects. You just need to instantiate the class:

```
>>> Download("ftpexample.com","ftpdirectory")
```

And that's it! With this brief snippet, you've just declared the particular FTP domain and the internal FTP directory where the data is located. After you execute this last line, a list appears, giving you data that you can manipulate and analyze as needed.

Checking out some useful Python libraries

In Python, a *library* is a specialized collection of scripts that were written by someone else to perform specialized sets of tasks. To use specialized libraries in Python, you must first complete the installation process. After you install your libraries on your local hard drive, you can import any library's function into a project by simply using the `import` statement. For example, if you want to import the `ftplib` library, you write

```
>>> import ftplib
```

REMEMBER

Be sure to import the library into your Python project before attempting to call its functions in your code.

After you import the library, you can use its functionality inside any of your scripts. Simply use *dot notation* (a shorthand way of accessing modules, functions, and classes in one line of code) to access the library. Here's an example of dot notation:

```
>>> ftplib.any_ftp_lib_function
```

The dot notation you see above tells the computer to open the "any_ftp_lib_function" that is found in the ftplib library.

REMEMBER

Though you can choose from countless libraries to accomplish different tasks in Python, the Python libraries most commonly used in data science are MatPlotLib, NumPy, Pandas, Scikit-learn, and SciPy. The NumPy and SciPy libraries were specially designed for scientific uses, Pandas was designed for optimal data analysis performance, and MatPlotLib library was designed for data visualization. Scikit-learn is Python's premiere machine learning library.

Saying hello to the NumPy library

NumPy is the Python package that primarily focuses on working with *n*-dimensional array objects, and SciPy, described next, extends the capabilities of the NumPy library. When working with plain Python (Python with no external extensions, such as libraries, added to it), you're confined to storing your data in 1-dimensional lists. If you extend Python by using the NumPy library, however, you're provided a basis from which you can work with *n*-dimensional arrays. (Just in case you were wondering, *n-dimensional* arrays are arrays of one dimension or of multiple dimensions.)

REMEMBER

To enable NumPy in Python, you must first install and import the NumPy library. After that, you can generate multidimensional arrays.

To see how generating *n*-dimensional arrays works in practice, start by checking out the following code snippet, which shows how you'd create a 1-dimensional NumPy array:

```
import numpy
>>> array_1d=numpy.arange(8)
>>> print(array_1d)
[0 1 2 3 4 5 6 7]
```

The numpy.arange method returns evenly spaced values from within a user specified interval. If you don't specify a number for numpy.arange to start with, then it starts with 0. In this case we specified that we want 8 values, so numpy.arange returns [0 1 2 3 4 5 6 7]

After importing numpy, you can use it to generate *n*-dimensional arrays, such as the 1-dimensional array just shown. One-dimensional arrays are referred to as *vectors*. You can also create multidimensional arrays using the reshape method, like this:

```
>>> array_2d=numpy.arange(8).reshape(2,4)
>>> print(array_2d)
[[0 1 2 3]
 [4 5 6 7]]
```

The preceding example is a 2-dimensional array, otherwise known as a 2 × 4 *matrix*. The only difference between this and the preceding example is that we called the .reshape method, and passed in a 2 and a 4 value — telling numpy to take the array and transform it into a 2*4 matrix.

REMEMBER

Standard matrix notation is m*n, where m is the number of rows and n specifies the number of columns in the matrix.

Using the .arange and reshape method is just one way to create NumPy arrays. You can also generate arrays from lists and tuples.

In the snow dataset that I introduce in the earlier section "Having fun with functions," I store my snow depth data for different locations inside three separate Python lists — one list per month:

```
>>> december_depth=[0,120,140,0,150,80,0,10]
>>> january_depth=[20,180,140,0,170,170,30,30]
>>> february_depth=[0,100,100,40,100,160,40,40]
```

It would be more efficient to have the measurements stored in a better-consolidated structure. For example, you can easily put all those lists in a single NumPy array by using the following code snippet:

```
>>>depth=numpy.array([december_depth,january_depth,february_depth])
>>> print(depth)
[[  0 120 140   0 150  80   0  10]
 [ 20 180 140   0 170 170  30  30]
 [  0 100 100  40 100 160  40  40]]
```

Using this structure allows you to pull out certain measurements more efficiently. For example, if you want to calculate the average of the snow depth for the first location in each of the three months, you'd extract the first elements of each horizontal row (values 0, 20, and 0, to be more precise). You can complete the extraction in a single line of code by taking a slice of the dataset and then calculating the mean by way of the NumPy mean function. The term slicing refers to taking a slice out of dataset. Here's an example:

```
>>> numpy.mean(depth[:,1])
133.33333333333334
```

With the above code, we've instructed the computer to go to column index position 1 and calculate the mean of the value in that column. The values in the column at column index 1 are 120, 180, and 100. When you calculate the mean value of the numbers, you get 133.3.

Beyond using NumPy to extract information from single matrices, you can use it to interact with different matrices as well — applying standard mathematical operations between matrices, for example, or even applying nonstandard operators, such as matrix inversion, summarize, and minimum/maximum operators.

REMEMBER

Array objects have the same rights as any other objects in Python. You can pass them as parameters to functions, set them as class attributes, or iterate through array elements to generate random numbers.

Getting up close and personal with the SciPy library

SciPy is a collection of mathematical algorithms and sophisticated functions that extends the capabilities of the NumPy library. The SciPy library adds some specialized scientific functions to Python for more specific tasks in data science. To use SciPy's functions within Python, you must first install and import the SciPy library.

TECHNICAL STUFF

Some sticklers out there consider SciPy to be an extension of the NumPy library. That's because SciPy was *built on top of* NumPy — it uses NumPy functions but adds to them.

SciPy offers functionalities and algorithms for a variety of tasks, including vector quantization, statistical functions, discrete Fourier transform-algorithms, orthogonal distance regression, airy functions, sparse eigenvalue solvers, maximum entropy fitting routines, n-dimensional image operations, integration routines, interpolation tools, sparse linear algebra, linear solvers, optimization tools, signal-processing tools, sparse matrices, and other utilities that aren't served by other Python libraries. Impressive, right? Yet that's not even a complete listing of the available SciPy utilities. If you're dying to get hold of a complete list, running the following code snippet in Python opens an extensive help module that explains the SciPy library:

```
>>> import scipy
>>> help(scipy)
```

REMEMBER

You need to first download and install the SciPy library before you can use this code.

The `help` function used in the preceding code snippet returns a script that lists all utilities that comprise SciPy and documents all of SciPy's functions and classes. This information helps you understand what's behind the prewritten functions and algorithms that make up the SciPy library.

TIP

Because SciPy is still under development, and therefore changing and growing, regularly check the `help` function to see what's changed.

Peeking into the Pandas offering

The Pandas library makes data analysis much faster and easier with its accessible and robust data structures. Its precise purpose is to improve Python's performance with respect to data analysis and modeling. It even offers some data visualization functionality by integrating small portions of the MatPlotLib library. The two main Pandas data structures are described in this list:

>> **Series:** A Series object is an array-like structure that can assume either a horizontal or vertical dimension. You can think of a Pandas Series object as being similar to one row or one column from an Excel spreadsheet.

>> **DataFrame:** A DataFrame object acts like a tabular data table in Python. Each row or column in a DataFrame can be accessed and treated as its own Pandas Series object.

Indexing is integrated into both data structure types, making it easy to access and manipulate your data. Pandas offers functionality for reading in and writing out your data, which makes it easy to use for loading, transferring, and saving datasets in whatever formats you want. Lastly, Pandas offers excellent functionality for reshaping data, treating missing values, and removing outliers, among other tasks. This makes Pandas an excellent choice for data preparation and basic data analysis tasks. If you want to carry out more advanced statistical and machine learning methods, you'll need to use the Scikit-learn library. The good news is that Scikit-learn and Pandas play well together.

Bonding with MatPlotLib for data visualization

Generally speaking, data science projects usually culminate in visual representations of objects or phenomena. In Python, things are no different. After taking baby steps (or some not-so-baby steps) with NumPy and SciPy, you can use Python's MatPlotLib library to create complex visual representations of your dataset or data analysis findings. MatPlotLib, when combined with NumPy and SciPy, creates an excellent environment in which to work when solving problems using data science.

Looking more closely at MatPlotLib, I can tell you that it is a 2-dimensional plotting library you can use in Python to produce figures from data. You can use Mat-PlotLib to produce plots, histograms, scatterplots, and a variety of other data graphics. What's more, because the library gives you full control of your visualization's symbology, line styles, fonts, and colors, you can even use MatPlotLib to produce publication-quality data graphics.

REMEMBER

As is the case with all other libraries in Python, in order to work with MatPlotLib, you first need to install and import the library into your script. After you complete those tasks, it's easy to get started producing graphs and charts.

To illustrate how to use MatPlotLib, consider the following NumPy array (which I came up with in the "Saying hello to the NumPy library" section, earlier in this chapter):

```
>>> print(depth)
[[  0 120 140   0 150  80   0  10]
 [ 20 180 140   0 170 170  30  30]
 [  0 100 100  40 100 160  40  40]]
```

With the following few lines of code, using just a `for` loop and a MatPlotLib function — `pyplot` — you can easily plot all measurements in a single graph within Python:

```
>>> import matplotlib.pyplot as plt
>>> for month in depth:
    plt.plot(month)
>>> plt.show()
```

TECHNICAL STUFF

Heads up for MacOS users who may have recently upgraded to Big Sur and already used MatPlotLib before (but didn't update), the first line of code generates a "Segmentation Error 11." The best way to fix this is to uninstall & re-install MatPlot-Lib. Learn more here: https://stackoverflow.com/questions/64841082/segmentation-fault-11-python-after-upgrading-to-os-big-sur

This code snippet instantly generates the line chart you see in Figure 6-2.

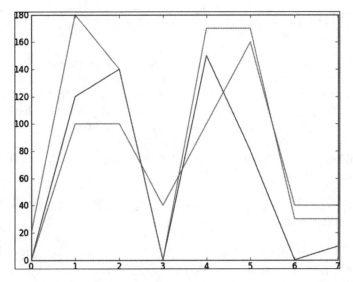

FIGURE 6-2:
Time-series plot of monthly snow depth data.

Each line in the graph represents the depth of snow at different locations in the same month. The preceding code you use to build this graph is simple; if you want to make a better representation, you can add color or text font attributes to the plot function. Of course, you can also use other types of data graphics, depending on which types best show the data trends you want to display. What's important here is that you know when to use each of these important libraries and that you understand how you can use the Python programming language to make data analysis both easy and efficient.

Learning from data with Scikit-learn

Scikit-learn is far and away Python's best machine learning library. With it, you can execute all sorts of machine learning methods, including classification, regression, clustering, dimensionality reduction, and more. The library also offers a preprocessing module that is wonderfully supportive whenever you need to prepare your data for predictive modeling. Lastly, Scikit-learn offers a model selection module that's readily available with all sorts of metrics to help you build your models and choose the best-performing model among a selection.

TECHNICAL STUFF

You'll want to write clear, concise documentation within your Python code, to detail how and why the code works. We discuss more on documentation in Chapter 9, but for now — just know that you can write comments within your Python code simply starting the comment line with a *hash symbol* — the # symbol. Anything written after the # will be ignored by the Python interpreter.

Using Open Source R for Data Science

R is an open-source, free statistical software system that, like Python, has been widely adopted across the data science sector over the past decade. In fact, a somewhat never-ending squabble takes place among data science types about which programming language is best suited for data science. Practitioners who favor R generally do so because of its advanced statistical programming and data visualization capabilities — capabilities that simply can't be replicated in Python. When it comes to data science practitioners, specifically, R's user base is broader than Python's.

You can download the R programming language and the packages that support it from http://cran.r-project.org.

R isn't as easy to learn as Python, but R can be more powerful for certain types of advanced statistical analyses. Although R's learning curve is somewhat steeper than Python's, the programming language is nonetheless relatively straightforward. All you really need to do is master the basic vocabulary used to describe the language and then it shouldn't be too hard to get a grasp on how the software works.

TIP

Again, this book wasn't designed to teach readers the mechanics of programming and implementing machine learning algorithms. I have, however, included plenty of helpful coding demonstrations and course recommendations over on the companion website, www.businessgrowth.ai. If you want a deeper dive into how to use R programming language to implement data science, you may want to check it out.

Comprehending R's basic vocabulary

Although the vocabulary associated with R may sound exotic at first, with practice you can quickly become comfortable with it. For starters, you can run R in one of two modes:

» **Non-interactive:** You run your R code by executing it as an .r file directly from the command line. (The .r file extension is the one that's assigned to script files created for execution by the R program.)

» **Interactive:** You generally work in a separate software application that interacts with you by prompting you to enter your data and R code. In an R session using interactive mode, you can import datasets or enter the raw data directly; assign names to variables and data objects; and use functions, operators, and built-in iterators to help you gain some insight into your source data.

REMEMBER

R is an *object-oriented* language, which simply means that the different parts that comprise the language belong to classes — each class has its own, specific definition and role. A specific example of a class is known as an *instance* of that class; as an instance, it inherits the class's characteristics. Classes are also referred to as *polymorphic,* meaning the subclasses of a class can have their own set of unique behaviors yet share some of the same functionality of the parent class. To illustrate this concept, consider R's print function: print( ). Because this function is polymorphic, it works slightly differently depending on the class of the object it's told to print. Thus, this function and many others perform the same general job in many classes but differ slightly according to class. In the section "Observing how objects work," later in this chapter, I elaborate on object-oriented programming and its advantages, but for now I want to simply introduce objects by giving you their names and definitions.

Here goes!

R works with the following main object types:

» **Vector:** A *vector* is an ordered list of the same mode — character (alphanumeric), numeric, or Boolean. Vectors can have any number of dimensions. For instance, the vector A = ["a", "cat", "def"] is a 3-dimensional Character vector. B = [2, 3.1, -5, 33] is a 4-dimensional Numerical vector. To identify specific elements of these vectors, you can enter the following codes at the prompt in Interactive mode to get R to generate the following returns: A[[1]] = "a" or A[[2]] = "cat" or A[[3]] = "def" or B[[1]] = 2 or B[[2]] = 3.1 or B[[3]] = -5 or B[[4]] = 33. R views a single number as a vector of dimension one. Because vectors can't be broken down further in R, they're also known as *atomic vectors*. Vectors are the R equivalent of the list objects I discuss in the earlier section on "Lists in Python." R's treatment of atomic vectors gives the language tremendous advantages with respect to speed and efficiency (as I describe in the section "Iterating in R," later in this chapter).

>> **Matrix:** Think of a *matrix* as a collection of vectors. A matrix can be of any mode (numerical, character, or Boolean), but all elements in the matrix must be of the same mode. A matrix is also characterized by its number of dimensions. Unlike a vector, a matrix has only two dimensions: number of rows and number of columns.

>> **List:** A *list* is a list of items of arbitrary modes, including other lists or vectors.

TECHNICAL STUFF

Lists are sometimes also called *generic vectors* because some of the same operations performed on vectors can be performed on lists as well.

>> **Data frame:** A data frame is a type of list that's analogous to a table in a database. Technically speaking, a data frame is a list of vectors, each of which is the same length. A row in a table contains the information for an individual record, but elements in the row most likely won't be of the same mode. All elements in a specific column, however, are all of the same mode. Data frames are structured in this same way — each vector in a data frame corresponds to a column in a data table, and each possible index for these vectors is a row.

There are two ways to access members of vectors, matrices, and lists in R:

>> **Single brackets** [ ] give a vector, matrix, or list (respectively) of the element(s) that are indexed.

>> **Double brackets** [[ ]] give a single element.

R users sometimes disagree about the proper use of the brackets for indexing. Generally speaking, the double bracket has several advantages over the single bracket. For example, the double bracket returns an error message if you enter an index that's out of bounds — or, in other words, an index value that does not exist within the given object. If, however, you want to indicate more than one element of a vector, matrix, or list, you should use a single bracket.

Now that you have a grasp of R's basic vocabulary, you're probably eager to see how it works with some actual programming. Imagine that you're using a simple EmployeeRoll dataset and entering the dataset into R by hand. You'd come up with something that looks like Listing 6-2.

LISTING 6-2: **Assigning an Object and Concatenating in R**

```
> EmployeeRoll <- data.frame(list(EmployeeName=c("Smith, John","O'Bannon,
  Tom","Simmons, Sarah"),Grade=c(10,8,12),Salary=c(100000,75000,125000),
  Union=c(TRUE, FALSE, TRUE)))
> EmployeeRoll
EmployeeName Grade Salary Union
1 Smith,John 10 100000 TRUE
2 O'Bannon, Tom 8 75000 FALSE
3 Simmons, Sarah 12 125000 TRUE
```

The combined symbol <- in the first line of Listing 6-2 is pronounced "gets." It assigns the contents on its right to the name on its left. You can think of this relationship in even simpler terms by considering the following statement, which assigns the number 3 to the variable c:

```
> c <- 3
```

Line 1 of Listing 6-2 also exhibits the use of R's concatenate function — c( ) — which is used to create a vector. The concatenate function is being used to form the atomic vectors that comprise the vector list that makes up the EmployeeRoll data frame. Line 2 of Listing 6-2, EmployeeRoll, instructs R to display the object's contents on the screen. (Figure 6-3 breaks out the data in more diagrammatic form.)

DATA FRAMES, LISTS & VECTORS IN R

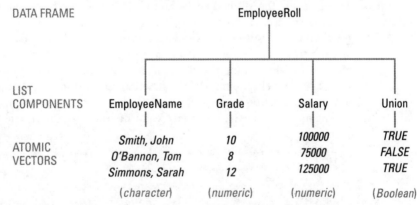

FIGURE 6-3: The relationship between atomic vectors, lists, and data frame objects.

One other object within R is vitally important: the function. *Functions* use atomic vectors, matrices, lists, and data frames to accomplish whatever analysis or computation you want done. (In the following section, I discuss functions more thoroughly. For now, you should simply understand their general role.) Each analysis you perform in R may be done in one or more sessions, which consists of entering a set of instructions that tells R what you want it to do with the data you've entered or imported. In each session, you specify the functions of your script. Then the blocks of code process any input that's received and return an output. A function's input (also known as a function's *arguments*) can be any R object or combination of objects — vectors, matrices, arrays, data frames, tables, or even other functions.

Invoking a function in R is known as *calling* a function.

TECHNICAL STUFF

Commenting in R works the same as in Python. (I cover Python earlier in this chapter.) As an R coder, you'd insert any comments you may have on the code by prefixing them with a *hash symbol* — the # symbol, in other words. The text or numbers that proceed the # on a single line of code all get ignored.

Delving into functions and operators

You can choose one of two methods when writing your functions: a quick, simple method and a more complex, but ultimately more useful, method. Of course, you achieve the same result from choosing either approach, but each method is advantageous in its own ways. If you want to call a function and generate a result as simply and as quickly as possible and you don't think you'll want to reuse the function later, use Method 1. If you want to write a function that you can call for different purposes and use with different datasets in the future, use Method 2 instead.

To illustrate the difference between these two methods, consider again the EmployeeRoll dataset defined in Listing 6-2. Say you want to come up with a function you can use to derive a mean value for employee salary. Using the first, simpler method, you call a single function to handle that task: You simply define an operation by writing the name of the function you want to use and you then include whatever argument(s) the function requires in the set of parentheses following the function name. More specifically, you call the built-in statistical function mean( ) to calculate the mean value of employee salaries, as shown here:

```
> #Method 1 of Calculating the Mean Salary
> MeanSalary1 <- mean(EmployeeRoll$Salary)
> MeanSalary1
[1] 1e+05
```

In this method, the mean( ) function calculates and saves the average salary, 100,000 (or 1e+05, in scientific notation) as an object (a vector, of course!) named MeanSalary1.

The $ symbol points R to a particular field in the dataset. In this example, it points R to the `Salary` field of the `EmployeeRoll` dataset.

Method 2 illustrates a more complicated but possibly more useful approach. Rather than define only a single operation, as in Method 1, Method 2's function can define a series of separate operations if they're needed; therefore, the method can oftentimes grow quite complex. In the following chunk of code, the statement `MeanSalary2 <- function(x)` creates a function named `MeanSalary2`, which takes one argument, x. The statements between the curly braces ({ }) make up this function. The job of `{return(mean(x))}` is to calculate the mean of some entity x and then return that value as a result to the computer screen:

```
> #Method 2 of Calculating the Mean Salary
> #This method allows the user to create a custom set of instructions for R that
  can be used again and again.
> MeanSalary2 <- function(x) {return(mean(x))}
>
> MeanSalary2(EmployeeRoll$Salary)
[1] 1e+05
```

The argument of the function definition isn't the `Salary` field from the `EmployeeRoll` dataset, because this type of function can be called and used for different purposes on different datasets and different fields of said datasets. Also, nothing happens when you finish typing the function and press Return after entering the ending curly brace; in the next line, you just get another prompt (>). That's because you set up the function correctly. (You know it's correct because you didn't get an error message.) You now can call this function when you actually need it — that's what the last instruction entered at the prompt in the preceding code does. Typing `MeanSalary2(EmployeeRoll$Salary)` is a *function call,* and it replaces the function's placeholder argument x with `EmployeeRoll$Salary` — a real object that allows the function to generate a solution.

Of course, the function that's written in Method 2 yields the same mean salary as did the function in Method 1, but the Method 2 function can now be reused for different applications. To illustrate how you'd use this same function on a different dataset, imagine that you have another business with its own payroll. It has five employees with the following salaries: $500,000; $1,000,000; $75,000; $112,000; and $400,000. If you want to call and use the `MeanSalary2` function to find the mean salary of these employees, you can simply write

```
> MeanSalary2(c(500000,1000000,75000,112000,400000))
[1] 417400
```

As instructed in Method 2, the MeanSalary2 function quickly generates a mean value for this new dataset — in this case, $417,400.

The primary benefit of using functions in R is that they make it easier to write cleaner, more concise code that's easy to read and more readily reusable. But at the most fundamental level, R is simply using functions to apply operators. Although applying operators and calling functions both serve the same purpose, you can distinguish the two techniques by their differing syntaxes.

Speaking of operators, R uses many of the same ones used in other programming languages. Table 6-1 lists the more commonly used operators.

TABLE 6-1: ## Popular Operators

Operation	Operator
Plus	+
Minus	–
Times	*
Divide	/
Modulo	%%
Power	^
Greater than	>
Greater than or equal to	>=
Less than	<
Less than or equal to	<=
Equals	==
Not equals	!=
Not (logical)	!
And (logical)	&
Or (logical)	|
Is assigned; gets	<-
Is assigned to	->

REMEMBER

Operators act as functions in R. (I *warned* you that learning the vocabulary of R can be tricky!)

The code snippet shows several examples of where operators are used as functions:

```
> "<"(2,3)
[1] TRUE
> "<"(100,10)
[1] FALSE
> "+"(100,1)
[1] 101
> "/"(4,2)
[1] 2
> "+"(2,5,6,3,10)
Error in `+`(2, 5, 6, 3, 10) : operator needs one or two arguments
```

In the preceding snippet, the Boolean operators less-than (<) and greater-than (>) return a value of either TRUE or FALSE. Also, do you see the error message that's generated by the last line of code? That error happened because the operator + can take only one or two arguments, and in that example, I provided three arguments more than it could handle.

TIP

You can use the + operator to add two numbers or two vectors. In fact, all arithmetic operators in R can accept both numbers and vectors as arguments. For more on arithmetic operators, check out the following section.

Iterating in R

Because of the way R handles vectors, programming in R offers you an efficient way to handle loops and iterations. Essentially, R has built-in iterators that automatically loop over elements without the added hassle of your having to write out the loops yourself.

To better conceptualize this process, called *vectorization*, imagine that you want to add a constant c = 3 to a series of three numbers that you've stored as a vector, m = [10, 6, 9]. You can use the following code:

```
> c <- 3
> m <- c(10, 6, 9)
> x <- m + c
> x
[1] 13 9 12
```

The preceding method works because of an R property known as *recyclability:* If you're performing operations on two vectors of different lengths, R repeats and reuses the smaller vector to make the operation work. In this example, c was a 1-dimensional vector, but R reused it to convert it to a 3-dimensional vector so that the operation could be performed on m.

Here's the logic behind this process:

```
10 + 3 = 13
6 + 3 = 9
9 + 3 = 12
```

This method works also because of the vectorization of the + operator, which performs the + operation on the vectors m and c — in effect, looping through each of the vectors to add their corresponding elements.

Here's another way of writing this process that makes the vectorization of the + operator obvious:

```
> x <- "+"(m,c)
```

TIP

R vectorizes all arithmetic operators, including +, −, /, *, and ^.

When you're using conditional statements within iterative loops, R uses vectorization to make this process more efficient. If you've used other programming languages, you've probably seen a structure that looks something like this:

```
for (y = 1 through 5) { if (3*y <= 4) then z = 1 else z = 0}
```

This loop iterates the code within the brackets ({ }) sequentially for each y equal to 1, 2, 3, 4, and 5. Within this loop, for each y-value, the conditional statement $3*y <= 4$ generates either a TRUE or a FALSE statement. For y-values that yield TRUE values, z is set to 1; otherwise, it's set to 0. This loop thus generates the following:

```
| y | 3*y | 3*y <= 4 | z |
| 1 | 3 | TRUE | 1 |
| 2 | 6 | FALSE | 0 |
| 3 | 9 | FALSE | 0 |
| 4 | 12 | FALSE | 0 |
| 5 | 15 | FALSE | 0 |
```

Now check out how you can do this same thing using R:

```
> y <- 1:5
> z <- ifelse(3*y <= 4, 1, 0)
> z
[1] 1 0 0 0 0
```

It's much more compact, right? In the preceding R code, the y term represents the numerical vector [1, 2, 3, 4, 5]. As was the case earlier, in the R code the operator <= is vectorized, and recyclability is again applied so that the scalar 4 is treated as a 5-dimensional vector [4, 4, 4, 4, 4] to make the vector operation work. As before, only where y = 1 is the condition met and, consequently, z[[1]] = 1 and z[2:5] = 0.

TIP

In R, you often see something that looks like 1:10. This *colon operator* notates a sequence of numbers — the first number, the last number, and the sequence that lies between them. Thus, the vector 1:10 is equivalent to 1, 2, 3, 4, 5, 6, 7, 8, 9, 10 and 2:5 is equal to 2, 3, 4, 5.

Observing how objects work

R's object-oriented approach makes deploying and maintaining code relatively quick and easy. As part of this object-oriented functionality, objects in R are distinguished by characteristics known as *attributes*. Each object is defined by its attributes; more specifically, each object is defined by its class attribute.

As an example, the USDA provides data on the percentages of insect-resistant and herbicide-tolerant corn planted per year, for years ranging from 2000 through 2014. You could use a linear regression function on this information to predict the percentage of herbicide-tolerant corn planted in Illinois during 2000 to 2014, from the percentage of insect-resistant corn planted in Illinois during these same years. The dataset and function are shown in Listing 6-3.

LISTING 6-3:   **Exploring Objects in R**

```
> GeneticallyEngineeredCorn <- data.frame(list(year=c(2000, 2001, 2002, 2003,
   2004, 2005, 2006, 2007, 2008, 2009, 2010, 2011, 2012, 2013, 2014),Insect
   =c(13, 12,18,23,26,25,24,19,13, 10, 15, 14, 14, 4, 3), herbicid
   e=c(3,3,3,4,5,6,12,15,15,15,15,17,18,7,5)))
> GeneticallyEngineeredCorn
   year Insect herbicide
1  2000    13        3
2  2001    12        3
```

(continued)

LISTING 6-3: *(continued)*

```
 3  2002    18       3
 4  2003    23       4
 5  2004    26       5
 6  2005    25       6
 7  2006    24      12
 8  2007    19      15
 9  2008    13      15
10 2009    10      15
11 2010    15      15
12 2011    14      17
13 2012    14      18
14 2013     4       7
15 2014     3       5
> PredictHerbicide <- lm(GeneticallyEngineeredCorn$herbicide ~
            GeneticallyEngineeredCorn$Insect)
> attributes(PredictHerbicide)$names
 [1] "coefficients"  "residuals"     "effects"      "rank"
 [5] "fitted.values" "assign"        "qr"           "df.residual"
 [9] "xlevels"       "call"          "terms"        "model"
> attributes(PredictHerbicide)$class
 [1] "lm"
> PredictHerbicide$coef
                 (Intercept) GeneticallyEngineeredCorn$Insect
    10.52165581                          -0.06362591
```

In Listing 6-3, the expression `PredictHerbicide <- lm(GeneticallyEngineered Corn$herbicide ~ GeneticallyEngineeredCorn$Insect)` instructs R to perform a linear regression and assign the results to the `PredictHerbicide` object. In the linear regression, `GeneticallyEngineeredCorn` is defined as the source dataset, the `Insect` column acts as the independent variable, and the `herbicide` column acts as the dependent variable.

R's `attribute` function returns information about an object's attributes. In this example, typing in the function `attribute(PredictHerbicide)$names` instructs R to name all attributes of the `PredictHerbicide` object, and the function `attribute(PredictHerbicide)$class` instructs R to identify the object's classes. You can see from Listing 6-3 that the `PredictHerbicide` object has 12 attributes and has class `lm` (which stands for *linear model*).

R allows you to request specifics on each of these attributes; but to keep this example brief, simply ask R to specify the coefficients of the linear regression equation. Looking back, you can see that this is the first attribute that's provided for the `PredictHerbicide` object. To ask R to show the coefficients obtained by fitting the linear model to the data, enter `PredictHerbicide$coef`, as shown in Listing 6-3, and R returns the following information:

```
(Intercept) GeneticallyEngineeredCorn$Insect
 10.52165581                      -0.06362591
```

In plain math, the preceding result translates into the equation shown in Figure 6-4.

FIGURE 6-4:
Linear regression coefficients from R, translated into a plain math equation.

$$\left(\% _{\text{herbicide-resistant corn}}\right)_{\text{Illinois, 2000-2014}} = 10.52165581 - 0.06362591\left(\% _{\text{insect-resistance corn}}\right)_{\text{Illinois, 2000-2014}}$$

Translated into mathematical terms, this is equivalent to the following:

Percentage of Genetically Engineered Herbicide-Tolerant Corn = 10.5 – 0.06 * Percentage of Genetically Engineered Insect-Resistant Corn

Thus the relationship between the two variables appears rather weak, so the percentage of genetically engineered, insect-resistant corn planted wouldn't provide a good predictor of the percentage of herbicide-resistant corn planted.

This example also illustrates the polymorphic nature of generic functions in R — that is, where the same function can be adapted to the class it's used with, thus making that function applicable to many different classes. The polymorphic function of this example is R's `attributes( )` function. This function is applicable to the `lm` (linear model) class, the `mean` class, the `histogram` class, and many others.

REMEMBER

If you want to get a quick orientation when working with instances of an unfamiliar class, R's polymorphic generic functions can come in handy. These functions generally tend to make R a more efficiently mastered programming language.

Sorting out R's popular statistical analysis packages

R has a plethora of easy-to-install packages and functions, many of which are quite useful in data science. In an R context, *packages* are bundles composed of specific functions, data, and code suited for performing specific types of analyses or sets of analyses, including forecasting, multivariate analysis, and factor analysis The CRAN site lists the current packages available for download at `http://cran.r-project.org/web/packages`, along with directions on how to download and install them. In this section, I discuss some popular packages and then delve deeper into the capabilities of a few of the more advanced packages that are available.

Let me start with R's `forecast` package, which contains various forecasting functions that you can adapt to use for AutoRegressive Integrated Moving Average (ARIMA) time series forecasting, or for other types of univariate time series forecasts. Or perhaps you want to use R for quality management? You can use R's Quality Control Charts package (`qcc`) for quality and statistical process control.

In the practice of data science, you're likely to benefit from almost any package that specializes in multivariate analysis. If you want to carry out logistic regression, you can use R's *multinomial logit model* (`mlogit`), in which observations of a known class are used to "train" the software so that it can identify classes of other observations whose classes are unknown. (For example, you can use logistic regression — discussed in Chapter 4 — to train software so that it can successfully predict customer churn, a data science use case that you can read more about in Chapter 11.)

If you want to use R to take undifferentiated data and identify which of its factors is significant for some specific purpose, you can use factor analysis. To better illustrate the fundamental concept of factor analysis, imagine that you own a restaurant. You want to do everything you can to make sure its customer satisfaction rating is as high as possible, right? Well, factor analysis can help you determine which exact factors have the largest impact on customer satisfaction ratings — those could coalesce into the general factors of ambience, restaurant layout, and employee appearance, attitude, and knowledge. With this knowledge, you can work on improving these factors to increase customer satisfaction and, with it, brand loyalty.

REMEMBER

Few people enter data manually into R. Data is more often imported from either Microsoft Excel or a relational database. You can find driver packages available to import data from various types of relational databases, including RMySQL, and RODBC, RPostgreSQL, RSQLite, as well as packages for many other RDBMSs. One of R's strengths is how it equips users with the ability to produce publication-quality graphical illustrations or even just data visualizations that can help you understand your data. The `ggplot2` package, for example, offers a ton of different data visualization options; I tell you more about this package later in this chapter.

For information on additional R packages, check out the R Project website at www.r-project.org. You can find a lot of existing online documentation to help you identify which packages best suit your needs. Also, coders in R's active community are making new packages and functions available all the time.

Examining packages for visualizing, mapping, and graphing in R

If you've read earlier sections in this chapter, you should have (I hope!) a basic understanding of how functions, objects, and R's built-in iterators work. You also should be able to think of a few data science tasks that R can help you accomplish. In the remainder of this chapter, I introduce you to some powerful R packages for data visualization, network graph analysis, and spatial point pattern analysis.

Visualizing R statistics with ggplot2

If you're looking for a fast and efficient way to produce good-looking data visualizations that you can use to derive and communicate insights from your datasets, look no further than R's ggplot2 package. It was designed to help you create all different types of data graphics in R, including histograms, scatterplots, bar charts, boxplots, and density plots. It offers a wide variety of design options as well, including choices in colors, layout, transparency, and line density. Admittedly, ggplot2 probably isn't the best option if you're looking to do data storytelling or data art, but it's definitely useful for data showcasing. (For better options for data storytelling or data art, see Chapter 20.)

To better understand how the ggplot2 package works, consider the following example. Figure 6-5 shows a simple scatterplot that was generated using ggplot2. This scatterplot depicts the concentrations (in parts per million, or ppm) of four types of pesticides that were detected in a stream between the years 2000 to 2013. The scatterplot could have been designed to show only the pesticide concentrations for each year, but ggplot2 provides an option for fitting a regression line to each of the pesticide types. (The regression lines are the solid lines shown on the plot.) You can also have ggplot2 present these pesticide types in different colors. The colored areas enclosing the regression lines represent 95 percent confidence intervals for the regression models.

The scatterplot chart makes it clear that all pesticides except for ryanoids are showing decreasing stream concentrations. Organochlorides had the highest concentration in 2000, but then exhibited the greatest decrease in concentration over the 13-year period.

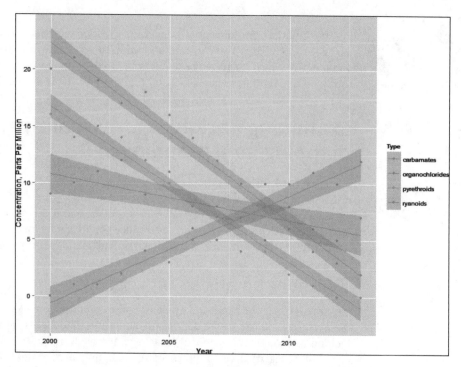

FIGURE 6-5:
A scatterplot,
generated in the
ggplot2 package.

Analyzing networks with statnet and igraph

Social networks and social network data volumes have absolutely exploded over the past decade. Therefore, knowing how to make sense of network data has become increasingly important for analysts. Social network analysis skills enable you to analyze social networks to uncover how accounts are connected and the ways in which information is shared across those connections. You can use network analysis methods to determine how fast information spreads across the Internet. You can even use network analysis methods in genetic mapping to better understand how one gene affects and influences the activity of other genes or use them in hydraulic modeling to figure out how to best design a water-distribution or sewer-collection system.

Two R packages were explicitly written for network analysis purposes: statnet and igraph. You can use either one to collect network statistics or statistics about network components. Figure 6-6 shows sample output from network analysis in R, generated using the statnet package. This output is just a simple network in which the direction of the arrows shows the direction of flow within the network, from one vertex to another. The network has five vertices and nine *faces* — connections between the vertices.

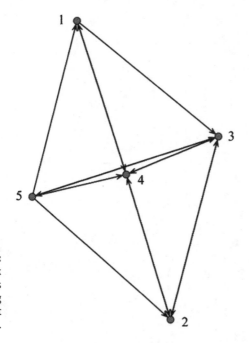

FIGURE 6-6:
A network
diagram that was
generated using
the statnet
package.

Mapping and analyzing spatial point patterns with spatstat

If you want to analyze spatial data in R, you can use the spatstat package. This package is most commonly used in analyzing the patterns of spatial data points — also called *point pattern data* — but you can also use it to analyze line patterns, pixels, and linear network data. By default, the package installs with geographical, ecological, and environmental datasets that you can use to support your analyses, if appropriate. With its space-time point pattern analysis capabilities, spatstat can help you visualize a spatiotemporal change in one or several variables over time. The package even comes with 3-dimensional graphing capabilities. Because spatstat is a geographic data analysis package, it's commonly used in ecology, geosciences, and botany, or for environmental studies, although the package could easily be used for location-based studies that relate to business, logistics, sales, marketing, and more.

Chapter **7**

Generating Insights with Software Applications

I n this day and age, when it seems that every company wants to hire data scientists with extensive experience programming in R and Python, it only makes sense for technology vendors to offer tools that help democratize the data insights that are generated by data scientists. There simply aren't enough data scientists to go around, and even if there were — the whole world doesn't need to be a data scientist. We need to be able to show up and create value in our own areas of expertise. The business world needs that from us as well.

In this chapter, you see some incredibly powerful low-code or no-code tools for generating more profits, faster, from the data you're already working with, without the downtime of needing to learn to build complicated predictive models in R or Python.

Choosing the Best Tools for Your Data Science Strategy

Data science strategy can best be described as a technical plan that maps out each and every element required to lead data science projects that increase the profitability of a business. In Chapter 6, I talk about how R and Python are often part of the plan, which may make you think that, when it comes to data science strategy, Python and R are the obvious answers to this question: "Which tools do I need for my strategy to succeed?" Is the obvious answer always the best answer? I think not. A data strategy that relies *only* on data science to improve profits from data is a limited one, cutting itself off at the pass by insisting on the use of code to monetize data.

For example, imagine that a human resources (HR) professional, without needing to write even one line of code, is able to build a software application that automatically collects applicant data, reads that data into an Applicants SQL database, and then executes an automated response to each applicant based on the manual determination of the HR personnel who is processing employment applications. Where appropriate, the software automatically moves candidates forward in the hiring process. This no-code application eliminates the need for manual data entry, data clean-up, email follow-up, and candidate forwarding. That's a lot of time (money, in other words) saved right there.

Do you know of any prebuilt software whose vendor could come in and configure it to create this type of system setup in-house? Yes, you probably do, but that's a lengthy, expensive, and inflexible route to take, considering that the same outcome is now possible in a no-code environment like Airtable — a collaborative, intuitive, cloud-based SQL-esque solution that acts and works like both a spreadsheet and database at the same time. These days, in my business, all of our data warehousing and project management take place inside Airtable, and I'm able to build applications off that platform while collaborating with ten team members, all for just $10 per month.

No-code is a type of development platform that leverages graphical user interfaces in a way that allows both coders and noncoders alike to build their own software applications. If your start-up or small business has no complex data architecture, it's entirely possible to house your company's data in a no-code environment and not have to worry about integrating that data and platform with other data systems you might have.

If your company is larger and more mature, you may want to look into *low-code* options — platforms that allow users to build applications without needing to use any code whatsoever, but that do require a small bit of code to configure on the back end in order to enable data integration with the rest of the company's data systems and sources. Commonly used low-code solutions are Google Forms and Microsoft Access for self-service data collection and integration.

With respect to data strategy, what we're really talking about here is leveraging low-code and no-code solutions to deploy and directly monetize more of your company's data, without needing to train existing team members, or hire experienced data scientists. The idea is to equip all knowledge workers with intuitive data technologies they can use right away to start getting better results from data themselves, without the intervention of data specialists — a true democratization of data and data monetization across the business, in other words.

Bridging the gap between no-code, low-code, SQL, and spreadsheets, SQL databases and spreadsheet applications such as Excel and Google Sheets provide just the no-code and low-code environments that knowledge workers can start using today to increase the productivity and profitability of their company's data. These technologies are so accessible and represent so much upside potential to modern businesses that I'm including high-level coverage of them in the pages that follow.

Getting a Handle on SQL and Relational Databases

Some data professionals are resistant to learning SQL because of the steep learning curve involved. They think, "I am not a coder and the term *Structured Query Language* sure sounds like a programming language to me." In the case of SQL, though, it is *not* a programming language — as you'll soon see. As far as the upside potential goes of learning to use SQL to query and access data, it's worth the small degree of hassle.

SQL, or *Structured Query Language,* is a standard for creating, maintaining, and securing relational databases. It's a set of rules you can use to quickly and efficiently query, update, modify, add, or remove data from large and complex databases. You use SQL rather than Python or a spreadsheet application to do these tasks because SQL is the simplest, fastest way to get the job done. It offers a plain and standardized set of core commands and methods that are easy to use when performing these particular tasks. In this chapter, I introduce you to basic SQL concepts and explain how you can use SQL to do cool things like query, join, group, sort, and even text-mine structured datasets.

REMEMBER

Although the SQL standard is lengthy, a user commonly needs fewer than 20 commands, and the syntax is human-readable — for example, if you need to pull data on employees in the Finance department who earn more than $50,000 per year in salary, you could use a SQL statement like the one shown in Figure 7-1. Making things even easier, SQL commands are written in ALL CAPS, which helps to keep the language distinct and separate in your mind from other programming languages.

```
SELECT*FROM employees WHERE salary>50000 AND department=finance;
```

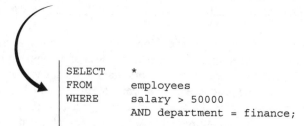

FIGURE 7-1:
An example of how SQL is human-readable.

```
SELECT      *
FROM        employees
WHERE       salary > 50000
            AND department = finance;
```

Although you can use SQL to work with structured data that resides in relational database management systems, you can't use standard SQL as a solution for handling big data. (Unfortunately, you just can't handle big data using relational database technologies.) I give you more solutions for handling big data in Chapter 2, where I discuss data engineering and its components. For now, suffice it to say that SQL is simply a tool you can use to manipulate and edit structured data tables. It's nothing exceedingly innovative, but it can be helpful to use SQL for the data querying and manipulation tasks that often arise in the practice of data science. In this chapter, I introduce the basics of relational databases, SQL, and database design.

REMEMBER

Although the name Structured Query Language suggests that SQL is a programming language, don't be misled. SQL is not a programming language, like R or Python. Rather, it's a language of commands and syntax that you can use to create, maintain, and search relational database systems. SQL supports a few common programming forms, like conditionals and loops, but to do anything more complex, you'd have to import your SQL query results into another programming platform and then do the more complex work there.

TECHNICAL STUFF

SQL has become so ubiquitous in the data field that its passionate users commonly debate whether SQL should be pronounced "ess-cue-el" or "see-quel." Most users I've met lean toward the latter.

One fundamental characteristic of SQL is that you can use it on only structured data that sits in a relational database. SQL database management systems (DBMSs) optimize their own structure with minimal user input, which enables blazing-fast operational performance.

REMEMBER

An *index* is the lookup table. You create it in order to index, point to, and "look up" data in tables of a database. Although SQL DBMSs are known for their fast structured database querying capabilities, this speed and effectiveness are heavily dependent on good indexing. Good indexing is vital for fast data retrieval in SQL.

Similar to how different web browsers comply with, add to, and ignore different parts of the HTML standard in different ways, SQL rules are interpreted a bit differently, depending on whether you're working with open-source products or commercial vendor software applications. Because not every SQL solution is the same, it's a good idea to know something about the benefits and drawbacks of some of the more popular SQL solutions on the market. Here are two popular open-source SQL implementations commonly used by data scientists:

» **MySQL:** By far the most popular open-source version of SQL, MySQL offers a complete and powerful version of SQL. It's used on the back end of millions of websites.

» **PostgreSQL:** This software adds object-oriented elements to SQL's relational language, making it popular with programmers who want to integrate SQL objects into their own platforms' object model.

REMEMBER

Other powerful commercial SQL implementations, such as Oracle and Microsoft SQL Server, are great solutions as well, but they're designed for use in a more traditional business context rather than as a data science tool.

As you might guess from the name, the most salient aspect of relational databases is that they're *relational* — they're composed of related tables, in other words. To illustrate the idea of a relational database, first imagine an Excel spreadsheet with rows, columns, and predefined relationships between shared columns. Then imagine having an Excel workbook with many worksheets (tables), in which every worksheet has a column with the same name as a column in one or more *other* worksheets. Because these worksheets have a shared relationship, if you use SQL you can use that shared relationship to look up data in all related worksheets. This type of relationship is illustrated in Figure 7-2.

REMEMBER

The *primary key* of a table is a column of values that uniquely identifies every row in that table. A good example of primary keys is the use of ISBN numbers for a table of books or employee ID numbers for a table of employees. A *foreign key* is a column in one table that matches the primary key of another and is used to link tables.

Foreign Key

Lake Name	Max Water Depth (ft)	Average Annual Depth Change (in)
Lake Monroe	...	...
Lake Lilly	...	...
Lake Conway	...	...

Primary Key

Lake Name	Alkalinity (mEq/L)	Total Dissolved Solids (ppm)	Phosphates (u g/L)
Lake Monroe	...	...	...
Lake Lilly	...	...	...
Lake Conway	...	...	...

Foreign Key

Lake Name	Subdivision Name	Taxing District
Lake Monroe	...	...
Lake Lilly	...	...
Lake Conway	...	...

FIGURE 7-2:
A relationship between data tables that share a column.

Keeping the focus on terminology, remember that proper database science often associates particular meanings to particular words, as you can see in this list:

>> **Columns,** called fields, keys, and attributes

>> **Rows,** called records

>> **Cells,** called values

REMEMBER

Database science uses a *lot* of synonyms. For simplicity's sake, I try to stick to using the words *column, row,* and *cell.* And because *primary key* and *foreign key* are standard terms, I use them to describe these two special column types.

The main benefits of using relational database management systems (RDBMSs, for short) is that they're fast, they have large storage and handling capacity (compared to spreadsheet applications such as Excel), and they're ideal tools to help you maintain *data integrity* — the consistency and accuracy of data in your database. If you need to make quick-and-accurate changes and updates to your datasets, you can use SQL and a RDBMS.

Let the following scenario serve as an illustration. This data table describes films and lists ratings from viewers:

```
id    title            genre    rating timestamp        rating
1     The Even Couple  NULL     2011-08-03 16:04:23      4
2     The Fourth Man   Drama    2014-02-19 19:17:16      5
```

```
2    The Fourth Man    Drama       2010-04-27 10:05:36   4
3    All About Adam    Drama       2011-04-05 21:21:05   4
3    All About Adam    Drama       2014-02-21 00:11:07   3
4    Dr. Yes           Thriller    NULL
```

What happens if you find out that *All About Adam* is a comedy rather than a drama? If the table were in a simple spreadsheet, you'd have to open the data table, find all instances of the film, and then manually change the genre value for that record. That's not so difficult in this sample table because only two records are related to that film. But even here, if you forget to change one of these records, this inconsistency would cause a loss of data integrity, which can cause all sorts of unpredictable problems for you down the road.

In contrast, the relational database solution is simple and elegant. Instead of one table for this example, you'd have three:

```
Film     id    title
         1     The Even Couple
         2     The Fourth Man
         3     All About Adam
         4     Dr. Yes


Genre    id    genre
         2     Drama
         3     Drama
         4     Thriller


Rating   timestamp              id    rating
         2011-08-03 16:04:23    1     4
         2014-02-19 19:17:16    2     5
         2010-04-27 10:05:36    2     4
         2011-04-05 21:21:05    3     4
         2014-02-21 00:11:07    3     3
```

The primary key for the Film and Genre tables is id. The primary key for the Rating table is timestamp — because a film can have more than one rating, id is not a unique field and, consequently, it can't be used as a primary key. In this example, if you want to look up and change the genre for *All About Adam*, you'd use Film.id as the primary key and Genre.id as the foreign key. You'd simply use these keys to query the records you need to change and then apply the changes systematically. This systematic approach eliminates the risk of stray errors.

Investing Some Effort into Database Design

If you want to ensure that your database will be useful to you for the foreseeable future, you need to invest time and resources into excellent database design. If you want to create databases that offer fast performance and error-free results, your database design has to be flawless, or as flawless as you can manage. Before you enter any data into a data table, first carefully consider the tables and columns you want to include, the kinds of data those tables will hold, and the relationships you want to create between those tables.

REMEMBER

Every hour you spend planning your database and anticipating future needs can save you countless hours down the road, when your database might hold a million records. Poorly planned databases can easily turn into slow, error-ridden monstrosities — avoid them at all costs.

Keep just a few concepts in mind when you design databases:

>> Data types

>> Constraints

>> Normalization

In the next few sections, I help you take a closer look at each topic.

Defining data types

When creating a data table, one of the first things you have to do is define the data type of each column. You have several data type options to choose from:

>> **Text:** If your column is to contain text values, you can classify it as a Character data type with a fixed length or a Text data type of indeterminate length.

>> **Numerical:** If your column is to hold number values, you can classify it as a Numerical data type. These can be stored as integers or floats.

>> **Date:** If your column is to hold date- or time-based values, you can designate this as a Date data type or Date-Time data type.

REMEMBER

Text data types are handy, but they're terrible for searches. When you use a text field to do a search or select query, SQL will cause the computer to call up each of the data objects individually, instead of searching and sorting through them *in-memory* — in other words, processing data within the computer's memory, without actually reading and writing its computational results onto the disk.

Designing constraints properly

Think of constraints, in the context of SQL, as rules you use to control the type of data that can be placed in a table. As such, they're an important consideration in any database design. When you're considering adding constraints, first decide whether each column is allowed to hold a NULL value. (NULL isn't the same as blank or zero data; it indicates a total absence of data in a cell.)

For example, if you have a table of products you're selling, you probably don't want to allow a NULL in the Price column. In the Product Description column, however, some products may have *long* descriptions, so you might allow some of the cells in this column to contain NULL values.

Within any data type, you can also constrain exactly what type of input values the column accepts. Imagine that you have a text field for Employee ID, which must contain values that are exactly two letters followed by seven numbers, like this: SD0154919. Because you don't want your database to accept a typo, you'd define a constraint that requires all values entered into the cells of the Employee ID column to have exactly two letters followed by seven numbers.

Normalizing your database

After you've defined the data types and designed constraints, you need to deal with *normalization* — structuring your database so that any changes, additions, or deletions to the data have to be made only once and won't result in anomalous, inconsistent data. There are many different degrees and types of normalization (at least seven), but a good, robust, normalized SQL database should have at least the following properties:

>> **Primary keys:** Each table has a primary key, which is a unique value for every row in that column.

>> **Nonredundancy of columns:** No two tables have the same column, unless it's the primary key of one and the foreign key of the other.

>> **No multiple dependencies:** Every column's value must depend on only one other column whose value does not in turn depend on any other column. Calculated values — values such as the total for an invoice, for example — must therefore be done on the fly for each query and should not be hard-coded into the database. This means that zip codes should be stored in a separate table because they depend on three columns — address, city, and state.

>> **Column indexes:** As you may recall, in SQL an index is a lookup table that points to data in tables of a database. When you make a column index — an

index of a particular column — each record in that column is assigned a unique key value that's indexed in a lookup table. Column indexing enables faster data retrieval from that column.

It's an excellent idea to create a column index for frequent searches or to be used as a search criterion. The column index takes up memory, but it increases your search speeds tremendously. It's easy to set up, too. Just tell your SQL DBMS to index a certain column, and then the system sets it up for you.

TIP

If you're concerned that your queries are slow, first make sure that you have all the indexes you need before trying other, perhaps more involved, trouble-shooting efforts.

» **Subject-matter segregation:** Another feature of good database design is that each table contains data for only one kind of subject matter. This isn't exactly a normalization principle per se, but it helps to achieve a similar end.

Consider again the film rating example, from an earlier section:

```
Film     id    title
         1     The Even Couple
         2     The Fourth Man
         3     All About Adam
         4     Dr. Yes


Genre    id    genre
         2     Drama
         3     Drama
         4     Thriller


Rating   timestamp              id    rating
         2011-08-03 16:04:23    1     4
         2014-02-19 19:17:16    2     5
         2010-04-27 10:05:36    2     4
         2011-04-05 21:21:05    3     4
         2014-02-21 00:11:07    3     3
```

I could have designated Genre to be a separate column in the Film table, but it's better off in its own table because that allows for the possibility of missing data values (NULLs). Look at the Film table just shown. Film 1 has no genre assigned to it. If the Genre column were included in this table, then Film 1 would have a NULL value there. Rather than have a column that contains a NULL value, it's much easier to make a separate Genre data table. The primary keys of the Genre table don't align exactly with those of the Film table, but they don't need to when you go to join them.

TIP

NULL values can be quite problematic when you're running a SELECT query. When you're querying based on the value of particular attribute, any records that have a NULL value for that attribute won't be returned in the query results. Of course, these records would still exist, and they may even fall within the specified range of values you've defined for your query, but if the record has a NULL value, it's omitted from the query results. In this case, you're likely to miss them in your analysis.

Any data scientist worth their salt must address many challenges when dealing with either the data or the science. SQL takes some of the pressure off when you're dealing with the time-consuming tasks of storing and querying data, saving precious time and effort.

Narrowing the Focus with SQL Functions

When working with SQL commands, you use *functions* to perform tasks, and *arguments* to more narrowly specify those tasks. To query a particular set from within your data tables, for example, use the SELECT function. To combine separate tables into one, use the JOIN function. To place limits on the data that your query returns, use a WHERE argument. As I say in the preceding section, fewer than 20 commands are commonly used in SQL. This section introduces SELECT, FROM, JOIN, WHERE, GROUP, MAX(), MIN(), COUNT(), AVG(), and HAVING.

The most common SQL command is SELECT. You can use this function to generate a list of search results based on designated criteria. To illustrate, imagine the film-rating scenario mentioned earlier in this chapter with a tiny database of movie ratings that contains the three tables Film, Genre, and Rating.

To generate a printout of all data FROM the Rating table, use the SELECT function. Any function with SELECT is called a *query*, and SELECT functions accept different arguments to narrow down or expand the data that is returned. An asterisk (*) represents a wildcard, so the asterisk in SELECT * tells the *interpreter* — the SQL component that carries out all SQL statements — to show every column in the table. You can then use the WHERE argument to limit the output to only certain values. For example, here is the complete Rating table:

Rating	timestamp	id	rating
	2011–08–03 16:04:23	1	4
	2014–02–19 19:17:16	2	5
	2010–04–27 10:05:36	2	4
	2011–04–05 21:21:05	3	4
	2014–02–21 00:11:07	3	3

If you want to limit your ratings to those made after a certain time, you'd use code like that shown in Listing 7-1.

LISTING 7-1: **Using SELECT, WHERE, and DATE() to Query Data**

```
SELECT * FROM Rating
WHERE Rating.timestamp >= date('2014-01-01')
timestamp              id    rating
2014-02-19 19:17:16    2     5
2014-02-21 00:11:07    3     3
```

In Listing 7-1, the DATE() function turns a string into a date that can then be compared with the timestamp column.

You can also use SQL to join columns into a new data table. Joins are made on the basis of shared (or compared) data in a particular column (or columns). You can execute a join in SQL in several ways, but the ones listed here are probably the most popular:

>> **Inner join:** The default JOIN type; returns all records that lie in the intersecting regions between the tables being queried

>> **Outer join:** Returns all records that lie outside the overlapping regions between queried data tables

>> **Full outer join:** Returns all records that lie both inside and outside the overlapping regions between queried data tables — in other words, returns all records for both tables

>> **Left join:** Returns all records that reside in the leftmost table

>> **Right join:** Returns all records that reside in the rightmost table

REMEMBER

Be sure to differentiate between an inner join and an outer join, because these functions handle missing data in different ways. As an example of a join in SQL, if you want a list of films that includes genres, you use an inner join between the Film and Genre tables to return only the results that intersect (overlap) between the two tables.

To refresh your memory, here are the two tables you're interested in:

```
Film    id    title
        1     The Even Couple
        2     The Fourth Man
```

```
        3    All About Adam
        4    Dr. Yes


Genre    id    genre
         2     Drama
         3     Drama
         4     Thriller
```

Listing 7-2 shows how you'd use an inner join to find the information you want.

LISTING 7-2: **An Inner JOIN Function**

```
SELECT Film.id, Film.title, Genre.genre
FROM Film
JOIN Genre On Genre.id=Film.id
id    title            genre
2     The Fourth Man   Drama
3     All About Adam   Drama
4     Dr. Yes          Thriller
```

In Listing 7-2, I name specific columns (Film.title and Genre.genre) after the SELECT command. I do this to avoid creating a duplicate id column in the table that results from the JOIN — one id from the Film table and one id from the Genre table. Because the default for JOIN is inner, and inner joins return only records that are overlapping or shared between tables, Film 1 is omitted from the results (because of its missing Genre value).

If you want to return all rows, even ones with NULL values, simply do a full outer join, like the one shown in Listing 7-3.

LISTING 7-3: **A Full Outer JOIN**

```
SELECT Film.id, Film.title, Genre.genre
FROM Film
FULL JOIN Genre On Genre.id=Film.id
id    title             genre
1     The Even Couple   NULL
2     The Fourth Man    Drama
3     All About Adam    Drama
4     Dr. Yes           Thriller
```

To aggregate values so that you can figure out the average rating for a film, use the GROUP statement. (GROUP statement commands include MAX( ), MIN( ), COUNT( ), or AVG( ).)

Listing 7-4 shows one way you can aggregate values in order to return the average rating of each film. The SELECT function uses the AS statement to rename the column to make sure it was properly labeled. The Film and Ratings tables had to be joined and, because *Dr. Yes* had no ratings and an inner join was used, that film was left out.

LISTING 7-4: **Using a GROUP Statement to Aggregate Data**

```
SELECT Film.title, AVG(rating) AS avg_rating
FROM Film
JOIN Rating On Film.id=Rating.id
GROUP BY Film.title


title           avg_rating
All About Adam  3.5
The Even Couple 4.0
The Fourth Man  4.5
```

To narrow the results even further, add a HAVING clause at the end, as shown in Listing 7-5.

LISTING 7-5: **A HAVING Clause to Narrow Results**

```
SELECT Film.title, AVG(rating) AS avg_rating
FROM Film
JOIN Rating On Film.id=Rating.id
GROUP BY Film.title
HAVING avg_rating >= 4


title           avg_rating
The Even Couple 4.0
The Fourth Man  4.5
```

The code in Listing 7-5 limits the data your query returns so that you get only records of titles that have an average rating greater than or equal to 4.

MINING TEXT WITH SQL

In this era of big data, more and more analysis is being done on larger and larger amounts of raw text — from books to government procedures and even Twitter feeds. You can use the `tm` and `nltk` packages in R and Python, respectively, to process such data, but as scripting languages, they can be rather slow. That's why users commonly do some text mining in SQL. If you want to generate quick statistics on word counts and frequencies, you can use SQL to your advantage.

When the first SQL standard was published, its originators likely had no idea it would be used for these purposes, but the boundaries of SQL are being pushed and expanded all the time. This flexibility is yet another reason why SQL maintains its place as an indispensable tool among data science practitioners.

TECHNICAL STUFF

Though SQL can do some basic text mining, packages such as Natural Language Toolkit in Python (NLTK, at `www.nltk.org`) and General Architecture for Text Engineering (GATE, at `https://gate.ac.uk`) are needed in order to do anything more complex than count words and combinations of words. These more advanced packages can be used for preprocessing data in order to extract linguistic items such as parts of speech or syntactic relations, which can then be stored in a relational database for later querying.

Making Life Easier with Excel

Microsoft Excel holds a special place among data science tools. It was originally designed to act as a simple spreadsheet. Over time, however, it has become the people's choice in data analysis software. In response to user demands, Microsoft has added more and more analysis and visualization tools with every release. As Excel advances, so do its data munging and data science capabilities. (In case you're curious, *data munging* involves reformatting and rearranging data into more manageable formats that are usually required for consumption by other processing applications downstream.) Excel 2013 includes easy-to-use tools for charting, PivotTables, and macros. It also supports scripting in Visual Basic so that you can design scripts to automate repeatable tasks.

The benefit of using Excel in a data science capacity is that it offers a fast-and-easy way to get up close and personal with your data. If you want to browse every data point in your dataset, you can quickly and easily do this using Excel. Most data scientists start in Excel and eventually add other tools and platforms when they find themselves pushing against the boundaries of the tasks Excel is designed to do. Still, even the best data scientists out there keep Excel as an important tool in their tool belt. When working in data science, you might not use Excel every day, but knowing how to use it can make your job easier.

TIP

If you're using Excel spreadsheets for data analysis but finding it to be rather buggy and clunky, I recommend that you instead test out Google Sheets — Google's cloud-based version of an Excel spreadsheet. It can be run offline on your computer, and it offers an ease-of-use and a set of collaborative features that simply aren't available within the Microsoft Office environment today. Google Sheets offers all the same functions discussed in this chapter, using all the same commands as Excel spreadsheets, but most users find Sheets to be a far more intuitive, extensible tool for data analysis, visualization, and collaboration.

REMEMBER

Although you have many different tools available to you when you want to see your data as one big forest, Excel is a great first choice when you need to look at the trees. Excel attempts to be many different things to many different kinds of users. Its functionality is well-compartmentalized in order to avoid overwhelming new users while still providing power users with the more advanced functionality they crave. In the following sections, I show you how you can use Excel to quickly get to know your data. I also introduce Excel PivotTables and macros and tell you how you can use them to greatly simplify your data clean-up and analysis tasks.

Using Excel to quickly get to know your data

If you're just starting off with an unfamiliar dataset and you need to spot patterns or trends as quickly as possible, use Excel. Excel offers effective features for exactly these purposes. Its main features for a quick-and-dirty data analysis are

>> **Filters:** Filters are useful for sorting out all records that are irrelevant to the analysis at hand.

>> **Conditional formatting:** Specify a condition, and Excel flags records that meet that condition. By using conditional formatting, you can easily detect outliers and trends in your tabular datasets.

>> **Charts:** Charts have long been used to visually detect outliers and trends in data, so charting is an integral part of almost all data science analyses.

To see how these features work in action, consider the sample dataset shown in Figure 7-3, which tracks sales figures for three employees over six months.

Salesperson	Month	Total Sales
Abbie	Jan	$ 10,144.75
Abbie	Feb	$ 29,008.52
Abbie	Mar	$ 208,187.70
Abbie	Apr	$ 21,502.13
Abbie	May	$ 23,975.73
Abbie	Jun	$ 20,172.20
Brian	Jan	$ 9,925.44
Brian	Feb	$ 9,183.93
Brian	Mar	$ 12,691.39
Brian	Apr	$ 19,521.37
Brian	May	$ 16,579.38
Brian	Jun	$ 14,161.52
Chris	Jan	$ 2,792.18
Chris	Feb	$ 5,669.46
Chris	Mar	$ 4,909.24
Chris	Apr	$ 8,731.14
Chris	May	$ 11,747.29
Chris	Jun	$ 13,856.17

FIGURE 7-3: The full dataset that tracks employee sales performance.

Filtering in Excel

To narrow your view of your dataset to only the data that matters for your analysis, use Excel filters to filter out irrelevant data from the data view. Simply select the data and click the Home tab's Sort & Filter button, and then choose Filter from the options that appear. A little drop-down option then appears in the header row of the selected data so that you can select the classes of records you want to have filtered from the selection. Using the Excel Filter functionality allows you to quickly and easily sort or restrict your view to only the subsets of the data that interest you the most.

Take another look at the full dataset shown in Figure 7-3. Say you want to view only data related to Abbie's sales figures. If you select all records in the Salesperson column and then activate the filter functionality (as just described), from the drop-down menu that appears you can specify that the filter should isolate only all records named Abbie, as shown in Figure 7-4. When filtered, the table is reduced from 18 rows to only 6 rows. In this particular example, that change doesn't seem so dramatic, but when you have hundreds, thousands, or even a million rows, this feature comes in very, very handy.

Salesperson	Month	Total Sales
Abbie	Jan	$10,144.75
Abbie	Feb	$29,008.52
Abbie	Mar	$208,187.70
Abbie	Apr	$21,502.13
Abbie	May	$23,975.73
Abbie	Jun	$20,172.20

FIGURE 7-4:
The sales performance dataset, filtered to show only Abbie's records.

WARNING

Excel lets you store only up to 1,048,576 rows per worksheet.

Using conditional formatting

To quickly spot outliers in your tabular data, use Excel's Conditional Formatting feature. Imagine after a data entry error that Abbie's March total sales showed $208,187.70 but was supposed to be only $20,818.77. You're not quite sure where the error is located, but you know that it must be significant because the figures seem off by about $180,000.

To quickly show such an outlier, select all records in the Total Sales column and then click the Conditional Formatting button on the Ribbon's Home tab. When the button's menu appears, choose the Data Bars option. Doing so displays the red data bar scales shown in Figure 7-5. With data bars turned on, the bar in the $208,187.70 cell is so much larger than any of the others that you can easily see the error.

If you want to quickly discover patterns in your tabular data, you can choose the Color Scales option (rather than the Data Bars option) from the Conditional Formatting menu. After correcting Abbie's March Total Sales figure to $20,818.77, select all cells in the Total Sales column and then activate the Color Scales version of conditional formatting. Doing so displays the result shown in Figure 7-6. From the red-white-blue heat map, you can see that Abbie has the highest sales total and that Brian has been selling more than Chris. (Okay, you can't see the red-white-blue in my black-and-white figures, but you can see the light-versus-dark contrast.) Now, if you only want to conditionally format Abbie's sales performance relative to her own total sales (but not Brian and Chris' sales), you can select only the cells for Abbie (and not the entire column).

Excel charting to visually identify outliers and trends

Excel's Charting tool gives you an incredibly easy way to visually identify both outliers and trends in your data. An XY (scatter) chart of the original dataset (refer to Figure 7-3) yields the scatterplot shown in Figure 7-7. As you can see, the outlier is overwhelmingly obvious when the data is plotted on a scatter chart.

Salesperson	Month	Total Sales
Abbie	Jan	$ 10,144.75
Abbie	Feb	$ 29,008.52
Abbie	Mar	$ 208,187.70
Abbie	Apr	$ 21,502.13
Abbie	May	$ 23,975.73
Abbie	Jun	$ 20,172.20
Brian	Jan	$ 9,925.44
Brian	Feb	$ 9,183.93
Brian	Mar	$ 12,691.39
Brian	Apr	$ 19,521.37
Brian	May	$ 16,579.38
Brian	Jun	$ 14,161.52
Chris	Jan	$ 2,792.18
Chris	Feb	$ 5,669.46
Chris	Mar	$ 4,909.24
Chris	Apr	$ 8,731.14
Chris	May	$ 11,747.29
Chris	Jun	$ 13,856.17

FIGURE 7-5: Spotting outliers in a tabular dataset with conditional formatting data bars.

Salesperson	Month	Total Sales
Abbie	Jan	$ 10,144.75
Abbie	Feb	$ 29,008.52
Abbie	Mar	$ 20,818.77
Abbie	Apr	$ 21,502.13
Abbie	May	$ 23,975.73
Abbie	Jun	$ 20,172.20
Brian	Jan	$ 9,925.44
Brian	Feb	$ 9,183.93
Brian	Mar	$ 12,691.39
Brian	Apr	$ 19,521.37
Brian	May	$ 16,579.38
Brian	Jun	$ 14,161.52
Chris	Jan	$ 2,792.18
Chris	Feb	$ 5,669.46
Chris	Mar	$ 4,909.24
Chris	Apr	$ 8,731.14
Chris	May	$ 11,747.29
Chris	Jun	$ 13,856.17

FIGURE 7-6: Spotting outliers in a tabular dataset with color scales.

Alternatively, if you want to visually detect trends in a dataset, you can use Excel's Line Chart feature. The data from Figure 7-6 is shown as a line chart in Figure 7-8. It's worth mentioning, I've fixed the outlier in this line graph, which is what allows the Y-axis to have a more readable scale compared to Figure 7-7.

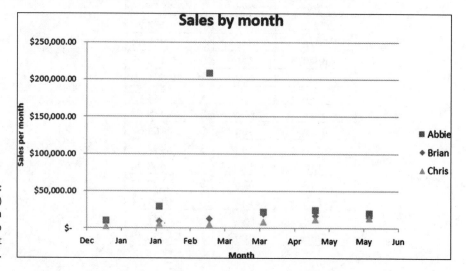

FIGURE 7-7:
Excel XY (scatter) plots provide a simple way to visually detect outliers.

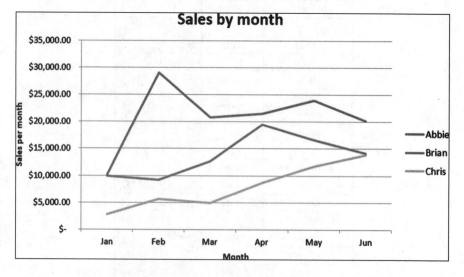

FIGURE 7-8:
Excel line charts make it easy to visually detect trends in data.

As you can clearly see from the figure, Chris's sales performance is low — last place among the three salespeople but gaining momentum. Because Chris seems to be improving, maybe management would want to wait a few months before making any firing decisions based on sales performance data.

Reformatting and summarizing with PivotTables

Excel developed the PivotTable to make it easier for users to extract valuable insights from large sets of spreadsheet data. If you want to generate insights by quickly restructuring or reclassifying your data, use a PivotChart. One of the main differences between a traditional spreadsheet and a dataset is that spreadsheets tend to be wide (with a lot of columns) and datasets tend to be long (with a lot of rows). Figure 7-9 clearly shows the difference between a long dataset and a wide spreadsheet.

Long format:

Salesperson	Month	Total Sales
Abbie	Jan	$ 10,144.75
Abbie	Feb	$ 29,008.52
Abbie	Mar	$ 208,187.70
Abbie	Apr	$ 21,502.13
Abbie	May	$ 23,975.73
Abbie	Jun	$ 20,172.20
Brian	Jan	$ 9,925.44
Brian	Feb	$ 9,183.93
Brian	Mar	$ 12,691.39
Brian	Apr	$ 19,521.37
Brian	May	$ 16,579.38
Brian	Jun	$ 14,161.52
Chris	Jan	$ 2,792.18
Chris	Feb	$ 5,669.46
Chris	Mar	$ 4,909.24
Chris	Apr	$ 8,731.14
Chris	May	$ 11,747.29
Chris	Jun	$ 13,856.17

Wide format:

Salesperson	Jan	Feb	Mar	Apr	May	Jun
Abbie	$10,144.75	$29,008.52	$208,187.70	$21,502.13	$23,975.73	$20,172.20
Brian	$ 9,925.44	$ 9,183.93	$ 12,691.39	$19,521.37	$16,579.38	$14,161.52
Chris	$ 2,792.18	$ 5,669.46	$ 4,909.24	$ 8,731.14	$11,747.29	$13,856.17

FIGURE 7-9: A long dataset and a wide spreadsheet.

REMEMBER

A *PivotTable* is a table that's derived from data that sits within a spreadsheet. The pivot allows for grouping, rearrangement, display, and summary of the raw data that's stored within the underlying spreadsheet.

The way that Excel is designed leads many users to intuitively prefer the wide format — which makes sense because it's a spreadsheet application. To counter this preference, however, Excel offers the *pivot table feature* so that you can quickly convert between long and wide formats. You can also use PivotTables to quickly calculate subtotals and summary calculations on your newly formatted and rearranged data tables.

TIP

Creating PivotTables is easy: Just select all cells that comprise the table you seek to analyze. Then click the PivotTable button on the Insert tab. This action opens the Create PivotTable dialog box, where you can define where you want Excel to construct the PivotTable. Select OK and Excel automatically generates a PivotField Interface on the page you've specified. From this interface, you can specify the fields you want to include in the PivotTable and how you want them to be laid out.

The table shown in Figure 7-10 was constructed using the long-format sales performance data shown in Figure 7-9. It's an example of the simplest possible PivotTable that can be constructed, but even at that, it automatically calculates subtotals for each column and those subtotals automatically update when you make changes to the data. What's more, PivotTables come with *PivotCharts* — data plots that automatically change when you make changes to the PivotTable filters based on the criteria you're evaluating.

FIGURE 7-10:
Creating a wide
data table from
the long dataset
via a PivotTable.

Total_Sales	Month						
Salesperson	Jan	Feb	Mar	Apr	May	Jun	Grand Total
Abbie	$10,144.75	$29,008.52	$20,818.77	$21,502.13	$23,975.73	$20,172.20	$125,622.10
Brian	$9,925.44	$9,183.93	$12,691.39	$19,521.37	$16,579.38	$14,161.52	$82,063.03
Chris	$2,792.18	$5,669.46	$4,909.24	$8,731.14	$11,747.29	$13,856.17	$47,705.48
Grand Total	$22,862.37	$43,861.91	$38,419.40	$49,754.64	$52,302.40	$48,189.89	$255,390.61

TIP

You can do a lot more sophisticated analytical work in Excel than just creating PivotTables, although they are handy. Over on the companion website to this book, http://www.businessgrowth.ai/, I give you some basic training in how to use Excel and XLMiner to implement data science without needing to touch a single line of code.

Automating Excel tasks with macros

Macros are prescripted routines written in Visual Basic for Applications (VBA). You can use macros to decrease the amount of manual processing you need to do when working with data in Excel. For example, within Excel, macros can act as a set of functions and commands that you can use to automate a wide variety of tasks. If you want to save time (and hassle) by automating Excel tasks that you routinely repeat, use macros.

To access macros, first activate Excel's Developer tab from within the Options menu on the File tab. (In other words, after opening the Options menu, choose Customize Ribbon from your choices on the left and then click to select the Developer check box in the column on the right.) Using the Developer tab, you can record a macro, import one that was created by someone else, or code your own in VBA.

To illustrate macros in action, imagine that you have a column of values and you want to insert an empty cell between each one of the values, as shown in Figure 7-11. Excel has no easy, out-of-the-box way to make this insertion. Using Excel macros, however, you can ask Excel to record you while you step through the process one time, and then assign a key command to this recording to create the macro. After you create the macro, every time you need to repeat the same task in the future, just run the macro by pressing the key command, and the script then performs all required steps for you.

Before macro:	After macro:
one	one
two	
three	two
four	
five	three
six	
seven	four
eight	
nine	five
ten	
	six
	seven
	eight
	nine
	ten

FIGURE 7-11:
Using a macro to insert empty cells between values.

REMEMBER

Macros have an Absolute mode and a Relative mode. The Absolute mode refers to a macros routine that runs absolutely the way you recorded it — all the way down to the spreadsheet cell positions in which the routine was recorded. Relative mode macros run the same routine you record but can be placed in whatever cell position you need within the spreadsheet.

TIP

When you record a macro, it records in Absolute mode by default. If you want it to record the macro in Relative mode instead, you need to select the Use Relative References option before recording the macro.

For a more formal definition of Absolute and Relative macros, consider this:

>> **Relative:** Every action and movement you make is recorded as relative to the cell that was selected when you began the recording. When you run the macro in the future, it will run in reference to the cell that's selected, acting as though that cell were the same cell you had initially selected when you recorded the macro.

>> **Absolute:** After you start recording the macro, every action and movement you make is repeated when you run the macro in the future, and those actions or movements aren't made in any relative reference to whatever cell was active when you started recording. The macro routine is repeated exactly as you recorded it.

In the preceding example, the macro was recorded in Relative mode. This enables the macro to be run continuously, anywhere, and on top of results from any preceding macros run. Since, in this scenario, the macro recorded only one iteration of the process, if it had been recorded in Absolute mode, every time it was run the macro would have kept adding a space between only the one and two values. In other words, it would not have operated on any cells other than the ones it was recorded on.

WARNING

Macro commands aren't entered into Excel's Undo stack. If you use a macro to change or delete data, you're stuck with that change.

TIP

Test your macros first and save your worksheets before using them so that you can revert to the saved file if something goes wrong.

Excel power users often graduate to programming their own macros using VBA. Because VBA is a full-fledged programming language, the possibilities from pairing Excel with VBA are almost endless. Still, ask yourself this question: If you're going to invest time in learning a programming language, do you need to work within the confines of Excel's spreadsheet structure? If not, you might consider learning a scientific computing language, like R or Python. These open-source languages have a more user-friendly syntax and are much more flexible and powerful.

Chapter **8**

Telling Powerful Stories with Data

A ny standard definition of data science will specify that its purpose is to help you extract meaning and value from raw data. Finding and deriving insights from raw data is at the crux of data science, but these insights mean nothing if you don't know how to communicate your findings to others. Data visualization and storytelling are excellent means by which you can visually communicate your data's meaning. To design effective data visualizations and stories, however, you must know and truly understand the target audience and the core purpose for which you're communicating with members of that audience. You must also understand the main types of data graphics that are available to you, as well as the significant benefits and drawbacks of each one. In this chapter, I present you with the core principles of data visualization and data storytelling design.

A *data visualization* is a visual representation that's designed for the purpose of conveying the meaning and significance of data and data insights. Because data visualizations are designed for a whole spectrum of different audiences, different purposes, and different skill levels, the first step to designing an effective data visualization is to *know your audience*. Audiences come in all shapes, forms, and sizes. You might design a data visualization for the young-and-edgy readers of *Wired* magazine or convey scientific findings to a research group. Your audience might consist of board members and organizational decision makers or a local grassroots organization.

The one thing that's consistent across all audiences, however, is the process you should follow when creating your data visualization, as spelled out here:

1. Determine the type of data visualization you will create, based on your audience and the purpose of your visualization.

2. Decide on a design style for your data visualization.

3. Choose which graphics make the most sense for your audience.

4. Test out different types of data graphics with the data, and then pick the ones that display the most clear and obvious answers.

5. Arrange your data graphics within the data visualization.

6. Where appropriate, add context to enhance the meaning of the visualization.

In this chapter, I walk you through each and every step in sequential order.

Data Visualizations: The Big Three

Every audience is composed of a unique class of consumers, each with unique data visualization needs, so you have to clarify for whom you're designing. (See Table 8-1.) I first want to introduce the three main types of data visualizations, and then I explain how to pick the one that best meets the needs of your audience.

TABLE 8-1: ## Types of Data Visualization, by Audience

Audience	Data Storytelling	Data Showcasing	Data Art
	Less-technical business decision-makers	Data implementers, analysts, engineers, scientists, or statisticians	Idealists, dreamers, and social change-makers

Data storytelling for decision makers

Sometimes, you have to design data visualizations for a less technical-minded audience, perhaps in order to help members of this audience make better-informed business decisions. The purpose of this type of visualization is to tell your audience the story behind the data. In data storytelling, the audience depends on you to make sense of the data behind the visualization and then turn useful insights into visual stories that they can easily understand.

With *data storytelling*, your goal should be to use data visualization, words, and presentation skills to create a narrative that tells the story — the *meaning*, in other words — of the data insights you seek to convey. With respect to the data visualization you use within a data story, you want it to be a clutter-free, highly focused visualization that enables your audience members to quickly extract meaning without having to make much effort. These visualizations are best delivered in the form of static images, but more adept decision makers may prefer to have an interactive dashboard that they can use to do a bit of exploration and what-if modeling.

Data storytelling involves more than just data visualization design, though. You need to use words and presentation skills to communicate the data story as well. You'll want to use words sparingly within annotations on the data visualization itself. Maybe you present the data story with an accompanying slideshow, or maybe not — but you should present it with effective presentation skills.

In Chapter 1, I talk about the three main data superhero archetypes: data implementer, data leader, and data entrepreneur. Data storytelling falls within the data leader suite of skill sets. I could write a whole book on the data leader skill set, but to keep it brief, your presentation design should be part of the broader work you're doing with respect to stakeholder management — the process of developing and maintaining the trust of those key stakeholders whom your data work is meant to support, so that you can bring your data insights to life by ensuring that they're seen, heard, and heeded in decision-making across your company.

TIP

For more on the importance of stakeholder relationships, be sure to check out the Selling to Stakeholders Formula and Executive Relationship Management Planner I've left for you over on `businessgrowth.ai`.

Data showcasing for analysts

If you're designing for a crowd of data implementers, or other logical, calculating analysts, you can create data visualizations that are rather open-ended. The purpose of this type of visualization is to help audience members visually explore the data and draw their own conclusions.

When using *data showcasing* techniques, your goal should be to display a lot of contextual information that supports audience members as they make their own interpretations. These visualizations should include more contextual data and less conclusive focus so that people can get in, analyze the data for themselves, and then draw their own conclusions. These visualizations are best delivered as static images or dynamic, interactive dashboards.

Designing data art for activists

You might design for an audience of idealists, dreamers, and change-makers. When designing for this particular audience, you want your data visualization to make a point! You can assume that typical audience members aren't overly analytical. What they lack in math skills, however, they more than compensate for in solid convictions.

These people look to your data visualization as a vehicle by which to make a statement. When designing for this audience, data art is the way to go. The main goal in using *data art* is to entertain, to provoke, to annoy, or to do whatever it takes to make a loud, clear, attention-demanding statement. Data art has little to no narrative and offers no room for viewers to form their own interpretations.

REMEMBER

Data scientists have an ethical responsibility to always represent data accurately. A data scientist should never distort the message of the data to fit what the audience wants to hear — not even for data art! Nontechnical audiences don't even recognize, let alone see, the possible issues. They rely on the data scientist to provide honest and accurate representations, thus amplifying the level of ethical responsibility that the data scientist must assume.

Designing to Meet the Needs of Your Target Audience

To make a functional data visualization, you must get to know your target audience and then design precisely for their needs. But to make every design decision with your target audience in mind, you need to take a few steps to make sure that you truly understand your data visualization's target consumers.

To gain the insights you need about your audience and your purpose, follow this process:

1. **Brainstorm.**

   Think about a specific member of your audience and make as many educated guesses as you can about that person's motivations.

TIP

   Give this (imaginary) audience member a name and a few other identifying characteristics. I always imagine a 45-year-old divorced mother of two named Eve.

2. **Define the purpose of your visualization.**

   Narrow the purpose of the visualization by deciding exactly what action or outcome you want audience members to make as a result of the visualization.

3. **Choose a functional design.**

Review the three main data visualization types (discussed earlier in this chapter) and decide which type can best help you achieve your intended outcome.

The following sections spell out this process in detail.

Step 1: Brainstorm (All about Eve)

To brainstorm properly, pull out a sheet of paper and picture an imaginary audience member — "Eve," for example. Let's practice together in creating a more functional and effective data visualization. You'd want to start by answering the more important questions we could ask about Eve in order to better understand her and thus better understand and design for your target audience.

Start by forming a picture of what Eve's average day looks like — what she does when she gets out of bed in the morning, what she does over her lunch hour, and what her workplace is like. Also consider how Eve will use your visualization. These things tell you a little bit about her *psychographics* — the psychological characteristics that drive her high-level needs and wants.

To form a more comprehensive view of who Eve is and how you can best meet her needs, you can pull from the following question bank:

>> Where does Eve work? What does she do for a living?

>> What kind of technical education or experience, if any, does she have?

>> How old is Eve? Is she married? Does she have children? What does she look like? Where does she live?

>> What social, political, cause-based, or professional issues are important to Eve? What does she think of herself?

>> What problems and issues does Eve have to deal with every day?

>> How does your data visualization help solve Eve's work problems or her family problems? How does it improve her self-esteem?

>> Through what avenue will you present the visualization to Eve — for example, over the Internet or in a staff meeting?

>> What does Eve need to be able to do with your data visualization?

Because we're doing this together, I'll answer these questions for you by telling you that Eve is the manager of the zoning department in Irvine County. She is 45 years old and a single divorcee with two children who are about to start college. She is deeply interested in local politics and eventually wants to be on the county's board of commissioners. To achieve that position, she has to get some major "oomph" on her county management résumé. Eve derives most of her feelings of self-worth from her job and her keen ability to make good management decisions for her department.

Until now, Eve has been forced to manage her department according to her gut-level intuition, backed by a few disparate business systems reports. She isn't extraordinarily analytical, but she knows enough to understand what she sees. The problem is that Eve lacks the visualization tools she needs in order to display all the relevant data she should consider. Because she has neither the time nor the skill to code something herself, she's been waiting in the lurch. Eve is excited that you'll attend next Monday's staff meeting to present data insights you've discovered that she hopes will enable her to make more effective data-driven management decisions.

Step 2: Define the purpose

After you brainstorm about the typical audience member (see the preceding section), you can much more easily pinpoint exactly what you're trying to achieve with your data visualization. Are you attempting to get consumers to feel a certain way about themselves or the world around them? Are you trying to make a statement? Are you seeking to influence organizational decision makers to make good business decisions? Or do you simply want to lay all the data out there, for all viewers to make sense of, and deduce from it what they will?

Returning to the hypothetical Eve: What decisions or processes are you trying to help her achieve? Well, you'd first need to make sense of her data and uncover relevant data insights. Then you'd need to present those data insights to her in a way that she can clearly understand and use for improved decision-making. So, looking at the data — what do you see that's happening within the inner mechanics of her department? Once you've discovered some clear trends and predictions, it'd be time to use data visualization skills to guide Eve into making the most prudent and effective management choices.

Step 3: Choose the most functional visualization type for your purpose

Keep in mind that you have three main types of visualization from which to choose: data storytelling, data art, and data showcasing. Remember that, if you're designing for organizational decision makers, you'll most likely use data storytelling to directly tell your audience what their data means with respect to their line of business. If you're designing for a social justice organization or a political campaign, data art can best make a dramatic and effective statement with your data. Lastly, if you're designing for analysts, engineers, scientists, or statisticians, stick with data showcasing so that these analytical types have plenty of room to figure things out on their own.

Back to Eve — because she's not extraordinarily analytical and because she's depending on you to help her make excellent data-driven decisions, you need to employ *data storytelling* techniques. Create either a static or interactive data visualization with some, but not too much, context. The visual elements of the design should tell a clear story about her business unit, such that Eve doesn't have to work through tons of complexity to get the point of what you're trying to tell her about her department.

TIP

My best practices for effective dashboard design are available to you over on `https://businessgrowth.ai/`.

Picking the Most Appropriate Design Style

If you're the analytical type, you might say that the only purpose of a data visualization is to convey numbers and facts via charts and graphs — no beauty or design is needed. But if you're a more artistic-minded person, you may insist that you have to *feel* something in order to truly understand it. Truth be told, a good data visualization is neither artless and dry nor completely abstract in its artistry. Rather, its beauty and design lie somewhere on the spectrum between these two extremes.

To choose the most appropriate design style, you must first consider your audience (discussed earlier in this chapter) and then decide how you want them to respond to your visualization. If you're looking to entice the audience into taking a deeper, more analytical dive into the visualization, employ a design style that induces a calculating and exacting response in its viewers. But if you want your data visualization to fuel your audience's passion, use an emotionally compelling design style instead.

Inducing a calculating, exacting response

If you're designing a data visualization for corporate types, engineers, scientists, or organizational decision makers, keep the design simple and sleek, using the data showcasing or data storytelling visualization. To induce a logical, calculating feel in your audience, include a lot of bar charts, scatterplots, and line charts. Color choices here should be rather traditional and conservative. The look and feel should scream "corporate chic." (See Figure 8-1.) Visualizations of this style are meant to quickly and clearly communicate what's happening in the data — direct, concise, and to the point. The best data visualizations of this style convey an elegant look and feel.

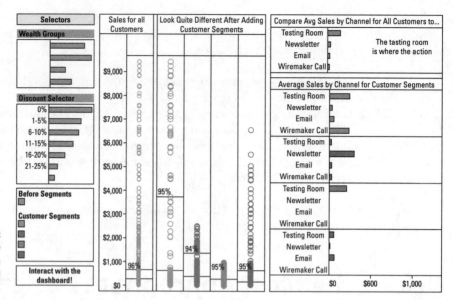

TIP

If you're looking for guidance on the best web applications for data visualization and storytelling, be sure to check out my *Web-Based Data Visualization Design Tools: Top 10 Guide.* I left it for you at this book's companion website, at https://businessgrowth.ai/.

Eliciting a strong emotional response

If you're designing a data visualization to influence or persuade people, incorporate design artistry that invokes an emotional response in your target audience. These visualizations usually fall under the data art category, but an extremely creative data storytelling piece can also inspire this sort of strong emotional response. Emotionally provocative data visualizations often support the stance of one side of a social, political, or environmental issue. These data visualizations include fluid, artistic design elements that flow and meander, as shown in Figure 8-2. Additionally, rich, dramatic color choices can influence the emotions of the viewer. This style of data visualization leaves a lot of room for artistic creativity and experimentation.

TIP

Keep artistic elements relevant — and recognize when they're likely to detract from the impression you want to make, particularly when you're designing for analytical types.

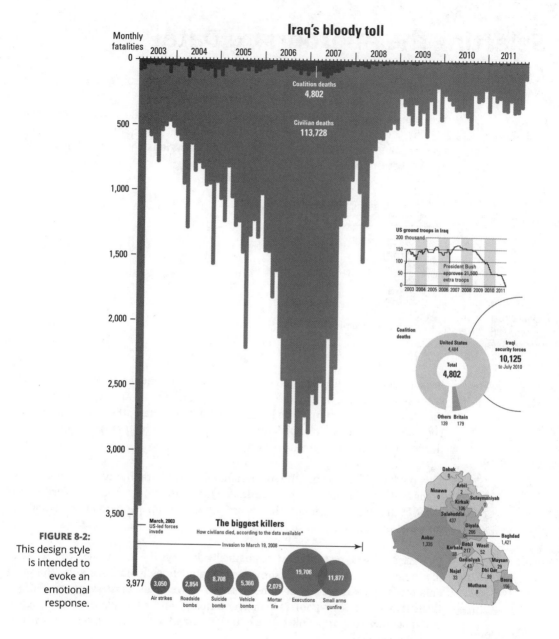

Iraq's bloody toll

FIGURE 8-2: This design style is intended to evoke an emotional response.

Selecting the Appropriate Data Graphic Type

Your choice of data graphic type can make or break a data visualization. In case it's unclear, a *data graphic* is the graphical element that depicts your data insight in visual format. (See Figure 8-3.) Most data visualizations have more than one data graphic within them.

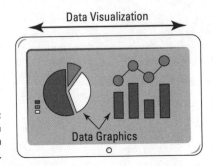

FIGURE 8-3:
Data visualization versus data graphics.

Because you probably need to represent many different facets of your data, you can mix-and-match among the different graphical classes and types. Even among the same class, certain graphic types perform better than others; therefore, it's a good idea to create several different mockups to see which graphic type conveys the clearest and most obvious message.

WARNING

This book introduces only the most commonly used graphic types (among hundreds that are available). Don't wander too far off the beaten path. The further you stray from familiar graphics, the harder it becomes for people to understand the information you're trying to convey.

REMEMBER

Pick the graphic type that most dramatically displays the data trends you're seeking to reveal. (Figure 8-4 lists some general guidelines.) You can display the same data trend in many ways, but some methods deliver a visual message more effectively than others. The point is to deliver a clear, comprehensive visual message to your audience so that people can use the visualization to help them make sense of the data presented.

Among the most useful types of data graphics are standard chart graphics, comparative graphics, statistical plots, topology structures, and spatial plots and maps. The next few sections take a look at each type in turn.

Data Graphic Types	Visualization Element	Data Storytelling audience: less-technical business decision-makers	Data Showcasing audience: data implementers, analysts, engineers, scientists, or statisticians	Data Art audience: idealists, dreamers, and social change-makers
Standard Chart Graphics	Bar Chart	☑	☑	☑
	Line Chart	☑	☑	☑
	Pie Chart	☑	☐	☑
Comparative Graphics	Bubble Plots	☑	☑	☑
	Packed Circle Diagrams	☐	☑	☐
	Gantt Charts	☑	☑	☐
	Stacked Charts	☐	☑	☐
	Tree Maps	☐	☑	☐
	Word Clouds	☑	☑	☑
Statistical Plots	Histogram	☐	☑	☐
	Scatter Plot	☐	☑	☐
	Scatter Plot Matrix	☐	☑	☐
Topology Structures	Linear Topology Structures	☑	☑	☑
	Graph Models	☐	☑	☑
	Tree Network Topology	☑	☑	☑
Spatial Plots and Maps	Cloropleth	☑	☑	☑
	Point	☑	☑	☑
	Raser Surface	☐	☑	☐
Contextual Elements	Contextual Data Graphics	☐	☑	☑
	Annotations	☑	☑	☐
	Trend Lines	☑	☑	☑
	Single-Value Alerts	☑	☑	☐
	Target Trend Lines	☑	☑	☐
	Predictive Benchmarks	☑	☑	☐

FIGURE 8-4: Types of data graphics, broken down by audience and data visualization type.

Standard chart graphics

When making data visualizations for an audience of non-analytical people, stick to standard chart graphics. The more complex your graphics, the harder it is for non-analytical people to understand them. And not all standard chart types are boring — you have quite a variety to choose from, as the following list makes clear:

>> **Area:** An area chart (shown in Figure 8-5) is a fun-yet-simple way to visually compare and contrast attribute values. You can use this type to effectively tell a visual story when you've chosen data storytelling and data showcasing. Not all area charts are 3-D like the one shown in Figure 8-5, but they all represent numerical values by the proportion of area those values consume visually on the chart.

>> **Bar:** Bar charts (see Figure 8-6) are a simple way to visually compare and contrast values of parameters in the same category. Bar charts are best for data storytelling and data showcasing.

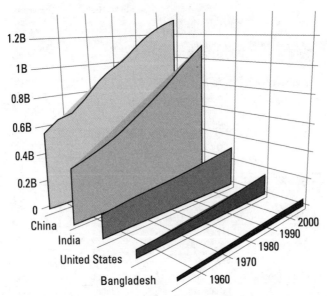

Population from 1957 to 2007 [Gapminder]

FIGURE 8-5:
An area chart in three dimensions.

Source: Lynda.com, Python for DS

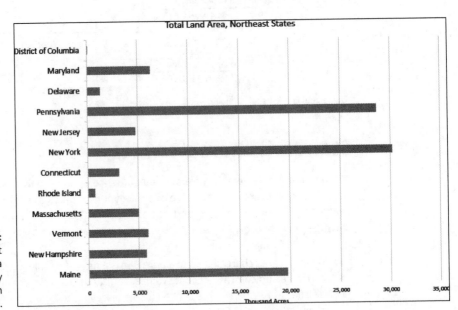

Total Land Area, Northeast States

FIGURE 8-6:
A bar chart showing the area of US states by their acreage, in thousand acres.

>> **Line:** Line charts (see Figure 8-7) most commonly show changes in time-series data, but they can also plot relationships between two, or even three, parameters. Line charts are so versatile that you can use them in all data visualization design types.

>> **Pie:** Pie chart graphics (see Figure 8-8), which are among the most commonly used, provide a simple way to compare values of parameters in the same category. Their simplicity, however, can be a double-edged sword; deeply analytical people tend to scoff at them, precisely because they seem so simple, so you may want to consider omitting them from data-showcasing visualizations.

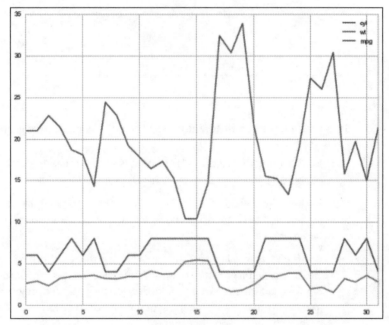

FIGURE 8-7: A line chart.

Source: Lynda.com, Python for DS

Comparative graphics

A *comparative graphic* displays the relative value of multiple parameters in a shared category or the relatedness of parameters within multiple shared categories. The core difference between comparative graphics and standard graphics is that comparative graphics offer you a way to simultaneously compare more than one parameter and category. Standard graphics, on the other hand, provide a way to view and compare only the difference between one parameter of any single category. Comparative graphics are geared for an audience that's at least slightly analytical, so you can easily use these graphics in either data storytelling or data showcasing. Visually speaking, comparative graphics are more complex than standard graphics.

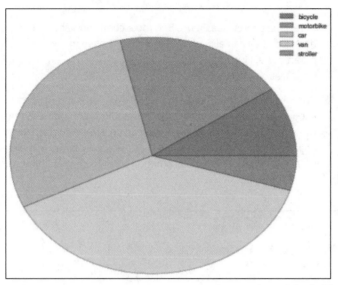

FIGURE 8-8:
A pie chart.

Source: Lynda.com, Python for DS

This list shows a few different types of popular comparative graphics:

>> **Bubble plots** (see Figure 8-9) use bubble size and color to demonstrate the relationship between three parameters of the same category.

>> **Packed circle diagrams** (see Figure 8-10) use both circle size and clustering to visualize the relationships between categories, parameters, and relative parameter values.

>> **Gantt charts** (see Figure 8-11) are bar charts that use horizontal bars to visualize scheduling requirements for project management purposes. This type of chart is useful when you're developing a plan for project delivery. It's also helpful in determining the sequence in which tasks must be completed in order to meet delivery timelines.

TIP

Choose Gantt charts for project management and scheduling.

>> **Stacked charts** (see Figure 8-12) are used to compare multiple attributes of parameters in the same category. To ensure that it doesn't become difficult to make a visual comparison, resist the urge to include too many parameters.

>> **Tree maps** aggregate parameters of like categories and then use area to show the relative size of each category compared to the whole, as shown in Figure 8-13.

>> **Word clouds** use size and color to show the relative difference in frequency of words used in a body of text, as shown in Figure 8-14. Colors are generally employed to indicate classifications of words by usage type.

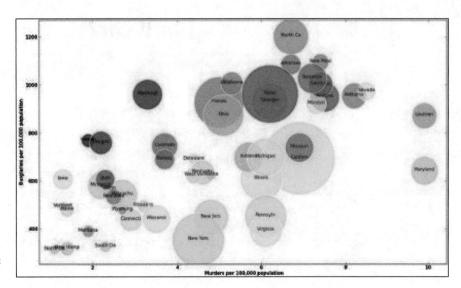

FIGURE 8-9:
A bubble chart.

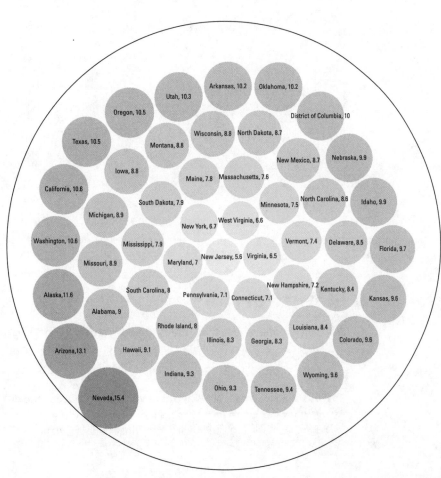

FIGURE 8-10:
A packed circle
diagram.

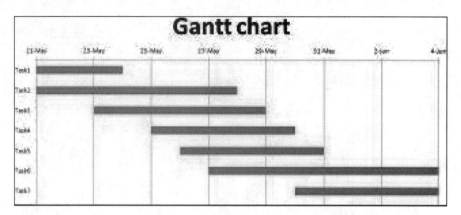

FIGURE 8-11:
A Gantt chart.

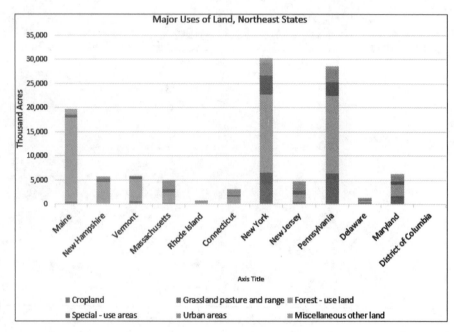

FIGURE 8-12:
A stacked chart.

Statistical plots

Statistical plots, which show the results of statistical analyses, are usually useful only to a deeply analytical audience (and aren't useful for making data art). Your statistical-plot choices are described in this list:

> **Histogram:** A diagram that plots a variable's frequency and distribution as rectangles on a chart, a histogram (see Figure 8-15) can help you quickly get a handle on the distribution and frequency of data in a dataset.

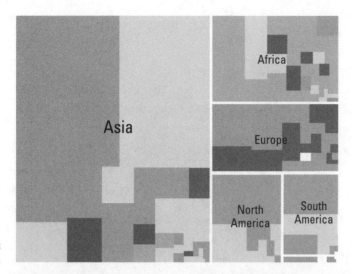

FIGURE 8-13:
A tree map.

FIGURE 8-14:
A simple word cloud.

TIP

Get comfortable with histograms. You'll see a lot of them in the course of making statistical analyses.

>> **Scatterplot:** A terrific way to quickly uncover significant trends and outliers in a dataset, a scatterplot plots data points according to their x- and y-values in order to visually reveal any significant patterns. (See Figure 8-16.) If you use data storytelling or data showcasing, start by generating a quick scatterplot to get a feel for areas in the dataset that may be interesting — areas that can potentially uncover significant relationships or yield persuasive stories.

>> **Scatterplot matrix:** A good choice when you want to explore the relationships between several variables, a scatterplot matrix places a number of related scatterplots in a visual series that shows correlations between multiple variables, as shown in Figure 8-17. Discovering and verifying relationships between variables can help you to identify clusters among variables and identify oddball outliers in your dataset.

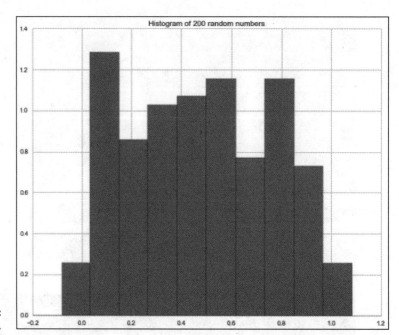

FIGURE 8-15:
A histogram.

Source: Lynda.com, Python for DS

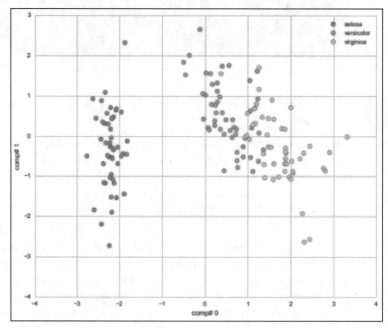

FIGURE 8-16:
A scatterplot.

Source: Lynda.com, Python for DS

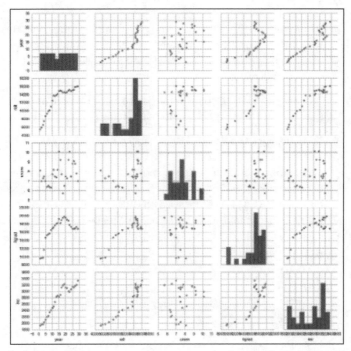

FIGURE 8-17:
A scatterplot
matrix.

Source: Lynda.com, Python for DS

Topology structures

Topology is the practice of using geometric structures to describe and model the relationships and connectedness between entities and variables in a dataset. You need to understand basic topology structures so that you can accurately structure your visual display to match the fundamental underlying structure of the concepts you're representing.

The following list describes a series of topological structures that are popular in data science:

>> **Linear topological structures:** Representing a pure one-to-one relationship, linear topological structures are often used in data visualizations that depict time-series flow patterns. Any process that can occur only by way of a sequential series of dependent events is linear (see Figure 8-18), and you can effectively represent it by using this underlying topological structure.

FIGURE 8-18:
A linear topology.

>> **Graph models:** These kinds of models underlie group communication networks and traffic flow patterns. You can use graph topology to represent many-to-many relationships (see Figure 8-19), like those that form the basis of social media platforms.

In a *many-to-many* relationship structure, each variable or entity has more than one link to the other variables or entities in that same dataset.

>> **Tree network topology:** This topology represents a *hierarchical* classification, where a network is distributed in top-down order — nodes act as receivers and distributors of connections, and lines represent the connections between nodes. End nodes act only as receivers and not as distributors. (See Figure 8-20.) Hierarchical classification underlies clustering and machine learning methodologies in data science. Tree network structures can represent one-to-many relationships, such as the ones that underlie a family tree or a taxonomy structure.

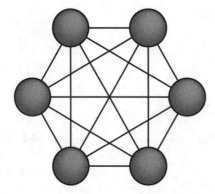

FIGURE 8-19:
A graph mesh network topology.

Spatial plots and maps

Spatial plots and maps are two different ways of visualizing spatial data. A *map* is just a plain figure that represents the location, shape, and size of features on the face of the earth. A *spatial plot*, which is visually more complex than a map, shows the values for — and location distribution of — a spatial feature's attributes.

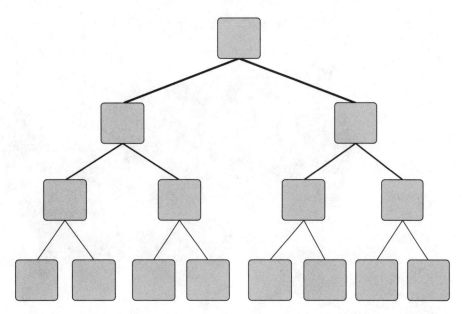

FIGURE 8-20:
A hierarchical
tree topology.

The following list describes a few types of spatial plots and maps that are commonly used in data visualization:

>> **Cloropleth:** Despite its fancy name, a Cloropleth map is really just spatial data plotted out according to area boundary polygons rather than by point, line, or raster coverage. To better understand what I mean, look at Figure 8-21. On this map, each state boundary represents an *area boundary* polygon. The color and shade of the area within each boundary represents the relative value of the attribute for that state — where red areas have a higher attribute value and blue areas have a smaller attribute value.

>> **Point:** Composed of spatial data that is plotted out according to specific point locations, a point map presents data in a graphical point form (see Figure 8-22) rather than in a polygon, line, or raster surface format.

>> **Raster surface:** This spatial map can be anything from a satellite image map to a surface coverage with values that have been interpolated from underlying spatial data points. (See Figure 8-23.)

TIP

For a training on how to make maps from data using free and QGIS, an open-source geographic information system (GIS) application, visit `https://businessgrowth.ai/`.

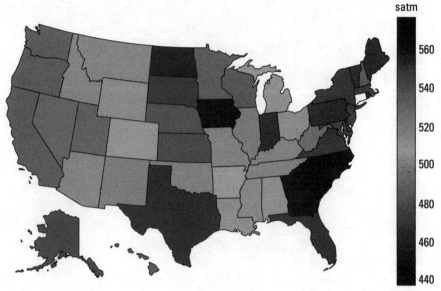

FIGURE 8-21:
A Cloropleth map.

Average SATm Score for Graduating High School Student

Source: Lynda.com, Python for DS

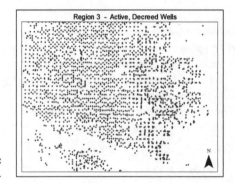

FIGURE 8-22:
A point map.

REMEMBER

Whether you're a data visualization designer or a consumer, be aware of some common pitfalls in data visualization. Simply put, a data visualization can be misleading if it isn't constructed correctly. Common problems include pie charts that don't add up to 100 percent, bar charts with a scale that starts in a strange place, and multicolumn bar charts with vertical axes that don't match.

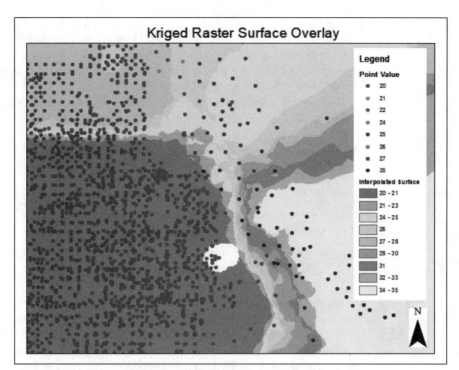

FIGURE 8-23:
A raster
surface map.

Testing Data Graphics

Your data visualizations must convey clear and powerful visual messages. To make that happen, you have to test various data graphics and select only the most effective ones to include in the final data visualization. For example, the two data graphics shown in Figure 8-24 represent exactly the same statistic.

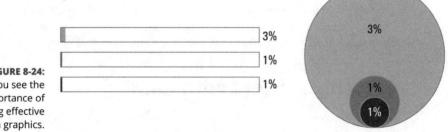

FIGURE 8-24:
Here you see the
importance of
selecting effective
data graphics.

Notice how the data graphic on the right does a much better job of visually emphasizing the difference in numeric values? You should always test different data graphics, to make sure that you use the one that most clearly and effectively displays your data. The graphic on the left is *not* effective. To choose only the most effective data graphics for inclusion in your data visualization, simply follow these four steps:

1. Make a list of the questions that your data is meant to answer.

2. Determine the data visualization type: data storytelling, data showcasing, or data art.

3. Select options from among appropriate data graphic types for that type of data visualization.

4. Test those data graphics with your data — see for yourself which graphic type displays the most clear and obvious answers to your questions.

TIP

After testing different data graphics and deciding what you want to use, you need to arrange those graphics within your data visualization. You can do that using either Python or R or a spreadsheet, as discussed in Chapter 6. Alternatively, to create your data visualization using an online data visualization design tool, you may find my guide helpful: *Web-Based Data Visualization Design Tools — Top 10.* I left it for you over at this book's companion website, at https://businessgrowth.ai/.

Adding Context

Once you know exactly which data graphics you'll use, you need to decide whether and how you'll create the necessary context to add more meaning to the data visualization. Adding context helps people understand the value and relative significance of the information your data visualization conveys. Adding context to calculating, exacting data visualization styles helps to create a sense of relative perspective, but in pure data art you may consider omitting additional context. That's because, with data art, you're only trying to make a single point and you don't want to add information that would distract from that point.

Creating context with data

In data showcasing, you should include relevant contextual data for the key metrics shown in your data visualization — in a situation where you're creating a data visualization that describes conversion rates for e-commerce sales, for example. The key metric would be represented by the percentage of users who convert to customers by making a purchase. Contextual data that's relevant to this metric might include shopping cart abandonment rates, average number of sessions before a user makes a purchase, average number of pages visited before making a purchase, or specific pages that are visited before a customer decides to convert. This sort of contextual information helps viewers understand the "why and how" behind sales conversions.

Adding contextual data tends to decentralize the focus of a data visualization, so add this data only in visualizations that are intended for an analytical audience. These folks are in a better position to assimilate the extra information and use it to draw their own conclusions; with other types of audiences, context is only a distraction.

Creating context with annotations

Sometimes, you can more appropriately create context by including annotations that provide a header and a small description of the context of the data that's shown. (See Figure 8-25.) This method of creating context is most appropriate for data storytelling or data showcasing. Good annotation is helpful to both analytical and non-analytical audiences alike.

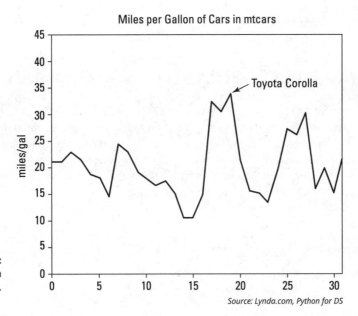

FIGURE 8-25:
Using annotation to create context.

Creating context with graphical elements

Another effective way to create context in a data visualization is to include graphical elements that convey the relative significance of the data. Such graphical elements include moving average trend lines, single-value alerts, target trend lines (as shown in Figure 8-26), and predictive benchmarks.

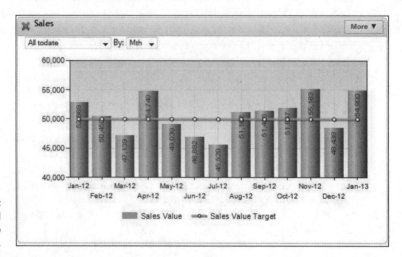

KNOWING WHEN TO GET PERSUASIVE

Persuasive design needs to confirm or refute a point. It leaves no room for audience interpretation. Persuasive data visualizations generally invoke a strong emotional response. Persuasive design is appropriate for both data art and data storytelling, but this type of design isn't helpful for data showcasing. Use persuasive design whenever you're making data visualizations on behalf of social, political, or cause-based organizations.

3

Taking Stock of Your Data Science Capabilities

IN THIS PART . . .

Improve your business acumen.

Use data science to create operational efficiencies.

Increase marketing ROI with better use of data.

Use data science to support decision-making.

Monetize data resources and skills.

Chapter **9**

Developing Your Business Acumen

D ata science is somewhat of a cross between software engineering and busi-ness consulting: You have to know enough code to do *ad hoc* analysis and build accurate predictive models, and you also have to know enough about the business to understand the context in which your work creates value for the company. That combination requires you to have coding skills, statistics chops, and, last but not least, business savvy. In this chapter, you'll see the extent to which you need business acumen to be successful working in the data science field — and what you can do to bolster your business knowledge in record time.

Bridging the Business Gap

Not all data scientists work inside businesses. Some are in academia and nonprof-its, and some work in scientific companies where business know-how simply isn't relevant to their work. Let me start this chapter by taking a look at what business acumen is and letting you know when it's especially important for data science professionals.

Contrasting business acumen with subject matter expertise

Over in Chapter 1, I say that — in order to practice data science effectively — you need the analytical know-how of math and statistics, the coding skills necessary to work with raw data, and an area of subject matter expertise. That's actually the first definition of the data scientist role, which was espoused by Drew Conway back in 2013, in his infamous data science Venn diagram. (You can see a re-creation of this diagram in Figure 9-1.)

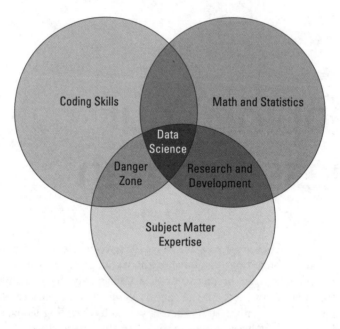

FIGURE 9-1:
The data science
Venn diagram.

So that's data science in a nutshell, but this reference to *subject matter expertise* is rather vague, is it not? I mean, what if you work as a data scientist in the Greenpeace Tech Lab? Imagine how different your subject matter expertise would be if you were working for an environmental nonprofit rather than as a data scientist for an investment bank like Barclays. The difference in requisite subject matter expertise between these two positions is almost indescribable.

Consequently, I need to tighten up this language a bit by defining the type of subject matter expertise I'm talking about. Luckily for you, however, if I'm talking about data science that's being used to support a business, the term *subject matter expertise* is just a placeholder for *business acumen* — the keen ability to understand business dealings in terms of risks and opportunities to a company when it comes to protecting and increasing its profits and adhering to its business mission.

I scope out the definition of *business acumen* in greater detail in the next section.

Defining business acumen

Short of a keen ability to understand business dealings, what does it *really* look like for a data professional to have strong business acumen? One clear way to answer this question is to define the characteristics that this data professional would exhibit, such as

- » **Executive mentality:** When I talk about executive mentality, what I'm referring to is your ability to think on a business big-picture level. In other words, you're able to see how all integral processes and components in a business function together to generate business profits and fulfill your company's mission.

- » **Financial savvy:** Financially literate professionals understand the core drivers of profit, growth, and cash flow across a business. They understand how to not only interpret these financial statements but also formulate strategy and take decisive action in order to boost a business's bottom line.

- » **Leadership skills**: Leadership skills involve product management or project management skills, as well as an exceptional ability to work with teams and stakeholders to deliver profit-forming projects or products that are within scope, on time and, hopefully, under budget.

If you're like most data professionals. you're probably feeling like a fish out of water while reading about the characteristics of a truly business-savvy data professional. Not to worry, though: The extent to which you need business acumen depends heavily on your role and function within your company.

For example, if you're a data science project manager or product manager, you can bet your paycheck that you need strong competency in the three areas I list in this section. If you're a data entrepreneur and your company stays in business for any extended period, chances are good that you will be forced to develop these competencies as a byproduct of the work you do every day to grow your company.

On the other hand, if you find yourself called deeper and deeper into data implementation work — and you love it — you're probably a pure data implementation person. One core benefit of data implementation roles is that they don't require many people skills, leadership skills, business acumen, and the rest. If you're a data implementation person and you can cover the documentation requirements for data implementers — discussed later in this chapter — that's about all the business savvy you should need. Next, let's take a closer look at how different roles within the data space function to support a business in reaching its goals.

Traversing the Business Landscape

The first thing you need to realize when it comes to the business world is that the core function of any business is to generate a profit. Within corporate environments, employees are heavily discouraged from discussing how much money they earn. At many companies, discussing your salary can be grounds for termination. So, it's no wonder that data professionals aren't naturally attuned to concepts and mechanics related to making money for a business.

REMEMBER

The goal and primary purpose of any business is to generate profits.

Data is used to generate profit for a company in one of two main ways:

» **Revenue-generation:** The idea here is to build and monetize new products and services.

» **Cost savings:** Here, the emphasis is on increasing profit margins by improving efficiency or decreasing risk.

In the next section, I show you exactly how various data roles support businesses in turning a profit.

Seeing how data roles support the business in making money

When discussing how data roles support a business to make money, I limit my discussion to a few primary roles. I discuss the data scientist role (of course) as well as the data analyst role, and I look at the role of data project manager and data product manager. And I need to help you consider the business analyst role as well as the role of data engineer and machine learning engineer. Figure 9-2 diagrams how each of these data roles supports the others and supports the business in generating a profit.

When considering each of these data roles, note that — although all these roles are data-intensive — they act on different levels within a business and support different types of actors within the business.

Data product managers manage products that directly generate revenues. Data project managers sometimes manage projects that result in cost savings, and at other times they manage data services that generate revenues directly. Data implementation people — like data analysts, data scientists, data engineers, and machine learning engineers — do the coding, building, and sophisticated machine learning work that's required in order to create the products and complete the projects led and managed by these data project and product managers. Business analysts use data analysis skills and strong business acumen to define the business's needs and support those internal projects that have been launched in order to increase profits by saving costs within the business's internal operations.

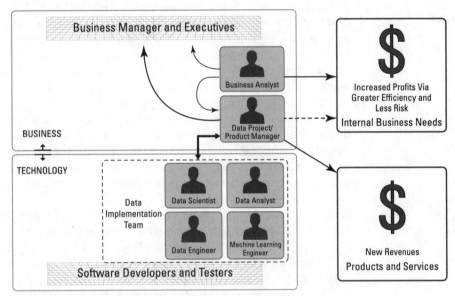

Because the business analyst is fundamentally closest to the pure business roles — roles like those occupied by business managers and executives — I'll ask you to consider this role first. Business analysts use existing business data and strong communication skills to fulfill a cross-collaborative role between teams. It's a people-oriented role, and business analysts are expected to have solid skills in persuasion. Business analysts collaborate between the business and technology, but sit firmly on the business-side. They scope the internal needs of the business, define requirements, and work to ensure that the technology portion of the business is doing the things that are needed to support the business. Business analysts gather requirements for internal business projects — in other words, projects that support and improve the internal operations of the business. The role involves using existing data to analyze processes, systems, organizational units, and overall problems throughout a business in order to help create effective business solutions to those problems. Business analysts support project managers and product managers as well as business managers and executives.

Data project managers work to manage and support the delivery of data implementation projects, whereas data product managers act as mini-CEOs of data products that are owned and sold by the company. Both of these roles function on the business side, but they interface directly with the technology side. People in these roles work to ensure timely and accurate delivery of their projects or products, and it's through those products and projects that people in these roles boost a business's bottom line.

Although these roles have lots of similarities between them, they're fundamentally different. In terms of similarities, both product managers and project managers support data implementation teams in getting their needs met as they build out the respective data science product or project. Both of these roles are responsible for working closely with business managers and executives. Data product managers, however, manage products that are for sale and consumption directly by the business's customers. They generally don't work to support the internal business needs of the company. In contrast, data science project managers often deliver projects that support the internal operations of a business as well as customer-facing data science services. In the context of my discussion of the data superhero archetype over in Chapter 1, both data science product managers and data science project managers would be considered data leaders.

Both data scientists and data analysts are on the technology side of the business, but they are far closer to the business than professionals who work in pure engineering or software development roles. Their work supports data product managers as well as data project managers, and they often provide *ad hoc* analytical support as needed for various personnel on the business side. These folks help a company generate profits by successfully implementing the requirements that are laid out for them, and that are managed by their data project or data product managers. Though both are data implementation roles, data analysts tend to do more business consulting work, whereas strict data scientists often spend most of their time focusing on the data. You need business acumen to work as either a data scientist or a data analyst, but you don't need it to the same degree as a data project manager, product manager, or business analyst. That said, data analysts, and especially data scientists, need quite a bit more technical chops than their more business focused counterparts. Data scientists and data analysts are both data implementation roles.

One step deeper into the technology side of the business lie the machine learning engineer and data engineer. (I discuss both roles in greater detail in Chapter 2.) People in these roles are almost all purely technical data implementers. There's little need for business acumen when you're doing the in-depth, detailed work of coding up decision engines or building data systems. Those aspects of your product or project dealing with requirements gathering or consulting are generally handed to you by a data project manager, data product manager, or business analyst. Despite this low bar for business acumen, data and machine learning engineers are still required to produce documentation to support the systems and products they build for the business. I help you dig into those requirements later in this chapter.

Leveling up your business acumen

Chances are, if you're an aspiring data science leader or entrepreneur, you're curious about the actions you can take to beef up your business acumen. The good news is that you don't need to go out and get an MBA to make this happen. The bad news is that, like all great things in life, it takes some work.

To increase your business acumen, you first need to start by understanding the levels that make up this thing called *business acumen.* Don't worry! It's a piece of cake — a 3-layer cake, to be exact. Figure 9-3 shows those three layers of the business acumen cake.

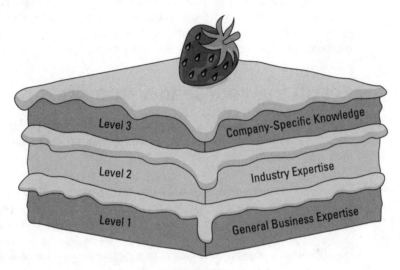

FIGURE 9-3:
The three layers
of the business
acumen cake.

On Level 1, at the base of the business acumen cake, you need to develop general business expertise. (This is on par with the executive-level mentality I talk about earlier in this chapter.) Basically, you'll want to understand the mechanics by which various business units function to improve a business's bottom line. Luckily, the purpose of this entire section of the book is to show you exactly how data science impacts business functions to improve business profits. In Chapter 10, you can see how data science projects are used to improve operations, and in Chapter 11, you can see how data science supports improved returns from a company's marketing activities. In Chapter 12, I talk about the decision-support function, and Chapter 13 is all about finance improvements. (This last bit of expertise is transferable across industries and companies you support, so you should make it a priority.)

On Level 2, in the middle of the cake, you want to develop business expertise that's relevant to your industry. Throughout the remainder of this section, you can see examples of how data science is improving profitability for businesses in a wide variety of industries — from food and beverage to software and everything in between. Industry-level expertise is extremely valuable because, as long as you stay working within the same industry, the expertise itself is transferable between companies. If you hop into a new industry, though, be forewarned that most of this expertise is longer relevant.

At the top of the cake, on Level 3, you have your company-specific expertise. This knowledge is critical to the success of data projects at the company, but has little value to you outside the company if you want to switch jobs. In fact, this company-specific knowledge is usually covered under a nondisclosure agreement (NDA) as proprietary intellectual property that cannot be disclosed to people outside of the company. In Chapter 15, I talk more about how to collect information about your company. That information you collect can go a long way in satisfying the company-specific expertise you need to lead successful data science projects.

Fortifying your leadership skills

Truth be told, I could write an entire book on the topic of leadership in data science, but if I had to summarize my tips in one short bullet-point list, I'd recommend the following:

>> **Invest in relationship:** If you're a data leader, you're in the business of relationships. You're responsible for cultivating and maintaining meaningful relationships with business leaders, project stakeholders, and data team members. Take it seriously. Additionally, don't neglect the broader data science community. Join a local data professional organization and network with other data science leaders by lending your expertise.

TIP

Over on https://businessgrowth.ai/, I give you some communication best practices as well as an email template to help you manage your relationships with project stakeholders. Also, I show you my Mini-Black Book of Data Professional Organizations, which lists some groups you may want to consider joining.

>> **Stay educated on new data use cases and case studies:** Never jump into data implementation head-first. Before each new project, take the time to get strategic by exploring and evaluating the latest relevant data science use cases and case studies. (I discuss how to do this in Chapter 16.)

>> **Cultivate a data-enthusiastic culture:** Even if your data science project is managed and implemented to perfection, if your company's culture doesn't inspire and excite employees to want to do their jobs on a more data-informed basis, your project is likely to face user-adoption challenges. Though you will want to make sure you've created a top-down enforcement approach,

you can supplement it with a bottom-up corporate culture that helps inspire employees to want to become more data-empowered by using your data science solution.

>> **Evangelize for your company's data project and teams:** Similar to the bottom-up approach I just mentioned, when you evangelize your company's data projects, you help spread data literacy and enthusiasm across its workforce. If you're serious about your data projects having a big impact on the company's bottom line, be the evangelist for your team and its data science projects.

Surveying Use Cases and Case Studies

It's time that I introduce you to my 4-step framework for initiating and maintaining profit-forming data science projects. I came up with this framework, the STAR framework, after many years traveling the globe and helping companies plan and kick off their own successful, profit-forming data science initiatives. The STAR framework is shown in Figure 9-4.

FIGURE 9-4: My STAR framework, for managing profit-forming data science projects.

The STAR acronym is created from these terms:

>> **Survey:** You need to know what's out there in terms of successful data science use cases and case studies. Part 3 is your opportunities to practice surveying the data science use case landscape.

>> **Take stock:** The second phase of the STAR framework is on gathering important information about your company. (You find out how to do that in Chapter 15.)

>> **Assess:** After you take stock of your company, you enter the third phase of the STAR framework, where you access your company's current state. (That topic is covered in Chapters 16.)

>> **Recommend:** The final phase of the STAR framework is where you recommend a plan for using data science to generate a new or improved profit for your company. (I cover that aspect in Chapter 17.)

This is the part of the chapter where I sometimes mention Big Ideas, so let me throw another conceptual linchpin your way — it may prove helpful as you move forward. It's the five main routes by which data science impacts business, as illustrated in Figure 9-5.

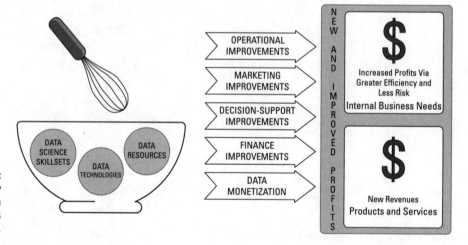

FIGURE 9-5: Five routes by which data science impacts business.

Building on the cake metaphor in Figure 9-3, Figure 9-5 summarizes the five main routes through which data science impacts (and improves) a business's bottom line. The following list points you to the chapters of this book that cover each topic:

>> **Operational improvements:** Chapter 10

>> **Marketing improvements:** Chapter 11

>> **Decision-support improvements:** Chapter 12

>> **Finance improvements:** Chapter 13

>> **Direct data monetization:** Chapter 14

To boost a profit-forming data science project off the ground, you need these three key ingredients:

>> **Data science skills and expertise:** You need data science professionals to both manage and implement your project.

>> **Data technologies:** You need data storage and processing tools for your data professionals to build out and maintain the solution.

>> **Data resources:** Last but not least, you need actual data that can be used to build out your predictive solutions.

Before jumping full-throttle into the STAR framework, however, you definitely need to get a few more business basics under your belt so that the rest of the book makes sense to you. Simply put, no matter what type of data science professional you are, when contemplating a new data science project, you should always start by reviewing the latest data use cases and case studies. And, if you're a data implementation person, go the extra mile to make sure you're baking business value into your data science code by documenting it properly. In this section, you dive deeper into data science use cases, case studies, and coding documentation best practices.

Though the documentation requirements for data leaders are different from those for data implementers, the documentation itself supports the same goal — to protect and preserve your company's return on investment (ROI) into its data operations. Let's take a look at what type of documentation you need to prepare and how that documentation works to protect your company's ROI.

REMEMBER

The goal of documentation is to protect and preserve your company's return on investment into its data operations.

Documentation for data leaders

Familiarity with data use cases and case studies is imperative for a data science leader, but if you want to be a well-rounded data science implementer, you simply have to take the time to stay up-to-speed with data use cases and case studies as well. The importance of use cases and case study evaluation comes down to feasibility. Alas, the data science landscape is awash with shiny objects that may or may not work well for your company. The key to your success as a data leader is to select the most promising data science use case for your company, given its current capabilities with respect to data resources, technology, and skill sets. Chapter 16 goes into great detail about how to go about doing that. For now, what you need to know is that, if you choose a data science use case that turns out not to be feasible, your company is highly likely to invest at least tens of thousands of dollars in deploying a use case that fails and ends up generating nothing but a massive waste of time and money. Step 1: Make sure the data science use case you choose is feasible, by taking the time to research current data science use cases and case studies. This research can help shed light on which use cases may offer promising results for your company.

WARNING

If you attempt to execute a data science use case that's not feasible for your specific situation, your project will probably fail and generate nothing but costly losses for your company.

What *is* a use case? Think of it as a recipe or set of instructions on how to build something — a set of instructions designed to benefit the business in a clear and specific way. A use case includes a list of sequential actions that need to take place in order for a system to operate properly. Technical use cases also should come with basic technology specifications: details regarding which types of technologies are required in order to implement the use case. Because use cases are written in plain language that anyone can understand, they can be extremely helpful when it comes to establishing clear communications with stakeholders as well as developers and managers.

Let's take a deeper look into the elements that can be included in a thorough data use case:

>> **Use case title:** The title should be descriptive of exactly how the use case benefits the business.

>> **Description:** The description should consist of one or two sentences that describe what the use case does and the benefit it renders.

>> **Actor:** An actor can be a person interacting with the system or the system itself. An actor is essentially an agent who takes action to support an outcome from the system. With respect to actors, you should document who the primary actors are as well as any supporting actors and offstage actors.

>> **Pre- and post-conditions:** Preconditions document the things that must be true in order for the system to work, and post conditions summarize the output of the system after it's built and running successfully.

>> **Main success scenario:** The main success scenario should include actor intentions as well as a clear statement of the success scenario. (*Actor intentions* are a series of sequential steps that the actors take in order to operate the system; the *success scenario* is simply the output capability of the system after it's built and running properly.)

>> **Industries and functions:** A comprehensive use case needs to document both the industries and business functions for which they are relevant.

>> **Use case diagram:** The business use case diagram is a visual depiction of how the actors interact with this system in a series of sequential steps in order for the system to work properly and achieve its outcome goal. (Check out Figure 9-6 for an example of a use case diagram.)

>> **Technology specifications:** For data use cases, also include information about the technology that's required in order to make these systems work as well as the data science methodologies of any relevant vendors and any integrations that this system offers.

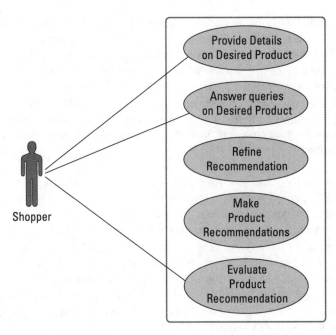

FIGURE 9-6:
A simple business use case diagram.

TIP

I've created a reusable data use case template to help you build out your own data use case collection. It's over on the companion website, at `https://business growth.ai/`, if you'd like to use it.

Case studies, the companion piece to use cases, are designed to function as written narratives that describe the use case in story format. A case study should document the problem the business was facing, how it went about solving that problem, the solution that was implemented, and the outcome the business saw. An important aspect of case studies is that they should be engaging narratives that demonstrate the power of the use case without requiring readers to have any technical expertise. Case studies should be powerful and persuasive communication tools when you're trying to sell your data science project idea to executives and business leaders. (I provide you with tons of examples of case studies and data science use cases in Part 3.)

Documentation for data implementers

Earlier in this chapter, I talk about the documentation that's most relevant to data science leaders and consultants. I still have lots to discuss, however, about how data implementation professionals can use documentation to create more value for the business.

All great data implementation professionals know the value of *coding documentation*: written and illustrative documentation that describes how your code works and what needs to be true in order for it to work successfully. Let's start by discussing why coding documentation is necessary in terms of business value. First off, you might need to pick back up on what you're working on in a year from now and, if you have good documentation, you won't need to spend tons of time retracing your steps to figure out why you made the decisions you made. That time is money for your company, so in this way, good documentation can save you a ton of money.

Additionally, when you use data science code to produce a product, that product is actually owned by your company. When you eventually leave the company, you need to be able to hand it over to others in a useful way and without a lot of downtime. Your coding documentation helps the next person in line understand how the product works, and how to use it properly. This protects the investment of resources that the company made in having you build that product, because it ensures that you're leaving behind a working prototype that can be used with or without you. And it ensures that the knowledge required to use that prototype doesn't get lost. Now let's look at the two types of details you should include in your data science documentation:

>> **Details regarding the data itself:** Document details about the data's source, its variable types, any outliers and missing value treatments, the data reformatting and clean-up that's required, and variable relationships within the data.

>> **Details regarding the data science**: Describe the business question that your model solves and how it goes about answering that question. Describe the models as well as their performance metrics. Include details on the *hyperparameters* (the parameters you set to tune model performance) and how they perform, as well as any feature engineering you did when building the model. Lastly, describe the final model you selected, and why you selected it.

TIP

No need to get too fancy with your documentation tool. You can easily document your data science code using a Google Doc or Word document. Other robust and easy options include Notion and GitHub. If you'd like to test out my favorite Notion templates, see the ones I've left for you over on http://businessgrowth.ai.

Chapter **10**

Improving Operations

What company doesn't want to operate more efficiently? What company doesn't want to spend (or waste) fewer resources on the internal processes it needs in order to produce its assets or services and sell them in exchange for money? None. All businesses want to improve and refine their operations so that they can make better profits with the same levels of input resources. That's business, and it's why data science is used extensively in making improvements to business operations. In fact, operational improvement is one of *the* most important types of use cases for data science and AI. In this chapter, you'll do a shallow dive into how data science is being used to optimize operations with respect to manufacturing, business processes, logistics, and media. Within each of these cases, you'll also take a deeper dive into operational improvements, use cases, technology specifications, and how data science is supercharging operational efficiency across multiple industries.

Establishing Essential Context for Operational Improvements Use Cases

Every time you begin making plans to take on a new data science project, you'll want to refresh your awareness of what's happening across the data science industry. This is especially true if your company is looking to you to help make operational improvements. That's because, operational improvements often come in the form of AI-infused automation, and this is a rapidly evolving area within data science.

Before diving into the nuts-and-bolts of data-science-driven operational improvements, let's talk about you and how this chapter applies to where you are in your data career. If you've read about the data superhero type earlier, in Chapter 1, you probably have already self-identified as either a data implementer, a data leader, or a data entrepreneur. Now, implementing an operational improvement use case at this time may — or may not — be the most appropriate choice, depending on where you work and the current priorities of that business. In either case, the knowledge shared in this chapter is valuable to you, personally, as an up-and-coming data expert. Here's how:

>> **Data implementers**: It's worth the time and effort to tap into the technology and machine learning aspects introduced within this chapter as a jumping-off point for explorations into demand across the data sector. If a particular aspect of this chapter looks especially interesting to you, I recommend that you do some market research to establish how much demand exists for these sorts of implementation skills. Just because an operational use case may not make sense for your company at this time doesn't mean that you can't incorporate the use cases' underlying technologies and methodologies to make improvements or create more efficiencies within the day-to-day work you're doing as a data science implementation worker.

>> **Data leaders**: The thing to understand about operational improvement use cases is that, although they may be proven by case studies in industries different from your own, it's possible that these use cases can be applied to drive improvements in your industry as well. While reading up on operational improvements use cases, be sure to continually "check in," by asking yourself, "Where might this fit into our company as it is today? Can this use case possibly be retrofitted to create value for the company as well? If so, how?"

>> **Data entrepreneurs**: It doesn't matter what sort of business you run, or plan to run; you'll continually look for ways to make operational improvements on your business. If you have a *business-to-business (B2B)* company — a company that works with and supports other companies, usually larger corporations — chances are good that you're selling products or services geared to make some sort of operational improvement for your client's company. If you see promising information in this chapter, I recommend looking deeper into its associated costs as well as *time-to-market* — the time required to set up a product or service and get it operationalized and out into the market.

Now that I've established the ground rules for how to use this chapter, let's get into all the glorious details about how data science is successfully being used to improve business operations!

Exploring Ways That Data Science Is Used to Improve Operations

When I talk about business operations with respect to data science, what I'm talking about are the operational processes within a business that are required to

>> Create and increase recurring revenues.

>> Increase the monetary value of existing assets.

>> Preserve the existing revenues and overall valuation of the business.

Beyond that, operational improvements come in many flavors. From quality assurance to improved forecasting, the improvements a company makes on an operational level subsequently feed into every single line of business that the company maintains. What's more, operational improvements are available to help businesses across every industry under the sun.

Table 10-1 provides you with more concrete examples of real-life operational improvement use cases for data science across a wide variety of industries.

Now let's take a closer look at ways in which data science is being used to improve operational efficiency in manufacturing.

TABLE 10-1   **Operational Improvement Use Cases for Data Science, by Industry**

Industry	Operational Improvement	Company
Transportation	Hundreds of millions of US dollars saved per year	United Postal Service (UPS)
Government, healthcare	A 120x reduction in report generation time	US Centers of Disease Control (CDC)
Media, news, and entertainment	Fifteen-fold increase in news stories generated	Associated Press (AP)
Food and beverage	Fifteen % reduction in restocking trips	Coca-Cola
Business services	Thirty % to 70% increase in business processes automation	Deutsche Bank
Finance and credit	Detection acuity increased by 250% for criminal transactions	NASDAQ
Computer software	Saved 75% of overall GPU cost for visual search	Bing
Lawyers, law firms	Automated Round 1 of document review	BA-HR
Transportation	Substantial fuel costs saved and data wrangling reduced by 60%	Southwest Airlines
Oil and gas	Substantial improvement in company's overall performance	Shell Oil

Source: Data Use Case Collection Workbox, Data-Mania.com

Making major improvements to traditional manufacturing operations

Over the past decade, advancements in Internet connectivity, AI, and robotics automation have turned traditional manufacturing on its head, catapulting the world into what's come to be known as the *fourth industrial revolution* — a period in which AI technology is producing a profound and rapid overhaul of the traditional manufacturing industry, seeking to replace traditionally manual labor with automated control and execution of production via robots. It's good for business but bad for factory workers — in fact, you've probably seen a lot about factory layoffs on the news, and this AI-enabled robotics automation is to blame. This was as true pre-COVID as it is today.

Manufacturing started off as the customized production of goods and then moved into an era of mass production; this fourth industrial revolution, however, marks an era in which manufacturing companies are developing the full flexibility they need to actually carry out *mass customization production* — customized production on a massive scale. With mass production, long lines of mass-producing robots were fixed in an operational series, and that was adequate to meet production requirements, but things have changed. To meet the demands of mass customization production, manufacturing robots must collaborate and be designed with the flexibility they need in order to integrate, change, and adjust production requirements autonomously and on demand.

When it comes to mass customization production, robot work can be performed within what's called a *robot workcell* — an autonomously operating work environment where robots can produce at their fullest speed and capacity without adherence to safety protocols that would generally be required in the presence of humans, as shown in Figure 10-1.

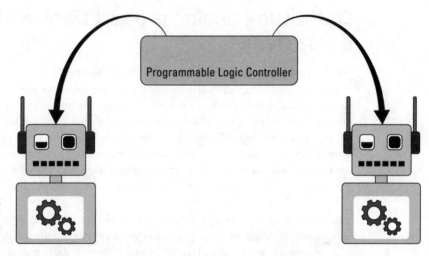

FIGURE 10-1:
AI-enabled robotics automation.

Within a robot workcell, predictive machine learning models can be run inside the programmable logic controller (PLC) — also known as the robot task controller. With machine learning making decisions in the PLC and the robots executing on those decisions in the physical world, you pass from industrial machine learning into full-fledged, honest-to-life artificial intelligence.

As machine learning advances, PLC units are able to offer increasingly more sophisticated robot task control. The following list describes just a few of the ways that industrial machine learning is making manufacturing operations dramatically more efficient:

>> **Defect analysis:** With the help of K-means clustering, you can categorize data on manufacturing parts to classify quality and reliability. For more on K-means clustering, refer to Chapter 5.

- **Production forecasting:** One strategy is to use regression analysis on historical production data in order to predict production levels from a system, or even any given process within that system. Regression analysis is covered in Chapter 4.

- **Self-tuning vision systems:** Neural networks are useful for *computer vision technology* — processes that use the automated extraction of information from images in order to support manufacturing units as they autoregulate and adapt based on data captured via live camera footage recorded during production work. Deep learning and neural networks are covered in Chapter 3.

Optimizing business operations with data science

Traditionally, it's been business process automation (BPA) solutions that are known for producing radical efficiencies within business processes. In case it's new to you, business process automation is the streamlining of day-to-day business operations by automating repetitive tasks that would otherwise be carried out manually. Though BPA is still a relevant and powerful force in the operational improvements space, data science has also stepped up as an outstanding companion to any business that seeks to optimize and improve its operations. The following are a few ways data science is being used to optimize business operations:

- **Automated document analysis:** Deep learning and neural networks are commonly implemented to produce computer vision applications that are capable of taking written reports, breaking them down to their most fundamental data points and then evaluating those data points in order to produce actionable insights from a written document without the need for human intervention.

- **Automated report writing:** It's now completely possible for businesses to take data from financial reports and apply natural language processing to automatically convert the raw financial data into fully customized written reports.

- **Automated customer service support:** Companies are now using machine learning to improve, personalize, and automate their client interaction processes. More details on this use case are discussed in the case study highlighted in the next section.

An AI case study: Automated, personalized, and effective debt collection processes

LendUp is a company specializing in financial technology, credit card, financial education, credit reporting, and loan services to lending clients. LendUp has developed a machine learning platform that prompts debtors to schedule and send debt payments through the use of personalized offers, repayment plans, and reminders. LendUp's mission is to promote AI technological approaches to real-world problems, and to deliver value-adding applications of AI technology. LendUp's main functions revolve around finding and implementing automated, technological solutions in the areas of account management and customer management.

As a financial tech company, LendUp wants to use a machine learning system to improve its credit card and loan services as well as its customer management mechanisms. To this end, LendUp sought out TrueAccord to utilize its machine learning platform. TrueAccord's system is capable of influencing customer behavior by publishing personalized reminders to make repayments of debts. This machine learning platform can also create and deliver customized debt repayment plans and personalized offers for LendUp's customers.

The solution

LendUp opted to work with TrueAccord because of the many benefits that its machine learning platform offers. TrueAccord's data-driven platform can increase LendUp's recovery rates, lower compliance-related risks, and optimize LendUp's customer experiences.

TrueAccord offers code-based and code-driven credit and other debt collection compliance measures, thus reducing LendUp's compliance risk and exposure levels. The platform also permits LendUp to fully monitor consumer behaviors. Additionally, it allows for quick and simple notifications to be sent and updates to be made as relevant requirements and regulations shift over time. Content that is prewritten and preapproved can be sent via TrueAccord's omnichannel approach (discussed further in Chapter 11), which can vastly reduce issues such as consumer complaints and the debt collection outreach frequency that's required to collect on loans due. During all of this, TrueAccord's system can log a complete record of the consumer interaction process that can be easily retrieved and reviewed by LendUp's teams.

With TrueAccord, LendUp can reach higher customer engagement levels and give consumers the tools that they need to clear up their debts by using on-demand and self-service features. TrueAccord's approach is consumer-centric, offering consumers personalized payment plans and offers that allow them to repay their debts more efficiently than would be the case if these machine learning systems weren't in place. LendUp is thus able to provide tailored, personal plans for its customers to guide them through the collections process and create successful debt payment arrangements, thus improving its recovery rates.

By working with TrueAccord, LendUp readily acknowledges that modern technology is now the norm in terms of consumer demands. Through a data-driven, digital-first collections approach, TrueAccord can further empower and engage LendUp's consumers by creating a tailored *contact strategy* — an automated procedure for directing consumers to self-service payment models and giving nurturing messages until their debts have been completely paid in full. In this way, LendUp's consumers can sustain high motivation levels with respect to paying off their loans or credit card debts and eventually reaching excellent financial health. The result is that LendUp gains valuable consumer loyalty while lowering its risks for losses in the present and future.

TrueAccord's decision engine, Heartbeat (patent pending), creates digital-first, personalized consumer experiences that are driven by machine learning. It chooses from internally generated and legally preapproved messages to keep track of real-time events related to each consumer, such as links clicked and emails opened. Its platform uses a *state machine* — a behavioral model that represents interactions as *transitions* and machine modes as *states* with the goal to reach a predetermined final state and produce a desired output. This state machine is used to craft a virtual interaction model with LendUp's consumers, and it uses a clustering engine to compare a given consumer to the over 1.5 million consumers who have interacted with the system in the past. Using data points that range in the hundreds of millions, TrueAccord's machine learning platform can offer actionable predictions when it comes to consumer reactions to elements such as content, communication timing, frequency, and channel. Through TrueAccord, LendUp has served over 2.5 million consumers and processed tens of millions of collections-related interactions.

The result

LendUp doesn't show it's cards by outright stating exactly how much money they are making from savings and increased revenue generation due to TrueAccord's Heartbeat solution, but let's review all of the ROI-generating outcomes their enjoying:

>> **Dramatic decrease in expenditures on payroll for customer service representatives:** TrueAccord automates customer service at mass-scale. What's more, Heartbeat uses machine learning to improve upon the results that human customer services agents would have produced. All of this means significantly less money spent on payroll as well as improved results.

>> **Increased conversion rates for new offers:** TrueAccord deploys machine learning to improve offer personalization. This results in more revenue, due to an increase in new loan contracts, as well as lower costs associated with customer acquisition.

>> **Improved customer satisfaction:** Customized debt repayment plans (delivered in a way that's not annoying to customers), self-service payment models, and nurturing messages that keep customers engaged and motivated . . . all of these result in lower customer churn, greater lifetime value per customer, and a net increase in loan repayment success.

But what does all this mean for you and your company? Well, your company might not be in the finance industry, but it probably does need to interact with its client regularly. In this case, it's possible that implementing a similar approach could streamline customer service operations and save the company lots of time and costs! It's definitely worth taking a deeper look into the types of tools, technologies, and techniques that are running under the hood. That's where the use case comes in, so let's take a quick look at it.

TIP

Anytime you see an especially promising case study, do some Internet research and try to map out a theoretical use case for it so that you can see how a particular data science win might be made reproducible in your own business. I did that in Table 10-2 for the LendUp case study I just introduced.

It's equally valuable to do some Internet research and dig into the types of tools, technologies, and data science methodologies that are required to build out this type of use case. Table 10-3 documents the theoretical technology stack that would support this type of debt-recovery use case.

If you're a data implementer and you like this use case, dig deeper into the technology specifications that are described in Table 10-3 above. If you're a data leader, you now have a blueprint for the people, processes, tools, and data resources you'd need to spearhead a project similar to this one for your company. Lastly, if you're a data entrepreneur, you could either explore ways to adopt processes from Table 10-2 to streamline your own customer service operations or you could decide to look into how feasible it is for your company to build and sell a similar but sufficiently unique product in a different vertical. That was easy! Now let's look at a few examples of how data science is being used to make operational improvements in industries outside financial services.

TABLE 10-2	Theoretical Business Use Case for Automating Client Interactions

A — BUSINESS USE CASE

Recover debt

B1: DESCRIPTION

This use case describes how a LendUp debt collector creates personalized reminders, repayment plans, and offers for consumers, using TrueAccord's Heartbeat algorithm. It begins when the debt collector inputs consumer information and ends when Heartbeat recommends a repayment plan and an offer to the consumer.

B2: ACTORS

Primary actor: Debt collector

Supporting actors: Heartbeat, content writer, legal reviewer

Offstage actor: Consumer

B3: PRECONDITIONS + POST-CONDITIONS

Preconditions

- **Heartbeat must be trained with historical collection information.**

- **Preapproved customer message templates to customer must exist.**

Post-conditions

- **Heartbeat custom message algorithm is updated based on actual consumer's reaction.**

C: MAIN SUCCESS SCENARIO

Actor intention

1. Debt collector inputs customer data into Heartbeat.

2. Heartbeat predicts consumer reaction.

3. Heartbeat selects from preapproved messages.

4. Legal reviewer and content writer review selected message.

5. Heartbeat sends preapproved message to consumer.

6. Heartbeat tracks real-time event from consumer.

7. Heartbeat recommends a repayment plan, reminders, and an offer for the consumer.

Success scenario

A personalized repayment plan, reminders, and an offer are created for the consumer.

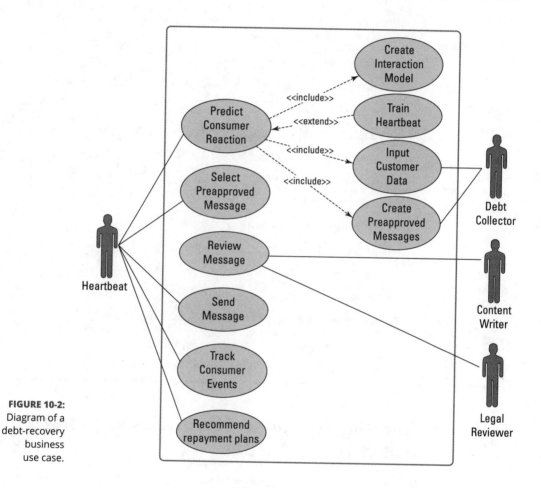

FIGURE 10-2:
Diagram of a debt-recovery business use case.

TABLE 10-3 **Theoretical Technology Stack for Automating Client Interactions**

Technology stack	**Data management**
	On-premise/cloud/hybrid data management
	<u>Big data</u>
	• NoSQL databases
	<u>Traditional data</u>
	• Relational database management systems (RDBMs)
	Analytics and visualization tools
	• <u>Data visualization:</u> Looker, Tableau, real-time stream analytics (Apache Spark)
	Machine learning technologies
	• <u>Predictive modeling programming languages:</u> Python, SQL
	• <u>Predictive modeling applications</u>: Jupyter Notebooks
	• <u>Deep learning</u>: TensorFlow
	• <u>Real-time predictive analytics</u>: Apache Spark
	Software engineering technologies
	• <u>Application development programming languages:</u> Java, Scala
Data science methodologies	• **Classification**
	• **Clustering:** KMeans, hierarchical
	• **Recommendation system methods:** Collaborative filtering, combinatorial optimization, linear and mixed-integer programming, content-based filtering, sentimental product recommendation, knowledge-based filtering
	• **Regression:** Linear, logistic, stepwise, multiple

Gaining logistical efficiencies with better use of real-time data

Given what you already know about data science, I'm sure you can already imagine some of the spectacular impacts AI has had on logistical operations. From Uber to UPS, the pace and scale of 21st century logistics is breathtaking. If successful today, these logistical operations are more than just cars, trains, freights, and delivery dates — they're also *data-intensive*. That means they run on parallel computing systems that are designed expressly to meet the processing and evaluation needs required to convert big data into big dollars. In this section, you get the chance to take a closer look at how UPS serves parcels on its data platter, but let's go broad first, by looking at various ways in which data science is used in supporting logistical operations. The most common logistical operations use cases for data science include these:

>> **Real-time optimized logistics routing:** Real-time routing is useful in all areas of transportation but has proven especially valuable when it comes to logistics operations involved in air freight, sea freight, and even ground parcel transportation. I help you take a deeper dive into a real-time optimized routing use case next. For now, just be aware that the use of AI is as beneficial to the environment as it is to a company's bottom line.

>> **Predictive maintenance:** Especially relevant in today's railway industry, transportation providers are now equipping freight locomotives with the cameras and predictive applications they need to identify physical objects and avoid potential collisions or derailments. To do this, they use neural networks to build a computer vision system that's capable of real-time object detection. This use of AI not only saves lives but also decreases the cost associated with unplanned and avoidable breakdowns.

>> **Optical character recognition to optimize delivery address sorting:** *Optical character recognition* is a form of computer vision that uses deep learning to detect handwritten and typed characters. Ground transport providers use this type of AI to "read" a parcel's address label and then automatically categorize and sort each parcel into groups based on similarities in geographic location (based on identifiers like zip code and city name). This use of AI decreases the person-hours spent in manual sorting and increases the speed and accuracy of the mail delivery service.

Another AI case study: Real-time optimized logistics routing

The United Parcel Service (UPS) is a multinational supply chain management company best known for its package delivery services. Beyond package delivery, it offers services in retail-centric shipping and packaging services (The UPS Store), freight-focused trucking operation (UPS Freight), and cargo airlines (UPS Airlines).

Each winter, UPS faces a daunting problem: how to handle the logistical complications of bad weather hitting major cities — such as nasty storms. Bad weather can disrupt many thousands of packages that are usually transported through a major city on their way to their ultimate destinations. If UPS had a way to know in advance that the bad weather would significantly impact its delivery-related operations, what would be the most efficient means of moving these packages, gifts, and online orders around the bad weather?

To do so, UPS has to take on the difficult task of selecting the facility that is best suited for handling an unexpected, large shipment and is capable of shipping these packages toward their destination. Several variables complicate this sort of decision: The packages' respective destinations, the types of packages, and their respective delivery deadlines. All these factors can slow down the logistical decisions of UPS engineers and can make it even harder to efficiently shift resources.

To manage the whole package-flow process, UPS employed several kinds of transportation planners and industrial engineers, including employees who set work hours and training for pilots and employees as well as employees who ran the coordination process for loading and unloading trucks. Teams used consumer software such as Microsoft Excel and Access, emailing lists to each other when the need arose. All this changed in September 2018, with the implementation of the initial version of UPS' Network Planning Tools, or NPT.

The solution

The NPT is an internal, cloud-based machine learning platform with multiple modules that provides a host of benefits to its networks and its customers — particularly, hub and route optimization benefits. One main benefit is that it allows UPS to create more efficient package routing and rerouting paths through its advanced algorithms. This allows UPS to reroute packages already in transit to a near- or at-capacity hub to a different hub that can handle the package. The system allows UPS's engineers to get a bird's-eye view of package distribution and volume across the entire network. It also allows UPS to make decisions based on real-time data year-round and through any number of volume fluctuations.

The NPT can also efficiently divert packages heading into bad weather to several different hubs that are out of harm's way, all while tracking the relative capacity levels of these hubs to not overwhelm any of these facilities. All this can be done in a way that still ensures that packages are delivered on time to their respective destinations. Essentially, the NPT serves as a comprehensive big data platform that includes a simulation function, informing employees of the impact of each work decision they make.

The result

The results of the NPT platform haven't been fully released, but UPS expected this platform to save the company hundreds of millions of dollars each year. NPT was also successful enough for UPS to add another feature to it: the Peak Volume Alignment Tool (PVAT). This analytical tool better pairs incoming volume flows with the available capacity of networks, improving operating efficiency and capacity utilization.

Now that you've seen this use case from the outside looking in, let's take a shot at creating a business use case that describes how this sort of thing would work in terms of business processes. Table 10-4 documents the theoretical technology stack that would support this type of route optimization use case.

TABLE 10-4: **Theoretical Business Use Case for Real-Time Optimized Logistics Routing**

A: BUSINESS USE CASE

Real-time optimized logistics routing

B1: DESCRIPTION

This use case describes how a UPS engineer uses network planning tools to route shipments to the facilities with the highest capacities.

B2: ACTORS

Primary actor: Engineer

Offstage actor: Customer

B3: PRECONDITIONS + POST-CONDITIONS

Preconditions

- Data on shipping variables exists, such as types of packages and their destinations, weight, volume, and delivery deadlines.

Post-Conditions

- Algorithm updates are based on feedback from customers, satisfaction, and cost.

C: MAIN SUCCESS SCENARIO

Actor intention

1. Engineer logs on to NPT to see package routes.

2. Available hubs for diversion are presented.

3. Engineer diverts package to another hub.

4. Notification is sent to engineers at the receiving hub.

5. Package sorting instruction is issued.

6. Outbound packages are grouped into smallest number.

7. Plane and truck pickup is scheduled.

8. Engineer decisions are analyzed for improvement.

Success scenario

- An appropriate route forecast is presented.

D: INDUSTRIES AND FUNCTIONS

Industries: Logistics and freight

Functions: Route planning

E: BUSINESS USE CASE DIAGRAM

See Figure 10-3.

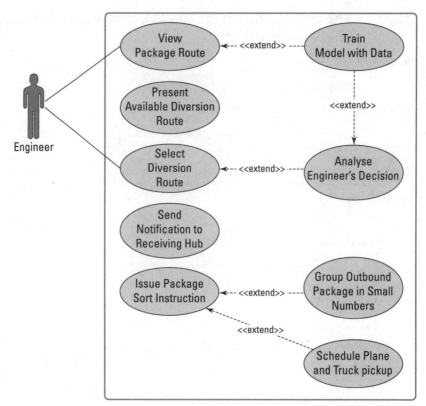

FIGURE 10-3:
Diagram of a
logistics-routing
business
use case.

Business use cases are all well and good, but because you're reading a book on data science, I'm sure you're itching to see the potential tools, technologies, and data science methodologies that are useful in this type of use case. Table 10-5 documents the theoretical technology stack you could build in order to support a route optimization use case like this one.

Google Search is your friend when you want to look into the sorts of technologies that go into building out a data science use case.

REMEMBER

Clearly, if you're a data implementation buff who is working in the logistics sector, you have a lot to play with here. Don't worry, though: I'm sure no one is expecting you to singlehandedly build a system like the one UPS came up with — that's not even possible! What you can do is start small — probably with a classification algorithm — and look to see how you can create some new efficiencies within your company's current logistical operations. Once you've achieved some small measure of success, you'll have some ground to stand on in terms of doing more.

TABLE 10-5	**Theoretical Technology Stack for Real-Time Optimized Logistics Routing**

Technology stack	**Data management**
	Cloud data management
	• Google Cloud (StackDriver)
	On-premise / cloud / hybrid data management
	<u>Big data</u>
	• Apache — Hadoop Distributed File System (HDFS), MapReduce
	• Kubernetes
	• NoSQL databases
	Machine learning technologies
	• Predictive modeling programming languages (Python, SQL)
	• Predictive modeling applications (H2O.ai, SAS, Stata)
	• Deep learning (TensorFlow)
	• Real-time predictive analytics (Apache Spark)
	Software engineering technologies
	• **Application development programming languages** (Java, Python, Scala)
Data science methodologies	• **Bayesian methods/networks**
	• **Classification**
	• **Clustering** (KMeans, hierarchical)
	• **Computer vision and image processing algorithms**
	• **Deep learning**
	• **Demand forecasting**
	• **Dimensionality reduction** (principal component analysis, factor analysis)
	• **Decision trees** (classification and regression trees)
	• **Gradient-boosting** (XGBoost, GBM, GLM, LightGBM, gradient boosted regression trees)
	• **Natural language processing**
	• **Network analysis** (network/graph mining)

(continued)

TABLE 10-5 *(continued)*

- **Random forests**

- **Recommendation system methods** (collaborative filtering systems, combinatorial recommender systems)

- **Optimization, linear and mixed-integer programming**

- **Regression** (linear, logistic, stepwise, and multiple)

- **Reinforcement learning**

- **Spatial network analysis, spatial mapping**

- **Text mining and analytics**

- **Time series analysis**

REMEMBER

When it comes to implementing new data use cases, always start small. Once you've achieved reproducible success on the small scale, you'll have a stronger sense of a solution's future feasibility when you start looking to implement your solution on a larger scale. (More on this topic in Chapter 17.)

Modernizing media and the press with data science and AI

Deep learning AI is in the process of turning the content, media, and press industry on its head, and the changes that are underway are utterly irreversible. From tiny online mom-and-pop shops to the largest media companies in the world, late-breaking advances in AI aren't just making for a level playing field — they're picking up the playing field and placing it into a whole new territory.

At the time of this book update, AI-assisted content creation tools are rapidly proliferating across the Internet. They're now available for free on a trial basis or at a very low cost so that even the smallest of small-business owners can benefit from the efficiencies these tools create. I'm talking about AI tools for written content creation, visual content creation, and everything in between. Let's start by looking at AI solutions that are available to small businesses, and then I'll introduce you to a case study and use case for building an AI solution for a behemoth-size media company like the Associated Press.

Generating content with the click of a button

"GPT-3." That has a ring to it, doesn't it? But that echo might just be the ringing sound of the final round in a content boxing match between humans and the machine. And machines? They're crushing it. If this sounds too apocalyptic to be true, let me explain.

GPT-3 is a language model that generates human-like language. Written in Python, it uses large amounts of text to generate new, similar text. It was developed by researchers from OpenAI — an AI research-and-deployment company determined to ensure that AI innovation benefits all of humanity, not just an unduly concentrated segment of rich-and-powerful business owners. On June 11, 2020, OpenAI announced user-friendly access to its API. Since then, many new data entrepreneurs have been busy building online businesses that sell automated AI content-generation services that run off the OpenAI API. These small data businesses are selling automated content services and making a good living helping content creators produce written content that can pass the *Turing test* — a standard set by famed mathematician and computer scientist Alan Turing in 1950. It says that machines will have achieved human-equivalent intelligence when they can produce outputs that are indistinguishable from similar outputs generated by humans.

OpenAI isn't just creating language models, though. It's also building models that can create visual images from text, called DALL·E, and Image GPT, a model that transforms partial images to full images by predicting and generating what would likely be contained in the missing portions of the images. What's more, these aren't the only types of AI-infused content generation tools, either. There are many others, like AI article spinners, AI content research tools, and AI grammar correction tools, just to name a few.

The $10 million dollar question here is, "Will AI put writers and content creators out of work permanently?" To that question, I reply with a resounding *no*. Though AI is now capable of creating human-esque, plagiarism-free content at the click of a button, it cannot generate the context that's required for humans to transform information into meaning. To gather meaning from information, humans need knowledge. Without knowledge or context being provided within a written piece of work, readers can't draw inferences or conclusions from the information the writing contains. In other words, will AI tools put non-experts and unskilled writers out of work? Probably. Will they be able to replace the human aspects required to generate an expert-level body of writing? It's unlikely.

A SAMPLE OF GPT-3 GENERATED CONTENT

What are the most lucrative data roles out there, and which ones will allow you to flourish emotionally? My data superhero quiz is here to help you find out. Answer a few questions about your work preferences and values, and then see which data role best suits you. You also gain access to recent research on more than 50 different data roles and their compensation packages and job trends.

GPT-3 and friends may be all well and good for small mom-and-pop shops, but it's not designed to support the operational needs of large media companies. For large companies, you almost always need to build out a robust, custom solution. That's exactly what the Associated Press did in order to generate a 15-fold increase in news stories it can generate per unit time. Let's take a deeper look into this remarkable win, shall we?

Yet another case study: Increasing content generation rates

The Associated Press (AP) is an industry leader in terms of journalism and news media. This organization's membership includes thousands of TV and radio broadcasters and roughly 1,400 daily newspapers around the US. Beyond the impressive amounts of news content that AP distributes, it's also an organization well-known for its style. Professionals in the fields of journalism and in other industries regard "AP style" as the quintessential writing standard.

For many years, Associated Press reporters had to report on the corporate earnings of US public companies every quarter, a time-consuming and stressful process. AP sought out a data-oriented automation solution that would free up its reporters' time, giving the reporters a chance to focus more on reporting quality news content.

The problem

Reporting on these quarterly corporate earnings created a number of external and internal problems for AP and its many reporters.

Externally, AP's main issue was the sheer volume of US public corporations that report their earnings, numbering in the thousands. Internally, AP business reporters were faced with a daunting task each quarter, where they would have to grab data from corporate earnings press releases, copy them, place them within pre-written templates, add headlines, and then promptly publish them. These actions needed to be performed quickly and early in the morning so that stock traders would be adequately informed on whether they should buy or sell a given stock.

On top of this process being time-consuming and unpleasant, the AP reporters would manage to create only around 300 news stories of these corporate earnings each quarter. Thousands of US corporate earnings reports were left by the wayside, so many traders lacked the information they needed.

Each quarter's news stories were crafted by interpreting financial information from the earnings reports of as many US corporations as the reporters could manage, but that still meant the stories for many companies went untold. Eventually,

AP decided that it needed to find a better way — for the sake of its reporters, its customers, and the company at large.

The solution

One reason for AP's ability to last so long compared to other news organizations is its recognition of the need to take advantage of new technologies and strategies. AP thus turned to automation as an innovative potential solution to its reporting problems.

AP had a plan that would lead to its reporters spending much less time on gathering data and numbers and devoting more time to producing high-quality articles and stories for its customers and subscribers. It was able to put its plan into action with Automated Insights' Wordsmith platform. Wordsmith uses natural language generation (NLG) to convert collected data into a written-out, plain-language story. It's capable of turning data from a corporate earnings report into an article worthy of being published at AP in only a fraction of a second. Wordsmith's products were able to meet AP's standards because the platform's team was able to customize the NLG engine in a way that matches AP style.

AP applied Wordsmith to different content areas at first. Over time, the Wordsmith platform was put through extensive and intensive testing, steadily reducing the error rates in the automated AP earnings reports. Eventually, testing was conducted on the automated earnings of corporations from Canada and from Europe.

The result

AP, working together with Automated Insights' Wordsmith platform, was able to achieve the following results:

» Produced 4,400 quarterly earnings stories

» Increased story generation rates by nearly 15-fold

» Freed up around 20 percent of the time that was spent by the reporting staff creating earnings reports each quarter

The Associated Press turned a problem into an opportunity to produce higher volumes of high-quality articles by way of automation. Through the automated NLG capabilities of Automated Insights' Wordsmith, AP converted raw corporate earnings data into thousands of AP news stories, creating many more stories about corporate quarterly earnings than previous efforts performed manually.

In terms of how the Associated Press was able to achieve this across the business unit, I've drawn up a theoretical business use case that could support the case study I just shared. Table 10-6 shows the fruit of my labors.

TABLE 10-6	Theoretical Business Use Case for Increasing Content-Generation Rates

A: BUSINESS USE CASE

Increase content-generation rates

B1: DESCRIPTION

This use case describes how a news company content writer can create a narrative from quarterly earnings data using Automated Insights' Wordsmith platform. It begins when the content writer uploads earnings data and ends when the content writer publishes a narrative created by Wordsmith.

B2: ACTORS

Primary actor: Content writer

Supporting actors: Wordsmith, domain expert

B3: PRECONDITIONS + POST-CONDITIONS

Preconditions

- Structured corporate earnings quarterly data must exist.
- A template of the narrative must have been created on Wordsmith.

Post-Conditions

- The Wordsmith template is updated based on the newly published narrative.

C: MAIN SUCCESS SCENARIO

Actor intention (basic flow)

1. Content writer uploads data into Wordsmith.
2. Wordsmith generates narratives.
3. Content writer and domain review narratives.
4. Content writer publishes narratives.

Exception flow (if content writer is dissatisfied with narratives in Step 3)

A. Content writer modifies data accordingly.
B. Wordsmith regenerates narratives.

Success scenario

A textual summary of earnings is produced from data.

D: INDUSTRIES AND FUNCTIONS

Industries: Media and publishing

Functions: General operations

E: BUSINESS USE CASE DIAGRAM

See Figure 10-4.

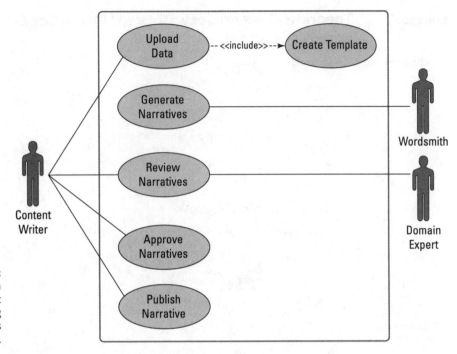

FIGURE 10-4:
Diagram of a
content
publishing
business
use case.

As helpful as this use case is to data leaders in the media industry, it probably doesn't wet the whistle of any data implementers out there. Let's look at Table 10-7 for some technology specifications for this use case, shall we?

That's the third and final technology specification for this chapter, and through them all, you've seen one overwhelmingly obvious trend: deep learning. In almost all the operations case studies I talk about, the company either utilizes, or wants to be utilizing, deep learning. Deep learning skills are clearly valuable and in demand, so if you're a data implementation person, now is a good time to boost your skillset in that subniche and find yourself some golden opportunities.

TIP

If you're a data professional in the news and media industry, it's time to open your eyes to the incredible breakthroughs that AI is facilitating across your industry. Whether you give GPT-3 a go or build out a custom data science solution, you have some major opportunities to use AI to get ahead of your competition as a professional in the media industry.

TABLE 10-7	**Theoretical Technology Stack for Increasing Content Generation Rates**	
Technology stack	**Data management**	
	Cloud data management	
	• Amazon Web Services (S3)	
	On-premise / cloud / hybrid data management	
	Big data	
	• Docker	
	Machine learning technologies	
	• Predictive modeling programming languages (Python)	
	• Deep learning (Caffe, Keras, PyTorch, TensorFlow)	
	Software engineering technologies	
	• Application development programming languages (C++)	
Data science methodologies	• Deep learning	
	• Natural language processing	

Chapter **11**

Making Marketing Improvements

ach and every customer has their own, unique set of preferences, needs, and wants. The better you can align your business and its offerings with the most intimate desires of your customers, the easier it is to convert leads into new customers and make repeat sales with existing customers. Luckily for you, data science, when combined with data analytics, is the perfect vehicle by which to offer the personalization that today's tech-savvy consumer craves. In this chapter, I have you look at several ways to go about using data science in marketing to improve the profitability of your company's marketing efforts.

Exploring Popular Use Cases for Data Science in Marketing

You can use data science in a lot of ways to increase your marketing return on investment. These are the most common marketing use cases for data science:

>> **Recommendation engines:** Whether you build them yourself or use a recommender application instead, recommendation systems use filtering to

segment customers according to shared characteristics. It's useful to segment customers in this way so that you can target offers for your customers' known preferences, in order to upsell and cross-sell your brand's offerings.

» **Churn reduction:** *Customer churn* describes the loss, or churn, of existing customers. *Customer churn analysis* is a set of analytical techniques that are designed to identify, monitor, and issue alerts on indicators that signify when customers are likely to churn. With the information that's generated in customer churn analysis, businesses can take preemptive measures to retain at-risk customers.

» **Content creation:** Though the use of AI for content creation isn't exactly new, it has become a lot more accessible lately. Natural language processing (NLP) is used in copy-writing applications as well as in applications that can read your copy back to you after you've written it. This is in addition to the NLP-generated text suggestions that we all have come to know and love inside of word processing applications like Word or Google Docs. Recently, even newer AI tools have emerged that can create new original content from a prewritten sample — GPT-3, for example, which is able to collect text on a single topic from many different sources, consolidate that to a single research finding and then write it out as copy that can, in some cases, pass for human-written copy. Refer back to Chapter 10 for more about GPT-3.

» **Lifetime value forecasting:** Modern lifetime value forecasting (LTV) involves using machine learning to predict the lifetime value — the total monetary value of a customer over their lifetime with your company, in other words — from existing customer data. Traditional approaches for LTV calculations used basic averages and groups to make predictions, but developments in data science have made it possible to generate much more accurate, reliable predictions of LTV using machine learning.

» **Hypertargeted advertising:** Hypertargeted advertising is a direct product of data science and machine learning. Social media platforms, like Facebook, have been utilizing its users' behavioral and interest data as well as data from its data partners to make predictions about which users are most likely to convert to customers, which are likely to opt in to become leads, and which are likely to become likely to opt in if they're made more aware of the problem solved and solutions offered by your company.

REMEMBER

Facebook takes all the heat, but if we consumers are truly being honest with ourselves, all the social platforms, search engines, and mobile apps out there are part of the race to monetize their platforms from either targeting ads or selling user data by way of data partnerships (a partnership between companies wherein data access is bought and sold). If you find yourself angered by this situation, just realize that there truly is no such thing as a free lunch. Someone has to pay to develop and maintain these free behemoth telecommunication tools we consumers are all so fortunate to use. If you're unwilling to be advertised to, you should be willing to pay for your usage. And if you're willing to be advertised to, what do you prefer — an ad that's extremely interesting to you about a product or service you didn't know existed and would love to purchase? Or an irrelevant ad spamming you about lame products you don't even like or want to know about? As someone who lived through the dotcom bubble, let me tell you: Nontargeted ads are spammy and no fun to experience.

» **Dynamic pricing:** In this form of real-time pricing optimization, machine learning models use clickstream data (and customer data, where available) to generate predictions for the optimal price point at which a customer will buy. A dynamic price is set in real-time, while the user is on the website, in order to maximize the likelihood of a sale.

» **Channel scoring:** Channel scoring helps you identify the best channels to use for the specific campaigns you're working on. By analyzing your current marketing strategy, you can identify where your customers are coming from and then assign a score to each channel. You can also identify channels that are performing better than others — as well as those that are putting a drag on your overall strategy. (There's a five-step process for how to do on channel scoring later in this chapter.)

» **Lead scoring:** Lead scoring is the practice of first assimilating data you have on a lead and then calculating out a score for each lead to indicate the stage of a lead — anywhere from cold to piping hot or (hopefully) already converted. Having this score on hand is helpful in categorizing your leads and predicting which type of marketing campaign will be most effective for each particular group in terms of converting people in those groups from leads to paying customers.

» **Marketing mix modeling:** Marketing mix modeling involves taking historical sales-and-marketing time series data and using statistical machine learning methods to uncover relationships between your core product and marketing features and sales made of those products. After you determine the nature of those relationships, you can predict future sales and tweak your company's marketing plans accordingly. (I cover marketing mix modeling in greater detail later in this chapter.)

» **Market basket analysis:** Market basket analysis involves analyzing transactional data to identify products that are commonly purchased together in pairs or small groups within a single checkout transaction. After uncovering these product pairings, retailers can then use that information in their product placement strategy to increase the number of items sold during a single customer visit. (This analysis is widely used to support in-store product placement.) Product placements should be done in such a way that the items frequently bought together are displayed next to each other so that customers are encouraged to buy them, resulting in a boost in sales.

TIP

For some coding demonstrations showing you how to build recommenders in both R and Python, be sure to check out the free training resources I've left for you over on http://businessgrowth.ai.

TIP

For a demonstration showing you how to do it in Excel, check out the free market basket analysis demonstration I've also left for you over on http://businessgrowth.ai.

Although I'd be delighted to write an entire book on the marketing data science topic, I have only a few pages to cover it within this chapter. For that reason, I've decided to do a deep dive into some of the more accessible methodologies — the ones that don't require you to purchase new software to get started, in other words. Those freebie methodologies are

» Omnichannel analytics

» Channel scoring

» Marketing mix modeling

I discuss each methodology in greater detail in later sections.

Turning Web Analytics into Dollars and Sense

Do you know which marketing and sales channels are driving the greatest number of new customers into your business? If your company is like most, the answer is no. In this section, I give you the lowdown on omnichannel marketing, channel analytics, and how to increase your marketing ROI with a simple 5-step approach to channel scoring that even the most novice data analyst could implement.

Web analytics is a generic term that represents the practice of tracking and evaluating website data in order to increase leads, make sales, and deliver excellent customer experiences. The use of visitor location and demographic data is the most basic form of web analytics, but basic won't get you very far — so let's focus on omnichannel analytics instead. It's a type of web analytics that has the highest likelihood of getting you traction — fast!

Getting acquainted with omnichannel analytics

Omnichannel analytics are a form of data analytics that clarifies your customer interests and expectations along each of your sales-and-marketing channels in the hope of directly increasing the number of leads and sales that are generated from your company's marketing endeavors.

An omnichannel approach assumes that you have several channels through which you market to customers and that you have data resources you can use to identify what your customers want to see on each channel. Through omnichannel marketing, you can provide your customers with different experiences on a channel-by-channel basis; thus allowing you to cater to your customers' different expectations and personalize their experience with your company based on where they're interacting with it and at what stage along their customer journey they find themselves.

Mapping your channels

To make sense of your customer interactions (often called "touchpoints" in marketing speak), you first need to map out where those "customer touches" take place online or in the physical world. With respect to omnichannel analytics, the term *channel* refers to either sales channels or marketing channels, or both. You'll want to start your journey in omnichannel analytics by first mapping out all your company's sales-and-marketing channels.

Sales channels are the channels through which your company generates sales and distributes its products and services to the buyer. Your company's sales channels might include these elements:

>> **Company website**: If your company offers products or services that are available for purchase online, then the web pages where sales are generated and the product or service is distributed is considered a sales channel.

>> **Company email list:** Technically, sales aren't made directly within email messages, but emails can be used as sales assets that directly trigger sales. It's often the case that, in the ecommerce industry, the distribution of the product or service happens by email, so consider your company's email list as a potential sales channel.

>> **Brick-and-mortar store:** If your company has a physical store where people enter and purchase tangible products or services, then each physical, *brick-and-mortar* store is considered a sales channel.

- » **Sales calls:** If your company offers sales calls that directly trigger new sales, the sales call is considered a sales channel.

- » **Live events:** Lots of companies host or sponsor live events as a way to directly trigger sales from attendees. If your company participates in an event with the intention of making sales, you should treat that live event as a sales channel.

Turning now to *marketing channels* — those channels through which your company generates leads as well as sales for your company — the most common ones are described in this list:

- » **Paid ads:** Paid ads are one of the most commonly used ways to increase brand awareness, generate leads, and drive sales. Each ads channel should be treated as a marketing channel.

- » **Website traffic from search engine optimization (SEO):** Search engines, like Google and Bing, are more than just tools for finding fast answers to your burning questions, like "Which came first — the chicken or the egg?" From a business and marketing perspective, in fact, search engines are useful tools that should be utilized and optimized in your company's favor to increase brand awareness, leads, and sales. Within omnichannel analytics, SEO traffic sources are definitely treated as a marketing channel.

- » **Website traffic from social media:** Your company's social media accounts are a primary touchpoint where brand representatives can interact with customers, create brand awareness, drive leads and even make sales. Within omnichannel analytics, your company's LinkedIn pages, Instagram pages, Facebook pages, and the rest — should each be treated as a separate marketing channel.

- » **Live events:** Most companies use live events as a way to increase brand awareness and word-of-mouth marketing as well as to generate a fresh set of warm leads. Regardless of whether you treat them as sales channels, all live events should be treated as marketing channels.

- » **Referral sites:** If your company offers engaging, free blog content on its website, if it has affiliate partnerships, or if it throws an occasional sales event, you should see some *referral sites* — referral traffic that's coming from other websites on the Internet — within your web analytics. These referral sites should be treated as marketing channels subject to omnichannel analytics.

Building analytics around channel performance

To build an effective omnichannel analytics strategy, you need access to data from a variety of sources. For sales channels, you need financial data that reflects the total dollar amounts of sales as well as details about where those sales were generated. Keep in mind that, if your company is running ads, the ad costs should be subtracted from the revenues generated along each channel in order to paint a more accurate picture of channel performance with respect to leads and sales per dollar invested into ads.

For marketing channels, you can rely heavily on Google Analytics for tracking how your online marketing channels are performing with respect to the behavior of website visitors, and how well each social or referral network is generating leads and sales. Unfortunately, evaluating your marketing channels isn't as simple as just looking at your Google Analytics data. You also need to lean on your social media analytics that are provided by each of the social platforms separately, or a third-party vendor that provides the intel to you. Lastly, for any live marketing events, you have to gather follow-up statistics from the marketing personnel in charge of the event.

REMEMBER

The purpose of omnichannel analytics is to support your company in providing your customers with different experiences on a channel-by-channel basis. The idea here is to allow you to cater to your customers' expectations and personalize their experience with your company. This type of personalization goes a long way in terms of creating brand trust.

Scoring your company's channels

Analyzing your current sales-and-marketing strategy means you'll be able to identify where your customers are coming from and then assign a score to each channel based on that channel's success. The scorecard you create then serves as a visual representation of the current importance of your various channels, relative to one another. The scores also help you identify and improve underperforming customer touchpoints. Armed with this knowledge, you can optimize and improve your marketing and sales strategy. Your overall strategy will not only make more sense but also provide a data-informed foundation for improving the ROI of your future multichannel marketing and sales campaigns.

You can go about scoring your sales channels in a number of ways, but I've created a simplified 5-step approach, just to give you a quick snapshot of what's involved. Here goes:

1. Map your channels.

Itemize all channels through which sales are generated. I discuss this step in the earlier section "Mapping your channels."

2. Score your channels.

Evaluate each of those channels and score them out, based on the characteristics of customers they generate. Important metrics to look at here may include these:

a. *Customer lifetime value*

Machine learning comes to the rescue when generating accurate LTV forecasts.

b. *Customer reviews and satisfaction metrics*

c. *Upsell, downsell, and subscription renewal rates*

d. *Ticket volume*

e. *Customer profitability*

These metrics help you understand the quality of the customers that are coming through each of your sales channels. Just looking at these metrics alone can help you identify areas of opportunity, as well as areas to avoid, if you want to attract better customers for your business.

3. Create a channel scorecard.

Summarize your findings for each of the metrics by creating a scorecard for each channel.

4. Define a customer avatar for each channel.

A customer avatar is a data-infused description of a company's ideal client — it describes both their demographic and their psychographic. Define your customer avatar by using your scorecard alongside behavioral analytics for each of your channels, making sure to also consider known attributes of existing customers within these channels, to make some educated guesses about what types of customers fit into each of the channels in your channel portfolio.

5. Tweak your sales-and-marketing strategy.

Looking at this customer avatar along with each channel scorecard, decide which changes you can make to improve a particular channel's performance so that it better supports your company's overall sales strategy and goals.

Figure 11-1 shows a sample of what your channel scorecard might look like after you've completed this 5-step process.

Scorecard Update for March 2021

	LinkedIn	**Search**	**Instagram**	**Email**
CONTENT PREFERENCES	Images, Mini-Trainings, Personal Stories	Coding Demonstrations, Long-Form Embedded Videos, Mini-Trainings	Photos, Personal Philosophy Posts, Personal Stories, Mini-Trainings	Quick Bytes on Professional and Business Topics
CONTENT DISLIKES	Long-Form Video, Announcements Promotional Content	General Tech FYI Content, Podcasts	Long-Form Video, Announcements Start-Up Advice	Revenue-Generation Topics, Promotional Content
CURRENT CHANNEL SCORE	C	A	A	A

FIGURE 11-1:
A channel scorecard.

Unfortunately, there is no exact, cut-and-dried formula to use for assigning a score to a particular channel. You really need to dig into your channel numbers and determine why particular channels are generating the most leads and sales — these metrics should be weighted in importance. Then look to see how that success is reflected in the channel data in terms of customer engagement statistics with your channels. Based on the numbers you collect for each channel, you then need to assign a relative score for all your sales-and-marketing channels.

TIP

I've left a handy Channel Scorecard Calculator template you can use to get started over on the companion website for this book at `http://businessgrowth.ai`.

What can scoring your company's channels in this way do to improve your company's sales-and-marketing strategy (and thus your company's bottom line)? I'm glad you asked. Here are the main advantages:

>> **Customer acquisition:** When you fine-tune your marketing strategy so that it aligns better with your customer desires and expectations along each channel, your marketing ROI immediately increases, as does the revenue associated with each new customer acquisition of new customer acquisitions from leads you're nurturing along each of those channels.

>> **Customer retention:** Fine-tuning your sales-and-marketing strategy so that your company keeps on pulse with changes and the evolution of its customer desires helps keep your existing customers coming back for more — driving an uptick in repeat purchases and word-of-mouth marketing.

>> **New product or service development:** By scoring your channels in the way I've just discussed, you have a much more granular view of your customer and their preferences. This perspective is, of course, helpful in designing products and services that your customers need, want, and adore.

Building Data Products That Increase Sales-and-Marketing ROI

Marketing optimization is one of the more popular use cases for data products. Unlike 30 years ago when 99 percent of products were tangible goods, today the word *product* has come to represent a wide variety of assets, including these:

>> **Tangible goods:** A tangible good is a physical item that is bought and sold on the open market.

>> **Software:** This one includes stand-alone applications, Software as a Service (SaaS) products, and even templates that are built on top of SaaS products.

>> **Software features:** In this context, a software feature is a functional unit within a software package that satisfies a business or user requirement. If you have product management experience, you're already aware that a feature is the product when you're managing software products.

>> **Digital products**: This category includes all forms of information products that come in electronic format, such as customized calculators, dashboards, courses, e-books, PDF documents, and slide decks.

When I talk about *data products*, I'm referring to monetizable products that are derived directly from any combination of data resources, technologies, and skill sets. Data products are a popular way to monetize data — a topic I cover in greater detail in Chapter 14. To name a few types of data products out there:

» **Software and software features:** Any sort of data-intensive software would qualify as a data product. This of course includes software packages that are exclusively designed for machine learning, data visualization, data clean-up, and so on. Most software these days includes at least some predictive AI or data visualization components. Regardless of what the rest of the software does, these features would themselves qualify as data products.

» **Digital products and certain tangible goods:** This includes all forms of digital products that rely heavily on data resources, technologies, or skill sets.

REMEMBER

A data product manager is someone who uses data science to generate predictive insights that better inform decision-making around product design, development, launch, and strategy. Because a data product manager uses data expertise to improve products in this way, you can get away with calling the products they manage *data products* regardless of the data resources and technologies that play a part in the product development and delivery.

Popular marketing data products include the obvious ones like Google Analytics and Adobe Analytics, but also less-obvious data products like marketing dashboards, data-intensive custom marketing strategies and plans, and even the social analytics features inside your social media accounts that tell you how your posts are performing. If you're curious how to go about using data and data expertise to build better marketing products and services, pay close attention to the first three chapters in Part 4.

TIP

In my own business, I use Google Data Studio and Segmetrics, both powerful yet affordable marketing analytics products. To make a free copy of the Google Data Studio templates I recommend, be sure to check out the Google Data Studio Template Recommendations on this book's website at http://businessgrowth.ai.

Increasing Profit Margins with Marketing Mix Modeling

You could say that *marketing mix modeling* (MMM) involves, in its simplest form, using machine learning methods on sales-and-marketing data to predict what combination of product features and marketing methods will directly result in the most sales. MMM is one of the most powerful marketing data science use cases today, but it ain't cheap.

Unless you hire a data scientist that specializes in MMM, or learn to do it yourself, the benefits of MMM are constrained mostly to larger companies with bigger marketing budgets that have sufficient allowances for costly vendor solutions. MMM's high costs are caused by several factors, the largest of which is the amount of manual data science work that's required. Several solution providers have built software solutions to help minimize the amount of work, but MMM is simply too complex to expect a SaaS solution to come in and do all the analytical work for you. My plan for this section is to give you a head start on figuring out how to do MMM in-house for your company.

Collecting data on the four Ps

When I talk about optimizing a marketing mix for more sales, what I'm talking about is identifying the exact mixture of product, place, promotion, and price — otherwise known in marketing as *the four Ps* — that are responsible for producing the most sales. The main thing you need to know about the *marketing mix* is that it should contain a mixture of features that are reflective of both your product and your marketing methods and that those features should be directly relevant to how well that product sells. Because the four Ps will comprise the variable in your machine learning models, it pays to look at each of them a little closer.

Inspecting important product features

The *product* here is, of course, the product you want to sell. In analyzing your product, you want to make sure it's high-quality and easy to use and exceeds the buyer's expectations. If your product is no good, it doesn't matter how you price or promote it — your buyers will be unhappy, sales will falter, and selling it will eventually tarnish your company's brand.

TIP

If you're selling services, you can technically use a service package as the product here. In that case, you'll probably want to extend to a *seven Ps* approach by adding variables that represent *process*, *people*, and *physical evidence*.

Playing with the price aspect

Price here is simply the price at which you sell your product. You can find lots of different pricing strategies out there, but the main thing to remember here is that you don't want to be in a race to the bottom. The price should reflect the value that the product provides its buyer as well as how much supply exists to meet its demand. Rather than lower prices, look for ways to increase the value of the product and improve your marketing messaging to enhance the product's positioning.

Generally, as prices increase, sales volumes decrease — so your distribution numbers (as represented by your *place* variables) would decrease. Simple math can tell you, however, that you can still end up seeing an increase in sales revenues anyway. That's one of the reasons it's important to include both price and distribution in the marketing mix.

REMEMBER

From my experience, and the experience of the countless entrepreneurs who've mentored me, when you drop prices, you tend to attract more sales with fewer marketing requirements, but the buyers are generally higher-maintenance customers. Under-pricing your offer erodes the profitability of the product because you draw more customers who all tend to require more support services — which has to be paid for out of the operations budget. In this case, the distribution numbers (as represented by your place variables) can go up, but the price would go down and the overall profitability of this product for your company would suffer. Obviously, this is a situation you want to avoid.

Placing your product

With respect to the place variable, I'm talking about the place where the sale was made and the place where the product is distributed to its buyer. So, if you have a digital business, the place is nearly equivalent to the sales channel. But if you're in retail and have a brick-and-mortar store in addition to an e-commerce store, place would designate the actual location where the sales and product distributions are made.

Promoting your offer

Promotion technically refers to how your company makes potential customers aware that the product is available for purchase. This often includes avenues such as organic marketing, paid ads, press releases, and how your brand appears in search engine results. Promotion is the vehicle by which these tactics are communicated to customers in order to produce an increase in sales.

Implementing marketing mix modeling

Simply put, machine learning for MMM involves deploying both linear and non-linear regression methods on product, marketing, and sales time-series. As with any other machine learning method, you start by selecting appropriate variables. (For more on regression methods, see Chapter 4.)

You use a regression method, so you need to select response and explanatory variables. Good options for response variables in MMM include these:

>> Number of sales, represented as a count

>> Sales revenue, in dollar amount

When it comes to explanatory variables, you need to select features that truly represent how each of the four Ps behaves. (To keep this description concise, I've listed these features in order of decreasing impact on total sales.)

Here are four good ways to represent product in a marketing mix model:

>> Product quality in terms of the quality of components that comprise it, represented as a percentage (%) of a desirable attribute

>> Product quality in terms of durability, represented as a count of the product life span in days

>> Product quality in terms of conformance to manufacturing requirements, represented with a *risk priority number (RPN)* — a numerical score that represents the risk associated with a manufacturing process and the steps that comprise it. These processes should conform to manufacturing specifications. When they don't, you get a higher RPN, and a greater risk of product defects.

>> Product newness, represented as a count of the number of days on the market

The place variable generally refers to distribution, so you'd want to explore representing it in any of the following ways:

>> Distribution volume, represented as the total number of units distributed and available for sale per location or per unit time — for example, per day, month, or quarter, depending on the time interval you'd like to use to represent the distribution volume.

>> Distribution in terms of the number of units purchased total, represented as a count

>> Distribution in terms of the number of units purchased per location, represented as a count per location

To represent price within the model, here are a few features to explore:

>> Unit cost, in dollar amount

>> Spending per customer, in dollar amount per sale

>> Product discount, in dollar amount or percentage (%)

And lastly, to represent promotion within the model, you need to home in on the activities your company engages in to increase product awareness and sales. Here are some features you might include:

>> Number of promotions

>> Cost per traditional promotion, in dollar amount, for TV ad spend, print ads, or outdoor campaigns, for example

>> Cost per digital promotion, in dollar amount, for Facebook or Instagram ads, Twitter ads, or paid search ads, for example

Unfortunately, if you want to take a single online course or read a comprehensive book on how to implement MMM, you won't find any yet. The good news is that you can learn for free if you're willing to use Google Search to track down a set of free online resources, like the one hosted over on the open-source R documentation website at https://rpubs.com/nihil0/mmm01.

TIP

I've compiled an entire listing of MMM learning resources for both R and Python. You can access that listing over on the website for this book, at http://businessgrowth.ai.

Increasing profitability with MMM

Because the entire point of MMM is to quantify direct relationships between your marketing mix and sales for your business, not much room remains for conflating the profitability issue. Once you've identified statistically (and economically) significant relationships between your marketing mix and actual sales for the business, you can reliably predict what marketing mix will produce even more sales — and then adjust your company's future marketing plans for improved ROI.

Chapter **12**

Enabling Improved Decision-Making

Business and data science are both complex topics in their own rights. You can easily find yourself getting caught up looking at the bark on the trees and accidentally forgetting to look for a way out of the forest. That's why, with each new data project, it's extremely important to stay focused on the goal. Ultimately, no matter the business function or industry you support, true north is always the same: business profit growth. Whether you achieve it by creating greater efficiencies or increasing sales rates and customer loyalty, the goal is to create a more stable, solid profit-growth rate for your business. In this chapter, I focus on showing you how to use data to increase business profit by improving decision support at your company.

Improving Decision-Making

Before discussing how to use data to help improve decision-making, it pays to take a closer look at decision support systems and whom they benefit. A *decision support system* is an information system that's capable of converting complex, raw data into data insights that inform business decision makers about the health of their operations and units. Back in the olden days, decision support products were only provided to business leaders, managers, and executives. These products fed them the intel they needed to make decisions on behalf of their companies. Nowadays, however, things have changed: Rapid innovation in data science and AI have made it relatively easy to improve decision support for workers at all levels of the business. The focus of this chapter is to explain how you can use data science, data analytics, and business intelligence to improve decision support for employees who serve in a wide variety of functions at businesses in all industries.

REMEMBER

Within the decision support route, it doesn't matter so much whether you're using business intelligence, analytics, or data science — the process of moving from raw data to improved business profit is similar. That process is mapped out in Figure 12-1.

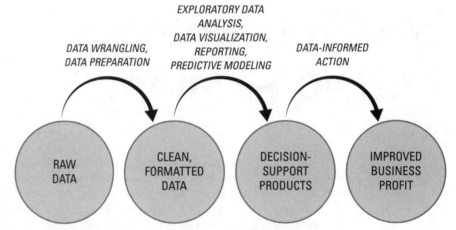

FIGURE 12-1:
The data-to-dollars flowchart.

As shown in the data-to-dollars flowchart in Figure 12-1, you always start with raw messy data, which you then need to clean and reformat in order to produce a meaningful result. Once it's ready, you can build data products that support and improve employees' decision-making at your company. The goal of this improved decision-making is, of course, to increase profits for the business — in other words, bring in more money, waste less money, or generate new revenue streams altogether. In a case study featured later in this chapter, you can see how data science was used to create decision support AI that resulted in improved customer satisfaction, thereby decreasing customer churn and driving up the customer lifetime value (the total revenue per customer, in other words).

Barking Up the Business Intelligence Tree

Between business intelligence, data analytics, and data science, business intelligence is the simplest way to support decision-making, so let's start there. In all honesty, until about 2013, the decision support function fell squarely within the responsibility of *business intelligence (BI)*, which I can handily define for you as the practice of transforming raw, historical business data into meaningful reports, data visualizations, and dashboards that decision-makers can use to guide them in deciding how to proceed to reach the business's goals. Within BI, business analysts (folks I discuss thoroughly in Chapter 9) use business intelligence tools to generate *descriptive analytics* — analytics based on historical and current data that seek to answer the question, "What happened in the near or distant past?" The goal of BI decision support products is to help decision-makers decide the next-best course of action based on what happened in the past.

The process by which business intelligence is useful in transforming raw data to improved profits is shown in Figure 12-2.

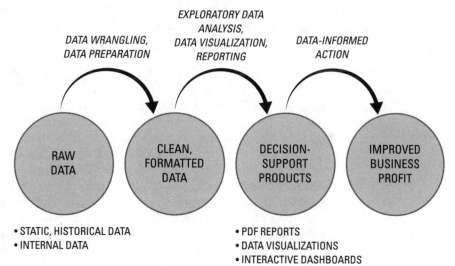

FIGURE 12-2: The business intelligence path within the data-to-dollars flowchart.

Four characteristics that help you distinguish BI from data analytics and data science — its more sophisticated cousins— are that BI generally involves these elements:

>> **Historical, static data:** Most traditional BI tools are designed to generate decision support products from existing data sets that sit inside structured RDBMSs or .csv files or within an Excel spreadsheet. They don't support

real-time data, moving data, unstructured data, or messy data. Data sets must be cleaned, transformed, and settled into a static data container before you can use traditional BI tools to generate decision support products from it.

>> **Internal data:** Traditional BI utilizes *internal* data — data that's generated as a by-product of your company's operations or that's generated from systems that your company runs in the course of doing business.

>> **Mostly small and medium-size data sets:** Traditional BI tools don't accommodate huge data sets. If you want to generate BI products from huge data sets, you need to wrangle and reformat the data to smoosh it down to the size your tool can accommodate. (I have more on data-wrangling later in this chapter.)

>> **Tools, technologies, and skill sets:** Certain keywords are a dead giveaway that someone is doing BI. Examples here are online analytical processing, ETL (extracting, transforming, and loading data from one database into another), data-warehousing, and information technology for business applications.

Figure 12-3 shows my favorite BI reporting tool that is used in my business, Segmetrics. (I use many BI reporting tools, but this is my favorite tool for rectifying marketing activities with their return on investment in terms of leads and sales for my business.)

Notice that this tool provides time stamps indicating when its source data was last updated. I've set up this BI tool so that, every two hours, it pulls structured data from various marketing and sales systems within my business. More specifically, it pulls *only* the most crucial sales and marketing data that I need from within these systems and leaves out all the rest. After that's done, it serves up the BI reports to me on a silver platter — interactive data tables, bar and line charts, and drill-downs. In this case, I am the business decision-maker, so I use the tool directly, but if I weren't technically oriented and had a data analyst helping me, the tool would provide that person with easy-to-use features for generating PDF reports or pulling the data in .csv format for their own analytical needs. The best thing about this tool is that it comes preconfigured. I spent 5 minutes hooking up my data sources and it was ready to roll. Pretty cool, huh?

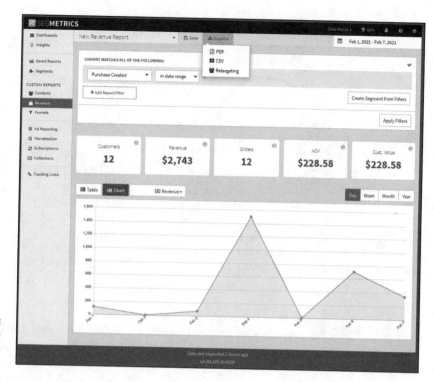

FIGURE 12-3:
An example
of a modern,
SaaS BI tool.

Using Data Analytics to Support Decision-Making

When you're on the quest to help support and improve decision-making across a company, data science is usually an unnecessarily complex route. In most cases, you can gain the insights you need faster by just using an analytics or business intelligence tool. In this section, I talk about how data analytics can still fit into the journey between raw, messy data and the dollars generated for your business. Similar to BI, *data analytics* is the practice of converting raw data to a usable format and then analyzing it to generate answers to business questions. The few notable differences between BI and analytics are shown in Figure 12-4.

Analytics are different from BI in several ways, as this list makes clear.

>> **Support both real-time data and historical, static data:** Analytics tools and techniques are more robust and sophisticated than traditional BI. You can use them to generate meaningful insights from real-time data moving through your systems as well as from existing data that sits static in a RDBMS.

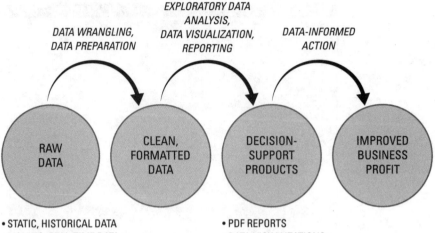

DATA WRANGLING,
DATA PREPARATION

EXPLORATORY DATA
ANALYSIS,
DATA VISUALIZATION,
REPORTING

DATA-INFORMED
ACTION

RAW
DATA

CLEAN,
FORMATTED
DATA

DECISION-
SUPPORT
PRODUCTS

IMPROVED
BUSINESS
PROFIT

FIGURE 12-4:
The analytics
path within the
data-to-dollars
flowchart.

- STATIC, HISTORICAL DATA
- MOVING, REAL-TIME DATA
- INTERNAL AND EXTERNAL DATA

- PDF REPORTS
- DATA VISUALIZATIONS
- INTERACTIVE ANALYTICS TOOLS

>> **Integrate external and internal data:** A key feature of analytics is that they can accommodate for, and generate insights from, external data — data that's highly relevant to your business but isn't generated from within your business directly.

>> **Can be generated from any size data set, even if it's unstructured:** Because analytics are more sophisticated, you can build them inside, or on top of, all sorts of software environments, allowing you to create meaningful data visualizations from data of almost any volume and variety.

>> **Big data tools, technologies, and skill sets:** Keywords that tend to represent data analytics include *Hive, Pig, Spark, big data, machine learning, predictive analytics, NoSQL, MongoDB, online analytical processing (OLAP),* and *SAP Analytics.*

The goal of analytics decision support products is to inform decision-makers about what happened in the past as well as what's happening now so that they can use that information to make better decisions on behalf of their companies and hopefully increase their profitability. An excellent example of what a quintessential analytics tool looks like is shown in Figures 12-5 and 12-6.

You might immediately recognize Google Analytics (GA) here, because it's one of the more popular data analytics tools. Part of that popularity lies in the fact that it offers real-time analytics about live activity on any web property where you've installed the GA tracking pixel. This tracking pixel collects website activity data and feeds it to the GA application. Additionally, GA integrates and generates analytics from relevant external data sources. (Refer to Figure 12-6.)

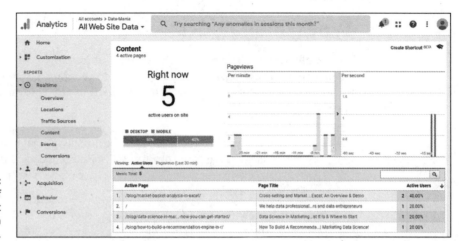

FIGURE 12-5:
An example of analytics that report on real-time data.

FIGURE 12-6:
An example of analytics that report on external data.

REMEMBER

GA is free and relatively easy to set up, but it can at times provide you with so much information that you end up distracted from the business goal you've set for yourself. A nice feature of this tool is that it provides externally sourced data — in the case of Figure 12-6, it's providing some detailed analytics about the interests of website visitors.

Types of analytics

Data analytics isn't a one-size-fits-all kind of enterprise — you have choices when it comes to the analytics type you want to generate. Listed here, in order of increasing complexity, are the four standard types (or *categories*) of data analytics:

- » **Descriptive analytics:** This one answers the question, "What happened?" Descriptive analytics are based on historical and current data. Business analysts, data analysts, and data scientists all base modern-day business intelligence on descriptive analytics.

- » **Diagnostic analytics:** You use this type of analytics to find answers to the question, "Why did this particular something happen?" or "What went wrong?" Diagnostic analytics are useful for deducing and inferring the success or failure of subcomponents of any data-driven initiative.

- » **Predictive analytics:** Although this type of analytics is based on historical and current data, predictive analytics go one step further than descriptive analytics. Predictive analytics can be generated using the correlation methods I mention in Chapter 4, and this simpler type of predictive analytics can be built by data analysts. More sophisticated predictive analytics involve complex model-building and analysis to predict a future event or trend. In a business context, these more sophisticated analyses would be generally performed by the data scientist.

- » **Prescriptive analytics:** This type of analytics aims to optimize processes, structures, and systems through informed action that's based on predictive analytics — essentially telling you what you should do based on an informed estimation of what will happen. Both business analysts and data scientists can generate prescriptive analytics, but their methods and data sources differ.

REMEMBER

Ideally, a business should engage in all four types of data analytics, but prescriptive analytics is where you can offer the most direct form of decision support.

Common challenges in analytics

Analytics commonly pose at least two challenges in the business enterprise: First, organizations often have difficulty finding new hires with analytics skills; second, even skilled analysts often have difficulty communicating complex insights in a way that makes intuitive sense to management decision makers.

To overcome these challenges, your organization must create and nurture a culture that values and accepts analytics products. The business must work to increase data literacy across all levels of the organization so that management not only has a basic concept of analytics but is also capable of seeing the successes that can be achieved by making well-informed decisions based on them. Conversely, data analysts and scientists must have a solid working knowledge about business in general and, in particular, a solid understanding of the business at hand. (For more on the need for a solid working knowledge of business, see Chapter 9.)

Data wrangling

Data-wrangling is another important portion of the work that's required in order to have data yield decision-support insights. To build analytics from raw data, you almost always need to use *data-wrangling* — the processes and procedures you have to use in order to clean and convert data from one format and structure to another so that the data is accurate and in the format that analytics tools and scripts require for consumption. The following list highlights a few of the practices and issues I consider most relevant when it comes to data-wrangling:

>> **Data extraction:** You have to first identify which data sets are relevant to the problem at hand and then extract sufficient quantities of the data that's required to solve the problem. (This extraction process is commonly referred to as *data mining.*)

>> **Data preparation:** Data preparation involves cleaning the raw data extracted via data mining and then converting it into a format that allows for a more convenient consumption of the data. (Six steps are involved, as you can see at the end of this section.)

>> **Data governance:** Data governance standards are used as a quality control measure to ensure that manual and automated data sources conform to the data standards of the model at hand. Data governance standards must be applied so that the data is at the right granularity when it's stored and made ready for use.

REMEMBER

Granularity is a measure of a data set's level of detail. It is determined by the relative size of the subgroupings into which the data is divided. For instance, if you're measuring brand loyalty for a certain product in the US is it going to be coarse-grained at the state or national level, or more fine-grained by neighborhood or ZIP code?

>> **Data architecture:** IT architecture is the key. If your data is isolated in separate, fixed repositories — those infamous data silos everybody complains about — then it's available to only a few people within a particular line of business. Siloed data structures result in scenarios where a majority of an organization's data is simply unavailable for use by most other people working in the company. (Needless to say, siloed data structures are incredibly wasteful and inefficient.)

TIP

When preparing to analyze data and generate decision support insights, be sure to follow this 6-step data preparation process:

1. **Import.**

   Read relevant data sets into your application.

2. **Clean.**

   Remove strays, duplicates, and out-of-range records, and also standardize casing.

3. **Transform.**

   In this step, you treat missing values, deal with outliers, and scale your variables.

4. **Process.**

   Processing your data involves data parsing, recoding of variables, recombining variables, and other methods of reformatting the data set to prepare it for analysis.

5. **Log the data.**

   In this step, you simply create a record that describes the data set. This record should include descriptive statistics, information that describes variable formats, the data source, collection methods, and more. Once you generate this log, store it in a place you'll remember, in case you need to share these details with other users of the processed data set.

6. **Back it up.**

   The last data preparation step is to store a backup of this processed data set so that you have a clean, fresh version — no matter what.

Increasing Profit Margins with Data Science

At its core, the process of progressing from raw data to improved business profits is the same for data science as it is for analytics and business intelligence. You can see some important distinctions, though, in Figure 12-7.

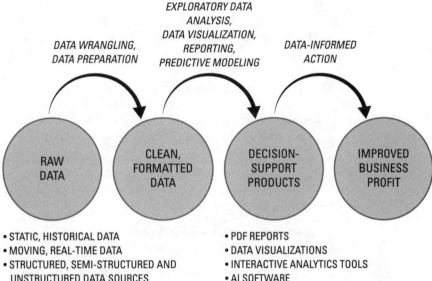

DATA WRANGLING,
DATA PREPARATION

EXPLORATORY DATA
ANALYSIS,
DATA VISUALIZATION,
REPORTING,
PREDICTIVE MODELING

DATA-INFORMED
ACTION

RAW
DATA

CLEAN,
FORMATTED
DATA

DECISION-
SUPPORT
PRODUCTS

IMPROVED
BUSINESS
PROFIT

FIGURE 12-7:
The data science
path within the
data-to-dollars
flowchart.

- STATIC, HISTORICAL DATA
- MOVING, REAL-TIME DATA
- STRUCTURED, SEMI-STRUCTURED AND
  UNSTRUCTURED DATA SOURCES
- INTERNAL AND EXTERNAL DATA

- PDF REPORTS
- DATA VISUALIZATIONS
- INTERACTIVE ANALYTICS TOOLS
- AI SOFTWARE

Though the process is the same, with data science you can actually codify a decision engine and deploy it within a software product. This means that, in addition to producing PDF reports, data visualizations, and interactive analytics tools, data scientists are able to generate predictive insights that support decision-makers directly, by way of a software application. (In all honesty, you almost certainly need a software developer and a machine learning engineer to help with the software side of the equation if you really want to make that happen.) You can then deploy this decision engine on many people's machines across your company, thus enabling you to use one solution to improve decision-making for many workers. What's more, you can take that same solution and sell access to it as a new product — thus generating new revenue streams on top of the improved revenues you're generating from better decision support systems. (For more on monetizing data, check out Chapter 14.)

REMEMBER

If you have large sets of structured and unstructured data that may (or may not) be complete and you want to convert that data into improved decision support, you'll want to call on a data scientist.

Seeing which kinds of data are useful when using data science for decision support

You can use data science to derive business insights from standard-size sets of structured business data (just like BI) or from structured, semistructured, and unstructured sets of big data. Data science solutions aren't confined to transactional data that sits in a relational database; you can use data science to create valuable decision support products from all available data sources, including these:

>> **Transactional business data:** A tried-and-true data source, transactional business data is the type of structured data used in traditional BI. It includes management data, customer service data, sales and marketing data, operational data, and employee performance data.

>> **Social data related to the brand or business:** The data covered by this rubric includes the unstructured data generated from email, instant messaging, and social networking such as Twitter, Facebook, LinkedIn, Pinterest, or Instagram.

>> **Machine data from business operations:** Machines automatically generate this unstructured data, like SCADA data, machine data, or sensor data.

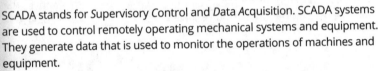

SCADA stands for *Supervisory Control and Data Acquisition*. SCADA systems are used to control remotely operating mechanical systems and equipment. They generate data that is used to monitor the operations of machines and equipment.

>> **Audio, video, image, and PDF file data:** These well-established formats are all sources of unstructured data. In the case study at the end of this chapter, you can see an incredible example of using data science to convert raw audio data to real-time decision support that decreases customer churn and increases customer lifetime value.

The type of data you should use depends on the use case you're implementing.

You may have heard of *dark data* — operational data that most organizations collect and store but then never use. Storing this data and then not using it is pure detriment to a business. On the other hand, with a few sharp data scientists and data engineers on staff, the same business can use this data resource for optimization, security, marketing, business processes, and more. If your company has dark data, someone should go ahead and turn the light on.

As with most topics, it's easier to show than to tell, so I've come up with a decision support use case for you to check out that utilizes data science and artificial intelligence to increase the lifetime value of customers. The next section gives the details.

Directing improved decision-making for call center agents

Data scientists build predictive models that convert real-time unstructured data into instantaneous real-time prescriptive analytics from within a software application that can be installed on an unlimited number of computers. I start off this particular discussion with a success story case study and then follow it up with the business and technology specifics that can support it.

Case study: Improving call center operations

Humana, which has provided health insurance to Americans for over 50 years, is a service company focused on fulfilling the needs of its customers. A great deal of Humana's success as a company rides on customer satisfaction, and the frontline of that battle for customers' hearts and minds is Humana's customer service center.

From an operational perspective, call centers are hard to get right. Many emotions rise to the surface during a customer service call, especially one relating to health or health insurance. Sometimes people are frustrated, sometimes they're upset, and sometimes the customer service agent (CSA) becomes aggravated and the overall tone and progression of the phone call go downhill, which is of course horrible for customer satisfaction.

THE NEED

Humana wanted to find a way to use artificial intelligence to monitor its phone calls and to help its CSAs do a better job of connecting with customers in order to improve customer satisfaction (and thus, customer retention rates and profit per customer).

THE ACTION

In light of its business need, Humana worked with Cogito, a company that specializes in voice analytics technology. Cogito offers a piece of AI technology called Cogito Dialogue, which has been trained to identify certain conversational cues as a way of helping the CSA and their supervisor stay actively engaged in a call with a customer. The AI listens to cues like the customer's voice pitch: If it's rising or if the CSA and the customer "talk over" each other, the dialogue tool sends out electronic alerts to the CSA during the call.

Humana fed the dialogue tool the customer service data from ten thousand calls and allowed it to analyze cues such as keywords, interruptions, and pauses, and then these cues were then linked with specific outcomes. For example, a representative who is receiving a particular type of cue is likely to earn a specific customer satisfaction result.

THE OUTCOME

Thanks to the data science project I outline in this section, Humana enjoyed a 28 percent increase in customer satisfaction and a 63 percent increase in employee engagement. From a revenue perspective, this project produced a net decrease in customer churn, and consequently, a significant increase in customer lifetime value. From a productivity perspective, this project improved both the employee engagement and the number of high-satisfaction outcomes per employee.

Customers were happier, and CSAs were more engaged. This automated solution for data analysis has now been deployed in 200 Humana call centers, and the company plans to roll it out to 100 percent of its centers. The initiative was so successful that Humana has been able to focus on the next steps in its data program. The company now plans to begin predicting the type of calls that are likely to remain unresolved so that they can forward those calls to management before they become frustrating to the customer and CSA alike.

What does Humana's success mean for you and your company? Well, if you're looking for new ways to generate value by improving decision support for personnel at your company, this is proof that the perfect data use case is out there somewhere to show you how! It's definitely worth taking a deeper look into the types of tools, technologies, and techniques that are running under the hood of this example. That's where the use cases come in handy. Because this particular data project involves both customer sentiment analysis and decision support, you can see separate reconstructed business use cases for both aspects, shown in Table 12-1 and Table 12-2.

TABLE 12-1 **Theoretical Business Use Case for Analyzing Customer Sentiment**

A: Business use case
Use case 1: Analyze customer sentiment
B1: Description
The system analyzes the sentiments of customers and CSAs who communicate by phone. The system collects data and generates reports. The aim is better customer retention and improved quality of customer handling.
B2: Actors
Primary actor: System
Supporting actors • Customer • CSA

B3: Preconditions and post-conditions

Preconditions

- Customer places call to the CSA.

- Interaction between the customer and the CSA happens over a phone call.

Post-conditions

- Collect data on customer sentiment and CSA call behavior.

- Generate reports on key call issues and key call parameters.

C: Main success scenario

Actor intention (basic flow)

1. The customer and CSA establish contact via call or text.

2. The system captures data points for sentiment analysis. For a call, collected data points include these:

    - Speech style

    - Pitch

    - Customer silence times

    - Estimated level of stress in customer's voice

    - Length of call

    - Speed of customer's speech

    - Quality indicators such as intonation or articulation

    - Agent silence times

    - Frequency of speech of agent

    - Agent's manner of speaking (monotonous, overexcited)

    - Overlaps in communication

3. The system analyzes the data collected using models for intent analysis, improvement in real-time communication, and customer engagement.

4. The system also generates a host of reports such as these:

    - Summary of key call issues

    - Call analysis report

Success scenario

Data regarding customer sentiment and CSAs successfully collected, stored, and analyzed

D: Industries and functions

Industries: Finance / credit companies, retail industry, counselling organizations, hospitals

Functions: Customer engagement, customer management, call center operations, counseling, critical care services, medical care services

TABLE 12-2	**Theoretical Business Use Case for Real-Time Decision Support**

A: Business use case

Use case 2 (decision support): Suggest action to CSA

B1: Description

Based on the data collected and analyzed on customer sentiments, the system offers real-time suggestions to arrive at courses of action that the CSA can take.

B2: Actors

Primary actor: System

Supporting actor: CSA

Offstage actor: Customer

B3: Preconditions and post-conditions

Preconditions

- Call-related data is collated and stored.

- AI models generate analysis on data points of the call experience.

Post-conditions

- Offer real-time suggestions to arrive at courses of action the CSA can take.

Actor intention (basic flow)

1. The system provides real-time suggestions to the CSA during the call or while responding via text. Here are some examples of suggestions:

   a. "Sound is tense."

   b. "Speed of speaking is high."

   c. "Overlap: Customer and CSA talking at the same time, which can lead to frustration in the customer."

Success scenario

Real-time suggestions are offered in order to improve call management and customer management.

D: Industries and functions

Industries: Finance or credit companies, retail industry, counseling organizations, hospitals

Functions: Customer engagement, customer management, call center operations, counseling, critical care services, medical care services

Table 12-1 is all about defining the problem in search of a solution — more specifically, a data intensive solution. Table 12-2 spells out the decision support component of this particular data science project.

Tables are nice, but sometimes an illustration gets the point across quicker. Figure 12-8 breaks things down to a much simpler level by plotting out the use case diagram.

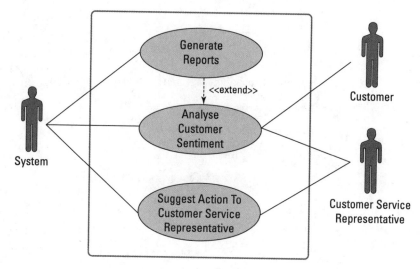

FIGURE 12-8: A business use case diagram for automated decision support AI for call center workers.

As for the data science and technologies that are likely required in order to make a system like this one function smoothly, I detail those in Table 12-3.

Naturally, data scientists and software engineers would be responsible for building the AI application that supports this use case. In this Humana example, however, they outsourced that data science and software engineering to the solution provider, Cogito. Imagine how much money you can save your company — and even *make* for your company — if you're able to build and deploy a system like this one in-house!

Technology Stack	**Data Management**
	Cloud data management:
	Amazon Web Services: Athena
	On-premise / cloud / hybrid data management:
	Big data
	• Apache: Hadoop distributed file system (HDFS), MapReduce
	Traditional data
	• Relational database management systems (RDBMS): PostgreSQL
	Analytics and visualization tools
	• Data visualization: Tableau
	Machine Learning Technologies
	• Predictive modeling programming languages: Python, R, SQL
	• Deep learning: PyTorch, TensorFlow
Data Science Methodologies	• Affective computing algorithms
	• Deep learning
	• Natural language processing

TABLE 12-3   **Theoretical Technology Stack for Automating Client Interactions**

Discovering the tipping point where the old way stops working

I've talked a lot about how business intelligence, analytics, and data science can potentially function to improve decision-making across a company. Now it's time to talk about when it's most appropriate to use each of these approaches. In all honesty, it doesn't matter whether you're a data leader, a data implementer, or a data entrepreneur, you need to know how to use and generate BI and analytics decision support products — even if it's just to support your own decision-making. The good news is that if you're already working with data regularly, BI and analytics are readily available to you without your company needing to sign off on a big budget. For business intelligence decision-support products, you can easily start off by creating them in Excel. As for analytics decision support products, those are a bit more sophisticated, but you can generate real-time analytics by using analytics software such as Tableau or Tableau Desktop.

I'll say it until it sticks: It doesn't matter whether you're a data leader, a data implementer, or a data entrepreneur, you need to know how to use and generate BI and analytics decision support products — even if it's just to support your own decision-making.

A breach of data privacy is a huge financial risk. Unless you've secured someone's official sign-off to use a SaaS tool on your company's data, it's a much better idea to gain permission and have the necessary software installed on your computer. If your company's data becomes breached because you took unauthorized actions to upload it to the cloud, it can be grounds for termination. (For more on data privacy and ethics concerns, check out Chapters 16.)

If you're a data implementor, utilizing machine learning within data science is mission critical. It's easy enough to learn the skills and build machine learning models on your computer, but don't attempt to implement a full-scale data science use case without discussing it with your manager first. If you want to build a little mini-product that demonstrates the power of your data science skills in providing decision support, I'm sure that effort will be well-received by higher-ups. That said, they also don't want you going off on "needless" tangents when you're supposed to be busy with implementation requests they've assigned you. It's advisable to keep them in the loop and stay on-point with what they're requesting of you.

Chapter **13**

Decreasing Lending Risk and Fighting Financial Crimes

The financial services industry is a treasure trove of opportunities for applying data science to achieve massive wins for your business. I start this chapter by showing you how one data scientist won big for himself and his company by pioneering a successful data science use case with his own two hands. After that, I introduce you to a financial use case that requires quite a bit more sophistication, but in exchange offers over a million dollars of ROI per year while protecting the investment marketplace from would-be scamsters.

If you're a data professional in the financial services industry, you're no doubt hearing about risk nearly daily. The good news is that data science offers several viable do-it-yourself options to assist you in your battle against fraud, suspicious behavior, and hidden lending risks. In cases where the scale of the problem is too big, some incredible SaaS solutions out there offer the AI capabilities you need. You're about to see examples of both these approaches.

Decreasing Lending Risk with Clustering and Classification

A data scientist singlehandedly taking down international criminal syndicates in southeast Asia? That may sound dramatic, if you've not yet met Vincent Lee. Vince was a big data and analytics strategy student of mine over in Kuala Lumpur, Malaysia. Technically, he was classified as a senior data analyst, but that didn't stop him from applying the data science strategy he learned in our week together. Within just three short months from that session, he'd built a data strategy plan and successfully executed on it to predict distress within financial institutions that managed the governance of the Central Bank of Malaysia. This use case helped the bank make more accurate predictions about the best bets to take when making federal lending decisions.

How'd Vince do it? After the workshop, he went back to business leaders at his company and spoke to them about the new options he'd learned were available to them. Traditionally, conversations about the data within the bank centered on which tools they should buy, which vendors they should hire, and so on. When Vince returned to his workplace, he began planting the seeds of possibilities within key stakeholders' minds about all the powerful results they could produce on their own with their data in-house. He used the processes covered in Chapters 15, 16, and 17 of this book, and worked with his business leaders to narrow down on a single quick-win data science use case. Vince was wearing his data science leadership hat as he navigated this portion of the journey.

Very quickly, the team was able to select a data science use case that looked extremely promising, given their current situation with respect to data resources, technology, and skillsets. It was then that Vince put on his data science implementation hat and got to work building the solution. Within three months, he'd built a risk analysis solution that was successful in helping lenders identify and avoid the financial risks incurred when they make loans to shaky institutions.

In terms of the data science that Vince used to make this solution work, that's between him and the Central Bank of Malaysia. I can only speak in general terms about how one could use machine learning to do risk analysis. Clustering and classification — both discussed in-depth in Chapter 5 — are the *de facto* go-to methods for both credit scoring, default prediction, and bankruptcy prediction. It can be a challenge to get the data resources you need for this type of evaluation, simply because of the way data privacy laws are set up and the (naturally) sensitive nature of financial data. If you work for a credit or lending institution, though, you probably already have access to all the data you'd need to produce a simple financial risk analysis prototype.

Whatever happened to Vince Lee? With rapid success like his, the Central Bank of Malaysia made a significant investment in him — by not only promoting him to senior data scientist but also sending him to the United States in order to receive his master's degree in analytics, data science at the University of Chicago Graham School of Continuing Liberal and Professional Studies. After earning his degree, he has kept up his fight against international money laundering for the Central Bank of Malaysia, as he continues working his way up the ranks there.

TIP

I managed to land Vince Lee for a podcast episode where he shared his full data career story. You can find it at businessgrowth.ai if you'd like to take a listen.

Preventing Fraud Via Natural Language Processing (NLP)

Natural language processing (NLP) has been proven an effective way to detect, interpret, and prevent fraud, but with that incredible superpower comes a significant threat to personal privacy. In this section, I talk about what NLP is, how it works, and how it's being used to detect and intercept criminal fraud. Following that, I touch lightly on the ethical implications of an AI solution that makes significant use of NLP. For demonstration purposes, I use Synthesys, a legendary SaaS product by Digital Reasoning, as a model.

What actually *is* NLP? The best way to describe it is to say that *NLP* is a computational approach to linguistics where machine learning models are trained to predict, read, and write in a human language. Building on that foundation, NLP uses deep learning to perform *affective computing* — an advanced focus area within data science where technologies are built for the purpose of reading and accurately predicting human emotion, person by person. (Figure 13-1 depicts the process graphically.)

In the case of Synthesys, the program deploys machine learning and patented deep learning neural architectures to deliver speech analytics and *sentiment analysis*, a form of NLP that generates predictions about an individual sentiment when taking an action. (In other words, it predicts their feelings.)

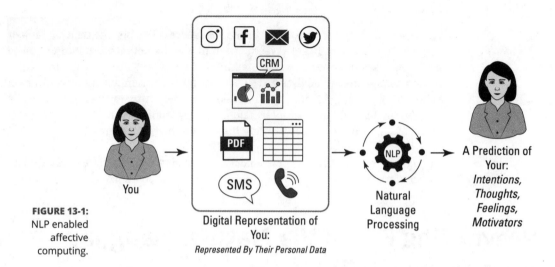

FIGURE 13-1:
NLP enabled affective computing.

Digital Representation of You:
Represented By Their Personal Data

You

Natural Language Processing

A Prediction of Your:
*Intentions,
Thoughts,
Feelings,
Motivators*

In layperson's terms, the Synthesys AI solution consumes data about an individual, perhaps while they're emailing, sending SMS messages, or using social media. The AI solution also consumes voice data from the individual's phone calls, applying NLP to transcribe it to written form for analysis and risk assessment. It consumes data in any spreadsheets, word processing documents, or PDF files an individual might generate. Lastly, the system can integrate any historical customer data a company might have on the individual within its customer relationship management (CRM) software. It then combines, scans, sorts, reads, reasons, and predicts what you're saying, thinking, and meaning, despite any vague references or code words you might use to be more polite or discrete in your word choices.

Translating that to "dataspeak," one would say that Synthesys consumes a virtually unlimited amount of *big data* — structured, unstructured, and semistructured data. This data would be classified as *personal data* — information that "relates to an identifiable live individual," as defined by the European Commission. (I tell you more about this topic in Chapter 16.) That personal data is then *ingested* — loaded, in other words — into a distributed computing environment that has the capacity to analyze 300,000 or more messages per day, per client instance. They call this an *e-surveillance platform*. As for the data storage architecture that supports the platform, it combines persistent storage as well as smart data caching in order to keep up with the accompanying high-paced data processing demands. (See the sentiment analysis flowchart in Figure 13-2.)

Synthesys has its own way of communicating how its NLP process works. It goes like this: Read, resolve, reason. It's a clever approach, so I'm adopting it as a model for discussing the data science that's involved in NLP.

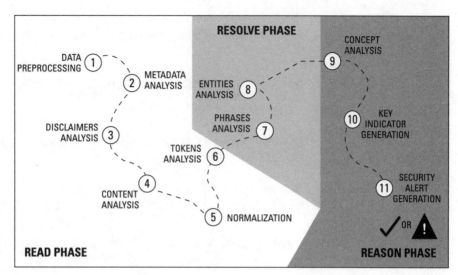

RESOLVE PHASE

FIGURE 13-2:
Sentiment
analysis
flowchart.

During the Read phase, the Synthesys AI solution is reading data associated with whichever individual trader is being overseen by the system. As with any other machine learning project, the first step is always *data preprocessing*. That generally requires the same 6-step process data preparation process I spell out in Chapter 12: Import the data, clean it, standardize it, transform it, process it, document it, and create a backup of it.

Next, the system reads and analyzes *metadata* — the data that describes the data, in other words. This data might describe the location where the data is stored, the data's author, that author's location, time stamps, relevant affiliations and what-have-you from the data sets that have been ingested into the system. Insights generated from metadata are helpful in creating context by providing categories that the system can use to sort and filter the information it generates. An example of metadata is shown in Figure 13-3.

The Digital Reasoning step of disclaimers analysis (refer to Figure 13-2) represents an extra layer of evaluation that's necessary when you're applying NLP to any sort of legal or compliance use case. The disclaimers set the rules for the system, so it knows what to flag as suspicious. *Content analysis* is exactly what it sounds like: the analysis of the user-generated text content that is contained within the data sets that have been ingested into the system.

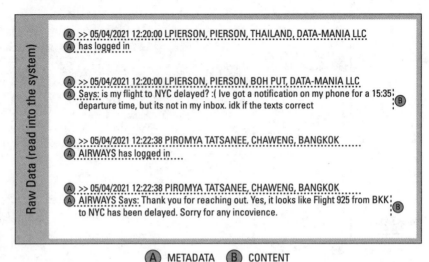

FIGURE 13-3:
An example of
raw data ingested
into an NLP
system.

Normalization is where you preprocess the text you intend to analyze. The standards that are applied in text preprocessing differ between NLP implementations, but, in general, this process involves transforming the text from its raw and imperfect format into a canonical standardized format that the NLP algorithms can use to make predictions. The transformation can involve correcting spelling and grammar errors, converting abbreviations to their long-form equivalents, reformatting casing, transforming emojis into their emotional equivalents, and more. Figure 13-4 provides an example.

is my flight to NYC delayed? :(Ive got a
notification on my phone for a 15:35 departure
time, but its not in my inbox. idk if the texts
correct

thank you for reaching out. Yes, it looks like Flight
925 from BKK to NYC has been delayed. Sorry for
any incovience.

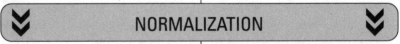

NORMALIZATION

Is my flight to New York City delayed? frown

Thank you for reaching out.

FIGURE 13-4:
An example
of text
normalization.

I have got a notification on my phone for a
15:35 departure time, but it is not in my
inbox. I do not know if the text is correct.

Yes, it looks like Flight 925 from Bangkok to
New York City has been delayed.

I am sorry for any inconvenience.

Token analysis, or *tokenization*, is where you break out the words from within the sentences in the normalized text and start treating them as separate string objects. (For more on string objects, check out Chapter 6.) An example of tokenization is shown in Figure 13-5.

I am sorry for any inconvenience.

"I" "am" "sorry" "for" "any" "inconvenience"

FIGURE 13-5:
An example of
text tokenization.

Within Synthesys's Resolve phase (refer to Figure 13-2), phrase analysis and entity analysis are used to gather context from text. With *phrase analysis*, meaningful phrases from within sentences are identified and broken out. In *entity analysis*, relevant entities — anything from people to places and from companies to titles and everything in between — are broken out and analyzed. Entities are useful for creating context around who and what is relevant within a body of text.

During both phrase and entity analysis, phrases are broken down into three units:

>> **N-gram:** A 1-word monogram

>> **Bi-gram:** A 2-word segment

>> **Tri-gram:** A 3-word combination that represents phrases, entities, concepts, or themes from within the text

Let me explain with an example. From the same sample data set, imagine that you have another conversation that's represented by the following excerpt:

>> "Holy cow"

>> "slow as molasses"

>> "Holy cow! The traffic is slow as molasses. I am never going to make it!"

Table 13-1 shows how these excerpts would be broken down into *n*-grams.

Looking at Table 13-1, you can easily see that monograms aren't helpful for creating meaning from 1-word phrases, but they do help answer questions about who ("I") and what ("traffic", "molasses"). Bi-gram phrases are usually more meaningful. For example, in Table 13-1, we have a "holy cow" phrase that infers a sentiment of surprise that is meaningful in deducing context. Additionally, the "slow as molasses" tri-gram is a phrase that infers that something ("traffic") is extra slow. In the concept analysis phase, the NLP program takes the most meaningful *n*-grams and bridges the gaps between them to deduce what the people who created the sentences were meaning, thinking, and feeling when the text was generated — *sentiment analysis,* in other words. In this phase of concept analysis, the program makes predictions about what's actually happening within the text and publishes indicators and alerts when those predictions are outside the bounds of the law and user policies.

TABLE 13-1: **An Example of *n*-grams in Phrase and Entity Analysis**

Sample Record	Monograms	Bi-grams	Tri-grams
"Holy cow"	cow	holy cow	
	holy		
"slow as molasses"	as	as molasses	slow as molasses
	molasses	slow as	
	slow		
"Holy cow! The traffic is slow as molasses. I am never going to make it!"	am	am never	as molasses I
	as	as molasses	am never going
	cow	cow the	cow the traffic
	going	going to	is slow as
	Holy	holy cow	going to make
	I	I am	holy cow the
	is	is slow	I am never
	it	make it	molasses I am
	to	molasses I	never going to
	make	never going	the traffic is
	molasses	slow as	to make it
	never	to make	traffic is slow
	slow	the traffic	
	The	traffic is	
	traffic		

In terms of the results that NLP technology like Synthesys can achieve for a business, take a look at Figure 13-6, where you can see that Forrester Research, Inc., estimated that Synthesys's NLP solution generated over $4 million in total benefits over three years for a US investment firm that has over $10 billion in assets under management.

TABLE 6 Total Benefits (Risk-Adjusted)							
Ref.	Benefit Category	Initial	Year 1	Year 2	Year 3	Total	Present Value
Atr	Analyst productivity savings	$0	$380,000	$380,000	$380,000	$1,140,000	$945,004
Btr	Savings from reduced downtime	$0	$73,077	$73,077	$73,077	$219,231	$181,731
Ctr	Direct cost avoidance — legacy systems	$0	$475,000	$475,000	$475,000	$1,425,000	$1,181,255
Dtr	Increased business agility — front-office time savings	$0	$181,731	$181,731	$181,731	$545,193	$451,938
Etr	Reduced security risk with lower probability of sanctions	$0	$0	$765,000	$0	$765,000	$632,231
	Total benefits (risk-adjusted)	$0	$1,109,808	$1,874,808	$1,109,808	$4,094,424	$3,392,159

FIGURE 13-6: Forrester's estimated ROI for a client.

Source: Forrester Research, Inc.

TIP

WARNING

Get the full 24-page Forrester Research, Inc., report at the companion site to this book: https://businessgrowth.ai.

There is always a trade-off between risk and reward. A high-risk data strategist would say that you should never bother with a new data science initiative unless you can see (from its use case) that the project is capable of increasing the company's bottom-line by 10-15 percent in one year. I am a professional engineer, so I am naturally more conservative in my technical strategy and planning approaches and, as a result, I do not agree with that rule of thumb. Clearly you want to have a significant ROI on any new projects, but after selecting a lowest-hanging fruit use case (something I show you how to select in Chapter 16), you should always start small — to test it out and make sure you can produce a return quickly and effectively on a small scale, and then look to expand the project's scope after you've gotten traction. A rule of thumb I like is this: If your new data project can increase business profits or save costs within 3 months, with no additional investments into data technologies, resources, or skill sets, then it represents a potential "quick win" for your company. Only after you and your company have several proven "quick wins" under your belt should you look into taking on higher ROI, higher-risk data science initiatives. And when you do, mitigate that risk by following a conservative approach to data science projects, and then look to increase your ROI after you've proven your approach to be fail-proof. The alternative to this is well represented in the great Hadoop debacle of 2012 – 2015 I talk about in Chapter 2.

Okay, now that you know how an NLP system like this one works and how helpful it can be in decreasing illegal fraud, what are your feelings? (Don't worry: I don't use sentiment analysis to determine the answer to that question!) Of course, when a system like this one is applied to reduce illegal activities, we can call that a massive win! But what about the downside risks related to even the mere existence of AI like this? How can you help ensure that it doesn't fall into the wrong hands? What if this type of technology is used for nefarious purposes one day? Does the means justify the end? What can we humans do, if anything, to mitigate that risk? We discuss answers to questions like these in the section about AI ethics in Chapter 15 and 16.

Chapter **14**

Monetizing Data and Data Science Expertise

"Data is the new oil." Clive Humby, a British mathematician and data science entrepreneur, said that all the way back in 2006! What did he know that most didn't? Well, he clearly must have seen the explosive potential for revenue generation that is available via the right combination of data resources, data expertise, and business-building know-how. I discuss Clive later in this chapter, but first I want to acquaint you with the various alternatives when it comes to monetizing data services, data products, and data partnerships. At the end of this chapter, I want to have a serious talk with you about AI ethics and their paramount importance in the survival of the planet, our businesses and societies, and the future of humanity. Make sure not to skip that part!

Setting the Tone for Data Monetization

Data monetization — the direct or indirect sale of data resources, technologies, or skill sets — isn't new *per se,* but what has changed is the variety of formats in which data is being monetized. In 2015, *MIT Technology Review* published a listing of the 50 Smartest Companies in the World. Over a quarter of those companies were *AI companies* — companies heavily dependent on AI to deliver their businesses' products and services. It isn't unreasonable to estimate that, these days, all of the world's smartest companies are in some way dependent on AI to help them in operating, growing, and scaling their business, products, and services.

Over the past several years, online listings and awards of the top AI start-ups have proliferated across the Internet. After spending only a few minutes browsing these listings, you or any other business-savvy data professional can see the obvious bias. Most of these listings only include AI SaaS products, and completely omit any mention of companies that in fact offer AI support but choose not to sell a particular AI SaaS solution — including service-based companies that build custom AI solutions for their clients or other forms of products that support companies in building out their AI products and services. Making matters worse, some of the companies listed as the top AI start-ups aren't even AI companies.

What has happened is that, since about 2017, the term *AI* became the holy grail buzzword that every technology company wanted to claim it offered its customers. And though most of these companies are surely *data companies* — companies that monetize some combination of data resources, technologies, or skill sets — they're not actually AI companies. For a SaaS solution to truly qualify as *artificial intelligence*, it needs to deploy machine learning within a software application, where the software application is the actor and the machine learning engine acts as the internal decision-maker. (For more on the difference between machine learning and AI, see Chapter 3.) Some of the SaaS companies in these listings of the top AI start-ups don't actually deliver any predictive or prescriptive analytics whatsoever — only descriptive analytics, which report what happened in the past. They might be more accurately described as top *BI* companies, but that label isn't *nearly* as sexy. (If all this talk of descriptive analytics and BI has you scratching your head, check out Chapter 12, where I discuss these topics in greater detail.)

Why then are non-AI data companies being highlighted and promoted as top AI companies? Well, I hate to say it, but that situation comes down to these three main factors:

» A widespread deficiency in data literacy

» Potentially questionable marketing alliances

» Investment money (the elephant in the room)

Most technology investors want to see that a company is AI-enabled. And many of these lists of top AI companies showcase data companies according to how much outside investment funding they've raised. It's only my opinion, but I believe that the *top* label should be assigned to companies that have generated the most positive impact on the world around them, not the companies who've managed to convince investors to give them the most amount of money. That said, despite COVID's disastrous impact on global economies in 2020, AI start-ups managed to raise record-breaking funding that totaled $33 billion dollars in 2020 alone. Needless to say, there is money to be had in the credibility conferred on you when you manage to get your company listed as a top AI start-up. That's marketing.

TIP

For a full listing of the research sources I've used in writing this book — including the resources I've used to investigate this whole idea of top AI start-ups — head over to https://businessgrowth.ai/.

It may sound harsh, but if it's not profitable, it's a hobby, not a business. And, though I can't speak to AI companies like Uber, which has maybe had a positive impact from a carbon-footprint perspective yet has never managed to turn an actual profit after seven years in operation, I can say that moving from big data hype (the negative consequences of which are discussed in Chapter 2) to AI hype is like switching rooms in the *Titanic:* Either room you're in, hype-based investment is a recipe for disaster.

Throughout the remainder of this chapter, you get a chance to move beyond the AI hype and learn about data monetization and the wide variety of alternatives out there to monetize data resources, data skills, and data technologies. Although AI SaaS is incredible — and I myself would love to own one — throughout this chapter, my goal is to educate you on the wide variety of ways to monetize data — including AI SaaS products as well as strategies with or without investors. Figure 14-1 shows the data monetization approaches I cover throughout the remainder of this chapter.

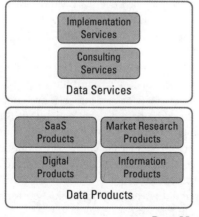
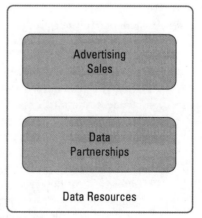

Data Monetization

FIGURE 14-1: The three main ways to monetize data.

Before tackling data monetization in earnest, let's turn back to Clive Humby for a moment and talk about where he fits within the data monetization picture. How did he know more about data's monetization potential back in 2006 than most people know even today? It's simple, actually. He emerged from university in 1972, with his degrees in applied mathematics and computer science in hand — but with a heart for business and leadership. What does any good entrepreneurial STEM graduate do? They naturally look for ways to turn their *Science*, *Technology*, *Engineering*, and *Mathematics* expertise into a business, of course! People who are of a mind to be a data leader or a data entrepreneur waste their talents when they spend their careers implementing data science solutions. Some people love to do data science implementation, and they're great at it. Other data science professionals love to solve big picture business problems, and often wind up being extremely successful leaders and entrepreneurs in the data space. As for Clive Humby, he's spent almost 50 years using his data science expertise to lead businesses or run his own. And for someone like that, "Data is the new oil" would be the most natural of conclusions — he just got a darned good head-start on the rest of us.

Monetizing Data Science Skills as a Service

If you've always worked as an employee in someone else's business, it can be difficult to see how your data science skills can translate to monetary value on the open market — that unlimited market that provides open access to buyers and sellers of all backgrounds, ethnicities, genders, and socioeconomic brackets. About ten years ago, there was no such a thing as "data science," and buying and selling data science services on the open market was a rare practice until about 2017. What has always been around, however, are vendors who sold services as add-ons to their product subscription packages. Most of these packages, though, were prohibitively expensive for small- and medium-size businesses.

The number of workers with data science expertise has grown incredibly fast since 2017. The good news about this expansion is that it has helped open up a space for businesses of all sizes to purchase and access data science support. Let's be real: Most businesses can afford to pay a data science consultant $20,000 to come in and build a few models for them. Heck, for that budget, you could be well on your way to building a data science product that you could monetize directly within your existing customer base. What most small- and medium-sized businesses *cannot* afford, however, is to pay $250,000 — maybe even multiple millions of dollars — per year for bloated data products and cookie-cutter services that miss the mark in terms of generating any measurable ROI.

And so you see, you have a wide gap in the market for data services, freelance data professionals, data services companies (agencies that sell data services), and data consulting companies (companies that sell data strategy consulting services). Throughout the rest of this section, you get a bird's-eye view of the data science services landscape — a landscape ripe for the picking for the entrepreneurs and businesses out there that have the expertise needed to fill that gap.

WARNING

Data science is a popular and important part of the data services sector, but you can offer data services many other ways that don't necessarily equate to "proper" data science. For brevity's sake, I've excluded these types of services from this discussion.

Data preparation services

I bet you didn't know that companies are outsourcing their data clean-up services, did you? They are. I'm not talking about the traditional type of email-list data validation and clean-up service, either — I'm talking about bona fide data-preparation-as-a-service businesses. Though still few and far between, these companies offer services like these:

>> **Data cleaning:** Removing strays, duplicates, and out-of-range records as well as standardizing casing

>> **Data transformation:** Treating missing values, dealing with outliers, and scaling variables

>> **Data normalization:** Preprocessing in order to transform data from its raw and imperfect format into a canonical standardized format

   The transformation can involve correcting spelling and grammar errors, converting abbreviations to their long-form equivalents, reformatting casing, transforming emojis into their emotional equivalents, and more.

>> **Data processing:** Data parsing, recoding of variables, concatenation, and other methods of reformatting your dataset to prepare it for analysis

>> **Data taxonomy services:** Manually assigning category labels to data points in a data set in order to create multiple, hierarchical relationships between data points in the data set

For perspective, let me point out that I took these offers from one service provider's website and elaborated on them. As you can see, service providers that offer similar services on a piecemeal basis have really just broken out the various steps involved in preparing data for data science and are then selling them as separate offers. You could structure these types of services in more profitable ways, but in the end, implementation-based services tend to be less scalable and have lower profit margins in the long run. This underscores the importance of diversity in revenue models in a data business.

TIP

I've created some mini trainings on optimal business models and revenue models for data businesses. If you'd like to see those, head over to the https://businessgrowth.ai/ website.

Model building services

Some companies offer the whole data science kit-and-caboodle. On top of preparing your data for analysis and machine learning, they also model it for you and present their findings. Machine learning model-building services can include these elements:

- >> **Data mining:** In data mining, you work to narrow down data sets by using pattern recognition techniques to identify and select only the most relevant data sources for the problem at hand. After you've identified these data sets, you have to extract enough of these select data resources in order to build a reliable model.

- >> **Data preparation:** I describe the steps for this process in the earlier section "Data preparation services."

- >> **Data ingestion:** This involves loading data into a system, platform, or environment. (For more on data ingestion, see Chapter 13.)

- >> **Machine learning model selection:** After testing out various machine learning algorithms, you then need to select the model that performs the best. This is what's known as model selection.

- >> **Machine learning model-tuning:** Model-tuning is where you adjust model parameters in order to achieve peak predictive performance from the model in terms of accuracy and reliability, without causing the model to be overfit or overgeneralized.

- >> **Ranking and scoring data:** The idea here is to figure out which data can provide the most benefit for you. I discuss in Chapter 4 the various statistical methods for ranking and scoring data.

- >> **Training and retraining machine learning models:** This is basically the whole kitchen sink, where the service provider starts by splitting your data into training and test sets, fits and tunes the model, and then selects for you the model that performs the best. In other words, it's a combination of all services in this list.

Again, these offers are based directly on what I saw on one company's website when I researched various online data science service providers. Similar to the data preparation services I discuss in the previous section, businesses that offer data science services in a piecemeal manner like this could restructure their service packages for better profitability. That said, in the model-building services I just described, the provider has made a move toward optimizing its offers.

REMEMBER

Way too many services in the model building area are the same, which confuses any service provider's would-be clients and can significantly decrease sales. I like the idea of a package for training and retraining machine learning models, because it represents a level up from all the other data services offered by combining them all into a single package. Hopefully, any provider offering it is selling it for a higher price but at a bit of a discounted rate than if the services were purchased separately. That strategy helps increase sales of the higher-priced package. Needless to say, most data entrepreneurs have much to learn when they first make the move from data science employee to data science entrepreneur. Everyone has to start somewhere, and often that means starting from the beginning.

TIP

I've created some mini trainings on how to best price and package data science services. If you want to see those, head over to https://businessgrowth.ai.

I could go on and on about monetizing data by selling data services. You could skin the data-science-as-a-service cat in about a million different ways. Though some companies out there are providing data science services on the open market, there's plenty of room (and plenty of need) for more providers. On top of that, most of what I've seen in terms of online data science service providers is way too generic. These small companies have, and sell, data science services, but they sell them to everyone. Don't do that.

REMEMBER

Attempting to sell to everyone is a bad business idea, and it flies in the face of the presumption that a data scientist has specific business expertise within an industry.

TIP

I've created a directory of online data service providers, and I always update it when I find exciting new examples of ways to sell data services on the open market. This includes data visualization services, data storytelling services, data strategy services, data management, data engineering, and so much more that I can't cover here. Feel free to peruse that directory over on the companion website to this book: https://businessgrowth.ai.

Summing things up, it's difficult to explain in words how much opportunity there is for data science service providers who specialize in their specific industry and who use that true expertise to deliver services that move the needle for their customers' businesses.

Selling Data Products

Most AI start-ups fall within the data monetization ecosystem. These companies utilize their sophisticated data skills, expertise, and technologies to build unique SaaS products for businesses that operate in a wide variety of industries, from government to retail, from healthcare to manufacturing, and everything in between. Most of these SaaS products offer some form of predictive analytics and would therefore be considered proper AI SaaS products. Other solutions, however, offer more simple reporting or data visualization capabilities. Although valuable in their own right, they cannot be considered true AI SaaS products.

REMEMBER

One interesting difference between data businesses that sell SaaS products and those that offer only data services is that the SaaS product businesses tend to be a lot more specialized and thus more focused on helping customers in a specific industry. That probably has a lot to do with the incredible amount of time and expense that goes into developing a SaaS product. The significant financial risk would drive most product owners to do their homework first.

Other data businesses, like SafeGraph (which I tell you more about later in this chapter), take raw data resources and then apply data skills and technologies to produce market research products — reports and dashboards that support businesses in making data-backed decisions on how to invest and develop, given current market conditions. Some of these products are developed from data that the company owns and uses for its own in-house purposes. Other market research products are derived solely from data that's sourced through one or more data partnerships. (This is the case with the SafeGraph example I'm about to describe.)

Another format in which data products are sold is the *digital product*, which can be any sort of data analysis, evaluation, visualization, or summary tool that's useful in creating value from data. A simple example is a plug-and-play dashboard that a customer can buy and install within their own environment to gain the insights they need without building the dashboard themselves.

Lastly, certain *information products* focus on data-intensive topics. These vehicles enable the transfer of data knowledge between one professional and another, which can include anything from books to self-service online courses, as well as done-for-you guides, action plans, or project management templates. (This book itself is an example of an information product.)

Direct Monetization of Data Resources

Companies directly monetize their data in two main ways: advertising and data partnerships. I cover both of these data monetization practices in this section, and I present you with a compelling case for why you should be interested in the collection, sale, and resale of your personal data — information that relates to you as "an identifiable, live individual" according to the European Commission.

Coupling data resources with a service and selling it

The most common way that data resources are directly monetized is via advertising, where advertising platforms bundle the right to access their audience with the right to access personal data on audience members in order to sell targeted advertising services to businesses. Without the data resources that describe a platform's user base, access to advertise to its users is almost worthless — you'd never be able to sort through and find the right users for whom your ad is relevant. That's why I categorize advertising as a form of direct data monetization rather than as a data service: The value is in the data, not the audience, as you can see in Figure 14-2.

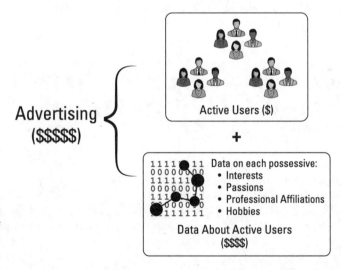

Advertising
($$$$$)

Active Users ($)

+

Data on each possessive:
- Interests
- Passions
- Professional Affiliations
- Hobbies

Data About Active Users
($$$$)

FIGURE 14-2: The value proposition of personal data in advertising.

Some popular data companies that monetize in this way are Facebook, Google, Snapchat, TikTok, and almost every other free communications application that people enjoy today. You pay nothing to use these marvels of technology, because advertisers are paying for you. Pretty cool, right? Well, after the Cambridge

Analytica scandal — a topic I cover in Chapter 11 — people have become increasingly wary when it comes to their data privacy and to how data about them is being used behind the scenes. (I discuss this important issue in greater detail later in this chapter.)

Making money with data partnerships

In a business context, a data partnership is an agreement between companies wherein they sell their data to other companies. The data that's sold by way of these partnerships almost always includes customer data — more specifically, their customer's *personal* data. With respect to data privacy and the potential misuse of personal data, there's a lot *not* to love about data partnerships. I'll let you decide for yourself after reading about the data business SafeGraph in the nearby sidebar, "Monetizing a product that's built solely from partners' data resources."

WARNING

Not surprisingly, most people feel violated when they learn that their location data has been collected, sold, and resold as an asset by various businesses. If you're considering developing this type of revenue model for your business, you're putting your company's reputation at risk in the long term. Application development companies do not now have a means by which to collect informed express consent from their users. They get by with it because people haven't been aware of what was happening. As you can see in the section on data privacy that follows, the freewheeling and highly profitable era of data collection and resale seems to me to be coming to a screeching halt.

MONETIZING A PRODUCT THAT'S BUILT SOLELY FROM PARTNERS' DATA RESOURCES

To give you a peek at what it looks like for a data buyer to monetize data resources purchased from data partners, let's look at SafeGraph, a top AI start-up, backed by the angel investor Peter Thiel. (It reportedly raised $45 million from a single presentation in its Series B funding round. That must have been a pretty compelling presentation, right?) To detail what investors bought into, let's take a closer look at how this Data-as-a-Service (DaaS) platform takes data resources from data partners and directly converts it into tens of millions of dollars per year in revenue.

SafeGraph buys people's location-based data from app developers who have collected that data about its users as part of running the application services they use on their phones. When you read the terms and conditions for your smartphone apps, you can see in there the wording that gives them the right to resell any data they collect on you, as part of the services run by each of your phone apps. You agree to this by the act of installing the application on your phone.

So SafeGraph comes in and, rather than waste time and money reinventing the wheel, forms partnerships with application developers to obtain your location data. SafeGraph then drills down into that data for your location-based activities around commercial spaces, like shopping malls, coffee shops, grocery stores, and the like. Once they've cleaned that data, they put it on their web-based mapping application and present it as a product available for purchase by retail companies. (See the sidebar figure for a clear picture of the flow of money and data between businesses.) These retail companies then use that information for the kinds of improved decision-making I talk about in Chapter 12.

SafeGraph's data tells them where you go, how frequently, how long you stay, and so much more. And the amount of data is far from small potatoes — SafeGraph collects data from tens of millions, if not hundreds of millions, of smartphones owned by Americans. Every single cell tower ping goes straight into SafeGraph's "file" on you, for lack of a better word — from tens to hundreds of trillions of pings per month, if you can imagine. All this location data has been openly aggregated and sold by SafeGraph since 2016, to the tune of hundreds of millions of dollars in revenue for this small, Colorado-based data company.

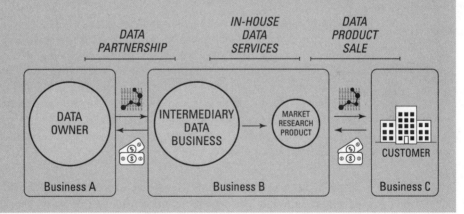

Pricing Out Data Privacy

The cookieless world is coming. You're seeing birthing pains now, with events such as Apple's iOS 14 software update, a data privacy change–maker where Apple put a full stop to user tracking for anyone using iOS 14 or higher software versions on their Apple products. With this move, Apple software no longer reports the user ID of its customers or any of their activities.

Consumers who opt not to share their data can heave a sigh of relief with the open assurance that their activities are no longer being recorded, tracked, or shared on the open market. Forced data privacy is coming!! Hooray, right? Unfortunately, within a data–intensive ecosystem like the Internet, things are never as they seem. You need to dig deeper into what's happening with personal data, technology businesses, and data businesses. My goal in this section is to help spread awareness about what's happening under the hood with respect to late–breaking data privacy developments.

The first thing you need to understand is the difference in business models for relevant actors in the data privacy war that rages in 2021. Though these businesses are all technology businesses, their business models are completely different. The most important of these now are described in this list:

>> **Hardware (that comes with software) product companies:** I'm talking here about Apple, Samsung, and the like. These hardware companies aren't now focusing on monetizing the personal data that they have on their users, but that's not to say they won't in the future. Rather than advertise to their customers on other platforms, they've built their own ecosystem in which they do indeed use personal data to advertise their products to their users.

>> **Data companies:** I'm talking here about companies like Facebook, Google, TikTok, Snapchat, and the like. These companies sell access to your personal data, including data that's collected via software on Apple and Samsung phones. For reasons shown earlier, in Figure 14-2, the only way companies like these can stay in business is because of the value of the data they collect from their users. Unlike hardware companies like Apple, they don't have much of a need to advertise their own products, because they already have the users — so they monetize by offering the chance for other businesses to advertise within their ecosystem.

In its highly contentious, politicized play, Apple recently thrust itself into the limelight as a data privacy champion in the eyes of most. Yet Apple continues using its customers' personal data to advertise to its own user base. Furthermore, by making this move, Apple has hurt its own customers and partners in at least two major ways:

>> **Hurting Apple application developers' bottom line:** Obviously, if you pay $1,000 or more for a cellular phone, you want it to come supplied with access to some awesome applications, right? As any iPhone user knows, Apple

doesn't "play friendly" with any non-Apple technology, so you can't download apps from Google Play — Google's application store for all Android users. Apple makes sure that you can get your applications only from its App Store. Well, the developers of those applications need customers in order to generate revenue and then reinvest a significant amount of that money into improving their applications. But where are most of these revenue-generating customers coming from? They come from ads that are run on data businesses like Facebook, Google, Snapchat, and others. Without these ads, how will application development companies stay in business?

» **Decreasing Apple iOS app quality:** To turn a profit, and subsequently reinvest in developing the best iOS applications possible, iOS app developers need customers. By cutting off user identification reporting, Apple's own app developers can no longer gather the conversion tracking data they need in order to run ads to attract more customers. This strategy results in fewer customers for them, leading to decreasing revenues and subsequently lower quality standards for any applications they want to develop. Maintaining an excellent software product costs money. When you lose a leads source, you see decreased sales and have less money to use for product maintenance. This change can't be good for Apple customers who are already trapped within the Apple ecosystem and unable to use any applications from elsewhere — the open-source Google Play Store, for example.

It almost seems as though Apple decided to cut off its own nose to spite its face, doesn't it? Though Apple's recent move means more privacy for its users, it also means less relevance with respect to advertisements those users see. It represents a complete loss of the ability to do any real-time advertising optimization. No one I know wants to see more ads for products they don't care about. Who out there hasn't discovered courses, products, or services that they absolutely adore but would never have known about if it weren't for the precision at which Facebook was able to match their interest and passions with various marketplace offers?

I'm just here to remind you that the much-ballyhooed data privacy initiatives coming down the pike will come at a great cost to consumers, given that you can expect to pay by being forced to repeatedly consume the same annoying, spammy ads that you have absolutely no interest in seeing ever again. Relevant advertisers will no longer be able to find you, and the ads that do make it through won't be optimized to conform with your desires, expectations, and preferences. Personally, it's hard to imagine wanting to make this trade-off, but I remember how bad spammy online advertising was 20 or so years ago, before we developed the data expertise and systems required to serve high-quality targeted online advertisements. Newer generations may not realize how bad the bad old days were — and perhaps are not sufficiently fearful about the prospect of their return.

As rollouts like these affect more and more platforms, they and their advertisers will have less and less data to use in evaluating what's working and what's not. Current estimates are that 30 to 40 percent of the conversion tracking data will be lost by the platforms and all businesses, brands, and advertisers that use them. Imagine paying $1,000 to run an ad and in return not getting any information whatsoever about how that ad performed or whether it generated any leads or sales for your business. Who would do that? For professionals who make their living helping companies create value from data, the enormity of problems that this cookieless society movement, so to speak, will create should be beyond obvious.

For data professionals, these changes are like taking food right out of our mouths. Data resources, skill sets, and technologies were the main drivers behind a company's ability to find new customers and to reach their existing ones. That meant an abundance of funding and opportunity for data professionals. But as businesses lose the ability to use targeted advertising to draw customers, they'll be forced to turn to more traditional marketing methods, which, coincidentally, don't require sophisticated data skills to perform. That's a net decrease in demand for data professionals in the online advertising industry.

The good news is that, although there will be less demand for data professionals in advertising, there will be more demand for data skills in marketing. (To learn more about organic data-intensive marketing methods that will increase in popularity with the loss of effectiveness in targeted advertising, check out Chapter 11.)

4

Assessing Your Data Science Options

Chapter **15**

Gathering Important Information about Your Company

The success of prospective data science projects heavily depends on whether those projects represent an implementation of your company's *lowest-hanging-fruit* use case — in other words, the most promising data science use case for your company, given its current capabilities with respect to data resources, technology, and skillsets. To ensure that your data science use case is the lowest-hanging fruit, though, you need to make sure that it offers the quickest and biggest bang for your company's buck — especially when you and your company are novices when it comes to leading profit-forming data science initiatives. For a new data science initiative to offer a solid return on investment in a short period, it should be something that your company can implement using its existing resources.

To make maximum use of existing resources, you first need to uncover what those resources are, as well as any hidden risks within them. In this chapter, you see the different types of information you should collect about your company so that you can assess that information and make an informed decision about which data science use case truly represents your lowest-hanging-fruit data science use case. *Do not skip* the last section of this chapter, because that's where you can find out the single most efficient way to collect the massive amount of information you need about your company before you can even *begin* trying to select a true lowest-hanging-fruit use case.

WARNING

Anytime your company has to make new investments into data technologies, skillsets, or resources, financial risk is introduced in the case that the project fails to deliver its estimated ROI. Decrease this risk by seeking to make maximum use of the resources your company already has on hand.

Unifying Your Data Science Team Under a Single Business Vision

One thing that new-and-aspiring data science leaders notice pretty quickly is that data implementation folks can sometimes struggle to see the forest for the trees. And, if you're doing data science implementation work, you've likely been frustrated to realize that nobody gives you a map of the forest — yet everyone expects you to find your way through it. If either of these two frustrations rings a bell, let me tell you that most companies' data teams face these frustrations every day! Figure 15-1 depicts the classic everyday struggle of most data teams.

FIGURE 15-1:
The classic power dynamic within a data science team.

Data Science Leader

Data Science Implementer

In Chapter 1, I spend some time clarifying the difference between data leaders, data implementers, and data entrepreneurs. Though it's true that my discussion there was meant to help you more quickly find your affinity within a wide variety of data science roles, there's more to it than that. From a business perspective, it's unrealistic to expect someone to act as both a data leader and a data implementer. Sometimes, smaller companies do have periods of overlap while they're still growing and lack the resources for separate dedicated team members for these roles — but the quicker you can segregate and delineate chains of responsibility between these two data science functions, the better.

If you're a data leader, you know that you're responsible for making sure that deliverables are managed effectively, to specification, on time, and within budget. Providing your data scientists, data analysts, and other data implementation workers with ample support is a huge part of making that happen. Though data science implementers are responsible for building data science solutions to business problems, they also have to be sure to communicate their progress, obstacles, and occasional misgivings. Data scientists don't have to worry much about how to pull it all together, or whether team members are completing their tasks on time, but everyone on the team needs to work together to help everyone along. This is how happy and efficient data science teams function.

A healthy dynamic between data science team members is essential, but there's more to leading successful data science projects than just that. You also need to understand where the data science team, as a whole, fits within the business (and I'm not talking about the organizational chart here!). The truth of the matter is that if your data science team members aren't supporting one another, or if the team itself isn't properly attuned to your business vision, it's entirely possible for the team to spend all its time tending to one lonely sapling of a data project — completely oblivious to whether that project actually moves the needle in terms of revenues or business vision.

I tend to talk a lot about how data leaders need to use data science to generate new or improved profit for their companies. I do that because earning money is the primary purpose of a business, though a business wouldn't be successful if all it did was focus on ways to make money.

REMEMBER

A business needs a mission and a vision. In this chapter, I take you one step further in the data science value chain by helping you ensure that your data science projects are profit-forming and, of equal importance, that these projects directly support your company's business vision.

Framing Data Science around the Company's Vision, Mission, and Values

A business needs a higher purpose that defines why it operates, and that purpose should not be solely to make money. A business that lacks a clear purpose (beyond just making money for its owners) might as well be called a parasite rather than a business. As shown in Figure 15-2, an equal exchange of money should take place for something of measurable, meaningful value to customers.

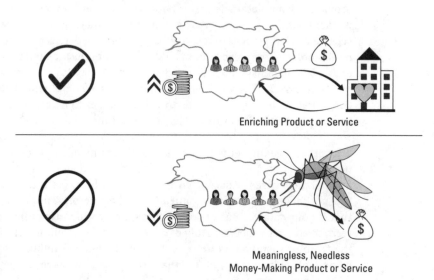

Enriching Product or Service

Meaningless, Needless
Money-Making Product or Service

FIGURE 15-2:
The need for business vision, mission, and values.

I don't care how much your company generates in revenue — if it's just a money extraction machine, it's not successful. True business success occurs whenever a company sells something that improves the lives or businesses of its customers, and the company, in exchange, makes a profit. One way to know whether a company sells products and services that truly enrich society is by looking at how people use the products or services. Are people able to use the products they purchased to help produce an increase in the net value of their communities? If the answer is yes, the products or services are enriching. The ultimate goal of a company should be to grow by enriching lives and societies.

On the other hand, if a company sells meaningless swag, in the long run its customers will see a net decrease in wealth and nothing of lasting value to show for it. If all businesses were run in this manner, societies would run dry of resources as companies grow richer and people become poorer. If you think of it on a large scale like this, I'm sure you'll agree that no one should support businesses like these. Enter the need for a clear business vision, mission, and values.

A *business vision* is a statement of a company's goals and aspirations for the future. A *mission statement* is an action-based description of a company's purpose for being in business, in terms of who it helps, how it helps them, and why it seeks to provide this type of support. A company's *values* are the moralistic principles that guide its initiatives. Getting back to data science, the goal of a data science project should be in direct support of your company in helping it reach its business vision. Because the company is a business, the goal of your project should be to improve revenues for the company, but only in ways that are aligned with the company's vision, mission, and values.

WARNING

If you see a way to use data science to make money for your company, yet you realize that this specific use case would somehow oppose the company's vision, mission, or values — do not proceed.

How do you know what your company's vision, mission and values are? These are the types of details that the folks in human resources usually indoctrinate you with when you first start as an employee. You can also check the company's website for these types of public-facing statements.

REMEMBER

For a company's data science project to be successful, it must (a) directly support the business vision and (b) generate new or improved profits for the company. Yes, it's that simple. Unfortunately, when you're busy with the details of trying to make something happen between many people and across multiple business units, you can easily get bogged down in the details. That's why you need a clearly defined process for repeatable success. In Chapter 9, I introduce my STAR framework, which may prove helpful in this context. (Figure 15-3 gives the details.) Think of it as a repeatable process you can apply to support you in delivering successful data science projects.

If you've read Part 3, you've completed the Survey phase of the STAR framework. In those chapters, I describe a wide variety of data science use cases that are applicable to multiple industries and that can support businesses in a wide variety of ways. By now, you should feel "stocked up" when it comes to ideas for new data science projects! The next phase of the STAR framework is where you take stock of your company and inventory its current data science capabilities. You can see how to do that throughout the rest of this chapter. Then, in the rest of Part 4, you can see how to work through the Access and Recommend phases of the STAR framework.

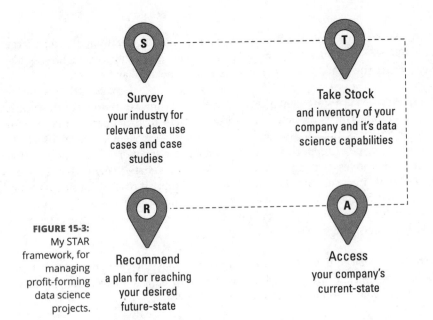

FIGURE 15-3:
My STAR
framework, for
managing
profit-forming
data science
projects.

S — Survey
your industry for
relevant data use
cases and case
studies

T — Take Stock
and inventory of your
company and it's data
science capabilities

R — Recommend
a plan for reaching
your desired
future-state

A — Access
your company's
current-state

Taking Stock of Data Technologies

Before you can pick a lowest-hanging fruit use case, you need to inventory all the data technologies that are already available at your company. You can get started on this task by first requesting your company's *enterprise IT architecture* — the low-level blueprint of the current state of your company's IT technology infrastructure. It describes the technologies your company owns and how they're utilized together to support the business requirements of your company. Also, be sure to request any *data infrastructure architecture* — the blueprint that details the technology architecture for the data solutions your company has in place, like the example shown in Figure 15-4.

You should be able to request an up-to-date copy of both the data/IT infrastructure architecture and the associated architecture standards from an IT manager or any relevant data architects. *Architecture standards* provide the metamodel and definitions around which the architecture is designed.

From the architecture artifacts, make a list of the data technologies that are in use at your company, and then conduct surveys and interviews of relevant personnel to fill in any gaps and uncover other data technologies. The purpose of this process is to unearth any "hidden" data technologies that are used within the business units of your company, but that may not be shown within the official architecture. As far as how to use surveys and interviews to collect the necessary information, I cover that topic in the last section of this chapter. As far as what data technology questions you may want to ask, they might include these:

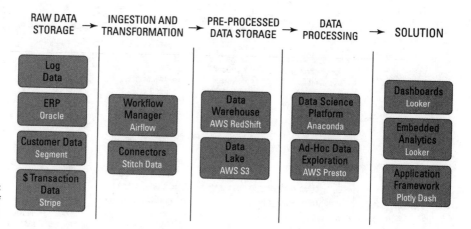

RAW DATA STORAGE → INGESTION AND TRANSFORMATION → PRE-PROCESSED DATA STORAGE → DATA PROCESSING → SOLUTION

FIGURE 15-4:
An example of data architecture.

>> What data technologies and tools do you use throughout the course of your work?

>> What other data technologies and tools do you know of that are being used by colleagues at the company?

>> In terms of file sizes, what are the biggest data sets you're working with?

>> How do you access the data you need to do your job?

>> Where are your data sets being stored?

>> How is data distributed across your company, and which data access issues are you aware of?

WARNING

When you ask personnel about file sizes, that's technically an attribute that describes the data resource, not the technology. Because file sizes heavily impact data technology selection, though, I listed that question in this section.

When interviewing and surveying personnel about data technologies they're using, map out a list of potential technologies. You can start with the ones shown in Figure 15-5 and add to it. Having a list like this one may help jog people's memories and capture the gist of what you're asking them to provide to you.

Beyond inventorying your company's data technologies, you also need to inventory all of its data resources to see how you might be able to utilize them in a lowest-hanging-fruit use case.

ETL and Data Integration Tools		Analytical Tools	On-Premise/Cloud/Hybrid Data Management	
• Apache Kafka • Microsoft Azure Data Factory • Microsoft SQL Server SSIS • Oracle Hyperion • Data Transformation Tools • Apache Airflow • Apache Samza • Analytics & Viz Tools	• Board • Looker • Microsoft PowerBI • MicroStrategy • Tableau • TIBCO • Qlik • Apache Mahout • Apache Samza • Apache Spark • Apache Storm	• Weka • Rapid Miner • Excel • Advanced Excel • Geographic Information Systems (GIS) • Business Intelligence Tools • SAS • Tableau • Matlab	• Apache: HDFS • Apache: MapReduce • Apache: Hive • Apache: Storm • Apache: Elasticsearch/Lucene • Apache: Maven • Apache: UIMA • Docker • Kubernetes	• NoSQL: Apache Cassandra • NoSQL: Neo4j • NoSQL: MongoDB • NoSQL: ObjectStore • NoSQL: Other • Redis • Oracle My SQL • PostgreSQL • SSRS • RDBMS: Other

Cloud Data Management	Predictive Modeling Applications	
• Amazon Web Services: S3, Athena, Redshift • Google Cloud: Big Query, StackDriver • IBM Cloud • Microsoft Azure Cloud Services • Snowflake	• Cloudera Data Science Workbench • Google Cloud AutoML • Gurobi • H2O.ai • IBM Watson	• Jupyter Notebooks • MATLAB Toolboxes • R-Studio • SAS • Stata • Weka

Inventorying Your Company's Data Resources

It's a safe bet to say that, if your company doesn't already own the data that's required in order to implement a data science use case, that use case isn't a lowest-hanging-fruit use case. That's why you need to make sure you're familiar with the data resources your company owns as well as with any known issues related to specific data sets within those resources. Only after you've collected and reviewed this information are you in a position to judge which potential data science use case truly represents the lowest-hanging fruit. In this section, you learn how to go about collecting the important information you need in order to leverage your company's data resources effectively.

Requesting your data dictionary and inventory

To wrap your head around the data resources your company is now storing, start by requesting a data dictionary and an inventory. A *data dictionary* is a central reference source that describes the company's data resources. Essentially, it's data that describes your company's data resources. Pretty meta, right? Well, actually, it *is* meta. It's *metadata* — the data that describes data sets. As shown in Figure 15-6, a data dictionary has a similar structure to the *Merriam-Webster* dictionary.

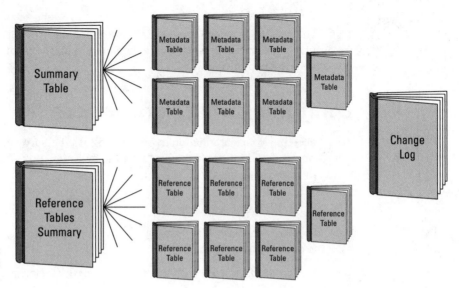

FIGURE 15-6:
The structure of a
data dictionary.

TIP

Some people call a data dictionary a *metadata repository*. No need for confusion! These terms mean the same thing.

Metadata tables provide detailed descriptions of the company's data in terms of the properties of each of the data elements. A *reference table* is a data table within the data dictionary that details the metadata describing the classification and description domains of the data defined within the data dictionary. Figure 15-7 shows how a data dictionary relates to the data sets it defines.

DATA

employee_id	first_name	last_name	nin	dept_id
44	John Doe	John Doe	HH 45 09 73 D	1
45	John Doe	John Doe	SA 75 35 42 B	2
46	John Doe	John Doe	NE 22 63 82	2
47	John Doe	John Doe	XY 29 87 61 A	1
48	John Doe	John Doe	MA 12 89 36 A	15
49	John Doe	John Doe	AT 20 73 18	2
50	John Doe	John Doe	HW 12 94 21 C	6
51	John Doe	John Doe	LX 13 26 39 B	6
52	John Doe	John Doe	YA 49 88 11 A	3
53	John Doe	John Doe	BE 08 74 68 A	1

DATA DICTIONARY (METADATA)

Column	Data Type	Description
employee_id	int	Primary key of a table
first_name	nvarchar(50)	Employee first name
last_name	nvarchar(50)	Employee last name
nin	nvarchar(15)	National Identification Number
position	nvarchar(50)	Current position title, e.g. Secretary
dept_id	int	Employee department. Ref: Departments
gender	char(1)	M = Male, F = Female, Null = unknown
employment_start_date	date	Start date of employment in organization.
employment_end_date	date	Employment end date.

FIGURE 15-7:
The relationship
between a
dataset and the
data dictionary
that describes it.

Once you get your hands on the data dictionary, give it a good once-over so that you gain a fundamental idea of which data sets to expect to hear about when you conduct surveys and interviews. This way, you can recognize when reported answers don't align with what's in the official file.

TIP

There's no need to do a deep dive looking into your company's data resources just yet. After a quick once over, set the data dictionary aside; I tell you what to do with it next over in Chapter 16.

Confirming what's officially on file

After collecting your data dictionary and giving it a cursory overview, the next thing you need to do is confirm what's on file by conducting surveys and interviews. Here are some questions you can ask:

>> What data do you have access to?

>> Of the data sets to which you have access, which do you use regularly? Name and describe the data set.

>> Does your work involve the utilization of any moving, streaming, or real-time data sources?

>> Does your work involve any unstructured data sources? This might involve building analytics or insights from PDF files, Word files, video files, audio files, or HTML web pages, for example.

>> Does your work involve using semistructured data sources? This might involve building analytics or insights from comma-separated values (.csv) files, tab-delimited files, log files, eXtensible Markup Language (XML) files, or JavaScript Object Notation (JSON) files.

>> Does your work involve the utilization of sensor data?

>> Is your work ever impeded by a lack of data access?

>> Do you know of data within other business units that you could use to create more value, if you only had access to it?

>> Do you have a clear record of how your data sets were captured, and when?

>> What data quality issues have you encountered? How have you worked to resolve or address them?

>> Does your work involve the use of data that stores personally identifiable information?

Unearthing data silos and data quality issues

There are a few sources of huge inherent risk to the success of any data science product. If the people who work at your company don't trust your data solution, they will be hesitant to rely on it. You may face user adoption issues, where you spend months building a solution that, once complete, seldom gets used. Even if you deploy a top-down approach to try to force personnel to use a solution, if they don't trust the results it generates, they may secretly waste time doing data analysis and processing manually to double-check that what the solution says is indeed correct.

Though lack of trust isn't the only reason that technology adoption suffers, it can be a big one. When it comes to trust and reliability with respect to data resources, the lack of data quality can be a huge contributing factor. Data silos, the data storage practice where a company stores its data in separate, unique repositories for each business unit, only aggravate this issue.

Let me illustrate this problem with a fictitious example, illustrated in Figure 15-8.

Back in May 2017, your company stored a data set in its central repository (the source data set shown in Figure 15-8). Unfortunately, the data within that data set had formatting errors as well as some missing values. User A, from Marketing, came along in June 2017 and cleaned up the formatting issues with the data set. He stored a copy of the formatted data set on his desktop and also on the repository for his business unit (which isn't the same central repository from whence he originally made a copy of the source data set). So now he has created two new versions of the file and saved them in two places that are known and understood only by him.

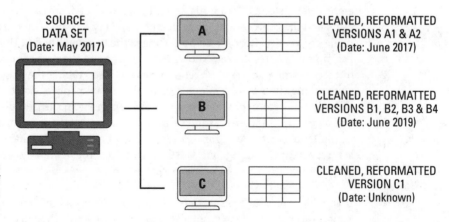

FIGURE 15-8: An example of data quality and silo issues.

User B, from Customer Service, comes along in June 2019. She finds the source data set on the central repository, and she, too, makes a copy of it. She reformats the data set (again), and then she goes one step further by using estimation techniques to fill in missing values. She's totally unaware of the reformatting work that User A did, so she reformats according to her own standards, which happen to be quite different from the ones chosen by User A. User B stores two versions of the file on her desktop, and two versions of the file on the repository for her business unit. Those two versions correspond to the reformatted version and the filled-in version. So now she has created four versions of the file, saved in two places that are known and understood only by her.

User C's situation is more mysterious. Also from Marketing, he originally made a copy of the source data set in 2018. Over time, he played with it, messed it up, tried to back out of his errors, reformatted it, and saved it in a heaping mess over on his desktop. That last time stamp on the data set says 2020, but he is sure that he has made no changes to it since 2018.

Is the problem clear yet? The source data set wasn't clean, and it had missing values, so it wasn't inherently trustworthy. Then three different employees from various business units come along and try to create value from it, thus creating duplicate versions of the data set — all with varying contents.

One big problem here is that, where possible, all the business units that access the data set should be able to use one another's efforts. If everything were centralized, standardized, and well-documented, User B and C could have just used Users A's reformatted version, without creating more file versions and without reinvesting more person-hours into a task that was already completed. This would solve the problem known as *duplication of effort*.

Here's another glaring issue: After Users A, B, and C are done, the company has eight versions of the same file saved in six locations, spread across two business units and the central repository. Versions span two years. The source data set is of mediocre quality. User A's reformatting is the best quality, but User B has filled in the missing values. No one knows which version of the data set is correct — if any of them is in fact correct. So, employees just keep taking the original source data and making their own versions. Eventually, no one knows exactly where the data actually came from, or whether it was ever any good in the first place. The data set and all the time and effort (and versions) that are wasted — no one trusts the data or wants to use it — and for this reason, no one can create value from it. The data set represents nothing but wasted effort for the company in terms of both employee-hours and operational expenses.

TIP

If you discover a data resource issue within your company, jot down the problem. Your awareness of these problems is extremely useful when deciding how to proceed. Only then can you generate more value from your company's data resources.

People-Mapping

When I talk about people-mapping, I'm talking about mapping out the structure of influential relationships, reach, and data skillset resources that are available within your company to help ensure that your data science project is a success. Resources aren't just your company's datasets, software packages, and hardware — resources are also measured by the level of expertise your people can bring to solving a problem.

Requesting organizational charts

Understanding organizational structure is an important part of understanding the people dynamic surrounding your future data science project. Be sure to ask for organizational charts. Get an executive-level organizational chart and an organizational chart for your particular business unit. (For one example of an organizational chart, see Figure 15-9.) After you've selected a use case — as discussed in Chapter 16 — be sure to also collect an organizational chart for the business units that your data science project will impact.

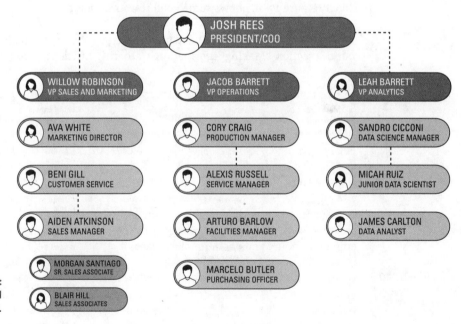

FIGURE 15-9:
An organizational chart.

REMEMBER

Organizational charts help you understand who you need to talk to when you conduct surveys and interviews. They also give you an idea of who is answering to whom and how that relationship dynamic potentially impacts your data science projects.

Surveying the skillsets of relevant personnel

To make maximum use of the data skillsets your company already has on hand, be sure to survey relevant existing employees.

REMEMBER

Anytime you can quickly create additional value from an existing company resource, that represents a win for your company. This is as true for data skillsets as it is of data resources and technologies.

When you survey personnel, you want to get a grasp on their data aptitudes and skills levels. You should ask questions about their formal education, which classes they took at university, and which technology skills they've utilized throughout the course of their careers. In terms of which exact skills and courses you can ask about, Figure 15-10 shows some good starter options.

For a closer look at the means and methodologies of surveys and interviews, check out the section "Making Information-Gathering Efficient," later in this chapter.

Math and Statistics Knowledge	Courses Completed	Tools	Coding Expertise	
• Algebra	• Calculus	• Advanced Excel (pivot tables, statistical analysis, etc.)	• Apache Hadoop/ MapReduce	• SciPy
• Geometry	• Cellular & Molecular Biology	• Business Intelligence Tools	• Apache Spark	• spaCy
• Pre-Calculus	• Chemistry	• Excel	• AWS	• SparkMLlib
• Probability and Statistics	• Data Engineering Courses	• Geographic Information Systems (GIS)	• C++/C#	• SPSS
• Quantitative Economics	• Data Science Courses	• Matlab	• Git/GitHub	• SQL
• Quantitative Marketing	• Data Visualization Courses	• Rapid Miner	• Go	• Stanford NLP
• Quantitative Psychology	• Differential Equations	• SAS	• HTML/CSS	• Web Development
	• Dynamics	• Tableau	• Java	• word-node2vec
	• Linear Algebra	• Weka	• Javascript	• XGBoost
	• Pharmacy		• Kotlin	
	• Physics		• MATLAB	
	• Statics		• NLTK	
	• Statistics for Engineers		• NodeJS	
	• Web Design		• NoSQL databases	
			• NumPy	
			• Pig/Hive	
			• Python	
			• R	
			• React JS	
			• Scala	
			• scikit-learn	

FIGURE 15-10: Some foundations from which great data professionals emerge.

Avoiding Classic Data Science Project Pitfalls

Two classic data science project pitfalls stem from (a) focusing too much on the data and technology and forgetting about the business and (b) failing to plan for the worst–case scenario.

Staying focused on the business, not on the tech

In the spirit of putting the business before the tech, let's look at how you can uncover business problems that you can readily solve with data science. To do this, you would again want to use surveys and interviews — this time, to collect feedback from the following individuals:

>> **Employees and contractors whose work has been directly affected by an inability to obtain or utilize data in a timely manner:** Get details about how the lack of data access has undermined their ability to get results.

>> **Organizational decision-makers and potential stakeholders:** Request details about the sort of data-driven improvements they'd like to see in an ideal future. Ask about their decision-support needs and how well those are being met. Inquire into their level of data literacy,

>> **Data professionals:** Ask them for their ideas on how the organization can make more effective use of data.

>> **HR managers:** Ask about how employee attrition may be adversely affecting the organization and what key factors they think are driving this attrition. Ask about talent sourcing, any problems in talent management, and how they think it could be improved.

>> **Sales and marketing professionals:** Ask for their thoughts on areas of opportunity with respect to marketing channels, sales optimization, and churn reduction.

>> **Business managers:** Ask about how a lack of data availability or predictive capabilities may be adversely affecting team member productivity or team outcomes. Also, look for ways that business process inefficiencies are adversely affecting business unit performance.

>> **IT professionals:** Collect documentation around security protocols, privacy policies, and current best practices that document the processes your company uses to ensure it meets General Data Protection Regulation (GDPR) requirements. More on GDPR in Chapter 16.

Drafting best practices to protect your data science project

Best practices are guidelines based on past experiences that, when put into practice, help protect and safeguard the success of future projects. To create best practices, you need to sit down with other personnel who have been part of past data and IT projects at your company. Speak with them about stumbling blocks that caused delays or failures in the past and why they believe these situations occurred. Ask them about what they think could have been done to avoid those setbacks in the first place. Ask them what people problems came up and how those problems adversely impacted the project. Ask them what technology components introduced the most risk to the overall success of their project. Make a list of these war stories.

After you've spoken to ten or so people about their experiences and opinions, compile their reports into one cohesive body of evidence. Review your findings and develop a set of best practices for your organization. How can you make your future data science project as efficient and effective as possible? Consider this from the perspective of both data skillsets and technology requirements. List at least three ways you can avoid implementation problems and delays. Describe which technology components are most likely to cause problems, and why. Describe three "people problems" that are likely to arise. Make sure your best practices are designed to help you preempt and prevent these potential problems. If you were to create at least ten rules to future-proof your future data science project, what would those rules be? Let those be your best practices.

REMEMBER

Your best practices should be practices you can put into place to ensure that your future data science project is as efficient and effective as possible, avoiding implementation problems and delays. Your final data science project plan should account for, preempt, and prevent the worst-case scenarios that may have plagued past technology projects at your company.

Tuning In to Your Company's Data Ethos

The last, but not least, important type of information you'll want to collect about your company relates to its data ethics. When I say *data ethics*, I'm referring to both data privacy rights and AI ethics. Although data privacy laws are still nebulous and ever-changing, the data privacy industry is considerably more mature than the industry that is growing up around the need for greater oversight into AI ethics. Let's have a look at data privacy first.

Collecting the official data privacy policy

During the information gathering mission across your company, be sure to collect any data privacy policies. Suffice it to say that your company's data privacy policy should fall on the side of full disclosure and affirmative consent. These policies should be complete, equitable, and enforceable. Not only should they be enforceable, but your company should also have the apparatus in place to enforce them. If that isn't the case, at this point it's a good idea to collect information about what is causing data privacy enforcement gaps. For now, just collect all this information and set it aside. In Chapter 16, I have you look at how to get started assessing your company's data privacy program.

Taking AI ethics into account

Obviously, if your project is the first-ever data science project at your company, you won't need to collect information about AI ethics. In that case, your company would have no AI project around which you could evaluate past ethical behavior. In Chapter 16, I talk about what it means for a company's AI to be ethical, and how to go about assessing the ethics of AI products and projects. For now, let's look at what sort of information you need to collect about your company's AI projects in order to ascertain the ethical standard of those projects.

For AI to be ethical, it should be accountable, explainable, and unbiased. To assess the accountability of your company's AI, start first by collecting the documentation that was published by the developers of the AI solution. Each solution should come with a report that documents the machine learning methodologies that the system deploys. Within that report, there should be model metadata that describes the models. This report should be open for all users to examine and evaluate. Snag that report and set it aside for now. I'll tell you what to do with it in Chapter 16. If this report doesn't exist, make note of that because this could become a serious problem one day.

Next collect the documentation that explains your AI solution in plain language. All AI solutions need a manual that explains how the predictions are actually generated by the machine. This manual needs to be in plain English, so all users and personnel can understand it without having to take a course in data literacy. Again, if this documentation doesn't exist, jot that down.

Moving into the last characteristic of ethical AI, your AI solutions need to produce unbiased outcomes. This can be tough to assess. For now, just look out for any documentation within your company (probably in the form of emails or meeting minutes) that details any concerns with a bias implicitly built into your company's AI solutions. If your AI solutions are provided by vendors, you can also do web research to track down any reports of biased outputs from the AI, as is common in AI domain applications, like healthcare.

REMEMBER

To put it plainly, you can't have ethical AI without good data governance supporting it. Why? Well, because in order for your AI to be explainable, unbiased, and accountable, it must be built from high-quality data that's been properly documented and maintained. You can think of data governance as a type of chain of custody that secures the integrity and reliability of your organization's data. *Data governance* standards are the standards and processes that ensure that your company's important data is entered according to the quality and management standards, as set forth by the data governance council. Collect a copy of your company's most up-to-date data governance policy.

Making Information-Gathering Efficient

Throughout this chapter, I talk a considerable amount about all the types of information you should collect about your company before looking into which data science use case might qualify as a low-hanging fruit. If not approached strategically, this type of information-gathering quest can go on for months and months, further extending your company's time-to-value on the future data science project that will be born of these efforts. It doesn't have to be that way. You can collect all the information you need by investing just in one or two weeks of effort.

REMEMBER

When I refer to the *commissioning manager,* I am referring to the manager who commissioned you to lead this information gathering mission on behalf of your business unit. If you're the head of data science, you're probably your own commissioning manager. At less data-mature companies, though, someone higher up is more likely to tap you to do this work on behalf of the data team. In this case, you're acting in a data leadership capacity without having been officially granted that title.

It's a little easier done than said, actually. Essentially, the process is to brainstorm, categorize, group, request, and receive the information in the form of email and/or survey responses.

TIP

If you want to use the question-and-asset request database that i built in order to illustrate this discussion, I've made it available to you at www.businessgrowth. ai. From there, you can sort, copy, and paste the questions as needed, or make a copy of the table and edit the data per your requirements.

All you need to do is plot out all the questions you need answered as well as the assets you need to collect in order to complete the information gathering process. Then, next to the question or asset request, detail from whom you need to request this information. (For an example of how this would work, see Figure 15-11.)

	Name	Question	Topic	RFI Recipient
1	The Business	**Asset Request:** Statement of Business Vision, Mission, and Values	The Business	Relevant Human Resources Personnel
2	Data Technologies	**Asset Request:** Enterprise IT architecture	Data Technologies	IT Manager
3	Data Technologies	**Asset Request:** Data infrastructure architecture	Data Technologies	Solution Architect
4	Data Technologies	**Asset Request:** Architecture standards	Data Technologies	IT Manager
5	Data Technologies	What data technologies and tools do you use throughout the course of your work?	Data Technologies	IT Professionals, Data Professionals, Relevant Human Resources Personnel, Relevant Sales & Marketing Personnel, Relevant Finance Personnel
6	Data Technologies	What other data technologies and tools do you know of that are being used by colleagues at the company?	Data Technologies	IT Professionals, Data Professionals, Relevant Human Resources Personnel, Relevant Sales & Marketing Personnel, Relevant Finance Personnel
7	Data Technologies	In terms of file sizes, what are the biggest data sets you're currently working with?	Data Technologies	IT Professionals, Data Professionals
8	Data Technologies	How do you access the data you need to do your job?	Data Technologies	IT Professionals, Data Professionals, Relevant Human Resources Personnel, Relevant Sales & Marketing Personnel, Relevant Finance Personnel

49 records

FIGURE 15-11: Questions and recipients inside my question-and-asset request database.

After you have all your questions and requests mapped out against the most appropriate recipients of those requests, you then filter the table by recipient to see who you need to send which questions to. Figure 15-12 shows the questions you may consider asking of relevant personnel in your finance department.

Finance Requests | Hide fields | 1 filter | Group | Sorted by 1 field | Color

	Name	Question	Topic
1	The Business	Do you think that a better use of data could create massive gains in your department? If so, how? (please describe)	The Business
2	Data Technologies	What data technologies and tools do you use throughout the course of your work?	Data Technologies
3	Data Technologies	What other data technologies and tools do you know of that are being used by colleagues at the company?	Data Technologies
4	Data Technologies	How do you access the data you need to do your job?	Data Technologies
5	Data Technologies	Where are your data sets being stored?	Data Technologies
6	Data Resources	What data do you have access to?	Data Resources

FIGURE 15-12: Some filtered questions, ready to send to relevant finance personnel.

You can then go in and, for each unique recipient group, just copy the appropriate questions and paste them into a survey tool. Proof them, and then send out a group email so that all appropriate members of that small recipient group receive a survey with the questions that are relevant to their specific role.

The questions in the following list are examples of what you might send to potential stakeholders and business unit managers:

>> Do you feel confident that you're getting the data and analytics you need to support you in making the best-informed decision on behalf of the company? If not, what would you like improved?

>> What sort of data-driven improvements would you like to see in an ideal future?

>> How is the lack of data availability and/or predictive capabilities adversely affecting your team members' productivity or team outcomes?

>> How are business process inefficiencies adversely affecting your business unit?

>> On a scale from 1 to 10 (where 1 is completely uncomfortable), how comfortable do you feel with your current level of data literacy?

>> Which data quality issues have you encountered? How have you worked to resolve or address those issues?

Once responses have been returned, start reviewing them. Look for some interesting responses and take note. These individuals may be people you should interview when you move into the assessment phase, which I talk about in Chapter 17.

Chapter **16**

Narrowing In on the Optimal Data Science Use Case

Selecting the best data science use case to implement first (or next) is one of the most important aspects of setting up your projects for success. To be in a position to do that successfully, you need to assess your company based on the evidence you've collected about its current state. Assuming that you're following the steps prescribed by the STAR framework, which I discuss in Chapter 15, at this point you've been authorized to propose a new data science project, you've surveyed the industry, and you've taken stock of your company's current state, as shown in Figure 16-1.

At this point in the process, you're ready to assess your company and identify the lowest-hanging-fruit data use case — the focus of this chapter. In Chapter 17, you can see how to make recommendations based on your assessment.

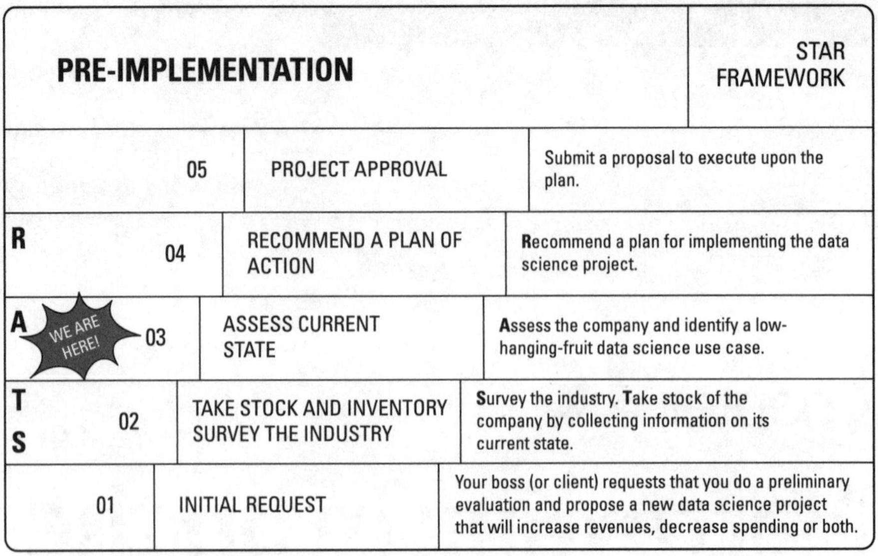

PRE-IMPLEMENTATION				STAR FRAMEWORK
	05	PROJECT APPROVAL	Submit a proposal to execute upon the plan.	
R	04	RECOMMEND A PLAN OF ACTION	Recommend a plan for implementing the data science project.	
A	03 WE ARE HERE!	ASSESS CURRENT STATE	Assess the company and identify a low-hanging-fruit data science use case.	
T S	02	TAKE STOCK AND INVENTORY SURVEY THE INDUSTRY	Survey the industry. Take stock of the company by collecting information on its current state.	
	01	INITIAL REQUEST	Your boss (or client) requests that you do a preliminary evaluation and propose a new data science project that will increase revenues, decrease spending or both.	

FIGURE 16-1: Assessing your company's current state.

Reviewing the Documentation

If you follow the instructions I lay out in Chapter 15 for researching your company, you end up with a lot of documentation describing the inner and outer workings of your company. That's great! That's just the strong foundation you need for meaningfully and accurately assessing your company's *current state*. If you're not familiar with this term, it's just consulting vernacular that refers to the state of your company, as it is now. This term is juxtaposed with a company's *future state* — the status of the company at some defined point in the future. When a company hires a consultant — data or otherwise — it's hiring someone to provide advice, strategic plans, or training (or all three) to help the company bridge the gap between its current state and future state.

After you have all that documentation on hand, it's time to review it. This process involves thoroughly reading and reviewing all the documentation you collected on your company. You can produce a SWOT analysis as you work through it, in order to make note of the key findings that jump out at you. (In case the term *SWOT* is new to you, it's just a simple set of notes you create about your company's strengths, weaknesses, opportunities, and threats that you notice while you're working your way through the documentation.) These notes can help you summarize your findings so that you can more easily identify the lowest-hanging-fruit data science use case.

Selecting Your Quick-Win Data Science Use Cases

After you have thoroughly reviewed all the documentation you've collected and have produced a high-level SWOT analysis, you should be in a good position to select some contenders for the lowest-hanging-fruit data science use case.

You can do that by bringing to mind the data science use cases you surveyed during Part 1 of the STAR framework. (For more on the STAR framework, see Chapter 15.) Consider all the data resources, technologies, and skillsets that are required in order to implement each case. If you conclude, based on your documentation review, that your company lacks (or cannot easily acquire) the data resources, technologies, and skillsets required in order to implement a particular data science use case, throw it out. It isn't the lowest-hanging-fruit use case you're looking for.

TIP

Review data science use cases thoroughly when you work through the Survey step of the STAR framework, for two reasons:

>> You want to have an idea of the best and worst of what's possible for your company with respect to the data science use cases it chooses to implement.

>> You need a sufficient number of data science use cases to choose from so that you can take "the best of the best" and quickly discard the ones that don't represent a quick win for your company.

After you've sifted through relevant data science use cases and removed the ones that aren't promising, you have to then apply your best judgment to select the top three data science cases that seem the most promising for your company — based on what you know about its current state. These three use cases are the final contenders for the lowest-hanging-fruit data science use case for your company's next successful data science project.

Zeroing in on the quick win

After you've narrowed the list to a set of three promising data science use cases, you then select the absolute best, most promising data science use case. If this is your first time being strategic about your data science project planning, you most definitely want this use case to be a quick win for your company. (When I say "quick win," I mean that you want the project to produce a positive, quantifiable return on investment, or ROI, in its first three months — this success establishes a solid foundation for you in gaining the confidence from business leaders that you need in order to lead even bigger data science projects.)

To assess these top three data science use cases against your company's current state, prudently produce an alternatives analysis, or at least some draft versions of one. For each of the potential data science use cases, first consider your working knowledge of your company as well as your findings from the documentation review, and then answer the following questions:

>> Is your use case based purely on big data technologies, or does it entail data science too?

>> How much data would this project require?

>> How much of that data does your company own?

>> Would you need to acquire outside data resources in order to implement this data science use case? If so, how feasible is it, in terms of cost and time, for these resources to be acquired?

>> Which data skillsets do you have on staff to help implement this data science use case?

>> Which skillsets would you need to acquire? How feasible is it, in terms of cost and time, for these skillsets to be acquired?

>> Which data technologies will you need in order to implement a particular data science use case?

>> Which technologies do you already own, and which ones will you need to acquire? How feasible is it, in terms of cost and time, for these technologies to be acquired?

Answering these questions should help narrow your data science use case options, but I suggest whittling them down further by using a POTI model.

Producing a POTI model

Before doing a final data science use case selection, you need to assess how each of the potential use cases will affect your company's POTI — its processes, organization, technology, and information, in other words. Let's look at each of these factors in greater detail:

>> **Processes:** Before deciding on a data science use case, you need to look at your company's operational models and processes. Describe how this data initiative will impact them. Which current business processes will be impacted by the implementation of this new data project? How will these business processes be modified or extended after the new data system is up and running?

>> **Organization:** Describe how this data initiative will impact the people and culture at your organization. Which people-requirements will be impacted by the implementation of this new data project? Document anticipated changes to these elements:

- Data skillset requirements

- Business culture

- Hiring requirements

- Team member repositioning

- Training requirements

>> **Technology:** Describe how this data initiative will impact technology across your organization. Which technologies will be required, eliminated, or augmented during the implementation of this new data project? How will these changes impact other business units or projects? What needs to be done to mitigate disruption of services across the business?

>> **Information:** Which information or data will be required by your company, in its future state, for this data science project to be considered a success? Describe how this data initiative will impact the type of information delivered to people and to business systems across your organization. Which information sources will be discarded? Which will need to be created? What changes are there to who-gets-which information? With respect to machine-to-machine systems, what changes take place to wherever information is sent? On which frequency does information need to be delivered? How do these changes in information requirements impact technology, people, and processes across the organization?

TIP

The data dictionary I recommend you use in Chapter 15 should come in handy here. Reference it when you're assessing the Information portion of the POTI model.

Based on your answers to these questions, it should be rather straightforward to pinpoint a data science use case that offers the greatest potential ROI for your company, in the shortest amount of time, with the lowest level of risk.

From there, I suggest one more stopgap assessment question. Does the data science use case support your company in better reaching its business mission and vision? If the answer to this question is yes, then let this use case be your lowest-hanging-fruit data science use case. If the answer to the question is no, step back to the second-most-promising data science use case.

A data science project ultimately has two goals: Increase revenue for the company and support the company in reaching its vision. Always be mindful of, and prepared to discuss, exactly how your data science projects are accomplishing these two requirements. If you can't do that, you may find yourself in hot water sometime in the near future.

If you've made it to this point in your data science journey, congratulations! You've identified the lowest-hanging-fruit data science use case for your company. That's a huge deal — and a lot of work you've accomplished to reach this point. If you've followed the documentation collection-and-review processes as I've described them, your decision-making will be well-supported with ironclad evidence. Furthermore, you created draft assessments before selecting a final use case. Be sure to keep all your documentation and draft assessments in a safe place. I recommend that you make them addendums to your data science project plan so that you have a full, comprehensive body of evidence to support any recommendations you might make. Before you reach that point, however, you still need to complete the assessment phase. The act of selecting your use case only marks the halfway point when it comes to assessments within the STAR framework.

If you made proper requests for information and could not gain access to all the documentation you need, document that aspect as well. Retain email records and meeting minutes that document the fact that you did your due diligence and that you simply were not granted the access you need. In case the documentation omission results in a downstream problem in your data science project plans, that documentation will defer responsibility to the responsible party (not to you!).

Picking between Plug-and-Play Assessments

The type of assessments you need depends heavily on the data science use case you've selected. Though you won't find a one-size-fits-all approach, I offer you some suggestions for assessments that I feel would be helpful in a wide variety of data science projects.

Most data professionals aren't working in a microcosm, where they have all the power and say-so about their company's data operations. To the contrary, I expect that most readers of this book are working in larger organizations where corporate politics menace their every move. The assessments I suggest in the remainder of this chapter are just that — suggestions. If you have the power and initiative to conduct these assessments, I am sure you will find them immensely helpful. But if you don't — just do what you can and move on.

The following assessment protocols are meant to be used as helpful plug-and-play suggestions that you can use according to your company's needs.

Carrying out a data skill gap analysis for your company

The STAR framework, which I talk about in Chapter 15, offers you a clear, repeatable process that you can use whenever you need to plan out a data science project. As part of this framework, you take stock of the data skillsets of the people who work at your company. Because you've already surveyed these individuals, you have a pretty good idea of the existing competencies to be found within the relevant human capital at your company. You also have already chosen a data science use case. With that use case selection, you've also narrowed in on a range of skills you'll need in order to support the data science project. In the best-case scenario, your company already has people with those skills, and those people have the capacity to help support your data science project. Another favorable outcome is that your company has people with the basic prerequisites needed to learn the data skills your project requires. And, in the worst-case scenario, your company needs to make one (or a few) new hires.

The reason that it's vitally important to select the lowest-hanging-fruit use case is so that you can achieve quick wins for your company without needing to make expensive and risky new hires or acquisitions. Especially if this is one of your first times leading a new data science project, I strongly recommend that you do *not* select a data science use case that requires your company to make new acquisitions of employees, technologies, or data resources. That's a good way to get your project put on hold indefinitely.

Assessing the data skillset requirements for the project is straightforward. You need to look at the technologies the project will require and the data science modeling approaches that are implicit in the use case you selected. With that step out of the way, all you then need to do is cross-reference those skillset requirements with your survey results to see who at your company can help deliver this project.

If you need your data science project to score a quick win for your company, you simply have to already have the requisite data skillsets, technologies, and resources on hand. There's no time for training, creating service agreements, or other related tasks. So, for your first few data science projects, make sure you select use cases that your company can implement right away and see a positive ROI within three months.

As you gain more experience and trust with respect to planning and leading data science projects, you earn a little more of an allowance in terms of resource allocation (or reallocation, as it were). In this situation, if your company has people who have the exact skills you need, you also need to address the other sticking point — their availability. If those individuals are completely locked down in supporting other teams and projects, adding one more project to their plate will be a tough sell to their superiors. You have to decide whether it's worth the risk to hire someone new to help. In other cases, you may find people with the available capacity who just don't have the exact skills that are needed. If it's possible that, with training, these individuals could support your data science project, that would eliminate the need for making a costly new hire. It would also create more value from that person's time (and your company's investment in retaining that time). In this case, you'd want to assess your survey results and produce a training plan for each of these workers in order to take them from their current competency to the higher competency levels your project requires.

Assessing the ethics of your company's AI projects and products

If you're working at a company that truly supports its mission, vision, and values and its leaders are data literate, those leaders will back initiatives that inquire about and reinforce higher ethical standards with respect to the company's AI solutions. Unfortunately, most leaders aren't all that data literate (which represents another opportunity for improvement in most companies' data strategies). In such cases, speak to them in a language they understand. Speaking strictly from a business perspective, gaps in AI ethics represent significant reputational risk to the company. If your company uses AI technology in a way that produces inequitable and/or biased outcomes and that grievance is discovered, you can expect the company to appear in media headlines — somehow, somewhere.

REMEMBER

AI is inherently risky — it's simply prudent to take proactive measures to mitigate any ethical issues related to your company's AI solutions. In this section, you get a head-start in assessing the ethics of your company's AI solutions.

In Chapter 15, I talk about how important it is for you to itemize all your company's active AI solutions as well as to collect reports and documentation that describes the machine learning processes and model metadata that each of these AI solutions deploys. I also talk there about the fact that you should collect, for each AI solution, user manuals, so to speak, that explain how each of these solutions works. Lastly, I make it clear in Chapter 15 that you have to gather any information that references potential biases produced by these solutions. After you've gathered all this requisite information, you can use it to do a preliminary assessment of your company's AI ethics. The next few sections point you in the right direction.

Illustrating the need for ethical AI

Accountable, explainable, unbiased: These words represent what your company's AI solutions need to be in order for them to be truly ethical. But what does "accountable, explainable, unbiased" AI actually mean, and why does it matter to real-life human beings? Let me explain with a true story.

REMEMBER

Though this scenario actually happened to someone in real life, the names and demographic details of the people involved are fictional.

Imagine yourself as a healthcare provider who's been tasked with treating Mr. Smith, a 65-year-old who has already been diagnosed with lung cancer and who experiences severe bleeding. You're working with one of the leading oncology clinics in the US, so you're privy to all the latest-and-greatest technologies. The latest gizmoid acquired by your clinic is IBM Watson for Oncology. You've been instructed to consult with this cutting-edge, costly software when making your treatment recommendation.

You follow orders, so you go in and feed Mr. Smith's patient data into the machine and await its recommendations. A few minutes later, it spits out a recommendation that the chemotherapy drug Bevacizumab should be administered to Mr. Smith as a form of treatment for his lung cancer. You stand back in complete shock because, experienced oncology specialist that you are, you know that Bevacizumab has a black box warning that it should never, *ever*, be used to treat cancer patients who experience severe bleeding.

This expensive technology is supposed to improve the quality and safety of the medical recommendations you make. Instead, its recommendation is downright dangerous. What if you hadn't been educated and aware of the medical contradiction for yourself? Do you see what a huge liability this machine could be setting you up for? Not to mention the negative impact on the lives of the people who depend on you to survive. I am sorry to break it to you, friends, but this scenario actually happened in real life. It's just one example of the real and present dangers you expose yourself to when you depend on AI solutions in the healthcare industry. Implicit risks like these, however, are baked into AI solutions that are used across every industry in existence. As users and beneficiaries of AI solutions, everyone must be extremely vigilant about their implicit risk.

What does that look like? I mean, what do you look for to determine whether an AI solution is trustworthy? Well, for starters, you have to take proactive measures to make sure that your AI system is, as I say a little earlier, accountable, explainable, and unbiased. (For more on this topic, see Chapter 15.)

Proving accountability for AI solutions

How can you identify whether your AI system is indeed accountable? You start by thoroughly reviewing the documentation you collected about the accountability of your company's AI solutions. Those are the reports you collected that describe the machine learning processes and model metadata that each of these AI solutions deploys. First read the documentation yourself, and jot down notes inside a draft SWOT analysis, just to get your own thoughts recorded, in a first pass, on paper. Then make another pass through the documentation — this time, answering the following questions:

>> Does each active AI solution come complete with its model metadata? And does that metadata detail where the datasets are stored, their filenames and version numbers, variable names, and some basics about underlying data set distributions?

>> Does the documentation detail what type of machine learning models are being used by the system? How about the steps that are required to prepro-cess the data before using it in the machine learning model? Does it include the parameter settings within the models? All this information is helpful if you need to either compare the system to others or rebuild it sometime in the distant future. (Heaven forbid!)

>> In terms of context, does the model metadata detail factors such as the programming language and version used to build the model, the source code, any dependencies, or the CPU/GPU and operating system in which the models were developed?

>> With respect to metrics, does the metadata detail the metrics that were used to evaluate the models that are included in your AI system?

>> Does the system come accompanied by a brief video that describes all these details?

You probably have guessed it, but your answer to all these questions should be a resounding yes! If any of the answers comes out as no, you have a gap in the accountability of your company's AI solutions. This gap represents risk to the business and should be remedied.

Vouching for your company's AI

Let me bring up the elephant in the room here: General Data Protection Regula-tion, otherwise known as GDPR. I talk about data privacy in Chapters 14 and 15, but never go so far as to name exact regulations. (There are a lot of them!) GDPR is a mammoth in terms of its elephant-ness, though, and it's one of the main drivers behind the need for explainable AI, so it pays to look at it in greater detail.

GDPR asserts data privacy rights for all EU citizens, regardless of where they reside in the world. According to Recital 71 of GDPR, "[the data subject should have] the right . . . to obtain an explanation of the decision reached" if their personal data was used in any part of reaching that decision — period. End of story.

GDPR extends to all EU citizens the right to an explanation anytime a predictive model is used in making a judgment about them. This right stipulates that EU citizens can demand an explanation for any judgments made that impact them, including for reasons such as credit risk scoring, autonomous vehicle behaviors, healthcare decisions, and what-have-you.

As for the financial risk to companies found in violation of GDPR, Article 83(4) of GDPR states that infringements shall be "subject to administrative fines up to 10 000 000 EUR, or . . . up to 2% of the total worldwide annual turnover of the preceding financial year, whichever is higher." Enough said?

Now that you understand the gravity of this explainable AI matter, I want to show you a couple of the ways that you can identify explainability in your company's AI systems. Read the documentation you've collected, and then answer the following questions:

>> Do all of your company's active AI solutions come with a manual that explains how the predictions are generated by the machine?

>> Is this manual written in plain English so that people who aren't data professionals can comprehend it without having to take a course in data literacy?

Having this manual comes in handy when inevitable questions arise about how and why recommendations are being made. In that case, the appropriate decision-maker can just explain their judgment and how the AI solution impacted it, providing a copy of the plain-language manual to supplement that response. In most cases, this type of explanation should be more than sufficient.

WARNING

Across the AI community, some deliberation takes place about whether AI systems really need to be explainable and interpretable. Because many data scientists are using a black box approach (they don't know all the details of the math and code that are implemented within the model), of course they can't explain them. This isn't a safe approach to AI.

Designated representatives of your company must be able to explain how its AI solutions work. If your company uses a vendor AI solution, the vendor who supplies the AI system must provide a plain-language manual explaining how it works, and in a way that makes sense to non-data people. If they can't, it's time for you to seek alternatives.

Unbiasing AI

To move into a description of one more characteristic of ethical AI, your AI system needs to produce unbiased results. This one is tough to explain, so let's start with a fictitious example.

An elderly man named Tom has been admitted to the hospital for medical testing related to a bronchitis diagnosis. The testing takes longer than expected, and Tom's loving family desperately want him to be released to them at home. In a few days, when it comes time for Tom to be released, he is discharged into a state-run nursing facility and isn't permitted to go home. When asked about this decision, the healthcare provider thoughtfully explains that, because Tom's household income is low, the AI system has predicted that he won't receive adequate support and care at home. The AI has determined that Tom should be discharged to a state care facility — where he will subsequently incur higher costs of services and a greater chance of readmission to the hospital. This is an example of an incredibly biased outcome.

Bias can be integrated into a predictive model in two main ways, when either of these statements is true:

>> **Training data isn't representative of the general population.**

>> **The AI relies heavily on demographics when making its predictions.**

>> **The cognitive bias of data professionals whose work impacts the project.**

Examples of variables that are at high-risk of producing bias are race, gender, skin color, religion, national origin, marital status, sexual orientation, education background, income, and age. Generally speaking, if your model requires these variables, be sure to evaluate its results for unfair bias. If you find bias, you have to go back to the drawing board and find another way to generate results — one that does not produce unfair discrimination of people based on their demographic.

As to what to look for when assessing whether your AI systems are biased, your best bet is to rigorously test the solution in trials that approximate real life as much as possible and then make some personal judgments about its outputs. It would be worth your time to assemble a user group to evaluate the level of potential bias. Here are some questions to consider when evaluating bias in AI outputs:

>> Is the model's training data representative of the general population?

>> Are the current AI systems relying heavily on demographics to make predictions about people?

>> What are the downstream implications of the outputs generated by the AI system?

>> What would a counterbiased system recommend?

>> What are the potential ramifications with respect to systemic bias, if this AI is implemented across a large swath of the population? Do you think it's fair? Would your peers think so?

>> How is your organization working to ensure that its current AI projects produce unbiased results?

If, by exploring these questions, you find troubling answers, I suggest that you take it on yourself to start brainstorming which measures your company can put into place to ensure that future AI projects are accountable, explainable, and unbiased. These are exactly the type of suggestions you'd want to include when you produce recommendations, a topic we cover thoroughly in Chapter 17.

Assessing data governance and data privacy policies

Here's the simple truth: You can't have ethical AI without good data governance supporting it. Why? Because in order for your AI to be explainable, unbiased, and accountable, it must be built from high-quality data that has been properly documented and maintained. If it helps to grasp this concept, think of data governance as a type of chain of custody that secures the integrity and reliability of your organization's data. To build explainable AI, you need to understand and, more importantly, *trust* the data that goes into it.

Being in a position to explain your AI to any doubters is one of the main benefits of insisting on good data governance, but there are other benefits as well, such as these:

>> Team members across the organization will trust the data as a credible and reliable source of information.

>> Your organization will have a unified set of data definitions. In other words, everyone will speak the same language when making reference to your organization's shared data resources.

>> Your organization's data will be maintained and will function as a consistently reliable source to end users.

>> You will have processes in place to centralize and simplify regular reporting processes.

You can assess your company's data governance by simply looking to see whether it exhibits the characteristics of good data governance I just outlined. Some signs of overly lax governance policies are redundant duplicate data sets running amok, poor data quality, and overall unmanageability in a company's data operations. Excessively strict data governance often makes itself known in the form of data bottleneck problems, where users can't access data without submitting a formal request from the IT department — a bureaucratic hoop that takes a long time to jump through. The result is that you and all the other business users wait in line to gain access to the basic data needed to do your jobs. If you see gaping data governance problems inside your company, you definitely need to address them in the planning and recommendations of your data science project.

As you might expect, data governance policies don't appear out of thin air — somebody has to come up with them. That's where the *data governance council* — a team of elected individuals who together decide on a company's data governance policies — comes into play. Any mature company has a data governance council in place, but in case your company is smaller or newer, you probably need to form one. When doing so, assess and identify those individuals best suited to serve on the council.

For starters, you should select people who have some mixture of the following characteristics:

>> **Educated and experienced in developing data policies and procedures**

>> **Capable of good communication with a knack for getting along with others**

   Look for some training background (so that the person can help educate the rest of the organization about the importance of data governance).

>> **Experienced with working with data coming from a wide variety of business units at your organization**

>> **Cognizant of operational ROIs related to data governance**

Data governance policies — or *data policies,* for short — are simply policies that document the rules and processes that should be followed in order for your data resources to remain consistent and of high quality. Document these rules and processes for every major data-intensive activity that happens within your business. Such rules and processes are often referred to as *data governance standards*. A mature company should be in a position to bring together the documentation for the entire set of major business activities into one data governance document — that's your organization's data policy. After being compiled, the data policy must be maintained and adjusted per changes in your organization. And again, data policy is but one of the fundamental constituents of solid data governance.

In this book, I don't tell you how to build solid data governance from an implementation perspective. Data governance is, however, a prerequisite to ethical AI. By selecting the right people to spearhead your data governance council, you set up your organization for success. And those right people? They should understand and make decisions to support the data science implementation requirements for your organization.

When it comes to your company's data privacy policies, that's a topic you definitely want to leave for the lawyers, because it's one that only they can develop, according to requirements by law. Your task is to assess how well those policies, when developed, are adhered to within your company. When looking to assess your company's data privacy policies, you may want to start by first answering the following questions:

>> What, exactly, are your company's data privacy policies?

>> How are these policies enforced?

>> Do the policies contain any hold-ups or gaps in enforcement?

>> Does the data privacy policy have any gaps that may pose a later financial or reputational risk to your company?

Document any potential gaps, omissions, or risks you can think of so that you can address them in the recommendations you'll surely make in line with your upcoming data science project. (For more on how to fashion these recommendations, check out Chapter 17.)

Chapter **17**

Planning for Future Data Science Project Success

Before putting the pedal to the metal with your new data science project, you *must* take the time to create a technical plan for all the implementation requirements involved in making this project a success. What you call this plan can vary: I've seen consultants call technical implementation plans lots of names — the most popular are technical plan, management plan, strategic plan, and plan of action. What you decide to name your plan is up to you, but make sure that you use your plan for its intended purpose. The purpose of your data science project planning document is to

» Document, summarize, and consolidate the company's data operations into one overarching, up-to-date plan

» Double-verify the feasibility of your intended project before proceeding into the implementation phase

» Secure the approvals needed for your project in order to proceed with the work

» Develop realistic benchmarks for measuring the delivery and performance of the data science project you recommend

WARNING

Much of the technical planning approach I share in this chapter is derived from my own professional experience in building plans and strategies for multimillion-dollar engineering projects for local and federal governments in the United States. The extent to which you need to preplan your data science project depends on its proposed costs. If you're planning and delivering this project as a team of one and it takes you fewer than eight weeks to complete the project, spending a month building a detailed implementation plan doesn't make sense. But if you're tasked with building and delivering a costly, resource-intensive data science project on behalf of your company, make sure to protect the company's investment (and the trust that has been placed in you) by following the STAR framework in its entirety. (If you're unsure what the STAR framework is all about, check out Chapter 15.)

Throughout the first part of this chapter, I focus on what you should include in your project plan. Following that, I have you take another pass through an alternatives analysis using the POTI model, interviews, and other approaches I talk about in Chapter 16. Though some of the approaches are the same as earlier in this chapter, I show you how to apply those approaches in new ways to map out precise implementation details that will be involved in executing your data science project plan.

Preparing an Implementation Plan

The implementation plan for your data science project is the last bit of work you need to complete before setting its wheels in motion. If your project is a small one, you'll still want to put together a draft planning document and secure preapproval before proceeding. If your project will require significant allocations of your company's data skillsets, resources, and technologies, however, knowing how to write a thorough data science technical plan may be even more important than the data science implementation work that proceeds from it. That's because the type of implementation plan you're about to see in this chapter protects the company from investing its capital in projects and technologies that may be ultimately doomed to failure. As shown in Figure 17-1, you're at the R step of the STAR framework, where you see how to make responsible recommendations for a plan of action for your proposed data science project.

Though I can't tell you exactly what you should include in, and exclude from, your specific data science project plan, I am happy to share with you the outline I use as part of the Data Strategy Plan Template I share with my clients inside my Data Strategy Starter Kit product. You can use and adopt the following outline so that it best meets your specific data science project needs:

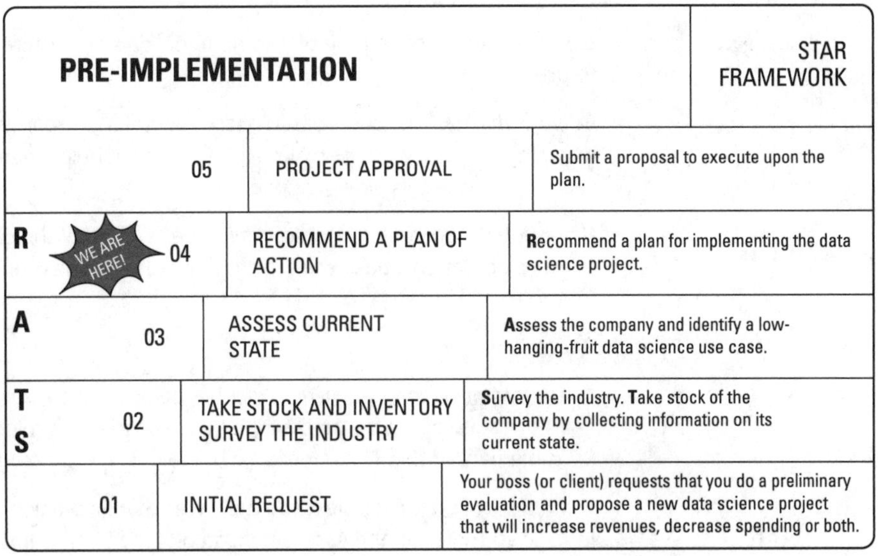

FIGURE 17-1:
Recommending a
plan of action.

>> **Table of Contents**

>> **Acronyms**

>> **Executive summary**

- *Current state summary statement:* This is a summary statement of the current state of your company and the problems you uncovered during the Assessment step of the STAR framework (covered in Chapter 16).

- *Recommendations summary:* This is a summary statement of the recommendations you set forth in this plan.

>> **Section 1: Introduction**

- *Applicability:* A statement describing the business units and problems to which this plan is applicable

- *Purpose:* A clear statement of the purpose and need for the project

- *Objective:* A statement describing the outcome goals for the project

>> **Section 2: Overview of your organization**

- *Background:* A description of the background of the company and why this data science project should happen now

- *Business vision:* A statement of a company's goals and aspirations for the future

- *Business mission:* An action-based description of a company's purpose for being in business, in terms of who it helps, how it helps them, and why it seeks to provide this type of support

- *Organization's operations and activities:* A description of the company's relevant operations, business activities, and the business units responsible for them

- *Future state*

  - *Future state vision statement:* Describe the optimal outcome for the future state of the business when this data science project plan is implemented to a T.

  - *Data science use case:* Describe the lowest-hanging-fruit data science use case you select in the Assessment step of the STAR framework. (I cover selecting a use case in Chapter 16.)

» Section 3: Legal, regulatory, and ethical framework

- *General Data Protection Regulation:* Describe relevant aspects of GDPR — a topic I discuss in Chapter 16.

- *AI ethics framework:* Introduce the accountable-explainable-unbiased AI ethics framework I talk about in Chapter 16.

- *Other applicable laws:* Look into other applicable data privacy laws — the California Consumer Privacy Act, for example. If local data privacy regulations impact your company, mention them here.

» Section 4: Your organization's current organizational structure

- *Organizational structure:* Describe the organizational structure of your company. (I recommend including a copy of the most relevant organizational charts collected as part of the Taking Stock step of the STAR framework I cover in Chapter 15.)

- *Chief executive officer:* Name and briefly describe the company's chief executive officer.

- *Chief information officer:* Name and briefly describe the company's chief information officer.

- *Data program/product managers:* Name and briefly describe the company's data program and product managers, as well as their respective responsibilities.

- *Data team roles and responsibilities:* Name and briefly describe the company's data team(s). Be sure to describe the purpose and function of each of the data teams, including their names and team members that comprise them.

- *Business units and intended users:* Describe the business unit and roles that will benefit most from the data science project you propose. (I talk about users and how best to go about designing for their needs in greater detail a little later in this chapter.)

- *Data governance committee and officers:* Describe the data governance council and name the members that comprise it. (For more on data governance, see Chapter 16.)

- *Data privacy compliance program:* If your company has a data privacy compliance program, describe it and its team members here.

>> **Section 5: Your organization's current data technologies**

Describe the primary tools now used within the company's data technology infrastructure. (For tips on how to carry out this step, read up on the Taking Stock step of the STAR framework in Chapter 15.)

>> **Section 6: Your organization's current data resources**

- *Data generation activities:* Describe how data is generated, stored, and handled across your company. Be sure to dig deep into the specifics of data generation activities with the business units that are most relevant to this data science project.

- *Data security processes:* Describe your company's current security protocols for protecting its data assets. (For more on this topic, see Chapter 16.)

>> **Section 7: Your organization's current data skillsets**

- *Methods:* Describe the methods used to collect information on the company's data skillsets. (The Data Skill Gap Analysis approach I talk about as part of the Assessment step of the STAR framework in Chapter 16 would be a help here.)

- *Data skillsets inventory:* Document the current data skillsets to be found among your workforce. (Again, the Data Skill Gap Analysis approach I talk about as part of the Assessment step of the STAR framework in Chapter 16 is helpful.)

>> **Section 8: Alternatives analysis**

Briefly describe the criteria you used to evaluate alternative solutions. (I cover alternatives analysis in greater detail later in this chapter.) Be sure to detail and describe all three alternatives you evaluated in the course of planning and making recommendations for this data science project.

» Section 9: Data program status and recommendations

In this section, outline your recommendations on how to go about implementing your data science project in order to take your company from current state to future state:

- *Requirements:* Describe the business requirements and needs that this data science project will satisfy.

- *Summary of goal status*: Describe the goals of this data science project, as well as the time frames in which these goals will be completed. These goals should include milestones and the statuses thereof, as well as indicators that designate the function of each of these within the project:

  - *Business mission goals:* Detail the outcome goals that demonstrate how this data science project helps move the business closer to its business vision.

  - *Data science project goals:* Define the milestones that represent success for this data science project.

- *Data technology recommendations:* Describe the data technologies you recommend for carrying out this data science project.

  - *Summary of technology recommendations:* Summarize the reasoning behind why you're recommending these specific data technologies as well as the alternatives you evaluated in the course of reaching this recommendation.

  - *Reference architecture:* This document is meant to embody accepted industry best practices, typically suggesting the optimal delivery method for the specific technologies you suggest for implementing this data science project. (For an example of what a reference architecture would look like, see Figure 17-2.)

- *Data resources recommendations:* Describe the data resources that will be required in order to carry out this data science project:

  - *Legal, regulatory, and AI ethics compliance recommendations:* Detail the measures that you recommend putting into place to protect the company's data privacy and AI ethics. Mention any legal concerns but defer responsibility for legal recommendations to your company's legal team.

  - *Data governance recommendations:* Detail any data governance recommendations you're making based on the assessment work you've completed. (For a look at how such work could be carried out, see Chapter 16.)

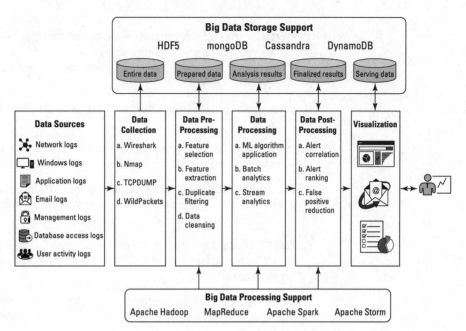

FIGURE 17-2:
An example of
reference
architecture.

- *Skillset and people recommendations:* Summarize the policies, roles, and responsibilities you recommend for successful implementation of this data science project:

  - *Use case skillset requirements:* Describe the data skillsets required in order to implement this specific data science use case.

  - *Training recommendations:* Describe who needs to receive which training in order for the company to implement (and take the most benefit from) this data science project. Publish all employee training plans:

    - Data team personnel training requirements: Summarize your training recommendations for data team personnel, as well as the recommended training workflows and training cost estimates.

    - User training requirements: Summarize your training recommendations for the end users of the data science solution as well as the recommended training workflows and training cost estimates.

    - Data literacy training requirements: If relevant, summarize your company-wide data literacy training recommendations, as well as the recommended training workflows and training cost estimates.

- *Personnel repositioning:* Summarize your recommendations for promoting existing staff to fulfill the skillset requirements of this data science project.

- *New hires:* Summarize your recommendation for making new hires to fulfill the skillset requirements of this data science project. Be sure to describe the roles, responsibilities, and skills requirements for all recommended new positions or hires.

- *Data teams:* Summarize any changes you recommend to the company's data teams.

- *Organizational culture:* Summarize your recommendations for improving the company culture with respect to data:

  - Top-down approach recommendations: Clarify a top-down strategy to gain buy-in and the adoption enforcement support needed to help your data science project succeed.

  - Bottom-up approach recommendations: Clarify a bottom-up strategy to secure buy-in and the user adoption needed to help your data science project succeed.

  - User adoption recommendations: Summarize your recommended best practices for making sure your data science solution gets used after it's ready.

- *Data initiative best practices:* Detail other best practices that need to be put into place to make sure that this project is successful where others have failed. (For more on best practices, see my discussion of the Taking Stock part of the STAR framework in Chapter 15.)

» Section 10: Data science project plan of action

Detail your plan of action for this recommended data science project. Be sure to include outcome goals and project milestones. Include an Action Plan Summary Table that details the action items that need to be completed, as well as their target dates, associated tasks, responsible parties, and outcome deliverables. Also include a project roadmap, which may or may not be delivered via the kinds of Gantt charts I discuss in Chapter 8.

» Section 11: Appendixes

- *Appendix A:* Document inventory. (See Chapter 15.)

- Appendix B: Skillset survey. (See Chapter 15.)

- *Appendix C:* Data dictionary. (See Chapter 15.)

- *Appendix D:* Proposed solution brief. (If you're recommending a vendor solution, include a brief on the solution you recommend.)

- *Appendix E:* Relevant use cases. (Include use cases for the three top-contender data science use cases you've assessed. For more on assessing use cases, see Chapter 16.)

- *Appendix F:* Alternatives analysis matrices, scorecards, and reference tables. (Include data to support your alternative analysis and the recommendations you made based on it.)

- *Appendix G:* Citations. (Document any external references you used for preparing your plan.)

- *Appendix H:* Supporting evaluation documents. (Include other relevant documentation that supports the data science project recommendations within this plan.)

WARNING

A comprehensive data science plan like this one isn't a one-and-done document. It's a living, breathing overview of your company's data operations and how effectively those operations support the company's bottom line. Because of the rapid pace of change in technology, data science strategic plans like this one should be updated every 18 months.

Supporting Your Data Science Project Plan

The outline I provide in the previous section should make it simple to know what you should include in your data science project plan, but it leaves out some important details about planning for your project. The truth is, I could write a whole book on how to plan and manage data science projects and products, and I have only one chapter at my disposal. So, what I've done is whittle down a veritable forest of technical planning approaches to a few that are sure to bring about the clarity you need to get started on creating a responsible plan for your data science project. Those approaches are alternative analysis, the POTI model, and interviews.

Analyzing your alternatives

Before you can make any recommendations, you need to carry out some detailed evaluations of what exactly will be involved in the implementation and how all the pieces and parts will work together to make your data science project a smashing success. In Chapter 16, I talk about how it's a good idea to consider at least three alternative data science use cases as part of your evaluations. The idea is for you to consider each use case separately and the downstream implications for your company if the use case is selected for implementation. The purpose of this lightweight form of alternatives analysis is to support you in selecting the lowest-hanging-fruit data science use case for your company — the data science use case that offers your company the biggest ROI in the shortest amount of time for the least amount of risk.

After having selected such a use case, it's time to get even more precise and exacting with your alternatives analyses. You should address four fundamental aspects in a good alternatives analysis for a data science project, as described in this list:

>> **Project objectives:** A final plan that must be written around a clear statement of purpose and the need for the project

>> **Criteria:** A clear and reasonable set of criteria for evaluating your alternatives

>> **Alternatives:** A clear and reasonable set of alternatives to be evaluated

>> **Documentation:** Sufficient documentation demonstrating that you've considered each alternative against the stated criteria

In terms of what type of alternatives you'd want to consider evaluating within your technical plan, no one-size-fits-all answer exists. The alternatives you choose depend greatly on the specifics of your company, project, and data science use case. I can, however, offer the following suggestions:

>> **Data technologies evaluation**: When it comes to data technology alternatives, you need to evaluate factors such as the cost, benefit, and feasibility associated with a range of alternative data technology solutions that would all potentially suffice. Which technologies do you already own, and which ones will you need to acquire? Within your alternatives, you need to consider which technology stack makes optimal use of your company's current investments.

>> **Data skillset evaluation:** Alternatives to evaluate with respect to data skillsets would mostly come down to evaluating the cost, benefit, and feasibility of various people configurations that would meet your project needs. Which skillsets do you have, and which will you need to acquire? Relevant criteria include hiring costs, availability of current data personnel, training costs, training timelines, and so on.

>> **Data resources evaluation:** Because of the cost and liability associated with storing data, when you evaluate alternatives based on their data resources requirements, you should look for ways to limit the amount of data that your company needs to store and secure. Consider how much data you need to acquire for each alternative. Consider which alternative makes the optimal use of your existing data, in terms of generating profit or savings in exchange for the expense and liability your company incurs by storing it.

The simpler approach here would be to produce a cost-benefit analysis for each alternative. If your proposed project is more costly, you'd probably want to get a lot more detailed with your alternatives analysis by adding the multicriteria decision-making/scoring approach I discuss in Chapter 4 as part of your alternatives evaluation.

Interviewing intended users and designing accordingly

In Chapter 15, I talk about the benefits of using surveys to take a detailed view of your company's current state. Surveys are precursors to interviews. Interviews are a similar information-gathering method, but the interview approach allows you to dig much deeper into what's happening under the hood and to see why key personnel are doing things a certain way. To put together a truly useful technical plan, you need to hear from people about what their needs are and how they are struggling to meet those needs, as well as their opinions about how particular issues are holding the company back from operating as efficiently as possible. These are the types of nitty-gritty details you need to understand if you're going to be successful in planning a data science solution to your company's business problems.

After you collect survey responses and read them thoroughly, you'll certainly be able to identify specific individuals who appear to have information and experience that you need to incorporate as part of your planning approach. Write down the names of those people and spend a good amount of time thinking about all the ways they're relevant to your proposed data science project. Prepare a custom set of interview questions for each interviewee. Be as creative as possible when thinking about questions to ask, because you want to gather information from this individual about every facet and aspect that they touch on with respect to your data science project.

After you have your questions put together, schedule an appropriate amount of time to speak with that person and hear their answers firsthand. When conducting your interview, try to think proactively about how your subject's words impact aspects of your project that you may not yet have considered. Jot down any ideas and questions as they come, and try to squeeze them in during the session, if possible. If you can manage to set aside two or three hours to spend with a key interview subject, that can do wonders for your understanding of the problem your data science solution is intended to solve (and your ability to craft a strategic plan for solving it).

In planning out your interview strategy, address data science product design. Your data science solution must be designed with its end users in mind, and pre-implementation planning is the time that you set these wheels into motion. When planning your interviews, make sure that you schedule time to sit with one or two key individuals who correspond to your idea of the perfect user of your data science solution. For example, if your solution has five different types of intended users (data professionals, executives, business managers, marketing professionals, and so on), you'd schedule time to interview one or two representatives of each of these user segments. Make sure that these individuals are a good representation of the needs and technical competencies of other users in their segment. Tell them about how the solution you're building will help them and then ask them how you can customize the new data science solution to make sure it best fits their needs. Consult with these individuals about their design preferences, outcome goals, and requests for features so that you can make sure that the data science solution is custom-tailored to their preferences and needs.

REMEMBER

The intended users of your data science solution are essentially your customers. Meeting their needs and desires is more important than most data professionals would imagine. If you don't build a solution for your customers according to their needs and preferences, they probably won't use it and, consequently, your project will fail. Avoid this outcome by interviewing your intended users in the project planning stage and taking their needs into account at every step of the development process.

POTI modeling the future state

I talk about the POTI model in Chapter 16 as part of my discussion of the Assessment stage of the STAR framework. It turns out that the POTI model can be as equally useful as part of the framework's recommendation, where you produce plans and recommendations for how to proceed with implementing the data science use case you've selected.

REMEMBER

POTI stands for *processes, organization, technology,* and *information.*

In this stage of the STAR framework, you use the same POTI model but you turn it on its head and consider the downstream implications of your project as you proceed through the implementation phase. In this sense, you're using POTI as a brainstorming tool to help you ensure that your final plan is comprehensive and accounts for all the changes that this new project will bring about within your company. Here are some examples of how you can use POTI as a brainstorming tool in the Recommendations phase:

>> **Processes**: When planning to implement your data science project, look at your company's operational models and processes. For each of the business's operations processes that will be impacted, you need to plan ahead for that impact. What can you do to minimize or avoid disruptions to services? What measures or programs need to be built to prepare impacted users for process modifications that will arise after your new solution is online? What measures can be taken to support those users now and in the future so that they feel comfortable, prepared, and maybe even excited for what's to come with this new data science solution:

>> **Organization:** What measures need to be taken in order to cultivate excitement among intended users of this new data science solution? Create a plan now and start watering those seeds as soon as possible so that when the solution is ready, you have a team (or teams) of people who are excited to use (and even advocate for) the new solution. How will you incentivize employees you plan to promote to a new role? What sort of community culture can you create around the training requirements this data science project will entail? How will you go about sourcing any new hires? What is your plan for creating both top-down and bottom-up reinforcements — to preempt any user adoption issues that might come your way? Detail plans for all these elements within your recommendations.

>> **Technology:** Write out detailed plans for ushering in technology changes. How do you prepare your company and its employees for temporary access restrictions, if applicable? How will you mitigate costly technology delays that you anticipate your project will create in other employees' workflows? How will you prepare employees for technology changes that your new project will inevitably create? How do you manage expectations among all the groups of technology users who will be impacted by this data science project? If your project involves cloud infrastructure or remote access requirements, what needs to be done to ensure that these are ready from day one? Your data science project plan needs to account for all the technology disruptions and changes that will occur because of this project.

>> **Information:** How do you avoid or mitigate information access issues that your data science project may create during the implementation phase? If certain data sources will be moved, how will you prepare the employee who depends on that information to do their job? If some data is slated for deletion, do parties need to be notified about this in advance? If the project expands or diminishes employees' access to data, how will you prepare them for these changes? Will they need training to use the new system? What topics do they need training on? Who will conduct that training, and at what cost? Include these details as part of your project plan as well. If the flow of information across your company will change, how will you manage these changes and the expectations of employees who rely on that information?

Executing On Your Data Science Project Plan

Building a data science project plan takes time, but that time pays off in dividends when it protects your company from costly missteps or project failures. After you take action on what I've been able to show you throughout this book, you will have a plan for implementing your data science project. After you secure approval to proceed with your plan, you move into the execution phase of your project. That's where you get to start applying all the concepts I talk about in Part 1 of this book.

Managing data science projects is a topic for another book, but I want to give you one important warning:

WARNING

Once you move into the execution phase, *keep a close eye on the project milestones* you set forth in your project plan. If you start running behind schedule or over cost projections, you need to go back to the drawing board right away and see what you missed in your planning efforts. Be sure to manage expectations as you execute the project, especially with stakeholders. And don't be afraid to admit weaknesses. If you missed something in the planning phase, you probably did a much better job of planning the project than 98 percent of the people on the planet could do. Be honest, make adjustments, and be fearless in communicating when you see something that may cause a problem later in the project.

REMEMBER

The method of technical planning you read about in this book could have helped many, many companies avoid getting drawn down by the huge Hadoop debacle I discuss in Chapter 2. Don't be a "yes person" if the answer is no. In the famous words of Kenny Rogers, "You've gotta know when to hold 'em, (and) know when to fold 'em." That's as true for data science projects as it is for anything else in life.

Chapter **18**

Blazing a Path to Data Science Career Success

I f you're just starting out on your career path or you're looking to break new ground career-wise and you're intrigued by the possibilities of a career in data science, this chapter is for you. Here you'll see some incredible examples of what's possible for you in your future data science career. You'll meet warm and inviting data science thought leaders, and you'll come up with ideas for how to make your way up the data science career ladder — regardless of whether you feel called to become a data implementer, a data leader, or a data entrepreneur.

Navigating the Data Science Career Matrix

Data science careers are anything but straightforward. There's no one-size-fits-all path to becoming a data science professional, but there are some well-trodden paths I'd like to share with you in this section. Figure 18-1 shows a wide variety of options you can take to move from entry-level to senior-level as a data implementation professional.

Of all the data science implementation career paths that can be taken, the most established, proven approach is this one:

Data analyst > Data scientist > Senior data scientist

Entry-Level	Mid-Level	Senior Level

Entry-Level
- Data Analyst
- Jr Data Scientist
- Data Science Intern
- Risk Analyst
- Analytics Engineer
- Statistical Analyst
- Applied Scientist
- Learning Analytics Scientist
- Research Scientist
- Statistician
- UX/UI Specialist

Mid-Level
- Algorithm Engineer
- Data Visualization Engineer
- (Clinical) Biostatistician
- Business Intelligence Engineer
- Data Engineer
- Enterprise Architect
- Solutions Architect
- Data Scientist
- Decision Scientist
- Quantitative Analyst

Senior Level
- Senior Data Scientist
- Machine Learning Engineer
- Senior Data Engineer

FIGURE 18-1:
Potential roles that can take you from entry-level to senior-level as a data implementer.

If data leadership is more aligned with your interests and personality, you have an equally diverse set of options to advance from entry-level to senior-level. Figure 18-2 shows you some of these options.

Entry-Level	Mid-Level	Senior Level

Entry-Level
- Data Journalist
- Public Health Analyst
- Sales and Marketing Analyst
- Data Steward
- Econometrician
- Marketing Operations Specialist
- Market Research Analyst
- GIS Analyst
- Statistician
- Data Manager
- Operations Analyst
- Continuous Improvement Manager
- Data Analyst
- Data Governance Analyst
- Data Privacy Analyst
- Insights Specialist
- Product Analyst
- GIS Manager
- Public Policy Research Analyst
- Financial Analyst
- Healthcare Analyst
- Data Product Owner

Mid-Level
- Reporting Analyst
- Marketing Manager
- Business Analyst
- Learning Analytics Scientist
- Metrics Analyst
- Business Intelligence Analyst
- Psychometrician
- Operations Manager
- Analytics Manager
- Data Governance Manager
- Data Architect
- Product Manager
- Technical Director
- Analytics Translator
- Data Product Manager

Senior Level
- Chief Data Officer
- VP of Analytics
- Chief Decision Scientist
- Data Product Manager
- Head of Data Science
- Head of Data Product

FIGURE 18-2:
Potential roles that can take you from entry-level to senior-level as a data leader.

TIP

To uncover which type of data path you should take, check out the fast, fun Data Superhero Quiz on the companion website, www.businessgrowth.ai.

Of all the data science leadership career paths that can be taken, the most common approach might look something like this:

Data analyst > Analytics manager > Head of data science

Lastly, if you're looking to do some data science freelancing or to become a data science entrepreneur, the fastest way to get going is to offer data science services. Figure 18-3 shows options for moving from entry-level to senior-level.

Entry-Level	Mid-Level	Senior Level
• Audit and Management Consulting Services • Business Analysis Services • Quantitative Business Consulting Services • Data Analysis Services • Data Journalism Services	• Data Pipeline Services • Learning Data Analysis Services • Econometric Advising Services • Data Cleaning Services • Data Visualization Services	• Machine Learning and Model-Building Services • Data Strategy Services • Machine Learning Engineering Services • Custom Chatbot Services

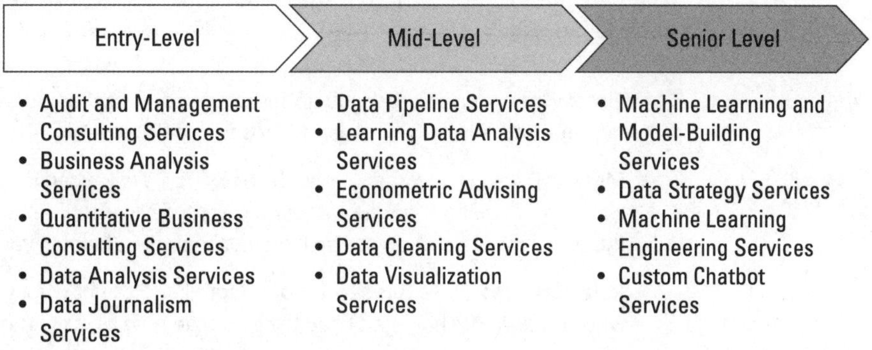

FIGURE 18-3: Potential roles that can take you from entry-level to senior-level as a data entrepreneur.

Of all the data science services you can offer, the easiest path is this one:

Audit services > Data cleaning services > Machine learning services

When I say that this is the easiest path, I mean that it's the easiest set of services to sell and deliver. That's mostly because the demand for these services is high, and the structure would naturally create simplicity in your service delivery workflow.

Now suppose that you've decided you want to take the traditional path of the data scientist and seek employment in that role. In the next section, I show you some of the communities, resources, and actions that are available to help you land the job.

Landing Your Data Scientist Dream Job

When I talk about data science jobs and careers, what I'm really talking about is business. When I talk about business, what I'm really talking about is wealth-generating activities. Maybe you've amassed all the wealth you'll ever need, but the primary reason that most people work is so that they can earn money to support themselves and their families, right? Make no mistake about it: When you set out to land a job in data science, what you're really doing is looking to use your data skills to generate wealth for yourself (and maybe the people you love). Nothing wrong with that! Cash earnings are a basic necessity, but there's so much more to wealth than just cash holdings, correct? Let's look a little deeper into what wealth actually is, and then I'll map it back to your quest for a dream job in data science.

When it comes right down to it, these four main types of currency can be used to generate wealth:

>> **Time:** When you look for a job and when you secure that job, you're exchanging your time for cash. Time is the most valuable currency of all four forms.

>> **Money:** Do you know the saying "Cash is king"? Well, when it comes to currency, if you have ample cash, you can save all your time by spending your money to inspire someone else to spend their time helping you.

>> **Relationships:** Does this saying sound familiar: "It's not what you know — it's who you know"? That age-old adage is as true now as ever. The more time, attention, and resources you can pour into building and maintaining relationships, the more those relationships pay off in the long run. Great relationships confer trust, which then confers influence.

>> **Audience:** The audience type is similar to relationships in that the more you give, the more you get. But they have some crucial differences between them. Whereas a relationship is a 1-to-1 type of interaction, the audience is a 1-to-many interaction. With relationships, you can develop a real depth and intimacy with another person, but with an audience, you're mostly looking to help people far and wide. You could equate the audience to what you see across the influencer industry, thought leadership industry, or, plainly, online creator space. These influencers, thought leaders, and creators amass an audience that they can then convert to money, time, or relationships. Ironic as it is, audience is more about reach than it is about influence. Influence comes from relationships.

For a graphical representation of the relationships between these four types of currencies, see Figure 18-4.

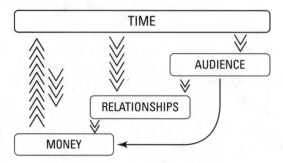

FIGURE 18-4:
The four types of currency.

What does all this have to do with your landing a job in the ubercompetitive world of data science? A lot, actually! Here's how it works: If you have some time and some data science skills, you can find a job in data science and earn money. If you take some of your time and spend it in developing meaningful relationships with other competent professionals in data science, at a later date those will likely convert to new professional opportunities for you and, hence, to more money. If you take your time and develop an audience, you will also later be able to convert it to money, in the form of new job opportunities or paid products and services in the case that you take the entrepreneurial route. As you can see in Figure 18-4, time is the scarcest form of currency because it's required in order to create all the other forms.

With the data scientist topic covered, it's time to direct your attention to my online peers in the data science space. Be prepared to have your mind blown by all the incredible things data science implementation professionals are doing within the communities they're building online.

Leaning into data science implementation

Beyond the fact that all the creators I discuss in this section work to support data implementers in advancing their data careers, they have something else in common: They're all relatively new to the online data science thought-leadership scene. All these creators have brought their data implementation expertise online and have built massive traction within their communities, in only the brief period since 2019!

Here are some community leaders I find particularly compelling:

>> **Danny Ma, founder of Sydney Data Science:** After several years of working as a data scientist and machine learning engineer, in 2020 Danny Ma began coaching other data professionals to level up in their own data science implementation careers. His dynamic LinkedIn community, called Data with Danny, is a great place to go for real-life input on everything from data science interviews and fine-tuning resumes to fun data memes and everything in between. If you're new to the data science field and looking to work in an implementation capacity long-term, make sure to follow Danny on LinkedIn https://au.linkedin.com/in/datawithdanny

>> **Harpreet Sahota, founder and host of the Artists of Data Science podcast:** Harpreet is the founder of Artists of Data Science — an online community and podcast that's exclusively focused on the personal growth and development of data scientists. Outside of growing his podcast community and carrying out his day job as a lead data scientist, he has spent several years mentoring aspiring data scientists inside the Data Science Dream Job

course. If you're looking to land a job as a data scientist (and you want to enjoy that process, despite its rigors), Sahota and his community can help get you there in comfort. Take a listen to his podcast:

```
https://theartistsofdatascience.fireside.fm
```

» **Ken Jee, creator of Ken Jee on YouTube:** Jee is a data scientist, based in Honolulu, Hawaii. He founded his YouTube channel in 2019 and grew it to 100,000 subscribers in just 12 months. He also has a podcast, cleverly named Ken's Nearest Neighbors Podcast. His magnetic YouTube channel helps new-and-aspiring data scientists prepare for seeking and landing a job in the industry. His videos are dedicated to data science implementation topics, like how to do well in Kaggle, pick the best portfolio projects, study to become a data scientist, and perfect your data science resume. His podcast features data scientists from all over the world serving in a wide variety of capacities — from data science leaders to implementers to entrepreneurs and everything in between. If you're looking to learn more about how to get started in your data science career, be sure to check out Jee's YouTube channel:

```
www.youtube.com/c/KenJee1
```

» **Zach Wilson, tech lead at Airbnb:** If you're thinking that data engineering is more your flavor, you'll love the LinkedIn community that Wilson has built. After several high-profile software and data engineering jobs for companies as lovable as Netflix and Airbnb, he made up his mind to do something about the dreadful lack of online communities in data engineering. He regularly shares valuable insider perspectives about his work and the job of a data engineer in order to help new-and-aspiring data engineers level up in their own data careers. I appreciate his down-to-earth and encouraging approach to career development in data engineering and software development. You can follow his LinkedIn community:

```
www.linkedin.com/in/eczachly
```

Acing your accreditations

My advice to you: If you want to get a job as a data scientist, save yourself a lot of time and trouble by making sure you have a STEM degree first. Figures 18-5 and 18-6 show why.

TIP

I've stored all links to my research findings for this book over on the companion website, www.businessgrowth.ai. Make a visit if you want to check them out and learn more about these studies.

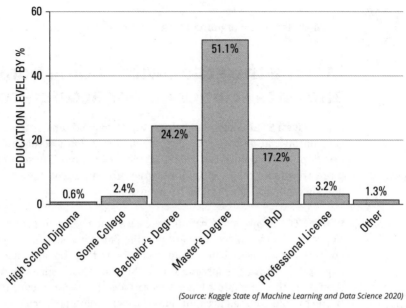

FIGURE 18-5:
Data scientists,
broken down by
degree types.

(Source: Kaggle State of Machine Learning and Data Science 2020)

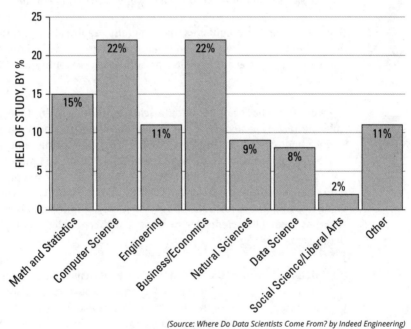

FIGURE 18-6:
Data scientists,
broken down by
field of study.

(Source: Where Do Data Scientists Come From? by Indeed Engineering)

The fundamentals that go into earning a STEM degree are the same fundamentals that make up the basics involved in doing data science. And because most data scientists have these degrees, it puts you at a serious disadvantage if you don't.

REMEMBER

STEM skills are the building blocks that form the foundation of data science.

Making the grade with coding bootcamps and data science career accelerators

If you have a STEM degree and don't want to spend tens of thousands of dollars to earn an official data science degree when you don't actually need one, another great option is to enroll in a data science boot camp. These programs tend to be more affordable than university degree programs, and they tend to evolve more quickly with changes in industry needs.

With a STEM degree, you can more or less teach yourself the extra skills you need to get into data science. If you take this path, invest some time in building out your own custom curriculum and making sure that the one you come up with is an appropriate fit for the job you'll inevitably seek. One nice benefit of boot camps, though, is that you don't have to worry about designing your own curriculum or trying to hold yourself accountable. You can generally develop an entire set of data science skills in about 16 weeks, via any one of the ample online boot camp options.

WARNING

Boot camps have prerequisites that generally require all applicants to hold a STEM degree before applying. If the boot camp program you're looking at doesn't require a STEM degree as a prerequisite for admission, I would question the program's validity.

If I were to go back and learn data science all over again, today in 2021, I would take the faster, easier route by simply enrolling in a boot camp program. Data science boot camps not only provide training, mentoring, and accountability but also help you land a job in the data science field after you graduate. As far as which data science boot camp I would pursue, I'm sure as heck not paying $16,000 for a data science training experience. I don't think any boot camp can provide enough value to compensate for that type of fee. After a modicum of research, I've identified these two data science boot camps that I'd consider joining if I were learning data science over again:

>> **UCLA Extension: 10-week data science intensive ($4,500):** This 4-course (16-unit) certificate provides training and education for pursuing a career in data science, with courses that cover data development and management, machine learning and natural language processing, exploratory data analysis, statistical models, data visualization, and inference. The program also provides hands-on training for handling real-life data science problems.

```
https://portal.uclaextension.edu/specialtyprogram/landingPage.do?method=lo
ad&specialtyProgramId=196400770
```

>> **Guru Path of the Data Science Bootcamp at Data Science Dojo ($3,000):**
This program offers instructional support, career counseling, and a verified certificate from the University of New Mexico, on top of the 16-week data science boot camp learning experience:

```
https://datasciencedojo.com/
```

I like both of these programs because, in addition to being reasonably priced, they're robust. They don't just rehash all the same old basics I've seen a hundred times. These programs are offered in a virtual environment, so I don't need to leave the comfort of my island villa. Lastly, these programs both appear to highlight fun and interesting practice problems that you don't see elsewhere on the Internet for free.

Networking and building authentic relationships

No question about it — diligent attention to professional networking and relationship-building affords you an unfair advantage when it comes to landing jobs in the data science field. Regardless, relationships don't form overnight, and they certainly don't form without concerted effort. If you haven't yet started building relationships in the data science space, don't worry: You can start today by joining, and actively contributing to, any of the professional networking associations listed here:

>> **Data Science Association (DSA):** DSA promotes data science to improve life, business, and government. Its guiding principles are to establish standards for the ethical professional practice of data science, ensure a base-level data scientist competency, advance data science to serve core values of the scientific method, and help shape a better future — not just for the powerful but also for the majority of people. If this sounds like an organization you can get behind, you can learn more about it here:

```
www.datascienceassn.org
```

>> **Research Data Alliance (RDA):** RDA's vision is to foster a safe and supportive community where researchers and innovators can openly share data and data expertise across technologies, disciplines, and countries to address the grand challenges of society. The Research Data Alliance (RDA) builds the social and technical bridges that enable the open sharing of data. Check them out:

```
www.rd-alliance.org
```

>> **Women in Data:** The international nonprofit organization Women in Data works to close the gender gap in technology and attract more women to the C-Suite — c-level roles within a company, such as CEO, COO, CFO, and so on. Rated as the number-one community for women in AI and tech, Women in Data is now in 17 countries with over 47 chapters and has a community of over 20,000 individuals. If you're a female in the data space, consider yourself invited to join this amazing community:

www.womenindata.org

I've included more professional networking options inside my Mini Black Book of Data Professional Organizations, available to you at businessgrowth.ai.

TIP

Developing your own thought leadership in data science

Thought leadership has become a bit of a buzzword lately, but don't let that lead you to believe that it's an ephemeral concept you can safely ignore. Thought leadership is real, and if you can put it to use for you, you can expand your audience and reach. Beyond wanting to make a positive impact on the world around them, there's a reason the number of people who aspire to become online thought leaders in the data science space is increasing: Audience confers opportunity. Whether that opportunity comes in the form of new job offers or the ability to start your own data science business, a significant audience is a verifiable form of currency.

For example, let me share a little about how it worked for me. With the intention of starting my own data business, I started building my data science audience back in 2012, before *data scientist* was dubbed "the sexiest job of the 21st century" by *Harvard Business Journal*. Within six months, I'd already grown my community to several thousand members and — because of the audience and relationships I was building — I scored a few freelance contracts to supplement my day job. At that job, I worked on a proof-of-concept data analytics project and on more sophisticated data science projects for my local county government. Throughout the 22 months that I worked there, I continued growing my data science community as well as my freelance client base. By the end of 2013, I had grown my data science community by several tens of thousands of members, and I'd established enough freelancing income to quit that job and convert to full-time in my business, Data-Mania. It has been nine years since I started working in data science — and the company is still going strong.

If the ability to establish one's financial independence in less than two years isn't sufficient proof of the value of an audience, consider this: Twenty months into that journey, I was being actively recruited to interview with Facebook for a data position based in Menlo Park. Before this job at local government, I had only a few years of work experience as a project engineer with a low-key environmental engineering consulting firm. To have a company like Facebook recruiting someone like me back then for a data position in Silicon Valley is quite the testament to the power of community-building in data science.

I didn't just build an audience, though. I actively contributed to the data science community, and I published the best data science portfolio I was capable of at that time. When you're looking to land a job as a data scientist, a great way to demonstrate your chops is by building a public data science portfolio. I tell you more about that topic in the next section.

Building a public data science project portfolio

Back in the early days of my own data science career, I grew and nurtured my audience by creating and publishing coding demonstrations. The purpose of this task was many fold. Here are some benefits to publishing a data science coding portfolio:

>> **Helping others:** Help other new and aspiring data scientists learn how to code and implement machine learning algorithms.

>> **Proving your competence:** Demonstrate your data science skills.

>> **Future-proofing your online hub:** Because coding demonstration content is extremely search-friendly, it will attract droves of traffic to your online hub for years to come.

>> **Growing your audience:** Publish and share this form of content to inevitably help increase the audience size, which can then confer new and better job opportunities later.

>> **Reeling in new job offers:** Hiring personnel often comb the Internet for coding demonstrations showing that the author has the specific skills and competencies required for a particular job. If your portfolio fits a company's needs, someone will actively try to reach you to see whether you're interested in the job. (That's a good reason it's important to publish a means by which they can contact you.)

REMEMBER

Prospective employers are looking to hire data scientists who can generate monetary value for the business by either reducing wasteful spending or increasing revenues. Although a data science portfolio isn't all you need to showcase the value of your skills, it can go a long way in terms of highlighting your valuable expertise and data science skills.

Showcasing your data science skills

Though each individual prospective employer is looking for something a little different, the good news is that skills in the following fundamental areas are common to most data science roles:

>> Programming in Python and/or R

>> Statistical programming

>> Machine learning and deep learning

>> SQL

>> Data visualization

Additionally, you'll want to find a way to show off your personality from within your coding portfolio. (Tough, I know!) Especially if you're a team player, problem-solver, or tenacious individual, you'll want to make those attributes shine. Just by taking the time to publish a coding portfolio, you're already showing potential employers that you're committed and passionate about the data science field. This dedication helps demonstrate that you have the personality attributes prospective employers are looking for.

Deciding which data science activities to publish

As far as what you should publish within your data science portfolio, you should build one that concisely demonstrates your ability to carry out all the essential data science tasks that'll be required of you. A good portfolio should make clear that you're quite capable of these activities:

>> **Data-wrangling:** In other words, this term refers to being able to show folks how to clean, restructure, and reformat raw data into the form needed for use in modeling and analysis. (For more on data-wrangling, see Chapter 12.)

>> **Describing and inferring:** Demonstrate how to use statistical methods to describe and make inferences from your cleaned datasets. (For more on this topic, see Chapter 4.)

>> **Data-showcasing and storytelling:** Here's where you show your proficiency at communicating data insights to different types of audiences. (For more on data showcasing and storytelling, see Chapter 8.)

>> **Predictive modeling and machine learning:** Demonstrate how you're able to use machine learning methods to make predictions (presumably, predictions that are relevant to business!). For more on these topics, check out Chapters 3 through 6.

TIP

You can put these activities together piecemeal or build an end-to-end project that walks you through each of the important components. The latter is probably the better bet.

Taking inspiration from the data science greats

When you're building a data science portfolio, it's always nice to look at some examples for inspiration. I have been quite impressed and inspired by Jake Vanderplas' GitHub portfolio. You can take a look at it for yourself on his GitHub site at https://github.com/jakevdp. Figure 18-7 gives a taste of what he's offering.

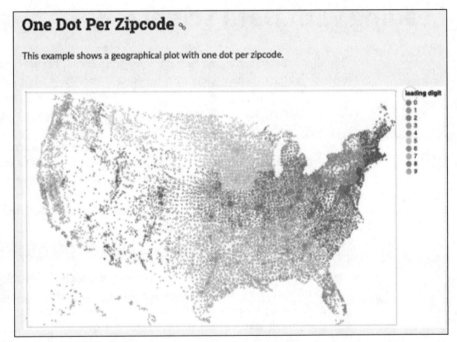

FIGURE 18-7:
A map from within Jake Vanderplas's instructional coding demonstrations on GitHub.

Jake Vanderplas is a long-standing software engineer at Google as well as the developer of a number of open-source Python projects. His portfolio stands out to me for many reasons. Right off the bat, having 12,000 followers on GitHub is awesome, but the real reason I admire the GitHub portfolio is the sentiment behind it. When you look over Jake's coding portfolio, you can clearly see that he is driven by a deep desire to help data professionals and the data industry at-large — making the learning of these skills more accessible to people around the world with no monetary gain for himself (although he does get paid for his work at Google). He takes time in his explanations and makes them all freely available on GitHub along with all the code to support his free demos. His portfolio demonstrates all the data science skills, activities, and personality traits of a data professional that any hiring manager would jump through hoops to hire.

TIP

For more sample portfolios, as well as a brief but powerful video session I created called Doing Data Science Freelancing Portfolios Right, be sure to visit the companion website to this book at `www.businessgrowth.ai`.

Leading with Data Science

I highlighted some amazing data implementers earlier in this chapter, but now let me highlight some data science professionals who know what it is to lead:

>> **Eric Weber, head of Experimentation, Economic Insights, and Metrics at Yelp:** Eric Weber is the perfect picture of what it looks like when you combine exceptional data science expertise, data leadership skills, and healthy dedication to a professional mindset. In his thriving LinkedIn community, he shares his insights about data science, data careers, interviews, hiring, and job opportunities. I most appreciate Eric's emphasis on maintaining the right mindset as well as his product-driven approach to leading in data science. You can follow Eric Weber on LinkedIn:

> `www.linkedin.com/in/eric-weber-060397b7`

>> **Cassie Kozyrkov, chief decision scientist at Google:** Cassie Kozyrkov was instrumental in developing a decision intelligence approach at Google, and she's a passionate advocate of the field, especially on LinkedIn, where she consistently contributes to her community of over 350,000 followers. The main focus of her content centers around high-impact data science and the data driven decision-making I discuss in Chapter 12. Or, to put it in her words, she's all about "making data useful and turning information into better actions." Join her community on LinkedIn to learn more about decision intelligence, machine learning, statistics, AI ethics, and the impact of data on society:

> `www.linkedin.com/in/kozyrkov`

- » **Felipe Flores, founder and host of the Data Futurology Podcast:** After 20 years of experience in data science implementation, consulting, and leadership, Felipe Flores started the Data Futurology Podcast back in 2018. As a fun and heartfelt host, Felipe uses this podcast as a means by which to help data enthusiasts, data scientists, and upcoming data science leaders advance their careers. He achieves this goal by inviting dynamic guests to share their stories and lessons learned with respect to data leadership, strategy, management, team building, stakeholder management, value delivery, and the skills required to be a truly great data scientist. If you're looking to become a better data science leader, the Data Futurology Podcast is right up your alley. Take a listen here:

  www.datafuturology.com

- » **Kirk Borne, chief science officer at DataPrime:** Kirk Borne has been an esteemed data science thought leader since 2013. He's most active over on Twitter, where he shares, for example, breaking news in AI and free data science learning resources. I am most appreciative of Kirk's emphasis on community, as well as his generosity and consistency as a long-standing community leader in data science. In addition to the work he does as chief science officer at DataPrime, Kirk has authored introductory-level data science courses with a company called AI+ Training. Follow and learn from Kirk Borne at:

  https://twitter.com/KirkDBorne

These individuals have created vibrant communities online where you can go to freely learn about what it takes to become a better data science leader. If you're like most readers, though, you have no interest in investing the overwhelming amount of time and resources it takes to grow and maintain an online community. That's great! You don't have to. You can start becoming a better data science leader here and now, in your current work environment. The nearby sidebar "Becoming your company's data science leader: A true story" shows you what it might look like.

BECOMING YOUR COMPANY'S DATA SCIENCE LEADER: A TRUE STORY

Heather Smith (www.linkedin.com/in/heatheralisonsmithpmp) now works as the associate managing director of innovation and data science at Moody's Investors Service, but not long ago she made her start in the data science field the same way you

(continued)

(continued)

are today: by thumbing through the pages of this very book, *Data Science For Dummies* (although she had the first edition and you're now reading the third).

When Heather was first introduced to data science, she had a job as an IT team leader in Seattle, Washington, for what has now become one of the world's largest telecommunications companies. Back then, the company was often cited as the worst-performing of any wireless service provider. Her daily work often revolved around helping the company test its products in order to strengthen its network and salvage the company's reputation. Complicating the issue, the company lacked the appropriate data science tools at that time. Heather and her team had to find their way out of the forest of problems using the resources they had at their disposal, which included grit, a healthy dose of IT strategy, and of course, a newly minted passion for data science.

Seven years later, that company is considered an industry leader. The rapid turnabout in success can be attributed, at least in part, to the work Heather and her team did back in those early days. Much of this work involved utilizing experimentation to make slow and steady improvements to the company's network reliability, and most of these experiments utilized the same data science techniques you can read about throughout this book. In my recent conversations with Heather, she mentioned using the first edition of *Data Science For Dummies* almost every day back then. The book was just the primer she needed to quickly familiarize herself with the broad data science ecosystem. She also used the book quite frequently whenever she needed to explain complex AI and machine learning concepts to business leaders who aren't technically oriented.

When asked about how the decision to develop data science skills impacted her career, Heather said, "[D]ata science has been life-changing. I'm constantly learning and getting to work on exciting projects. It's made me more curious and given me a greater sense of purpose and fulfillment in my work. My career took off when I became a data scientist. There are so many career pathways that did not exist in the early years of the field — I've been able to grow with intention and be more selective about where I work and the type of projects I take on. When I started, I was a part-time data scientist, part-time machine learning engineer. I was often a team of one. As my career evolved, though, I've been lucky to work with some incredible data scientists. Now I lead high-impact data science teams and help companies create and implement data strategy. Helping the next generation of data scientists mature their skills and plan their career paths has been incredibly rewarding."

To people newly entering the data science field, here's Heather's recommendation: "Have patience and don't be afraid to make mistakes. Grit will get you everywhere in this field. Be open to working with data scientists who are different — diversity leads to greater creativity and innovation."

Starting Up in Data Science

In this section, I share my insider perspective on how to go about starting your own data science business, without investors. This advice has limited applicability to funded start-ups, simply because investment money generally fast-tracks what is possible while also diverting the founder's autonomy over to the investors. In this section, you can read all about the business models and revenue models for data businesses. Additionally, I provide some input about which one makes the most sense for you, given your specific situation.

Choosing a business model for your data science business

Before going into any of the business models that work best for data science businesses, let me explain what a business model is. A *business model* is just a conceptual model that explains how a business delivers value in exchange for money. Figure 18-8 shows the four best business models for remote, self-funded data businesses — data businesses that you can operate from anywhere in the world, without investors. These are service-based businesses, information products businesses, consulting and advising businesses, and Software as a Service (SaaS) businesses. Of course, these are not binary classifications, so natural areas of overlap will occur between each of these business models.

FIGURE 18-8: The four best business models for remote, self-funded data science businesses.

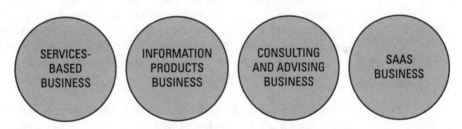

The most obvious of the business models is for service-based businesses, where the "services" I'm referring to are data implementation services. If you're already a data science freelancer, you already have a form of service-based business, but you're probably the only employee delivering the services. Another way to deliver data science services sounds something like "freelancing with a team." This strategy is akin to a data science services agency.

In terms of the pros of service-based data science businesses, service businesses are certainly the fastest way to start a data business. Additionally, you can easily make sales of high-dollar contracts with a data science services business because you're essentially selling your time, which is the most valuable resource you have to offer. Now, because you're a *data science* professional, you can sell your time for quite a bit of money. The base rate on that service? You need to sell your time for two times the amount of money you would make in take-home pay if you were doing the equivalent work as an in-house employee working within someone else's business.

When it comes to the cons of the service-based business model for data business, for starters you have the liability to think of in terms of anything you built. If it breaks, you have to figure out who will own responsibility for its repercussions. This can potentially amount to a huge degree of financial liability, so tread carefully. And, honestly, a services-based data science business isn't scalable in the long term. Though it's a great way to start your business and become profitable, you then need to start looking into how you shift your business model into one that's more scalable.

TIP

One way you can make a services-based data business more scalable is to transform it into an agency or SaaS.

As far as information products businesses go, in this business model you'd sell items such as data courses, data books (like the one you're reading now), and data digital products. The pros of starting an information products business is that it's generally easy to sell your products, and the business model is quite scalable. Looking at the drawbacks, however, most of your information products will generate a lower dollar amount per sale. To make sales in this type of business model, you must already have an audience that trusts you. That means if you haven't started to build up an audience, you shouldn't start an information products data business. In this case, you're better off starting by offering data science services and then making sure you go heavy on your thought leadership efforts in order to build up the audience you need to then sell information products.

When it comes to data businesses, trying to sell your data expertise to other data professionals is a bit like trying to sell blacksmithing expertise to a blacksmith. That's usually the exact kind of help they do *not* need. It's people from *other* industries, outside of the data professions, who need to hire out for the data expertise they don't already have.

TIP

If you want to grow your data science business extremely quickly, specialize in supporting professionals or businesses in other industries, outside of the data science industry.

Now let's look at data science consulting and advising as a business model. This is essentially strategy-level advising work that you offer as a service via your data business. When it comes to the pros on this type of model, it's easy to set up this type of offer, and the hourly pay rates can be quite decent. As for the drawbacks, advising packages tend to produce lower dollar amounts per sale compared to selling a product like enterprise-grade subscriptions to a SaaS product. And because you're still selling time here, you need to charge a relatively high rate — so it's tougher to make the sale.

Lastly, let's look at the SaaS business model for data businesses. In terms of what your business would sell under this type of model, that's some sort of data or AI software as a service that you deliver across a cloud environment. Now, the pros on this type of business model are, of course, that it can be *very* scalable and *very* profitable. The cons, however, are that SaaS generally has a long *time-to-market*, which means that it takes you a long time to build a software package as a service solution. It also requires a technical skillset, and that can get expensive. And, when you need to bring on other developers and data scientists to help you develop and maintain your product, you'll have even more capital, operational, and maintenance costs.

TIP

I created a mini training course, "The Secret to Building AI Software That Actually Sells," and left it for you at this page: `www.businessgrowth.ai`.

As far as which of these business models you should use to start your data science business — it depends. If you have no audience, definitely start with a services-based business. If you have an audience but need to monetize fast, a services-based business also works best. If you have strong data science expertise already and an audience, and if you have no urgent need to monetize, you might combine the information products model and the consulting-and-advising model. SaaS is the best option for established data businesses or founders who've already secured investment money to fund their research and development.

Selecting a data science start-up revenue model

Revenue models are all about the best ways to use your data science experience to quickly monetize within your small data science business or start-up. In this section, you see the best ways to monetize fast in your data science business. Before discussing any of the revenue models, you should know the difference between a revenue model and a business model. Simply put, a *revenue model* is just the portion of the business model that's responsible for bringing revenues into the business. Figure 18-9 illustrates some common revenue models.

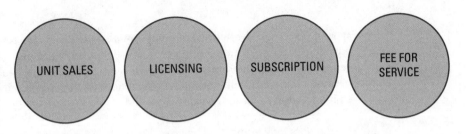

FIGURE 18-9:
The four best
business models
for remote,
self-funded data
science
businesses.

The first revenue model I want to discuss is *unit sales* — the direct sale of ownership of a product. It might be the sale of merchandise or the sale of a license to use a digital product, like a course or an e-book. The pros to this type of revenue model are that it's scalable and it has a high earning capacity. Another nice aspect is that you can automate or delegate most of the client delivery work so that it's not occupying any of your personal time to deliver the data products. In terms of negatives, however, this type of revenue model requires that you have an audience. Yes, of course, you can make the product and try to sell it, but if you have no audience, it makes that task difficult. Another risk in this type of revenue model is the product development time: Make sure that you validate your offer before taking all the time required to build it and take it to market.

Another revenue model is *licensing,* where you essentially sell a license to someone in exchange for their right to use your intellectual property. In other words, you're selling a license to your customer in exchange for the right to use your intellectual property as if it were their own. You're probably familiar with these types of data products. They come under the guise of white label products like Klipfolio's white label analytics dashboards (www.klipfolio.com/partner-features/white-label-reporting). The pros on this type of revenue model are that it can be easy to develop this type of product and you can use it to grow your audience as you make sales. The con to this type of revenue model is, of course, that this is no path to high ticket sales — it's a low-ticket earner.

TIP

I created a mini training course on how to implement these revenue models in your data business. It's at www.businessgrowth.ai.

As for the *subscriptions* revenue model, this is when you sell the right to access your product or service or community on a subscription or pay-as-you-go basis. In some cases, it can be something like a service retainer package. Now, the pros on this type of revenue model are that they're generally easy to sell and they're also a great way to get paid while you build out your product suite while testing it with users. It also has a small time-to-market — unless you're trying to sell SaaS subscriptions, of course.

Another benefit to the SaaS model is that it can be effective for making sales while you're growing your audience — simply because lower-priced versions would be an option that's easier to sell. The drawback to this type of revenue model is, of course, that it can be high-maintenance in terms of your customers. If your membership grows, you have to bring in team members to help you administer it — for example, people join and cancel all the time, ask questions or want to help, or request service. You must be clear in the contract about what the membership includes — and doesn't include.

The next revenue model is the services revenue model, or *fee-for-service*, where you essentially either sell your services according to a fixed price, as with a lump sum, or on an hourly basis.

WARNING

Never sell your time in exchange for money when you're doing implementation work — this is an easy way to get yourself a microboss. Then when you scale that offer, you'll attract many microbosses, all trying to micromanage the work you're doing on an hourly basis. (This is a good way to build a business that you detest.)

In terms of the positive aspects of fee-for-service, this is the fastest way to start a data business — or any other business, for that matter. Now, the negative aspect of fee-for-service is that it's not a scalable revenue model. You have only so many hours per day. At a certain point, if you start off with a fee-for-service revenue model and you want to keep rendering services, you have to switch to something like an agency or SaaS business model.

Taking inspiration from Kam Lee's success story

Kam Lee revels in all the trappings of success: A multiple six-figure income as a data scientist. A posh apartment in New York City. A glorious reputation that precedes him. Long and illustrious tales about his traveling adventures across the far reaches of the planet. Lee's work has been featured by media sites like Bloomberg and *Foundr* magazine. What's more, he's driven upward of $2 billion in revenue for his clients and has produced 40 percent year-over-year growth for some of the fastest-growing companies in financial technology, SaaS, e-commerce, and cloud security with econometrics, marketing mix modeling, lead scoring, and AI. In short, Lee's data science career is more fabulous and exciting than most data scientists would ever dare to dream possible.

And yet, less than a decade ago, he too was new to the data science field. By taking the time to learn to do data science, Lee made a complete 180-degree turnaround in his career — he went from marketer to marketing data science leader. I want to briefly highlight how he did it and pass on the words of wisdom he has to offer to new-and-aspiring data science professionals.

It was 2015 when he first started reading the books and taking the online courses that helped him develop skills in statistics and machine learning. In fact, Lee is the exact prototype of the person I had in mind when I created The Self-Taught Data Scientist Curriculum back in 2017.

TIP

The Self-Taught Data Scientist Curriculum is part of my free, 52-page e-book, *A Badass's Guide to Breaking into Data*, and I have left it for you to download at `www.businessgrowth.ai`.

So, how did Lee do it? I can tell you what he didn't do. He didn't spend two or three years and tens of thousands of dollars to earn a master's degree in data science. Nor did he devote a month's worth of sleepless nights trying to land one of those competitive corporate jobs as a data scientist.

As for what Lee *did* do (according to him, anyway), he started by following these three steps:

1. **Take online training courses on data science implementation.**

   For example, in 2018 he first took my LinkedIn Learning course on building a recommendation system with Python machine learning and AI. Because he was already working in e-commerce at the time, the course helped him adopt a more data-intensive approach to his marketing career. In other words, he became a marketing data scientist rather than the other clear option, which would have been to become a marketing strategist.

2. **Start taking contract work as an independent data scientist in the marketing industry (otherwise known as a "marketing data scientist").**

   In 2019, Lee began consulting on marketing analytics projects, delivering these services as an agency. After getting caught up in the low-budget hamster wheel, Lee could clearly see the error of his ways, which were these:

   - His offers weren't differentiated from market competitors.

   - His ideal customer profiles weren't clear.

   - He wasn't clearly presenting the monetary value of the results his services could generate.

3. **He invested in taking his data business to the next level.**

   In 2020, Lee joined my group mentorship program. Since March 2020, he closed 15 business-to-business (B2B) contracts valued at $310,000. He also presold $60,000 worth of annual contracts for his upcoming marketing optimization SaaS company, which is expected to go live in the fourth quarter (Q4) of 2021. Of the sales he has generated since joining, 67 percent has been pure profit. With the optimization of new, custom internal tools, he estimates that by the end of Q4 2021 (when he launches his software), he should be able to drive even more automation which should earn Lee's company anywhere between a 75 and 80 percent profit margin. Of all the work Lee did throughout the course of the mentorship, he attributes his remarkable success to the following core elements:

- *Market research:* He developed a concrete customer research study that helped him validate his minimum viable product. He built a competitor matrix and established clarity on his ideal customer profile and then used that profile to clearly define his *circle of influence* — in other words, the influencers, team members, and other close associates who have the ability to influence his outcomes. He also clarified the true Total Addressable Market (TAM) — the total market demand for his offers, expressed as an annual revenue estimate. After estimating the TAM, he crafted and executed a plan for meeting individuals wherever they are within that market.

- *Offer development and positioning:* He improved his offers with the help of his research findings and converted many of his previous services into products. He also made sure he was demonstrating the value of his marketing data science expertise to his growing online audience.

- *Operations optimization:* He came up with innovative ways to apply systems and technology such as Python, RPA, and data engineering to drive back-office operations for his company. As a result, he's been able to keep costs down and drive a high profit margin.

In 2020, Lee successfully converted his deep marketing data science expertise into a SaaS product that delivers both lead scoring and marketing mix modeling. The signature framework around which he is developing this AI SaaS has already helped several clients realize over $120 million in opportunities for predictable ROI and cost savings. By developing this marketing mix modeling and marketing optimization software, what he's doing is building clever ways to automate much of the existing successes he has already generated with data science services he offers in marketing attribution and marketing mix optimization, customer segmentation, customer lifetime value models, predictive models, cross-sell/upsell models (Buy-Till-You-Die for CLTV), market basket analysis, pricing and promo optimization, as well as web analytics and digital data.

REMEMBER

I like to stress the importance of *not* trying to sell data expertise to fellow data experts. Lee's story offers a perfect example of what's possible when you avoid this mistake. When asked, "To which market factors do you most attribute your rapid success as a data entrepreneur?" he responded:

> As a data entrepreneur, my thought leadership, case studies, and niche expertise have given me an edge against other marketers and data professionals in my

industry because I apply statistical knowledge to solve complex marketing and business strategy problems. A major gap in contextual knowledge occurs when it comes to marketing analytics, data science, and technical expertise. *Currently, teams typically rely on analysts who are not inherent marketers. This creates a knowledge gap between technical expertise, functional business knowledge, and being able to translate analysis into business results that truly add value.* Moreover, I've invested a lot of time and effort into developing the essential people skills and communication skills that are synonymous with analytics success. These skills are proven difference-makers across all career levels but are especially relevant as you enter the management and leadership ranks with data strategy.

And, to new data science professionals, Lee recommends that you differentiate yourself from the pack of other aspiring data scientists by developing and exhibiting the following ancillary skills:

>> **Data engineering:** These skills allow you to be useful in many dynamic ways.

>> **Business consulting:** These skills help you show up and become a trusted business partner to stakeholders by quantifying the impact of their work. Additionally, as you develop your business consulting skills, you naturally improve in other aspects that are vital to your career success in data science — skills like communication, organization/project management, and research skills that will help you solve complex statistical and technical problems.

Following in the footsteps of the data science entrepreneurs

I've highlighted quite a few examples of data science professionals in this chapter who have built strong and enormously helpful communities that help data professionals of all shapes and sizes. Now I want to introduce you to a list of people that exemplify what happens when you combine an entrepreneurial spirit with a love of data science and community-building:

>> **Kate Strachnyi, founder and CEO of DATAcated:** Strachnyi is the founder of the DATAcated community, whose powerful presence is predominantly active on LinkedIn. The vibrant DATAcated community is focused on helping data professionals improve both their data visualization and data storytelling skills. If you're looking to improve your visual and verbal skills in communicating data insights, take a peek at what's happening inside the DATAcated community, as well as the data storytelling courses offered at the DATAcated website. Personally, I've learned a lot from Strachnyi about the data community, and

what it means to be a good steward of that community. Be sure to join her LinkedIn community at www.linkedin.com/in/kate-strachnyi-data, and then listen and learn your way to data storytelling excellence.

» **Matt Dancho, founder and CEO of Business Science University:** Dancho is an engineering leader turned data entrepreneur. Fueled by a mission to empower data scientists, he founded his online training company back in 2017. Since then, he's helped educate over 2,000 data scientists. What I find particularly compelling about Dancho's program is that he is fully cognizant of, and committed to, helping data scientists deliver projects that positively impact their company's bottom line. His free social media community is a great place to go to learn more about technical details related to implementing data science solutions in business. If that sounds good to you, be sure to join his LinkedIn community at www.linkedin.com/in/mattdancho.

» **Sadie St. Lawrence, founder and CEO of Women in Data:** St. Lawrence, a serial entrepreneur in the data science space, runs a data consulting company where she has been a data science instructor since 2017 for Coursera, where she has educated over 300,000 data professionals. She also serves as a board member for multiple start-ups. Her other business is Women in Data, the nonprofit which was introduced earlier in this chapter. St. Lawrence's work has been featured in *USA Today* and the Dataversity website, and she is the recipient of the Outstanding Service award from UC Davis. She is most active on LinkedIn (www.linkedin.com/in/sadiestlawrence), where she offers a female perspective on career development in the data science field.

REMEMBER

Not all successful data entrepreneurs started off as data professionals and then became business owners. In fact, some data entrepreneurs started off as entrepreneurs and then grew their data expertise as they grew their businesses, eventually morphing those businesses into full-fledged data businesses. Such is the case with our next leader here, Jennifer Grayeb.

» **Jennifer Grayeb, CEO of The Nimble Company & COO of Funnel Gorgeous**: Back in just 2019, Jennifer left her senior HR strategy role at a Fortune 5 company where she held 5 roles in just 7 years. On the side of her work at that company, and in just 2 short years, she built a productivity blog that reached over 2 million pageviews per year. After selling that business, Jennifer founded The Nimble Company, a consulting group focused on helping online business owners better understand their marketing analytics so they can make data-driven and profit-generating marketing decisions. More recently, Jennifer has taken an advisory role on the C-Suite of another women-founded data-intensive marketing company called Funnel Gorgeous. Always generous with her analytics knowledge, Jennifer's most active free online community is on Instagram, where she shares valuable, free content that helps entrepreneurs use data to generate greater revenues. Check her out at www.instagram.com/jennifergrayeb/.

As you've probably already noticed, I myself fall into the data science entrepreneur camp. I started building my data science community in 2012 and grew it to 650,000 members as I worked as an independent data science consultant in my business, Data-Mania. After supporting 10 percent of Fortune 100 companies, after being featured in *Forbes*, *The Guardian*, and *Fortune* (and many more media outlets), and after helping educate over 1.2 million data professionals on data science and AI, I felt moved to switch the focus of my business away from data consulting to mentoring fellow data professionals. Our mission is to support data professionals in transforming to world-class data leaders and entrepreneurs. If that's you, and if you're thinking about ways to become a better data science leader, or even an entrepreneur, I invite you to join my LinkedIn community of over 350,000 like-minded data science professionals at www.linkedin.com/in/lillianpierson.

5

The Part of Tens

Locate the open data sources you need.

Incorporate external data.

Save money and time with free and low-cost data science tools.

Chapter **19**

Ten Phenomenal Resources for Open Data

O pen data is part of a larger trend toward a less restrictive, more open understanding of the idea of intellectual property, a trend that's been gaining tremendous popularity over the past decade. Think of *open* data as data that has been made publicly available and is permitted to be used, reused, built on, and shared with others. Maybe you've heard of open-source software, open hardware, open-content creative work, open access to scientific journals, and open science. Along with open data, they're all part of the aptly named *open movement* — a movement committed to the notion that content (including raw data from experiments) should be shared freely.

The distinguishing feature of open licenses is that they have copyleft instead of copyright. With *copyleft*, the only restriction is that the source of the work must be identified, sometimes with the caveat that derivative works can't be copyrighted with a more restrictive license than the original. If the second condition is in force, successfully commercializing the work itself becomes difficult, although people often find plenty of other indirect, creative avenues of commercialization.

WARNING

Be aware that sometimes work that's labeled as open may not fit the accepted definition. You're responsible for checking the licensing rights and restrictions of the open data you use.

People often confuse *open* licenses with Creative Commons licenses. *Creative Commons* is a not-for-profit organization that's dedicated to encouraging and spreading creative works by offering a legal framework through which usage permissions can be granted and obtained so that sharing parties are safe from legal risks when building on and using work and knowledge that's been openly shared. Some Creative Commons licenses are open, and some explicitly forbid derivative works and/or commercialization.

As part of more recent open government initiatives, governments around the world began releasing open government data. Governments generally provide this data so that it can be used by volunteer analysts and *civic hackers* — programmers who work collaboratively to build open-source solutions that use open data to solve social problems — in an effort to benefit society at large. In 2013, the G8 nations (France, the United States, the United Kingdom, Russia, Germany, Japan, Italy, and Canada) signed a charter committing themselves to open data, prioritizing the areas of national statistics, election results, government budgets, and national maps.

The open government movement promotes government transparency and accountability, nurtures a well-informed electorate, and encourages public engagement. To put it in computing terms, open government facilitates a read/write relationship between a government and its citizenry.

Digging Through data.gov

The Data.gov program (at www.data.gov) was started by the administration of former US president Barrack Obama to provide open access to nonclassified US government data. Data.gov data is being produced by all departments in the executive branch — the White House and all cabinet-level departments — as well as datasets from other levels of government. By mid-2014, you could search for over 100,000 datasets by using the Data.gov search. The website is an unparalleled resource if you're looking for US-government-derived data on the following indicators:

>> **Economic:** Find data on finance, education, jobs and skills, agriculture, manufacturing, and business.

>> **Environmental:** Looking for data on energy, climate, geospatial, oceans, and global development? Look no further.

>> **STEM industry:** Your go-to place for anything related to *science, technology, engineering,* or *mathematics* — data on energy science and research, for example.

>> **Quality of life:** Here you can find data on weather patterns, health, and public safety.

>> **Legal:** If your interests lean in a more legalistic direction, Data.gov can help you track down data on law and ethics.

TIP

Data.gov's data policy makes federal data derived from this source extremely safe to use. The policy says, "U.S. Federal data available through Data.gov is offered free and without restriction. Data and content created by government employees within the scope of their employment are not subject to domestic copyright protection." And because it comes in countless formats — including XLS, CSV, HTML, JSON, XML, and geospatial — you can almost certainly find something you can use.

Datasets aren't the only things that are open on Data.gov. You can also find over 60 open-source application programming interfaces (APIs) available on the platform. You can use these APIs to create tools and apps that pull data from government departments listed in the Data.gov data catalog. The catalog itself uses the popular open-source CKAN API. (CKAN here is short for Comprehensive Knowledge Archive Network.) Even the code used to generate the Data.gov website is open source and is published on GitHub (at `https://github.com/ckan/ckan`), in case you're interested in digging into that.

TIP

Data.gov allocates hundreds of thousands of dollars in prizes per year for app development competitions. If you're an app developer looking for a fun side project that has the potential to provide you with financial rewards while also offering you an opportunity to make a positive impact on society, check out the Data.gov competitions. Examples of popular apps developed in these competitions are an interactive global hunger map and an app that calculates and tracks bus fares, routes, and connections in Albuquerque, New Mexico, in real-time.

Checking Out Canada Open Data

For many decades, Canada has been a world leader for its data collection and publication practices. Both *The Economist* and the Public Policy Forum have repeatedly named Statistics Canada — Canada's federal department for statistics — as the best statistical organization in the world.

If you take a look at the Canada Open Data website (`http://open.canada.ca`), the nation's strong commitment to data is overwhelmingly evident. At this site, you can find over 200,000 datasets. Among the 25 most popular offerings on the site are datasets that cover the following indicators:

>> **Environmental:** Areas here include topics like natural disasters and fuel consumption ratings.

>> **Citizenship:** Permanent resident applications, permanent resident counts, foreign student entry counts, and other items can be found here.

>> **Quality of life:** Here you'll find cost-of-living trends, automobile collision statistics, and disease surveillance, for example.

WARNING

Canada Open Data issues its open data under an *open government license* — a usage license that's issued by a government organization to specify the requirements that must be met in order to lawfully use or reuse the open data that the organization has released. Canada Open Data releases data under the Open Government License — Canada. You are required to acknowledge the source every time you use the data, as well as provide backlinks to the Open Government License — Canada page, at

```
http://open.canada.ca/open-government-licence-canada
```

Diving into data.gov.uk

The United Kingdom got off to a late start in the open government movement. Data.gov.uk (`http://data.gov.uk`) was started in 2010, and by mid-2014, only about 20,000 datasets were yet available. Like Data.gov (discussed in the section "Digging through Data.gov," earlier in this chapter), data.gov.uk is also powered by the CKAN data catalog.

Although data.gov.uk is still playing catch-up, it has an impressive collection of ordnance survey maps old enough — 50 years or more — to be out of copyright. If you're looking for world-renowned, free-to-use survey maps, data.gov.uk is an incredible place for you to explore. Beyond its stellar survey maps, data.gov.uk is a useful source for data on the following indicators:

>> **Environmental (data.gov.uk's most prolific theme):** They provide a range of data sets, including data on weather, floods, rivers, air quality, and geology.

>> **Government spending:** The data sets in this collection include all payments of over £25,000 by government departments.

- >> **Societal**: These data sets include important information on employment rates, benefits, household finances, poverty, and population.

- >> **Health**: Visit this section to explore statistics about smoking, drugs and alcohol, medicine performance, and hospitals.

- >> **Education**: This section contains the data you'd need on students, training, qualifications, and the National Curriculum.

- >> **Business and economic**: This section of the website provides information on a variety of topics, including small business, industry, imports and exports, and trade.

Interestingly, the dataset most frequently downloaded from data.gov.uk is a dataset that covers the Bona Vacantia division — the government division charged with tracking the complicated processes involved in determining the proper inheritance of British estates.

WARNING

Like the Canada Open Data website (see the preceding section), data.gov.uk uses an Open Government License, which means you're required to acknowledge the data source every time you use it, as well as provide backlinks to the data.gov.uk Open Government License page at www.nationalarchives.gov.uk/doc/open-government-licence.

TIP

Although data.gov.uk is still young, it's growing quickly, so check back often. If you can't find what you're looking for, the data.gov.uk website has tools you can use to specifically request the datasets you want to see.

Checking Out US Census Bureau Data

The US Census is held every ten years, and since 2010, the data has been made freely available at www.census.gov. Statistics are available down to the level of the census block — which aggregates by 30-person counts, on average. The demographics data provided by the US Census Bureau can be extremely helpful if you're doing marketing or advertising research and need to target your audience according to the following classifications:

- >> Age

- >> Average annual income

- >> Household size

- >> Gender or race

- >> Level of education

In addition to its census counts on people in the United States, the bureau conducts a census of businesses. You can use this business census data as a source for practical industry research to tell you information such as the number of businesses, the number of employees, and the size of payroll per industry per state or metropolitan area.

Lastly, the US Census Bureau carries out an annual American Community Survey to track demographics with a statistically representative sample of the population during non-census years. You can check this data if you need specific information about what has happened during a particular year or set of years.

WARNING

Some census blocks have a population density that's far greater than average. When you use data from these blocks, remember that the block data has been aggregated over a person count that's greater than the average 30-person count of census blocks.

With respect to features and functionality, the US Census Bureau has a lot to offer. You can use QuickFacts (`www.census.gov/programs-surveys/sis/resources/data-tools/quickfacts.html`) to quickly source and pull government data from the US federal, state, county, or municipal level.

TIP

If you'd like to download and further explore US Census data as well as census and survey data from other countries, head over to IPUMS (`www.ipums.org/`). This organization stores data on countries the world over, including US Census data from 1850-present, but makes it all easily downloadable into R for free!

Accessing NASA Data

Since its inception in 1958, NASA has made public all its nonclassified project data. It has been in the open data game so long that NASA has tons of data! NASA datasets have been growing even faster with recent improvements in satellite and communication technology. In fact, NASA now generates 4 terabytes of new earth-science data per day — that's equivalent to over a million MP3 files. Many of NASA's projects have accumulated data into the petabyte range.

NASA's open data portal is called DATA.NASA.GOV (`http://data.nasa.gov`). This portal is a source of all kinds of wonderful data, including data about

>> Astronomy and space (of course!)

>> Climate

>> Life sciences

- » Geology

- » Engineering

Some examples from its hundreds of datasets are detailed data on the color of Earth's oceans, a database of every lunar sample and where it's stored, and the Great Images in NASA (GRIN) collection of historically significant photographs.

Wrangling World Bank Data

The World Bank is an international financial institution that provides loans to developing countries to pay for capital investment that will lead (one hopes) to poverty reduction and some surplus so that the recipient nations can repay the loan amounts over time. It provides loans to developing countries to pay for capital investment that will lead (one hopes) to poverty reduction and some surplus so that the recipient nations can repay the loan amounts over time. Because World Bank officers need to make well-informed decisions about which countries would be more likely to repay their loans, they've gathered an enormous amount of data on member nations. They've made this data available to the public at the World Bank Open Data page (http://data.worldbank.org).

If you're looking for data to buttress your argument in a truly interesting data-journalism piece that's supported by global statistics, the World Bank should be your go-to source. No matter the scope of your project, if you need data about what's happening in developing nations, the World Bank is the place to go. You can use the website to download entire datasets or simply view the data visualizations online. You can also use the World Bank's Open Data API to access what you need.

World Bank Open Data supplies data on the following indicators (and many, many more):

- » **Agriculture and rural development:** Here you'll find data on major contract awards, contributions to financial intermediary funds, forest area, and rural population size data.

- » **Economy and growth:** For the Big Picture — data on gross domestic product (GDP), gross capital formation, and agricultural value-added data, for example — no source is more exhaustive than World Bank Open Data.

- » **Environment:** Data here can tell you all about methane emissions, nitrous oxide emissions, and water pollution.

>> **Science and technology:** You can track patent applications and trademark applications data.

>> **Financial sector:** Research the health (or lack thereof) of a national economy by looking at a nation's bank capital-to-assets ratio, foreign direct investment, market capitalization, and new or supplemental project data.

>> **Poverty income:** For a clear sense of how a country's poorer population is faring, analyze the data associated with gross national income (GNI) per capita, income shares, and the poverty gap.

World Bank Data also includes *microdata* — sample surveys of households and businesses in developing countries. You can use microdata to explore variations in your datasets.

Getting to Know Knoema Data

Knoema (pronounced "no-mah") purports to be the largest repository of public data on the web. The Knoema platform houses a staggering 500+ databases, in addition to its 150 million *time series* — 150 million collections of data on attribute values over time, in other words. Knoema includes, but isn't limited to, all these data sources:

>> **Government data from industrial nations:** Data from Data.gov, Canada Open Data, data.gov.uk, and Eurostat.

>> **National public data from developing nations:** Data from countries such as India and Kenya.

>> **United Nations data:** Includes data from the Food and Agriculture Organization, the World Health Organization, and many other UN organizations.

>> **International organization data:** There's more to the international scene than the United Nations, so if you're looking for data from organizations such as the International Monetary Fund and the Organization for Economic Co-operation and Development, Knoema is where you want to be.

>> **Corporate data from global corporations:** Knoema offers data made public by private corporations such as British Petroleum and BASF.

Knoema is an outstanding resource if you're looking for international data on agriculture, crime statistics, demographics, economy, education, energy, environment, food security, foreign trade, health, land use, national defense, poverty, research and development, telecommunications, tourism, transportation, or water.

In addition to being an incredible data source, Knoema is a multifaceted tasking platform. You can use the Knoema platform to make dashboards that automatically track all your favorite datasets. You can use the platform's data visualization tools to quickly and easily see your data in a tabular or map format. You can use the Knoema Data Atlas (`http://knoema.com/atlas`) to drill down among categories and/or geographic regions and quickly access the specific datasets you need. As an individual, you can upload your own data and use Knoema as a free hosting service.

TIP

Although a lot of Knoema's data is pretty general, you can still find some surprisingly specific data as well. If you're having a hard time locating data on a specific topic, you might have luck finding it on the Knoema platform. Figure 19-1 illustrates just how specific Knoema data can be.

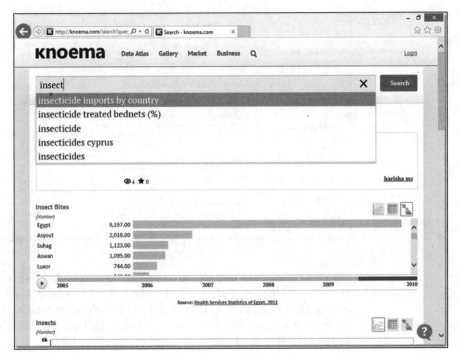

FIGURE 19-1: The index of insect records in Knoema's search.

Queuing Up with Quandl Data

Quandl (www.quandl.com) is a Toronto-based website that aims to be a search engine for numeric data. Unlike most search engines, however, its database isn't automatically generated by spiders that crawl the web. Rather, it focuses on linked data that's updated via *crowdsourcing* — updated manually via human curators, in other words.

Because most financial data is in numeric format, Quandl is an excellent tool for staying up-to-date on the latest business informatics. As you can see in Figure 19-2, a search for *Apple* returns over 4,700 datasets from 11 different sources with time series at the daily, weekly, monthly, quarterly, or annual level. Many of these results are related to the United Nations' agricultural data. If you're looking for data on Apple, you can narrow the scope of your search by replacing the *Apple* search term with the company's stock abbreviation, *AAPL*.

FIGURE 19-2:
The index of Apple records in a Quandl search.

The Quandl database includes links to over 10 million datasets (although it uses a generous metric in declaring what distinguishes one dataset from another). Quandl links to 2.1 million UN datasets and many other sources, including datasets in the Open Financial Data Project, the central banks, real estate organizations, and well-known think tanks.

You can browse Quandl data and get instant charts based on what you find. If you sign up for a free registered account, you can download as much data as you want or use the Quandl application programming interface (API). The Quandl Application Programming Interface (API) includes wrappers to accommodate platforms such as Java, Python, Julia, R, MATLAB, Excel, and Stata, among others. (In case you're new to *wrappers*, think of them as a collection of functions that make it easier to interact with an API. They're language-specific and are sometimes called "wrappers" because they wrap the API calls into easy-to-use functions.)

Exploring Exversion Data

Modeled after GitHub — the cloud-hosted platform across which programmers can collaboratively share and review code — Exversion aims to provide the same collaborative functionality around data that GitHub provides around code. The Exversion platform offers version control functionality and hosting services for uploading and sharing your data. To illustrate how Exversion works, imagine a platform that would allow you to first *fork* (or copy) a dataset and then make the changes you want. Exversion would be there to keep track of what has changed from the original set and every change that you make to it. Exversion also allows users to rate, review, and comment on datasets.

Datasets hosted on the Exversion platform are either provided by a user or created by a spider that crawls and indexes open data to make it searchable from a single application programming interface (API). As with GitHub, with a free user account, all the data you upload to Exversion is public. If you're willing to pay for an account, you can create your own, private data repositories. Also, with the paid account, you gain the option to share your data with selected users for collaborative projects.

TIP

When you work on collaborative projects, version control becomes vitally important — rather than learn this lesson the hard way, just start your project on a version-enabled application or platform. This approach will save you from a lot of problems in the future.

Exversion is extremely useful in the data-cleanup stage. Most developers are familiar with data-cleanup hassles. Imagine that you want to use a particular dataset, but in order to do so, you must insert tabs in all the right places to make the columns line up correctly. Meanwhile, the other 100 developers out there working with that dataset are doing exactly the same thing. In contrast, if you download, clean, and then upload the data to Exversion, other developers can use it and don't have to spend their time doing the same work later. In this way, everyone can benefit from each other's work, and each individual person can spend more time analyzing data and less time cleaning it.

Mapping OpenStreetMap Spatial Data

OpenStreetMap (OSM) is an open, crowd-sourced alternative to commercial mapping products such as Google Maps and ESRI ArcGIS Online. In OSM, users create, upload, or digitize geographic data into the central repository.

REMEMBER

The OSM platform is quite robust. Governments and private companies have started contributing to, and pulling from, the shared datasets. Even corporations as big as Apple are relying on OSM data. OSM now has over 1 million registered users. To illustrate how a person can create data in OSM, imagine that someone links the GPS system on their mobile phone to the OSM application. Because of this authorization, OSM can automatically trace the routes of roads while the person travels. Later, this person (or another OSM user) can go to the OSM online platform to verify and label the routes.

The data in OSM isn't stored as maps, but rather as geometric and text representations — points, lines, polygons, and map annotation — so all of OSM's data can be quickly downloaded from the website and easily assembled into a cartographic representation via a desktop application.

Chapter **20**

Ten Free or Low-Cost Data Science Tools and Applications

ecause data collection, analysis, and visualization comprise the crux of the data scientist's toolkit, it should come as no surprise that you can use quite a few free SaaS tools to carry out these tasks with greater ease. These simple applications can sometimes be useful to more advanced data scientists, but at other times, data science experts simply need more technical tools to help them delve deeper into datasets. In this chapter, I present ten free or low-cost applications you can use to complete data science tasks. You can download and install many of these applications on your personal computer, and most of the downloadable applications are available for multiple operating systems.

WARNING

Always read and understand the licensing requirements of any app you use. Protect yourself by determining how you're allowed to use the products you create with that app.

TECHNICAL STUFF

For more free and low-cost data science and analytics tool recommendations, be sure to check out the ones I've left over on the companion website, `https://businessgrowth.ai`.

Scraping, Collecting, and Handling Data Tools

Whether you need data to support a business analysis or for a new market research data product you're building, web-scraping can help you track down interesting and unique data sources. In web-scraping, you set up automated programs and then let them scour the web for the data you need. In this section, you get a quick peek at some amazing free tools you can use to capture data in the wild and start wrangling it into a useful format.

Sourcing and aggregating image data with ImageQuilts

ImageQuilts (`http://imagequilts.com`) is a Chrome extension developed in part by the legendary Edward Tufte, one of the first great pioneers in data visualization — he popularized the use of the data-to-ink ratio to judge the effectiveness of charts.

The task that ImageQuilts performs is deceptively simple to describe but quite complex to implement. ImageQuilts makes collages of tens of images and then pieces them all together into one "quilt" that's composed of multiple rows of equal height. This task can be complex because the source images are almost never the same height. ImageQuilts scrapes and resizes the images before stitching them together into a single output image. The image quilt shown in Figure 20-1 was derived from a Labeled for Reuse search for the term *data science* at Google Images.

ImageQuilts even allows you to choose the order of images or to randomize them. You can use the tool to drag-and-drop any image to any location, remove an image, zoom all images at the same time, or zoom each image individually. You can even use the tool to convert between image colors — from color to grayscale or inverted color (which is handy for making contact sheets of negatives, if you're one of those rare people who still processes analog photography).

FIGURE 20-1:
An ImageQuilts
output from the
Google Images
search term *data
science.*

Wrangling data with DataWrangler

DataWrangler (http://vis.stanford.edu/wrangler) is an online tool that's
supported by the University of Washington Interactive Data Lab. (At the time
DataWrangler was developed, this group was called the Stanford Visualization
Group.) This same group developed Lyra, an interactive data visualization environment you can use to create complex visualizations without programming
experience.

If your goal is to *sculpt* your dataset — clean things up by moving them around like
a sculptor would (split this part in two, slice off that bit and move it over there,
push this down so that everything below it gets shifted to the right, and so on) —
DataWrangler is the tool for you.

You can do manipulations with DataWrangler similar to the ones you can do in
Excel using Visual Basic. For example, you can use DataWrangler or Excel with
Visual Basic to copy, paste, and format information from lists you scrape from the
Internet.

DataWrangler even suggests actions based on your dataset and can repeat complex actions across entire datasets — actions such as eliminating skipped rows,
splitting data from one column into two, and turning a header into column data.
DataWrangler can also show you where your dataset is missing data.

REMEMBER

Missing data can indicate a formatting error that needs to be cleaned up.

Data-Exploration Tools

When I talk about data science, I tend to talk a lot about the free tools that people can use to visualize their data. And although visualization can help clarify and communicate your data's meaning, you need to make sure that the data insights you're communicating are correct — that requires great care and attention in the data analysis phase. In this section, I introduce you to a few free tools you can use for some advanced data analysis and data science tasks.

Getting up to speed in Gephi

Remember back in school when you were taught how to use graph paper to do math and then were told to draw *graphs* of the results? Well, apparently that nomenclature is incorrect. Those things with an *x*-axis and a *y*-axis are called *charts*. Graphs are *network topologies* — the same type of network topologies I talk about in Chapter 8.

If this book is your first introduction to network topologies, welcome to this weird and wonderful world. You're in for a voyage of discovery. Gephi (`http://gephi.github.io`) is an open-source software package you can use to create graph layouts and then manipulate them to get the clearest and most effective results. The kinds of connection-based visualizations you can create in Gephi are useful in all types of network analyses — from social media data analysis to an analysis of protein interactions or horizontal gene transfers between bacteria.

To illustrate a network analysis, imagine that you want to analyze the interconnectedness of people in your social networks. You can use Gephi to quickly and easily present the different aspects of interconnectedness between your Facebook friends. So, imagine that you're friends with Alice. You and Alice share 10 of the same friends on Facebook, but Alice has an additional 200 friends with whom you're not connected. One of the friends that you and Alice share is named Bob. You and Bob share 20 of the same friends on Facebook also, but Bob has only 5 friends in common with Alice. On the basis of shared friends, you can easily surmise that you and Bob are the most similar, but you can use Gephi to visually graph the friend links between you, Alice, and Bob.

In another example, imagine that you have a graph showing which characters appear in the same chapter as which other characters in Victor Hugo's immense novel *Les Misérables*. (Actually, you don't have to imagine it — Figure 20-2 shows just such a graph, created in the Gephi application.) The larger bubbles indicate that these characters appear most often — the more lines attached to a bubble, the more they co-occur with others. The big bubble in the center left is, of course, Jean Valjean.

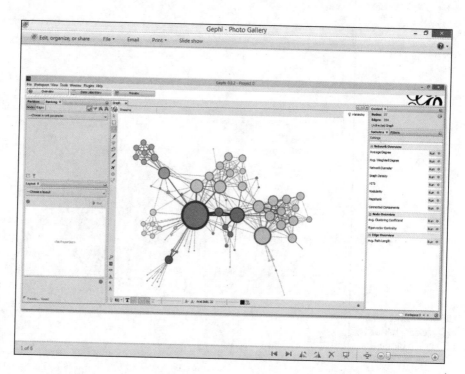

FIGURE 20-2:
A moderate-size graph on characters in the novel *Les Misérables*.

When you use Gephi, the application automatically colors your data according to different criteria. Looking to the upper left corner of Figure 20-2, the cluster of characters in blue (the somewhat darker color in this black-and-white image) are characters who mostly appear only with each other. (They're the friends of Fantine, such as Félix Tholomyès — if you've only seen the musical, they don't appear in that production.) These characters are connected to the rest of the book's characters by way of only a single character, Fantine. If a group of characters appear only together and never with any other characters, they would be in a separate cluster of their own and not be attached to the rest of the graph in any way.

To take one final example, check out Figure 20-3, which shows a graph of the US power grid and the degrees of interconnectedness between thousands of power-generation and power-distribution facilities. This type of graph is commonly referred to as a *hairball* graph, for obvious reasons. You can make it less dense and more visually clear, but making those kinds of adjustments is as much of an art as it is a science. The best way to learn is through practice, using trial-and-error.

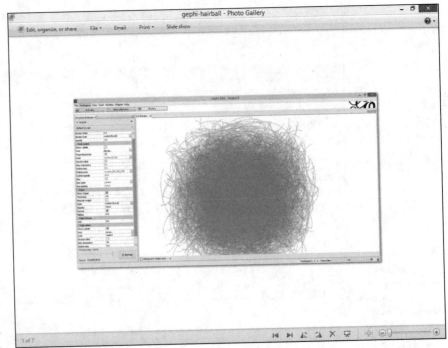

FIGURE 20-3:
A Gephi hairball graph of the US power grid.

Machine learning with the WEKA suite

Machine learning is the class of artificial intelligence that's dedicated to developing and applying algorithms to data so that the algorithms can automatically learn and detect patterns in large datasets. Waikato Environment for Knowledge Analysis (WEKA; www.cs.waikato.ac.nz/ml/weka) is a popular suite of tools that's useful for machine learning tasks. It was written in Java and developed at the University of Waikato, New Zealand.

You can use the stand-alone WEKA application to analyze patterns in your datasets and then visualize those patterns in all sorts of interesting ways. For advanced users, WEKA's true value is derived from its suite of machine learning algorithms that you can use to cluster or categorize your data. WEKA even allows you to run different machine learning algorithms in parallel to see which ones perform most efficiently. WEKA can be run through a graphical user interface (GUI) or by command line. Thanks to the well-written Weka Wiki documentation, the learning curve for WEKA isn't as steep as you might expect for a piece of software this powerful.

Designing Data Visualizations

Ready for the artsy stuff? Here are some tools you can use to create neat-looking web-based data visualizations.

Getting Shiny by RStudio

Once upon a time, you needed to know how to use a statistics-capable programming language like R if you wanted to do any kind of serious data analysis. And, if you needed to make interactive web visualizations, you'd have to know how to code in languages like JavaScript or PHP. Of course, if you wanted to do both simultaneously, you'd have to know how to code in an additional two or three more programming languages. In other words, SaaS data visualization based on statistical analyses was a cumbersome task.

The good news is that the situation has changed. Because of the work of a few dedicated developers, the walls between analysis and presentation have crumbled. After the 2012 launch of RStudio's Shiny package (http://shiny.rstudio.com), both statistical analysis and SaaS data visualization can be carried out in the same framework.

RStudio —by far the most popular integrated development environment (IDE) for R — developed the Shiny package to allow R users to create web apps. Apps made in Shiny run on a web server and are *interactive* — you can move sliders, select check boxes, or click the data itself in order to manipulate said data to your heart's desire. Because these apps run on a server, they're considered *live* — when you make changes to the underlying data, those changes are automatically reflected in the appearance of the data visualization. Web apps created in Shiny are also *reactive* — in other words, their output updates instantly in response to a user interaction, without the user having to click the Submit button.

If you want to quickly use a few lines of code to instantly generate a SaaS data visualization application, use R's Shiny package. What's more, if you want to customize your SaaS data visualization app to be more aesthetically appealing, you can do that by simply editing the HTML, CSS, and JavaScript that underlies the Shiny application.

REMEMBER

Because Shiny produces server-side web apps, you need a server host and the know-how to host your web app on a server before you can make useful web apps by using the package.

TIP

Over on `https://businessgrowth.ai`, I keep a listing of my favorite Shiny applications. They're useful if you're considering using Shiny to build your first data product.

TIP

Shiny runs the public web server ShinyApps.io (`www.shinyapps.io`). You can use that server to host an app for free, or you can pay to host there if your requirements are more resource-intensive. The starter level of service costs $9 per month and promises you 100 hours of application runtime per month.

Mapmaking and spatial data analytics with CARTO

If you're not a professional programmer or cartographer, just know that CARTO is about the most powerful online mapping solution that's available. People in information services, software engineering, media and entertainment, and urban development industries often use CARTO for digital visual communications.

By using CARTO, you can create a heat map by simply uploading or linking to a list of spatial coordinates. Likewise, if you want to create a choropleth map to show values for quantitative attributes, simply upload or link to a set of spatial coordinates that includes attribute data. (Choropleth maps show spatial data plotted out according to area boundary polygons rather than by point, line, or raster coverage. I discuss them in greater detail in Chapter 8.)

CARTO allows you to overlay markers and shapes on all sorts of interesting base maps. You can use it to make anything from simple outline maps of geographic regions to stylish, antiqued, glossy map books that come out looking like magazines. You can even use it to generate street maps from satellite imagery. CARTO's geocoding functionality is so well implemented that you can drill down to a location using individual addresses, postal codes, or even IP addresses.

REMEMBER

To get going in CARTO, you need to first set up a user account. You can do that via the CARTO home page (at `https://carto.com`).

More advanced users can use CARTO to

- Link to SQL databases.
- Customize Cascading Style Sheets (CSS).
- Incorporate other chart types in the form of superimposed graphs, outlines, and 3-dimensional surface plots.

Figure 20-4 shows CARTO's version of the sample choropleth map of a sample dataset derived from the number of people who moved within the same county in the US in 2011, and Figure 20-5 shows a bubble map of the same dataset.

REMEMBER

CARTO is interactive: It allows you to click features to see attribute information and turn map layers on and off in the same map interface.

TECHNICAL
STUFF

Map layers are spatial datasets that represent different features on a map. In shared areas, layers often overlap one another in the same spatial region. To better understand this concept, think again about a map that shows an election outcome. This type of map has a States layer and a Political Party layer. The States layer shows you the name and spatial boundary of the state. The Political Party layer, geographically overlaid on top of the States layer, tells you, state by state, how the majority of voters voted in the election. Although the layers overlap in physical location, both the States layer and the Political Party layer are based on separate, individual datasets. This is how layers work in mapping applications.

FIGURE 20-5:
An interactive
bubble map in
CARTO.

Talking about Tableau Public

Collaborative data visualization platforms are SaaS platforms you can use to design data visualizations and then share those visualizations with other platform users to get their feedback on the visualization's design or on the data insights conveyed.

Collaborative data visualization platforms have been described as the YouTube of data visualization, but these platforms are in reality far more interactive than YouTube. A collaborative data visualization platform is like a version of YouTube that lets you instantly copy and edit every video using your own software tools and then republish the video via your own social channels.

Collaborative platforms are quite efficient and effective for working in teams. Rather than have to email versions back-and-forth, or (heaven forbid) learn a dedicated version-control system like GitHub, you and your teammates can use the platform's sharing features to work on visualizations as a team.

Even if you don't need or want to work with collaborators, collaborative platforms still have much to offer in the way of useful data analysis and visualization tools. These tools are often as powerful as (and sometimes even more powerful than) comparable desktop packages — just keep in mind that they often require users to publicly share their data and results so that others can view, modify, or use those results for their specific needs.

TIP

Many sites offer free plans that allow you to keep your work private if you purchase a paid account.

Tableau Public (`www.tableausoftware.com/public`), a free desktop application, aims to be a complete package for chart-making. If its name sounds familiar, it may be because Tableau Public is the free version of the popular Tableau Desktop software program. As part of the freeware limitation, the application doesn't let you save files locally to your computer. All your work must be uploaded to Tableau Public's cloud server, unless you purchase the software.

Tableau Public creates three levels of document: the worksheet, the dashboard, and the story. In the worksheet, you can create individual charts from data you've imported from Access, Excel, or a text-format `.csv` file. You can then use Tableau Public to easily do things such as choose between different data graphic types or drag columns to different axes or subgroups.

WARNING

You have to deal with a bit of a learning curve when working with the flow of the application and its nomenclature — for example, *dimensions* are categorical data, and *measures* are numerical data.

Tableau Public offers many different default chart types: bar charts, scatter plots, line charts, bubble charts, Gantt charts, and even geographical maps. It can even look at the type of data you have and suggest types of charts you can use to best represent it. For example, imagine that you have two dimensions and one measure. In this situation, a bar chart is a popular choice because you have two categories of data and only one numeric measure for those two categories. But if you have two dimensions and two measures, a scatter plot might be a good option because the scatter plot data graphic allows you to visualize two sets of numerical data for two categories of data.

You can use a Tableau Public dashboard to combine charts with text annotations or with other data charts. You can also use the dashboard to add interactive filters, such as check boxes or sliders, so that users can interact with your data to visualize only certain time series or categories. With a Tableau Public story, you can combine several dashboards into a sort of slide show presentation that shows a linear story revealed through your data.

And at last, you can use Tableau Public's online gallery to collaborate and share all the worksheets, dashboards, and stories you generate within the application. You can also embed them into websites that link back to the Tableau Public cloud server.

Using RAWGraphs for web-based data visualization

You can use RAWGraphs, a unique and unusual web application, to make artistic and creative visualizations from your dataset. RAWGraphs' layout provides you with a simple drag-and-drop interface you can use to make unique and interesting data visualizations with just a few clicks of the mouse. If you want to get funky and cool with your data visualization but you lack the time or money it takes to learn how to code this sort of thing for yourself, RAWGraphs is the perfect data visualization alternative.

REMEMBER

Like I said, RAWGraphs is unique — it doesn't even offer standard bar chart visualizations. It does, however, offer clustered force diagrams, Voronoi tessellations, Reingold-Tilford trees, and other, less-well-known chart types.

To use RAWGraphs, first go to the RAWGraphs home page (at `https://rawgraphs.io/`) and then navigate to the Use It Now! button. You don't even need to create an account to use the application — just copy and paste your raw data into the application, and then choose the optimal chart types for that data. RAWGraphs makes it easy to choose between chart types by telling you the precise number of quantitative attributes, categorical attributes, and labels that are required to generate each plot.

This service wasn't designed for novices, but its simple, straightforward interface makes it a fun, user-friendly application for playing with your data and figuring out how to generate unique chart types. Even if you don't know a convex hull from a hexagonal bin, you can play around with settings, drag columns from place to place, and view how those changes affect the overall visualization. With enough practice, you may even end up using some of the visualization strategies you learn from RAWGraphs in other contexts.

REMEMBER

You can have fun getting cool and funky with visualization design, but always make sure that your visual result is easy to understand for the average viewer.

Figure 20-6 shows a diagram I created in RAWGraphs of the dataset I used for my CARTO example, earlier in this chapter. (*Note:* This is just about the only type of visualization RAWGraphs offers that would work with such a simple dataset!)

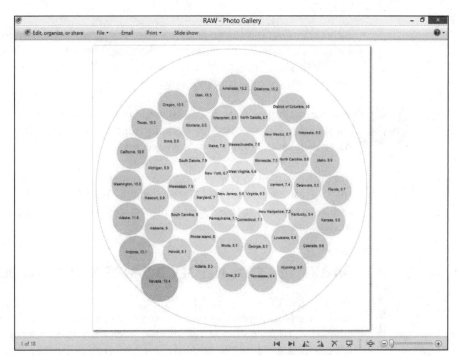

FIGURE 20-6:
A diagram from
RAWCharts.

Communicating with Infographics

Although the contextual difference between an infographic and a data visualization is often clear, even data visualization professionals can sometimes have a hard time distinguishing between the two. A good rule of thumb is that if the data graphics are primarily produced in an automated fashion using a data graphing application, it's a data visualization. But if you use a custom graphic design tool, such as Photoshop or Illustrator, to produce the final product, it's an infographic.

This categorization grows a bit more complicated, though. An infographic often incorporates one or more charts, making it more difficult to determine the manner in which the visualization was produced. Complicating the issue, online infographic design applications, such as Piktochart and Infogram, have dual functionality that allows for automated data graphing and customizable, artistic graphic design.

REMEMBER

An even broader rule of thumb is that if the visualization looks artfully designed, it's an infographic, but if it looks rather plain and analytical, it's a data visualization.

Although infographics can be dynamic or static, when you're designing a graphic for print, a slide for PowerPoint, or an image for social media syndication, just stick with static infographics. If you want to tell a story with your data or create data art, use a dynamic infographic.

You can easily and directly embed static graphics into a social media post. Social content that has an embedded graphic tends to get more attention and engagement than social content that's posted as text-only.

Applications used to create infographics provide many more creative alternatives than do traditional data visualization applications. In fact, this is as good a time as any to introduce you to a few of the better applications that are available for infographic design. Read on for all the details.

Making cool infographics with Infogram

You can use the online tool Infogram to make aesthetically appealing, *vertically stacked card infographics* — visualizations that are composed of a series of cards, stacked vertically on top of one another, each with its own set of data graphics, in other words. Because the cards are stacked vertically, one on top of the other, the end infographic is often longer than it is wide.

Infogram offers a variety of trendy color schemes, design schemes, and chart types. With Infogram, you can import your own images to make an infographic that's much more personalized. Infogram also provides you with sharing capabilities so that you can spread an infographic quickly and easily across social channels or via private email.

You can use Infogram to create stylish infographics that display bar charts, column charts, pie charts, line charts, area charts, scatter charts, bubble charts, pictorials, hierarchical charts, tables, progress displays, word clouds, tree maps, or even financial charts. To get started using Infogram, just head over to the home page (at https://infogram.com) and register for an account. Its freemium plan is robust enough to supply all your more basic infographic-making needs.

Figure 20-7 shows a bar chart of the (by now familiar) in-county moving dataset in Infogram.

If you want to check out some great Infogram examples before you get started, you can view a live feed of featured infographics at Infogram's Featured Infographics page (https://infogram.com/examples).

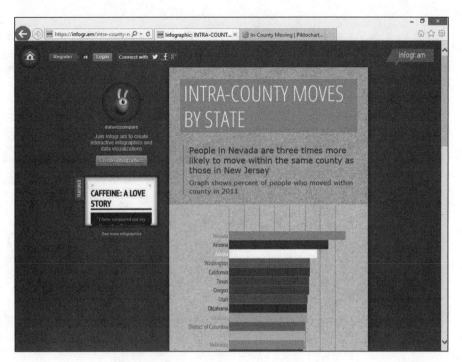

FIGURE 20-7:
A bar chart in
Infogram.

Making cool infographics with Piktochart

The Piktochart web application provides an easy-to-use interface that people like you and me can use to quickly create beautiful infographics. Piktochart offers a large selection of attractive templates, but be warned that only members who have paying accounts can access most of these templates. These templates are a great option if you want to save time and money on design but need to produce documents in an infographic format. Piktochart offers more creative flexibility than other comparable web applications, which makes Piktochart useful in a wide range of industries, from nonprofit grassroots to media and entertainment.

You can use Piktochart to make either static or dynamic infographics, and you can also link your infographics to Google Sheets for live updating. Piktochart offers the usual array of chart types, in addition to more infographic-oriented types, such as Venn diagrams, gauges, and matrixes.

If you use the free version of Piktochart to create your infographic, be warned that your infographic will be made available to the public. If you sign up for a paid account, however, you have the option of keeping your work private. You can register for Piktochart on the application's home page at `http://piktochart.com`.

Using Piktochart, you can create infographics that display bar charts, triangle charts, line charts, area charts, scatter charts, pie charts, Venn diagrams, matrixes, pyramids, gauges, donuts, swatches, and icons. Figure 20-8 shows a Piktochart version of a bar chart of the in-county moving dataset example.

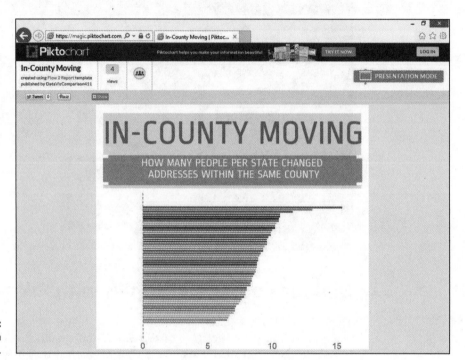

TIP

This list is awesome, but too short. It's only a list of 10. There are so many other tool options available to you out there. A few other places you might want to explore includes Datawrapper (www.datawrapper.de), which is used by *The New York Times*, *Wired*, and *Fortune* for their data visualizations. It lets you create charts, choropleth maps, tables, and so much more! Additionally, there is mapbox (www.mapbox.com) which is useful for creating high-quality geographic data and shapefiles for GIS.

Index

Symbols and Numerics

symbol, 120, 124

* (asterisk), in SQL, 147

2 × 4 matrix, generating with NumPy, 115

A

Absolute macros, Microsoft Excel, 159–160

accountability for AI solutions, 319–320

accreditations, 346–348

accuracy, degree of, 52

accuracy in representations, 164

activation function, 45

activists, data art for, 163

actors, 200

Adobe Analytics, 239

advertising, 230–231, 283–284

affective computing, 267, 268

AI. *See* artificial intelligence

algorithms for machine learning

  classification

    general discussion, 90–91

    instance-based learning classifiers, 90

    overfitting in, 92–93

    overgeneralization in, 92–93

    overview, 89

  clustering

    DBScan, 87–88

    general discussion, 78

    with hierarchical algorithms, 84–87

    kernel density estimation, 84

    k-means algorithm, 82–84

    overview, 79–81

    similarity metrics, 81–82

  decision trees, 44, 46, 88–89

  nearest neighbor

    average nearest neighbor algorithms, 94–97, 101–102

    k-nearest neighbor algorithms, 90, 97–100, 101

    overview, 93–94

    solving real-world problems with, 100–102

  random forest, 89

  selecting based on function, 44–48

  supervised, 42

  unsupervised, 43

alternatives analysis, 335–336

Amazon Redshift, 30–31

Amazon Web Services S3 platform, 23

analysts, data showcasing for, 163

annotations, including in data visualization, 185

AP (Associated Press) case study, 224–228

Apache Cassandra, 32

Apache Flume, 22

Apache Kafka, 22

Apache Spark, 35, 48–49

Apache Sqoop, 22

app development competitions, 371

appendixes, in technical plan, 334–335

Apple, 285–286

application files, 11

application programming interface (API), 371, 379

application step, in machine learning, 40

applications. *See also* Microsoft Excel; Structured Query Language

  CARTO, 388–390

  in data science strategy, 138–139

  DataWrangler, 383

  Gephi, 384–386

  ImageQuilts, 382–383

  Infogram, 394–395

  overview, 137, 381–382

  Piktochart, 395–396

  RAWGraphs, 392–393

  Shiny by RStudio, 387–388

  Tableau Public, 390–391

  WEKA, 386

Funnel Gorgeous, 365
future state of company, 312
future state vision statement, 330
fuzzy multiple criteria decision-making (FMCDM), 67

G

Gantt chart, 174, 176
GaussianNB, 56
General Architecture for Text Engineering (GATE), 151
General Data Protection Regulation (GDPR), 320–321, 330
generic vectors, 122
geometric metrics, 81
Gephi, 384–386
ggplot2 package, 133–134
GitHub portfolio, 353–354
Gmail, 47
goals of data science projects, 332
Google Analytics, 239, 250–251
Google BigQuery, 31
Google Data Studio, 239
Google Sheets, 152
government data, open, 370–373
GPT-3, 222–224, 230
graph mesh network topology, 180
graph models, 180
graphics, data. See data graphics
GraphX library, Apache Spark, 48
Grayeb, Jennifer, 365
grocery retail, use of average nearest neighbor algorithms by, 101–102
GROUP function, SQL, 150
Guru Path of the Data Science Bootcamp, Data Science Dojo, 349

H

Hadoop, 20, 33–34, 35
Hadoop distributed file system (HDFS), 22, 23, 33–34
hairball graph, 385, 386
hardware companies, use of personal data by, 286

hash symbol, 120, 124
HAVING function, SQL, 150
HDFS blocks, 33
Heartbeat algorithm, TrueAccord, 211–216
help function, SciPy library, 117
hidden layer, 45
hierarchical clustering algorithms, 79, 84–87
hierarchical tree topology, 180, 181
high-variety data, 22
hiring new employees, 317, 334
histogram, 176–177, 178
HR managers, feedback from, 305
Humana case study, 257–262
  need, 257
  results, 258
  solution, 257
  technology stack, 262
  use case diagram, 261
  use cases, 258–260
Humby, Clive, 275, 278
hyperparameters, 203
hypertargeted advertising, 230–231

I

icons, used in book, 4
igraph package, 134
ImageQuilts, 382–383
implementation plan. See technical plan
implementing data use cases, 222
implicit risk in AI, 319
independent variable (IV), 41
index, 141
inferential statistics, 52–53
Infogram, 394–395
infographic tools, 393–396
information, in POTI modeling, 315, 339
information products, 282
information products businesses, 358
information redundancy, 63
in-memory computing, 35, 48, 144
inner JOIN function, SQL, 148, 149
instance

regularization algorithms, 44, 46

reinforcement learning, 43

relational database management system (RDBMS), 8, 22–23, 26, 31, 141–143

relationship-building, 349–350

Relative macros, Microsoft Excel, 159–160

Remember icon, 4

report writing, automated, 210

Research Data Alliance (RDA), 349

researching company
  business vision, mission, and values, 294–296
  data ethics, 306–308
  data resources, inventorying, 298–302
  data science team, unifying, 292–293
  data technologies, inventorying, 296–298
  efficient process for, 308–310
  overview, 291–292
  people-mapping, 303–304
  project pitfalls, avoiding, 305–306

residuals, 68

Resolve phase, Synthesys AI, 271–272

resources, open data. *See* open data resources

retail stores, use of k-nearest neighbor algorithms by, 101

revenue model, choosing, 359–361

right JOIN function, SQL, 148

risk priority number (RPN), 242

robot workcell, 209

S

SaaS (Software as a Service), 26, 282

SaaS business model, 359

SafeGraph, 282, 284–285

Sahota, Harpreet, 345–346

sales calls, 234

sales channels, omnichannel analytics approach for, 233–238

sales professionals, feedback from, 305

sample, 53

scatterplot, 177, 178

scatterplot charts, 133–134

scatterplot matrix, 177, 179

Scikit-learn library, 119–120

SciPy library, 116–117

scoring channels, 231, 235–237

scraping websites, 14

script files, 11

sculpting data, 383

search engine optimization (SEO), 234

seasonality, 74

security cameras, use of k-nearest neighbor algorithms by, 101

security of cloud storage, 29

SELECT function, SQL, 147–148

self-learning networks, 45

Self-Taught Data Scientist Curriculum, 362

self-tuning vision systems, 210

semistructured data, 8, 22–23

sentiment analysis, 267, 269–273

SEO (search engine optimization), 234

sequences, 95

Series object, Pandas library, 117

serverless computing solutions, 29

service development, 237

service-based businesses, 357–358

services revenue model, 361

sets, Python, 109

shared variance, 63

Sheets, Google, 152

Shiny applications, RStudio, 387–388

showcasing, data. *See* data showcasing

silhouette coefficient, 83

similarity metrics, 81–82

single-link algorithm, 94

singular value decomposition (SVD), 59–62

skills
  alternatives analysis, 336
  coding portfolio, building, 351–354
  data skill gap analysis, 317–318
  of relevant personnel, surveying, 304
  in technical plan, 331, 333
  upgrading, 9

Smart-Reply, Gmail, 47

SME (subject matter expert), 10–11, 13–14, 190

Smith, Heather, 355–356

About the Author

Lillian Pierson is a CEO and data leader that supports data professionals to evolve into world-class leaders and entrepreneurs. To date, she's helped educate over 1.3 million data professionals on AI and data science.

The author of six data-oriented books from Wiley Publishing as well as eight data courses on LinkedIn Learning, Lillian has supported a wide variety of organizations across the globe, from the United Nations and *National Geographic* to Ericsson and Saudi Aramco and everything in between.

A licensed professional engineer in good standing, Lillian has been a technical consultant since 2007 and a data business mentor since 2018. She occasionally volunteers her expertise in global summits and forums on data privacy and ethics.

Dedication

To Vitaly Ivanov and Ariana Ivanov. I love you both so much — you make my world go round.

Author's Acknowledgments

I extend a huge thanks to all the people who've helped me produce this book. Thanks so much to Chris Levesque, for your technical edits. Also, I extend a huge thanks to Elizabeth Stilwell, Paul Levesque, Becky Whitney, and the rest of the editorial and production staff at Wiley.

Publisher's Acknowledgments

Acquisitions Editor: Elizabeth Stilwell

Senior Project Editor: Paul Levesque

Copy Editor: Becky Whitney

Editorial Assistant: Matthew Lowe

Sr. Editorial Assistant: Cherie Case

Project Coordinator: Ram Prabakaran

Cover Image: © ivanastar/Getty Images

Take dummies with you everywhere you go!

Whether you are excited about e-books, want more from the web, must have your mobile apps, or are swept up in social media, dummies makes everything easier.

Find us online!

dummies.com

dummies
A Wiley Brand

PERSONAL ENRICHMENT

Staying Sharp	Facebook	Guitar	Investing	Beekeeping	Digital Photography
9781119187790	9781119179030	9781119293354	9781119293347	9781119310068	9781119235606
USA $26.00	USA $21.99	USA $24.99	USA $22.99	USA $22.99	USA $24.99
CAN $31.99	CAN $25.99	CAN $29.99	CAN $27.99	CAN $27.99	CAN $29.99
UK £19.99	UK £16.99	UK £17.99	UK £16.99	UK £16.99	UK £17.99

Meditation	Pregnancy	Samsung Galaxy S7	iPhone	Crocheting	Nutrition
9781119251163	9781119235491	9781119279952	9781119283133	9781119287117	9781119130246
USA $24.99	USA $26.99	USA $24.99	USA $24.99	USA $24.99	USA $22.99
CAN $29.99	CAN $31.99	CAN $29.99	CAN $29.99	CAN $29.99	CAN $27.99
UK £17.99	UK £19.99	UK £17.99	UK £17.99	UK £16.99	UK £16.99

PROFESSIONAL DEVELOPMENT

Windows 10	AutoCAD	Excel 2016	QuickBooks 2017	macOS Sierra	LinkedIn	Windows 10
9781119311041	9781119255796	9781119293439	9781119281467	9781119280651	9781119251132	9781119310563
USA $24.99	USA $39.99	USA $26.99	USA $26.99	USA $29.99	USA $24.99	USA $34.00
CAN $29.99	CAN $47.99	CAN $31.99	CAN $31.99	CAN $35.99	CAN $29.99	CAN $41.99
UK £17.99	UK £27.99	UK £19.99	UK £19.99	UK £21.99	UK £17.99	UK £24.99

SharePoint 2016	Fundamental Analysis	Networking	Office 2016	Office 365	Salesforce.com	Coding
9781119181705	9781119263593	9781119257769	9781119293477	9781119265313	9781119239314	9781119933323
USA $29.99	USA $26.99	USA $29.99	USA $26.99	USA $24.99	USA $29.99	USA $29.99
CAN $35.99	CAN $31.99	CAN $35.99	CAN $31.99	CAN $29.99	CAN $35.99	CAN $35.99
UK £21.99	UK £19.99	UK £21.99	UK £19.99	UK £17.99	UK £21.99	UK £21.99

dummies.com

dummies®
A Wiley Brand